BI 3174181 9

C000275114

£2·50

BIRMINGHAM CITY
UNIVERSITY
DISCARDED

LONGMAN LINGUISTICS LIBRARY

# Experimental Phonetics

LONGMAN LINGUISTICS LIBRARY

*General editors*

**R. H. ROBINS**, *University of London*

**GEOFFREY HORROCKS**, *University of Cambridge*

**DAVID DENISON**, *University of Manchester*

For a complete list of books in the series, see pages vii & viii

# Experimental Phonetics

KATRINA HAYWARD

An imprint of **Pearson Education**

Harlow, England · London · New York · Reading, Massachusetts · San Francisco · Toronto · Don Mills, Ontario · Sydney
Tokyo · Singapore · Hong Kong · Seoul · Taipei · Cape Town · Madrid · Mexico City · Amsterdam · Munich · Paris · Milan

UNIVERSITY
INFORMATION
SERVICES
CENTRAL ENGLAND

**Pearson Education Limited**
Edinburgh Gate
Harlow
Essex CM20 2JE
England

and Associated Companies throughout the world

*Visit us on the World Wide Web at:*
pearsoneduc.com

First published 2000

© Pearson Education Limited 2000

The right of Katrina Hayward to be identified as author of this work has been asserted by
her in accordance with the Copyright, Designs and Patents Act 1988.

All rights reserved; no part of this publication may be reproduced,
stored in a retrieval system, or transmitted in any form or by any
means, electronic, mechanical, photocopying, recording, or otherwise
without either the prior written permission of the Publishers or a licence
permitting restricted copying in the United Kingdom issued by the
Copyright Licensing Agency Ltd., 90 Tottenham Court Road,
London W1P 0LP

ISBN 0-582-29137-2 PPR

**British Library Cataloguing-in-Publication Data**

A catalogue record for this book is available from the British Library

**Library of Congress Cataloging-in-Publication Data**

A catalog record for this book is available from the Library of Congress

Set by 35 in 10/12pt Times
Printed in Great Britain by T.J. International Ltd, Padstow, Cornwall

UNIVERSITY OF
CENTRAL ENGLAND

Book no.   31741819

Subject no.   612.78 May

INFORMATION SERVICES

#414

*to the memory of Eugénie Henderson*

LONGMAN LINGUISTICS LIBRARY

**General Editors:**

**R. H. ROBINS**
*University of London*

**GEOFFREY HORROCKS**
*University of Cambridge*

**DAVID DENISON**
*University of Manchester*

Introduction to Text Linguistics
ROBERT DE BEAUGRANDE and
WOLFGANG DRESSLER

Psycholinguistics
Language, Mind and World
DANNY D. STEINBERG

Principles of Pragmatics
GEOFFREY N. LEECH

The English Verb
*Second edition*
F. R. PALMER

Pidgin and Creole Languages
SUZANNE ROMAINE

General Linguistics
An Introductory Survey
*Fourth edition*
R. H. ROBINS

Generative and Non-linear
Phonology
JACQUES DURAND

Modality and the English Modals
*Second edition*
F. R. PALMER

Dialects of English
Studies in Grammatical Variation
PETER TRUDGILL and
J. K. CHAMBERS (eds)

An Introduction to Bilingualism
CHARLOTTE HOFFMANN

Linguistic Theory
The Discourse of Fundamental Works
ROBERT DE BEAUGRANDE

A History of American English
J. L. DILLARD

Aspect in the English Verb
Process and Result in Language
YISHAI TOBIN

The Meaning of Syntax
A Study in the Adjectives of English
CONNOR FERRIS

Latin American Spanish
JOHN LIPSKI

A Linguistic History of Italian
MARTIN MAIDEN

The History of Linguistics
All edited by GIULIO LEPSCHY

Volume I:
The Eastern Traditions of Linguistics

Volume II:
Classical and Medieval Linguistics

Volume III:
Renaissance and Early Modern
Linguistics

Volume IV:
Nineteenth Century Linguistics
ANNA MORPURGO DAVIES

*To come:*
Volume V:
The Twentieth Century

Modern Arabic
Structures, Functions and Varieties
CLIVE HOLES

Frontiers of Phonology
Atoms, Structures and Derivations
JACQUES DURAND and FRANCIS KATAMBA (eds)

An Introduction to the Celtic Languages
PAUL RUSSELL

Causatives and Causation
A Universal-typological perspective
JAE JUNG SONG

A Short History of Linguistics
*Fourth edition*
R. H. ROBINS

Grammar and Grammarians in the
Early Middle Ages
VIVIEN LAW

Greek
A History of the Language and its Speakers
GEOFFREY HORROCKS

The New Comparative Syntax
LILIANE HAEGEMAN (ed.)

The Structure and History of Japanese
LONE TAKEUCHI

The Acquisition of Syntax
Studies in Comparative Developmental
Linguistics
MARC-ARIEL FRIEDEMANN and LUIGI
RIZZI (eds)

Explaining Language Change:
An Evolutionary Approach
WILLIAM CROFT

Experimental Phonetics
KATRINA HAYWARD

# Contents

# Author's acknowledgements

A number of people have made contributions, directly or indirectly, to this work. I should particularly like to thank Sarah Hawkins, Mark Huckvale, Peter Roach, Iggy Roca, Burton Rosner and Justin Watkins for reading and providing suggestions on various chapters. Any mistakes or infelicities which remain are my own responsibility.

I am greatly indebted to Bernard Howard for technical support with regard to recording and production of spectrograms. Geoff Williams and Alan Hirson kindly provided assistance with LPC analysis. I should also like to thank the School of Oriental and African Studies for purchasing the *Mathematica* software for me, without which many of the illustrations could not have been prepared.

Bruce Ingham deserves particular thanks for generously lending his good spectrographic voice to the project. Martin Barry kindly recorded the EPG examples for Figure 8.15. I am also indebted to Muhammed El-Ashiry for allowing me to use to his recordings of Qur'anic recitation and to Keith Howard for advice on Korean musical terms in connection with Figure 8.9.

Special thanks are due to Nigel Phillips for unselfishly doing more than his share of our joint teaching and administrative duties, thus helping to bring the work to completion. It is impossible to mention everyone who has provided encouragement and moral support, but I should particularly like to thank Diana Flint, Jiyoung Shin and Lone Takeuchi for their understanding friendship and encouragement. Thanks are also due to my parents and friends outside the academic world, who uncomplainingly put up with less contact than they might reasonably have expected while the work was in progress.

To conclude, I should particularly like to thank Professor Bobby Robins, who persuaded me to undertake the work in the first place and whose confidence in me has been a source of strength in troubled times. The final thanks are for my husband, Dick, who remained encouraging while having to live with the work on a day-to-day basis, and who told me honestly how boring the first version was.

# Publisher's acknowledgements

We are grateful to the following to reproduce copyright material:

Blackwell Publishers for our Figure 5.10 which appeared in B. Delgutte's chapter in *The Handbook of Phonetic Sciences* edited by W. J. Hardcastle and J. Laver (1997); Oxford University Press for our Figure 8.2 from Peter Ladefoged's *Three Areas of Experimental Phonetics* (1987); The University of Chicago Press for our Figure 5.7 from Peter Ladefoged's *Elements of Acoustic Phonetics*, second edition (1996); Lawrence Erlbaum Associates Inc. for our Figure 7.8 from K. N. Stevens and S. E. Blumstein's contribution in *Perspectives on the Study of Speech* (1981) edited by P. Eimas and J. Miller.

Whilst every effort has been made to trace the owners of copyright material, in a few cases this has proved impossible and we take this opportunity to offer our apologies to any copyright holders whose rights we may have unwittingly infringed.

# Chapter 1

# Introduction: impressionistic phonetics and experimental phonetics

## 1.1 What is experimental phonetics?

Phonetics is the study of speech. Traditionally, phoneticians have relied on their ears and eyes, and their awareness of their own vocal organs, to study pronunciation. Increasingly, however, they have been using instruments of various types to supplement the information they derive from their own sensations. *Experimental phonetics*, as the term is commonly used, includes any investigation of speech by means of instruments. It is understood here that the instruments are used to visualise some aspect of the speech event, and possibly also to provide a basis for measurements. For example, making a tape recording for the purpose of repeated listening does not fall within the scope of experimental phonetics, but if the tape recording is fed into a computer and used to produce an acoustic analysis, the activity would be described as an experimental investigation.

There are four main reasons for studying experimental phonetics. The first of these is that speech is interesting in itself. The ability to produce and understand speech is a fundamental part of our identity, as individuals, as members of larger communities, and as human beings. However, many aspects of speaking and hearing are inaccessible without the aid of instruments.

The second reason for studying experimental phonetics is that it expands the range of contexts in which we can study speech. To give but two examples, speech is a highly skilled motor activity, which can be studied as part of the general study of movement. Speech is also a type of sound which can be compared with other types of sound from the perspective of general acoustics. Each of these contexts has its own theoretical perspective, to which the study of speech can contribute.

A third reason is provided by the numerous practical applications of experimental phonetics. Obvious examples are medical applications such as helping patients with disordered speech, applications in the fields of telecommunications and man–machine communication, and the development of audio-visual aids for improving pronunciation in language teaching.

The fourth reason, and the one which underlies this book, is the relevance of speech for the study of language in general. Theoretical linguistics operates with an inner world of language, in which discrete, inherently timeless elements such as words, sounds and even individual components of sounds are arranged in meaningful patterns in accordance with logical principles. This contrasts

1

markedly with the outer world of speech, where individual sounds are anchored in space and time and merge into one another, where boundaries become obscured, and where answers to questions tend to come from statistical, rather than logical, inference. As speakers and hearers, we constantly move between these two worlds, and the processes by which we do so are still not well-understood. However, the two worlds must necessarily influence each other, and it is doubtful that a full explanation of the abstract properties of language will ever be possible without an understanding of the more concrete properties of speech.

This book aims to provide an introduction to the methods of experimental phonetics, the nature of the data which experimental phoneticians must deal with, and the nature of the questions to which the data may provide answers. At the same time, it aims to avoid too many technical details, which may obscure the main points for readers new to the subject. Its orientation is primarily linguistic, but, because of limitations of space and time, it cannot cover all aspects of experimental phonetics which are relevant to linguists.

Since experimental phonetics is defined primarily by its methodology rather than by its subject matter, it is somewhat misleading to suggest that a clear-cut distinction can be drawn between experimental phonetics with non-experimental phonetics. Nevertheless, we shall assume such a division here. We shall use the term *impressionistic phonetics* to refer to the more traditional type of phonetic investigation which relies on the unaided skill of the phonetician in recognising and reproducing speech sounds. The purpose of the present chapter is twofold. Firstly, it aims to point out ways in which the availability of instruments has influenced the nature of research into speech. Secondly, it aims to provide an overview of the basic methodology and assumptions of impressionistic phonetics, since it will be necessary to build on these in the chapters which follow.

## 1.2  Impressionistic phonetics

The term *impressionistic* is taken from Abercrombie (1954, 1967), where it is applied to a style of phonetic transcription. In Abercrombie's usage, it is not meant to suggest any neglect of detail, but, rather, the absence of preconceived notions about the structure of the language being transcribed. For example, a linguistic field worker beginning work on a previously unstudied language would make a very detailed impressionistic transcription. In the present context, impressionistic is opposed to instrumental, and is meant to convey the idea of the phonetician relying entirely on his own impressions of sound, unaided by technology.

Impressionistic phonetics involves, first and foremost, acquiring and cultivating a skill in recognising, discriminating between, and performing, a wide range of speech sounds. For some practitioners, this skill is an end in itself. For others, it is an essential part of a larger, more theoretical enterprise of delimiting and classifying the set of possible speech sounds which may occur in human language. To quote Catford (1988: 2), 'What the competent phonetician *must* acquire is a deep, internally experienced, awareness of what is going on within the vocal tract – an ability to analyse, and hence describe and ultimately control, the postures and movements of organs that produce the sounds of speech ... the acquisition of these practical skills is by far the best way of acquiring a deep understanding of phonetic theory.'

Impressionistic phonetics has a long history, extending back to before the fifth century BC, at least in Ancient India (Allen 1953: 5). At the risk of being overly simplistic, we might say that the basic framework and methodology of the subject as it is taught and practised today were already in place by the early years of this century. In contrast, experimental phonetics is a young field. Convenient benchmark dates are the publication of *Principes de phonétique expérimentale* by Rousselot (often considered to be the father of the subject) in 1897–98 and, most importantly for the character of the subject today, the invention of the sound spectrograph in the 1940s. Experimental phonetics has built on the foundations of impressionistic phonetics, and has taken over much as regards orientation and basic assumptions. At the same time, the basic classificatory framework of impressionistic phonetics has itself been an object of study for experimental phoneticians. Some knowledge of impressionistic phonetics is therefore essential for the study of experimental phonetics, whereas the opposite is not true. It is possible to become a highly skilled impressionistic phonetician without ever setting foot in a phonetics laboratory.

In this section, I shall give a brief account of some of the basic assumptions which provide the foundation for impressionistic phonetics, and also of its methodology. An overview of the classificatory framework is given in the Appendix.

### 1.2.1  *Assumptions*

Impressionistic phonetics focusses on the positions and movements of the speech organs involved in the production of individual speech sounds. It is based on a number of assumptions about the nature of speech. Important among these are:

1   Speech can be represented as a series of segments.
2   Each segment has a target, and can be specified uniquely with reference to its target. Each target corresponds to a unique auditory percept in the mind of a trained observer.
3   Any segmental target can be specified using a limited number of dimensions. These dimensions do not need to be defined for each language individually. Instead, there is a universal set of dimensions which are relevant to all human languages.

For example, the English word **fan** might be represented as [fæn].[1] This implies that it is made up of a sequence of three segments, as, indeed, is suggested by the spelling. Let us now focus our attention on the first segment, represented by the letter **f**. It is produced by forcing air through a narrow opening between the lower lip and the upper teeth. The target may be described as: 'loose contact between lower lip and upper teeth, vocal folds open and not vibrating', and is conventionally specified as a *voiceless labiodental fricative*. Each term of this three-term label refers to one articulatory dimension. *Voiceless* refers to the fact that the vocal folds are not vibrating (the *voicing* dimension), *labiodental* to contact between the upper teeth and the lower lip (the *place of articulation* dimension), and *fricative* to the fact that the constriction between the lips and the teeth is sufficiently narrow for the rasping sound to be produced when air flows between them, but does not cut off the airstream entirely (the *manner of articulation* dimension). These three dimensions are crucial for the description of consonants in all known languages.

### 1.2.2  *Methodology*

Acquiring skill in impressionistic phonetics is, in many ways, like studying the pronunciation of a new language. For example, a native speaker of English who sets out to learn French must master the vowel sound which occurs in words such as **lune** 'moon' or **tu** 'you (familiar)', and which is pronounced rather like the vowel of English **see** but with closely rounded lips. There are three aspects to this mastery: (1) learning to pronounce the vowel oneself (2) learning to recognise the vowel when it is pronounced by native speakers of French and to distinguish it from the other French vowels and (3) learning to associate this particular articulatory-auditory package with the letter **u**, which is never pronounced in this way in English.

In more abstract terms, learning a new speech sound involves learning to get the speech organs to adopt a new position or to move in a new way, and to associate this new activity with a new and distinct auditory percept. In the process, students may be led to a new awareness of their own vocal organs, especially if they have not studied a foreign language before. (How many monolingual English speakers stop to think about the position of their tongue and lips when pronouncing the vowel of **see**?) The association with the letter **u** is also important because it helps to give students access to the representation of French words in writing.

Training in impressionistic phonetics aims to increase students' repertoire of speech sounds beyond what might be found in any particular language. In the ideal case, it would result in mastery of all possible speech sounds of all possible human languages. Students must concentrate on the proprioceptive (tactile and kinaesthetic) sensations associated with producing speech, in order to achieve an increased awareness of, and control over, the movements of their own vocal organs. Training should also result in an increased ability to distinguish between similar sounds and an increased awareness of the relationship between what the speech organs are doing and the auditory percept which results. Thus, the trained impressionistic phonetician, hearing an unfamiliar language for the first time, should be able to make an educated guess as regards what the speaker is doing with his or her vocal organs. This task is made easier if it is possible to look at the speaker. The guess can be refined by repeated listening and by trying to imitate the pronunciation to the satisfaction of a native-speaker informant.

The final elements in impressionistic phonetic training are learning to specify speech sounds in terms of universal articulatory dimensions and to use phonetic notation, most commonly the International Phonetic Alphabet (IPA). Once our trained impressionistic phonetician has worked out what the informant is doing with his or her vocal organs, he or she will want to communicate his or her observations to others. Most commonly, this will involve producing a transcription of the speech, that is, writing the speech down as a string of individual speech sounds (segments), each represented by its own alphabetic letter, as in the example of [fæn] above.

Both proprioceptive percepts of position and movement and auditory percepts of sound are entirely personal matters, and it is necessary to have a simple and convenient means of talking about them. In the example of the sound [f], discussed above, the relevant universal dimensions were voicing, place of articulation and manner of articulation, and the specification was *voiceless labiodental fricative*. If understood literally, the specification refers to the articulatory target for [f], that is, the position of the speech organs which results from the movement of the lower lip upwards to touch the upper teeth and the opening of the vocal folds (though the term *fricative* also refers to the rasping sound or *audible friction* which characterises this sound). However, in practice, the specification is also identified with the sound of [f].

It is obviously desireable that phonetic notation should not be tied to any particular language and should not vary between or within languages. For example, in writing English phonetically, the letter **f** would have to be used rather than **ph** for the initial sound of **phonetics**. Learning to write in IPA notation is, in some respects, easier than learning to write a foreign language. The relation between sounds and symbols is one-to-one; there are no inconsistencies such as the English use of both **f** and **ph** to spell the single sound [f]. (When letters are used with their universal values, it is customary to enclose them in square brackets, as will be explained below.) However, IPA notation is also more difficult because there are so many more symbols to remember and because it is necessary to concentrate on the individual sounds one by one rather than going for whole words.

The characteristic of impressionistic phonetics which we wish to call attention to here, and which distinguishes it from experimental phonetics, is the direct association between articulations and auditory percepts. In reality, of course, there is no direct contact between the speaker's vocal organs and the hearer's ears (except in the case of a speaker listening to him- or herself). The two are linked by a sound wave, which travels from the one to the other. However, without the aid of instruments, we have no access to the sound wave itself. Nor do we have a ready-made vocabulary for describing speech sounds in a precise way. If we want to refer to a particular sound there are three options. The first is to produce an imitation of the sound (which is not possible in writing). The second is to describe how the sound is produced: 'In English spelling, the letter combination **ph** is used to represent a *voiceless labiodental fricative* in words of Greek origin.' The third is to refer to the alphabetic or phonetic symbol which we would use to represent it: 'Young children acquiring English often substitute **w** for **r**.'

## 1.3    The scope of experimental phonetics

From what has been said already, it should be clear that the scope of impressionistic phonetics is limited by the capabilities of the human senses. Another potential shortcoming is the impossibility of verifying impressionistic-phonetic descriptions without access to the speakers whose pronunciation is being described. For example, if we read that the **t**-sound of language X, spoken by a small number of speakers in the depths of the Amazon jungle, is slightly retroflexed, we can only take the phonetician's word for it. Thus, one function of instrumental methods in phonetics has been to extend, back up, and provide a check on impressionistic methods. Ladefoged and Maddieson's monumental *Sounds of the World's Languages* (1996) is an outstanding example of this kind of use of experimental data.

In other ways, experimental methods have widened the scope of phonetic studies and have led to a change in perception of what phonetics is about. Here, it is useful to start from the idea of the *speech chain*, as formulated by Denes and Pinson (1993). Their diagram is reproduced in Figure 1.1. The

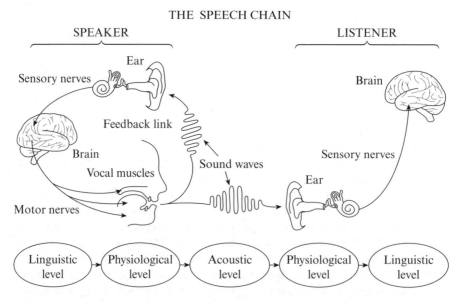

THE SPEECH CHAIN

FIGURE 1.1    The 'speech chain': stages in the transmission of a spoken message from the brain of the speaker to the brain of the listener. After Denes and Pinson (1993: 5).

speaker first conceives what he or she wants to say, and puts the message into linguistic form. The linguistic form is then translated into a set of motor commands, which ensure that the requisite muscles are activated at the necessary time. The result of all this motor activity is a sound wave, which travels to the ear of the listener. The sound wave, in its turn, brings about activity inside the ear. This results in nerve impulses which travel, via a complicated set of neural pathways, to the brain of the listener. Finally, the brain is able to interpret the nerve impulses as a message in linguistic form. Thus, speech communication is conceived of as a series of levels, with the output of one level serving as input to the next level. Denes and Pinson's diagram also takes into account the ability of speakers to monitor their own performance by including a feedback link which takes the sound from the speaker's mouth back to his or her own ears.

The sound wave – or, as it is often referred to, the *acoustic signal* – is at the very centre of the speech chain. Only at this stage does speech exist outside of the human body. When speech is in this form, we can achieve our most comprehensive knowledge of it. Furthermore, the acoustic signal defines the common ground between the study of speech production and the study of speech perception. For researchers into speech production, the acoustic signal is the endpoint, the output which they must try to explain with reference to the speech organs. For researchers into speech perception, the acoustic signal is the beginning, the input from which they must derive auditory percepts.

The acoustic signal is thus pivotal within experimental phonetics. For this reason, introductory university courses in experimental phonetics always include some study of acoustics, though they may differ greatly with regard to what else is covered and with what emphasis. As we move along the speech chain, away from the acoustic signal and in the direction of either the speaker's or the hearer's brain, it becomes increasingly difficult to say what falls within the scope of experimental phonetics and what belongs properly to some other field. For example, in the study of speech perception, it is difficult to draw a sharp line between phonetics and psychology (Chapter 5). It is only at the endpoints of the speech chain that we arrive within the domain of language proper and theoretical linguistics. The links between linguistic sound as it exists in the mind and the reality of sound as it exists outside the body, must therefore operate across the diverse layers of the speech chain. The nature of these links is not yet fully understood, and coming to such an understanding is an important research goal in both fields.

In any case, experimental phonetics includes at least some aspects of both the study of speech production and the study of speech perception, and I shall close this section by pointing out important differences between the two. Diagrams of the speech chain, such as Figure 1.1, might suggest that the two activities are the mirror image of each other and involve essentially the same stages in reverse order. This is misleading.

The problem of speech production is essentially one of coordination. It has often been pointed out that the organs of speech are quite diverse and that none of them has speaking as its primary biological function. For example, the primary function of the lungs is breathing and the structures of the mouth are primarily for eating. Furthermore, they vary greatly with regard to the nature of the tasks required of them, the speed at which they can move, and the time needed for messages to reach them from the brain via the appropriate nerves. Even pronouncing a simple monosyllabic word such as **fan** on its own requires a good deal of planning: among other things, the lungs must produce a sustained airstream of suitable strength; the lower lip must be brought into contact with the upper teeth for the [f], and this movement must be coordinated with the opening of the vocal folds; the tongue tip must move up to touch the ridge behind the teeth for the [n] just as the soft palate is lowering to open up the nasal cavity. Estimates of the number of muscles involved in speech production vary. Lenneberg (1967) puts the figure at over 100, and estimates that speaking may involve as many as 10–15 thousand neuromuscular events per minute.

Although the complexity of speech production poses a challenge for research, there is a compensating advantage in that the organs involved are relatively accessible. Indeed, it is possible to monitor the activity of just about any part of the speech-producing apparatus. Such monitoring might cause extreme discomfort to, or pose a health risk for, the subject, but it is not directly life-threatening. Phoneticians have often acted as their own subjects in production studies and have endured a variety of tortures such as tubes down the nose, wires stuck into the muscles of the tongue or larynx, needles through the rings of the trachea (windpipe), and even in one instance having dental-impression material inserted into the lower pharynx for the purpose of making a cast (Ladefoged *et al.* 1971)! While it is still not possible to make a truly comprehensive study of any particular speech act because it would not be practical to monitor *all* aspects of all the organs involved in speech production simultaneously, repeated experimentation is possible, and has provided a good idea of the complexities involved.

The case of speech perception is quite different. In this case everything depends on a single organ, the ear. No muscular activity is involved, and nerves take over from structures which respond to sound mechanically at an early stage of the process. Furthermore, the hearing mechanism is highly inaccessible, so that it is not possible to monitor what goes on as a living human being perceives speech. The great bulk of our knowledge of the processes of speech perception must therefore come from the more indirect methods of experimental psychology and from studies of experimental animals. For this reason, the perception of speech poses different kinds of difficulties than the production of speech.

At the linguistic level, there would appear to be no difference between the sounds we produce and the sounds we hear, and the two are also the same at the acoustic level. In between, however, the paths along the speech chain which mediate between them are very different.

The questions we have just raised are complicated, and much more research will be necessary before definitive answers can emerge. The point to be made here is that the questions could not even be asked if we had only the techniques of impressionistic phonetics at our disposal.

## 1.4    The representation of speech sounds

Sound of any kind is invisible and intangible and exists only as a pattern of changes through time. To study the sound of speech systematically, we must represent it in some more concrete and more permanent way which is accessible to the eye. Similarly, we can only study the movements of the speech organs, which give rise to the sound, by means of a more concrete visual representation of changing position through time (for example, a graph showing up-and-down movements of the jaw or the tip of the tongue). The visual representation of sound is the main topic of Chapters 2 and 3, and the representation of movement will be taken up in Chapter 8.

At the other end of the speech chain, it is clear that we must carry around some sort of representations of the sound of speech in our minds. Were this not the case, we should not be able to recognise points of similarity between new utterances and utterances which we have heard before. As will become clear in Chapter 5, the nature of these representations is a problem which occupies psychologists as well as linguists, and is highly controversial.

Theoretical linguists working within the general approach known as *Generative Grammar* hold that the grammar of every language, which the native speaker carries around in his or her head, includes a *lexicon*. Among other things, the lexicon relates abstract and invariant representations of pronunciation to meanings (whatever those are). The question of what such abstract representations might be like is of some importance for experimental phoneticians with a linguistic orientation, though it is usually considered to be outside the scope of phonetics proper. Within linguistics, teasing out the nature of mental representations falls within the province of phonology, which deals with the role of sound in language. Phonology has its home base, as it were, at the brain end of the speech chain, while phonetics is based at the acoustic end. The two must meet up somewhere in both production and perception pathways, and understanding the nature of that meeting is a research goal for practitioners in both fields. Such questions will occupy us particularly in Chapters 5 and 8 below. Later in this chapter (Section 1.4.2), I shall attempt to give a very brief and general summary of current views held by phonologists on the nature of mental representations.

In any case, it should be clear that the problem of representation is to be found at all levels of the study of speech. Indeed, many researchers would conceive of the speech chain as a series of translations from one type of representation into another. However, all areas of research into speech find a common point of reference in the representation of speech as a string of segments, represented by alphabetic letters, following the conventions of impressionistic phonetics. In fact, impressionistic phonetics recognises two major types of alphabetic representations, namely, *impressionistic*, also called *general phonetic*, and *phonemic*, also called *systematic*. We shall now give a brief account of these.

### 1.4.1  Segments and phonemes

The assumption that speech can be represented as a string of individual sounds or *segments* is fundamental to impressionistic phonetics. The justification for this assumption comes not from speech itself, but from the patternings which are observed in language. For example, poetic devices such as alliteration and rhyme, which depend on matching single segments or groups of segments, would provide one type of justification. Linguists have laid particular emphasis on the possibilities for substitution (sometimes referred to as *commutation*). For example, it is possible to move from the word **fan** to another word via three, and only three, types of substitution: (a) at the beginning, giving **pan**, **tan**, **dan**, etc.; (b) in the middle, giving **fin**, **fun**, **fen**, etc.; and (c) at the end, giving **fat**, **fad**, **fang**, etc. There are no smaller units on which substitution can operate. For example, the **f** portion cannot, as it were, be split in half. This justifies the statement that **fan** contains three segments.

One of the rules of impressionistic-phonetic representation is, as we have seen, that the same symbol should always be used to represent the same sound. Although this sounds simple enough, much hangs on what we mean by 'the same'. To some extent, this varies from language to language. For example, to a native speaker of English, the **k**-sound at the beginning of **kin** is the same as the **k**-sound of **skin**. However, for a native speaker of Hindi, the two would not be the same because the **k**-sound of **kin** is followed by a short **h**-like element, known as 'aspiration', while the **k**-sound of **skin** is not. This is because, in Hindi, the difference between aspirated **k** and unaspirated **k** is crucial for distinguishing between words (**khānā** 'food' vs. **kān** 'ear') while it is not in English. On the other hand, English speakers think of the **d**-sound of **den** and the **th**-sound of **then** ([ð]) as quite distinct while many native speakers of Spanish are unaware of a distinction between **d**-like sounds and ð-like sounds in their own language. In this case, the same type of explanation applies.

The trained impressionistic phonetician would side with the Hindi speakers in the first case and with the English speakers in the second case, while recognising that languages may treat two phonetically different sounds as varieties of 'the same' sound. In other words, languages not only vary as regards which sounds they use, they vary as regards the way those sounds are organised into a system. The term *phoneme* is used to refer to a grouping of sounds which are treated as the variants of one another within the system of a particular language. If two sounds contrast, that is, if substituting one for the other will result in another (real or potential) word, they must belong to different phonemes. For example, aspirated **k** and unaspirated **k** belong to the same phoneme in English, but they are different phonemes in Hindi. The question of how a linguist might decide that two sounds which he or she hears as different really are 'the same' in the system of the language he or she is studying is one which we cannot take up here.

From what has just been said, it should be clear that there are two distinct approaches to the problem of representing speech as a sequence of segments. One is to use a distinct symbol for each distinct sound, as defined by the system of the language concerned. This is known as a *phonemic transcription* or *phonemic representation*. Conventionally, phonemic transcriptions are set off by slashes (//). For example, the English words **pan** and **nap** would be represented as /pæn/ and /næp/ in phonemic transcription.

The second approach involves the use of a distinct symbol for each distinguishable sound, where 'distinguishable' is meant in a more universal way, without reference to the system of any particular language. This is known as *impressionistic transcription* or *impressionistic representation*. Conventionally, impressionistic transcriptions are set off by square brackets ([ ]). In this case, there is also a decision to be taken as to how much phonetic detail to represent. Transcriptions may be *narrow* (detailed) or *broad*, these two qualities being matters of degree. For example, relatively narrow transcriptions of the English words **pan** and **nap** in a Southern British pronunciation might be [pʰæn] and [næˀp̚] (where the superscript **h** indicates aspiration, the superscript **?** indicates that the [p] is accompanied by a 'glottal stop' and the ˺ indicates that the [p] is not released). Broad transcriptions would be [pæn] and [næp]. In this book, I shall use mostly phonemic representations (//), but in some cases general phonetic representations ([]) will be more appropriate.

### 1.4.2 Mental representations

As I have already said, the task of teasing out the nature of mental representations of the sounds of language belongs to the domain of phonology, a branch of theoretical linguistics. Hypotheses about mental representations are usually expressed in the form of diagrams (visual representations of supposed mental representations), and this makes phonology a very visual subject. Although a number of distinct schools of thought exist, they share a good deal of common ground. At the risk of oversimplification, I shall attempt to give an overview of some of this common ground which we shall need to refer back to at various points in the remainder of the book.

1  Structure is separated from phonetic-phonological content. For example, the English monosyllabic words **fan**, **cat** and **top** would all be considered to have the same structure, but to differ in content. The term *melody* is often used to refer to what we term *content*.

Structure is basically hierarchical, though individual phonologists would disagree as to the number of levels, precisely which constituents are involved at each level, and the 'rules of the game' for forming the structures. Figure 1.2 shows one possible view of the structure of the English word **fan**. In this formulation, the highest level in the structure is the syllable (σ). At the lowest

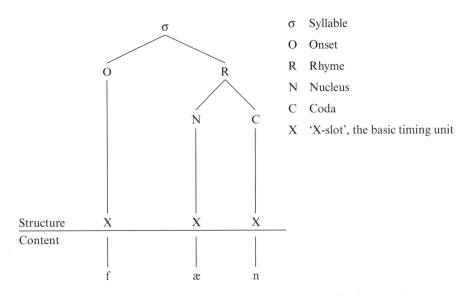

FIGURE 1.2    One possible representation of the structure of the English word **fan**.

end of structure is a series of *timing units* or *skeletal slots*, which serve to provide the link between structure and content. Usually, but not always, the slots are equivalent to the segments of impressionistic phonetics (a long vowel is one segment but occupies two skeletal slots). These slots are not related to physical time in an explicit way, though they do provide information about relative timing. For example, although two Xs will have a longer duration than one X, it is not expected that the duration of XX will be *exactly* twice the duration of X. X-slots also serve to indicate how the individual segments (melodic items) are ordered with respect to each other.

The hierarchical structure does not in fact end with the syllable. Syllables are organised into higher-level rhythmic units, consisting of alternating strong and weak elements. For example, the word **language** is a single *foot*, consisting of a strong first syllable and a weak second syllable. The compound **language teacher** is made up of two such feet. In this more complex structure, the first element (**language**) is stronger than the second (**teacher**). This approach can be taken further, building up higher-level units such as intonational phrases or even whole utterances. It is clear that some aspects of production and perception, such as intonation tunes, must be directly related to these higher-level units.

2    As regards content, segments are decomposable into more basic units, commonly referred to as *distinctive features*, which are said to be the *atoms* or *primes* of phonological representation. These features can be translated into the classificatory dimensions of impressionistic phonetics in a straightforward way, though the correspondence is not necessarily one-to-one. The features are not simply listed, as would be the case in an impressionistic description (or in

earlier theoretical approaches to phonology), but exist within a hierarchical structure.

Some controversy exists as to how the features should be defined and whether or not they should be expressed as binary oppositions. The philosophical issues involved cannot be discussed here. It should be remembered, however, that, whatever names are given to the features, and however they are represented visually, they are essentially abstract mental codings which we identify only by virtue of their translation equivalents at lower levels of the speech chain. For example, a nasal consonant might be specified by a positive-valued feature [+ nasal] or by a more abstract nasal element represented by capital N, and either of these might be defined with reference to speech production, the acoustic signal, or speech perception. We might choose the first option, and define the nasality feature with reference to a low position of the soft palate (which allows air to flow into the nasal cavity), but still *it is not the same thing* as a low position of the soft palate. Nor is it the same thing as a motor command to lower the soft palate.

Something of the nature of views on what lies below the X-slot can be seen in Figure 1.3, though, because the nature of segmental structure is continually subject to debate and revision, neither of the two diagrams can be taken as definitive. The figure contrasts two representations of an aspirated [pʰ], in impressionistic terms a *voiceless aspirated bilabial (plosive) stop*. Both are similar in that they have a tree structure, consisting of nodes at various levels, with the top node known as the *root node*. Diagram (a), taken from Kenstowicz (1994: 152), is formulated in the *Feature Geometry* framework. In this framework, features are defined as dimensions. The root node specifies that the segment is a non-sonorant consonant (terms not included in the conventional descriptive label, but which could be inferred from it). Otherwise, [− continuant] translates into *stop*, the presence of the node *labial* under the oral node translates into *bilabial*, [− voiced] translates into *voiceless*, and [+ spread glottis] translates into *aspirated*.

Diagram (b), based on Harris (1994), is within the framework known as *Government Phonology*. In this approach, the primes are called *elements* rather than *features*, and are conceived of as whole entities in their own right which are defined formally in terms of abstract acoustic properties. In this case, the upper-case **H** under the laryngeal node translates into *voiceless aspirated*, the **U** under the place node translates into *bilabial*, and the ʔ attached directly to the root node translates into *stop*. The lower-case **h** additionally specifies that the stop is released. The elements are more abstract than the features of (a), and their interpretation in terms of impressionistic-phonetic dimensions depends on what other elements they are combined with. For example, when small **h** appears without the ʔ, it translates into the impressionistic-phonetic dimension *fricative*.

3   It is necessary to distinguish between two levels of representation, *underlying representation* and *surface representation*. In this context, slashes (//) are often used for underlying representations and square brackets ([]) for surface

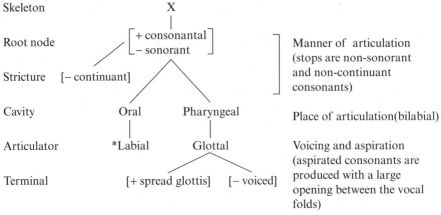

(a) The Feature Geometry framework, adapted from Kenstowicz (1994: 152). The asterisk indicates that the lips are the principal articulator.

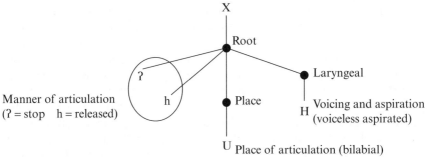

(b) The Government Phonology framework, based on Harris (1994: 127–138).

FIGURE 1.3    Two views of the phonological structure of a voiceless aspirated bilabial plosive ([pʰ]).

representations. This should be distinguished from the use of // for phonemic representations and [ ] for impressionistic representations described in Section 1.4.1. In this section, and here only, we shall follow the phonological convention of using // and [ ] for underlying and surface representations respectively.

Differences between underlying and surface representations arise when complex words or phrases are built up from simpler elements. To take a simple and often-discussed example, in English, there is a negative prefix which has the form **in-** when it is attached to a word beginning with a vowel, as in **ineligible**. However, its pronunciation varies when it is attached to a word beginning with a consonant: compare, for example, **impossible**, **intolerant** and **incomplete**. (In the last of these, the orthographic **n** is pronounced like the **ng** sound of **sing**, transcribed [ŋ].) On the one hand, we should like to think that there is only one prefix, but, on the other hand, we must account for the diversity in the way it is pronounced. Theoretical phonology offers a solution by allowing the prefix to exist on two levels. At the underlying level, it has only one form, while, on the surface level, it takes on a variety of forms. A crucial point here is that the surface form of the prefix is entirely predictable. For example, in the case of words beginning with stop consonants, the final nasal sound must agree with the initial consonant in place of articulation. Thus, only the bilabial nasal [m] (**im-**) may appear before the bilabial stop [p].

It is examples like this one which provide motivation for giving the status of independent primes to classificatory dimensions of sounds. For example, we might wish to claim that the prefix has the form **in-** at the deep level but is changed to **im-** at the surface level whenever a /p/ follows. However, this is not very insightful, because the change is only a minimal one. Like [n], [m] is a nasal consonant, and all that has changed is its place of articulation. It is simpler to say that what has changed is the specification for place (*bilabial* for *coronal*) rather than that the entire segment [m] has been substituted for /n/. In other terminology, the /n/ of the prefix has undergone a phonological process of assimilation to the following /p/.

An alternative would be to claim that the consonant of the prefix has no inherent place of articulation at the underlying level. It is only an abstract nasal consonant, which might be represented orthographically as **N**. In this case, it would only acquire its specification when it comes to be adjacent to /p/. Another way of putting the matter would be that the labial specification for place of articulation spreads from the /p/ to the adjacent nasal. Whichever of the alternatives we choose (changing specification or acquiring specification), such processes are easy to represent visually using diagrams such as those of Figure 1.3. Individual specifications may be *delinked* or *spread* at the level of any node.

An example which uses the same type of formalism as Figure 1.3 (a) is shown in Figure 1.4. This illustrates how an underlying sequence /np/ would be converted into a surface sequence [mp] in the Feature Geometry framework (based on Kenstowicz 1994: 150–151). The node for the coronal place of articulation is delinked in the feature tree for /n/. The node for the labial place of articulation from the adjacent /p/ is then associated with the 'mother' Oral node. The process would be described as 'changing specification' because the nasal consonant is specified as coronal /n/ underlyingly and is then changed to labial [m].

As many readers will be aware, the nature of underlying representations and the way in which they are converted to surface representations has been the subject of much debate. For example, some theoreticians would argue that surface representations are generated by applying sets of rules to underlying representations, while others would prefer to think in terms of constraints which rule out infelicitous possibilities. These issues cannot be taken up here.

To conclude this section, it is useful to ask what light experimental-phonetic data might be able to shed on the nature of mental representations. Firstly, since features can only be defined with reference to their translation equivalents at lower levels of the speech chain, experimental-phonetic data can be of

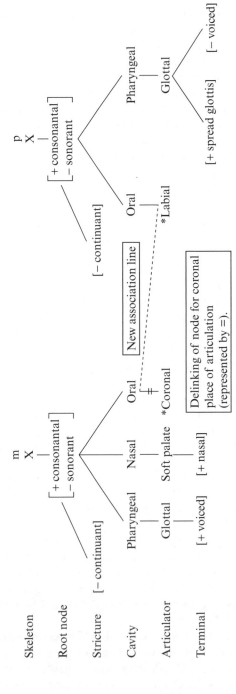

FIGURE 1.4   An example of how 'feature trees' may be used to represent assimilation (in the Feature Geometry framework). In this example, an underlying sequence /np/ is converted into a surface sequence of [mp]. A possible example from English would be the derivation of surface **impossible** from underlying /ɪn/ + **possible**. In this example, it is assumed that the /p/ is aspirated as in English.

use in suggesting and refining definitions. For example, the use of the feature [spread glottis] to define aspiration was suggested by experimental-phonetic research, as will be explained in Section 8.3.7. It is with reference to definitions of features that phonologists are most frequently moved to consult their phonetician colleagues. However, it is unlikely that experimental-phonetic data can provide crucial evidence for deciding between different theories about the nature of the features (binary or non-binary) or about how underlying representations are related to surface representations.

Secondly, experimental phonetics has provided more insight into the nature of structural units above the X-slot (*prosodic structure*), such as syllables (Figure 1.2), feet, and phrases. This has two aspects: (1) identifying special characteristics which mark out the beginnings and endings of such units and (2) investigating how the internal organisation of such units affects both articulatory organisation and the acoustic signal.

Thirdly, the techniques of experimental phonetics can be used to investigate the operation of phonological processes such as assimilation. Some examples of this type of data will be discussed in Section 8.5.

Fourthly, as already mentioned, experimental-phonetic data is crucial for understanding the link between phonetics and phonology within the paths of the speech chain. If it were to be shown that some hypothesized mental representations could not be translated into production or arrived at via perception in a straightforward way, this would provide a strong argument for rejecting the hypothesis in question. As yet, no such case has come to light. However, various proposals have been put forward which would, as it were, move phonetics higher up the speech chain into territory more usually considered to belong to the domain of phonology. Some examples will be considered briefly in Section 5.2.4.5 and Section 8.5.

## 1.5    Experimental phonetics and the structure of sound systems

We mentioned above that the sounds of any particular language form a system. If we compare systems across languages, a number of statistical tendencies emerge. To give a well-known example, languages appear to prefer rounded back vowels to unrounded back vowels, and no vowel systems have come to light which have only unrounded back vowels without also having rounded ones. Acoustic studies of vowel quality suggest an explanation: lip rounding makes back vowels more different from front vowels in acoustic terms and, consequently, they should be easier to distinguish from one another (Chapter 6).

Theories of mental representations have incorporated various devices for giving expression to such general preferences in the structure of systems. Such concerns are a major theme of Archangeli and Pulleyblank (1994). Experimental-phonetic data cannot provide decisive evidence for choosing between theoretical approaches, but it can suggest explanations as to why such preferences should occur. More generally, we imagine that language should have evolved to make maximally efficient use of human capabilities for producing and perceiving speech. What is efficient can be established only by means of experimental-phonetic methods. Considerations of efficiency arise particularly in the study of speech aerodynamics, which will be taken up in Chapter 8.

## 1.6   The structure and scope of this book

From what has been said already, it should be clear that experimental phonetics is an extremely diverse field, in which the study of the acoustics of speech plays a pivotal role. Any introduction to experimental phonetics must therefore begin with the acoustic signal, how it can be represented visually, and how it can be described in both qualitative and quantitative terms. These topics will be·the main focus of Chapters 2 and 3. Chapter 4 deals with the acoustics of speech production, while Chapter 5 provides an introduction to perception and hearing. Chapters 6 and 7 deal with the acoustic characteristics of vowels and consonants respectively. Chapter 8 is concerned with various aspects of speech production.

Probably the most important topic which has not been included is intonation, which is a major research interest for many experimental phoneticians, following on from work by Janet Pierrehumbert. This is partly for reasons of space and partly because the study of intonation arguably belongs much more to the domain of phonology than to the domain of phonetics proper. An excellent introduction to the study of intonation with substantial coverage of the work of experimental phoneticians in this field is Ladd (1996).

Another regrettable omission is an account of experimental-phonetic studies relating to prosodic structure (Section 1.4.2) and rhythm. Interest in these areas has been increasing in recent years, and they are likely to become more important. A good starting point for further reading are the volumes *Papers in Laboratory Phonology* (Kingston and Beckman 1990; Docherty and Ladd 1992; Keating 1994; Connell and Arvaniti 1995).

Finally, it should be mentioned that the book assumes a familiarity with the basic descriptive framework of impressionistic phonetics and the alphabet of the International Phonetic Association (IPA). A brief overview of impressionistic phonetic classification is given in the Appendix.

## 1.7   Further reading

A large number of books provide elementary introductions to the impressionistic-phonetic classification of speech sounds. Most of these also include an introduction to the phoneme and phonemic transcription. Such works include books specifically about phonetics, such as Abercrombie (1967), Ashby (1995), Ladefoged (1993) or O'Connor (1973); introductory textbooks on phonology, such as Gussenhoven and Jacobs (1998), Katamba (1989) or Spencer (1996);

introductory textbooks on general linguistics, such as Robins (1989) or O'Grady *et al.* (1997); and books aimed at improving the student's pronunciation of English or other languages, such as Roach (1991). A good introduction to phonetics and phonology for the absolute beginner is Davenport and Hannahs (1998). Clark and Yallop (1995) also covers both fields, and is more comprehensive.

Special mention should be given to Catford (1988), which is based on a carefully thought out and rigorous programme of phonetic experiments which are profitable for beginner and more advanced student alike. The most complete and in-depth treatment of impressionistic phonetics is Laver (1994), which also assumes no background knowledge on the part of the reader.

As regards theoretical phonology (within the tradition of Generative Grammar), a large number of books are available as well. To those already mentioned, I shall add Kenstowicz (1994), Roca (1994) and Roca and Johnson (1999). The second of these includes an introduction to the Government Phonology approach (illustrated in Figure 1.3), as does Harris (1994). A comprehensive reference work on phonology is the *Handbook of Phonological Theory*, edited by Goldsmith (1994). Finally, special mention should be made of Kelly and Local (1989), which discusses in some detail how one goes from a detailed narrow phonetic transcription to a more abstract phonological analysis.

## Note

1  Unless otherwise stated, references to 'English' will be based on Standard Southern British pronunciation and will not necessarily apply to all varieties of English.

**Chapter 2**

# The nature of sound

## 2.1 Introduction

The ability to represent sound visually and to describe it objectively, in a way that does not depend on human sensory perception, is central to modern experimental phonetics (Section 1.3). Accordingly, in this chapter, I shall concentrate on the nature of sound.

Sound is very elusive. It ultimately depends on very small and very quick movements of air particles, and movements exist only in time. The particles themselves are much too small to be seen with the naked eye and the movements are too quick to be perceived as separate events. In order even to begin talking about sound, it is necessary to be able to picture it on a much larger scale. It is important to add here that the same sound can be visualised and conceptualised in a number of different ways, just as the same object can be photographed from a number of different angles. Different representations of the same sound can be quite different in appearance and can also provide quite different types of information, just as different photographs of the same object do not look the same and may reveal quite different aspects of the object. To the experienced acoustic phonetician, this multiplicity of ways of viewing the same acoustic event is an advantage to be exploited, but to the beginner it can make the subject seem confusing.

Sound has a dual nature. It is at once a unified entity and a collection of individual components working together. We might suggest an analogy with an orchestra (or any musical ensemble), which is a unity with a single voice but is, at the same time, a collection of individual instruments, all contributing their own voices to the whole in various proportions. In this chapter, I shall present two ways of visualising a single sound, corresponding to these two aspects. The *waveform* corresponds to the first view of sound, and presents it as a single entity, evolving through time. The *spectrum* corresponds to the second view, and is essentially an overview of individual components, which also sets out the relative importance of each contribution to the whole.

## 2.2 Sound waves

To describe sound is to describe *sound waves*. Sound waves involve transmission of a pattern of motion through a medium. Within the medium, each

20

particle transmits its motion to its neighbour – there can be no sound in a vacuum. In most everyday situations, the medium is air. Air particles, too small to be seen, are set in motion by the sound-producing body. Each particle sets its neighbour in motion, with the result that, invisibly and with surprising speed, the pattern of motion travels through space and reaches the ears of any potential hearers.

Sound waves are difficult to visualise because the particles of air are moving back and forth in the same direction as the wave travels. The result is that, at any given point along the wave's path, air particles are continually coming closer together and then moving further apart. A good analogy is the movement of a disturbance down the length of a spring, which is easy to demonstrate using the toy springs known as 'Slinkys'. If you lay the spring out flat, take hold of one end, and move your hand back and forth repeatedly, a series of compressions, in which individual rings of the spring come closer together, appears to move down the length of the spring. The rings of the spring are moving back and forth, along the same line as the wave itself is moving. Although no individual ring of the spring moves very far, the compressions travel the whole length of the spring. Furthermore, the motion of each individual ring duplicates the original motion of your hand.

### 2.2.1  Describing a simple sound wave

Everyday experience tells us that many sounds originate from the vibration of objects. For example, when the string of an instrument such as a guitar or a harp is plucked, it can usually be seen to vibrate as the sound is produced.

The acoustician's usual example is the sounding of a tuning fork. A tuning fork is a small two-pronged fork which is tuned to a particular pitch, and which is used by musicians as an aid to tuning their instruments. When the fork is struck, or when its prongs are pinched, the prongs move in and out, as illustrated in Figure 2.1 (a). Let us now focus our attention on the right-hand prong. In the drawing, the outward movement is to the right. Each outward movement pushes the immediately adjacent air particles to the right. Each inward movement creates an unfilled space which will immediately be filled by a corresponding leftward movement of particles. In fact, the motions of the individual air particles will reproduce the motion of the prong of the fork.

To describe the motion of a prong of a tuning fork, we need to consider how its position changes with time. We start when the right-hand prong is moving through the upright position, which is also its position at rest (Position 1 of Figure 2.1 (a)). At this stage, it is moving with maximum speed. As it continues to move rightwards, it will gradually slow down until it reaches its maximum displacement (Position 2). At this point, it reverses direction and begins moving to the left, picking up speed and reaching maximum speed as it moves back through the upright position (Position 3). It continues moving leftwards, gradually slowing down, until it reaches its maximum leftward displacement (Position 4). It then reverses direction again, picking up speed as it

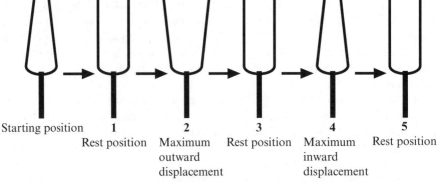

Starting position    1              2              3              4              5
                Rest position   Maximum      Rest position   Maximum      Rest position
                                outward                      inward
                                displacement                 displacement

(a) Movement of the prongs of a tuning fork after it has been made to sound by pinching the two prongs together. The prongs move outward (2) and inward (4), via the rest position (1, 3, 5).

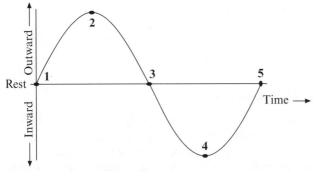

(b) Graph showing the inward and outward displacement of one of the prongs of a tuning fork such as that pictured in (a). On this graph, the baseline corresponds to the position at rest (that is, when the fork is not sounding). Outward movements of the prong correspond to upward movements on the graph, whereas inward movements of the prong correspond to downward movements on the graph.

FIGURE 2.1    Describing the motion of a prong of a tuning fork.

moves toward the upright position (Position 5). We are now back to where we started at Position 1. The prong of the fork has gone through one complete *cycle*.

Figure 2.1 (b) shows a graph illustrating this motion. The middle or baseline position, when the prong of the fork is upright, is represented by a straight horizontal line. Outward movements of the prong correspond to upward movements on the graph, while inward movements of the prong correspond to downward movements on the graph. The graph starts when the prong of the fork is upright (Position 1). The curve ascends to its maximum height as the prong of the fork moves outward to its maximum displacement (Position 2). It then reverses direction and moves down, crossing the baseline (Position 3), until it reaches its minimum, corresponding to the prong's maximum inward displacement (Position 4). Finally, it returns to the baseline (Position 5) and the cycle can begin all over again.

The curve which describes the motion of the tuning fork prong is called a *sine curve*, or *sinusoid* (meaning sine-like), and the prong of the tuning fork itself is said to move in *simple harmonic motion*. We would produce a graph of the same shape if we were to set out to describe the motion of a number of other simple oscillating objects such as the up-and-down movements of a weight on the end of a spring or the back-and-forth movements of a swing or pendulum. The sound produced by a tuning fork is known as a *pure tone*.

### 2.2.2 From movements to pressures

What is more important for our purposes is that the sine curve shown in Figure 2.1 (b) also describes the motion of the air particles immediately to the right of the right-hand prong. Moreover, these particles are setting their neigh- bours in motion, which are in turn setting their neighbours in motion, and so on. Thus, the graph describes the pattern of motion which is being transmitted from one layer of air particles to another. It gives us a visual representation of the pattern, and we can think of it as a picture of the sound wave which is being transmitted from the tuning fork. In this instance, we refer to the wave itself as a *sine wave* and to the picture which describes it as a *sinusoidal waveform* or a *sine waveform*. In practice, the distinction between *wave* and *waveform* may be blurred, and the two-dimensional representations of waves (i.e. waveforms) may be referred to simply as 'waves'.

Less obviously, the graph of Figure 2.1 (b) also describes variations in air pressure. As air particles move closer together and further apart, air pressure increases and decreases. Figure 2.2 shows how the spacing between air particles in a line will change over time during the transmission of a sine wave along the line. The double rows, numbered 1 to 12, show a series of particles in two parallel rows, at twelve points in time. Each individual particle moves a small distance, to the left or to the right, in simple harmonic motion, and performs just over half a complete cycle in the time between row 1 and row 12. The series of short curved lines labelled **c**, in the middle of the figure, pick out the motion of one pair of particles.

Each row contains alternating *compressions* (where the particles are more crowded together and the pressure is higher) and *rarefactions* (where the par- ticles are further apart and the pressure is lower), as illustrated in Figures 2.2 and 2.3. As we move in time from row 1 to row 12, the compressions appear to be travelling to the right. The distance from one compression to the next, however, remains constant. This is illustrated by the two lines at the bottom, labelled **d** and **e**, each of which runs between points of maximal compression. We shall return to this point below.

Now let us concentrate on the area enclosed by the two vertical lines **a** and **b**, which corresponds to a fixed position in space. The number of particles between the lines increases from time 1 to time 4 and then decreases. This

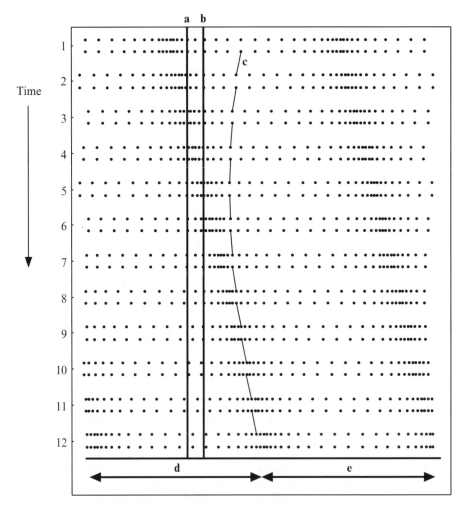

Movement of wave through space ⟶

FIGURE 2.2   The changing position of air particles during the transmission of a simple sound wave. The twelve rows represent a double row of air particles at twelve successive points in time. Each particle moves back and forth in simple harmonic motion. The short curved lines (**c**) pick out the motion of one pair of particles.

Each row contains alternating *compressions* (where the particles are crowded together and the pressure is higher) and *rarefactions* (where the particles are further apart and pressure is lower). The compressions appear to move gradually to the right, but remain equally spaced. Lines **d** and **e** run between points of maximal compression in row 12.

The area between the two vertical lines, **a** and **b**, corresponds to a fixed position in space. As we move from time 1 to time 12, particles become more crowded together, and then more dispersed, at this position. In other words, increasing pressure alternates with decreasing pressure.

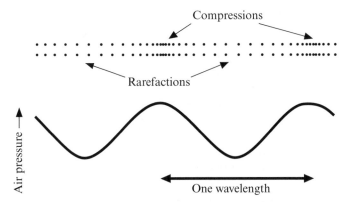

FIGURE 2.3    Spatial variation in air pressure during the transmission of a simple sound wave. The drawing at the top, which is identical to row 8 of Figure 2.2, represents a double row of air particles. The waveform below depicts the corresponding variation in air pressure. Like the graph of Figure 2.1 (b), it is a sine wave. The *wavelength* is the distance required to execute one cycle.

makes the point that, if we were to take up a fixed position in space and observe changes in air pressure as the wave travels by, we should find that the pressure goes up and down. A graph showing how air pressure increases and decreases with time will have exactly the same sinusoidal form as the graph which describes the motion of the individual particles or the motion of the prong of the tuning fork. The same holds true for more complicated patterns of motion.

Equipment for recording and displaying sound waves is based on responding to changes in air pressure and, for this reason, graphs representing sound waves are sometimes referred to as *pressure waveforms*. It is probably easier to think about sound waves as patterns of movement. It is easier still to think pictorially, in terms of a two-dimensional visual waveform like that of Figure 2.1 (b). Indeed, there is much to be said for this third view, since it is the *pattern* which is of primary importance rather than the particles or the pressure variations which may be involved in executing it.

As we shall see in Chapter 3, recording, displaying and analysing sound waves depends crucially on our ability to translate patterns of variation in pressure into patterns of varying electrical voltage, and by the time a 'sound wave' comes to be displayed on a computer screen, it is several translations away from the original variations in air pressure. Furthermore, the same principles which we use to analyse sound waves can also be applied to other things which vary through time such as rate of air flow. These must also be translated into patterns of varying electrical voltage before they can be displayed and analysed. Thus, it has become common to think and speak abstractly, not of displaying and analysing sound waves, but of displaying and analysing *signals*. The sound waves which we record are often referred to as 'acoustic signals'.

### 2.2.3  Sound waves in space

Whether we conceive of a waveform as depicting variation in pressure or movements of particles or variations in electrical voltage, we are thinking about a pattern of variation in one dimension through time. I have been at pains to make clear that it is the pattern itself which is of primary importance. It is also possible, however, to think about waveforms as patterns of variation in space. This is clear from diagrams such as Figure 2.2, which show a pattern of alternating compression and rarefaction moving through space. If we imagine taking a snapshot of the wave at any instant in time, we should see something like one of the rows of Figure 2.2. We could draw a graph in which distance, rather than time, was on the horizontal axis and air pressure was on the vertical axis, as in Figure 2.3. This graph has the same form as the graph of Figure 2.1 (b), which shows variation through time.

### 2.2.4  Some definitions

An important feature of sine waves is that they repeat themselves over and over again, so that they can be described as a series of *cycles*. Figure 2.4 shows ten cycles of a sine wave. The duration of a single cycle is called the *period*. It is often represented by the capital letter **T**, and may be measured in seconds or in milliseconds (thousandths of a second). The *frequency* is the number of cycles per second, and is represented by capital **F** or lower-case **f**. There is an important relationship between F and T, namely

$\mathbf{f} \times \mathbf{T} = \mathbf{1}$, which implies that
$\mathbf{f} = \mathbf{1/T}$ and $\mathbf{T} = \mathbf{1/f}$.

For example, in Figure 2.4, T is .01 seconds and F is 100 cycles per second (.01 × 100 = 1). In general, the shorter the period, the higher the frequency.

Frequency plays an important role in specifying the internal structure of speech sounds (Section 2.4.2). It is measured in *cycles per second*, abbreviated

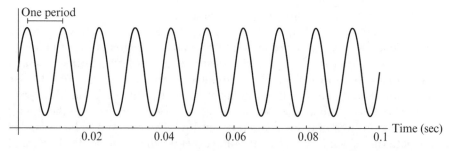

FIGURE 2.4    Ten cycles of a sine wave with frequency 100 Hz. The period (duration of a single cycle) is 0.01 sec. In this example, we have measured from the peak of the first cycle to the peak of the second cycle.

*cps*. However, it is very common to use the term *Hertz*, abbreviated *Hz*, and we shall do so in this book. This usage honours the memory of the German physicist Heinrich Hertz (d. 1894).

The period is important because it provides a means of determining frequency. For example, in the case of Figure 2.4, we can divide 1/.01 to obtain a frequency of 100 cycles per second. This is much easier than extending the graph to a full second of time and then counting up the number of cycles which occur within that second. In any case, it would be highly unusual for a speech sound to be prolonged to a duration of a full second. As regards the period, the formula given above (f = 1/T) requires that the period should be measured in seconds. It is common, however, to report durations in milliseconds (abbreviated *msec* or *ms*).

As already mentioned, sounds with sinusoidal waveforms are called *pure tones*. The *pitch* of a pure tone is related to its frequency; if the frequency increases, the pitch rises (Section 5.4). In principle, it is important to distinguish between frequency, which is a measurable characteristic of sounds as they exist in the physical world, and pitch, which is a psychological attribute of sounds and exists only in the mind. We cannot measure pitch directly; we can only measure frequency. Accordingly, frequency is often used to specify pitch, as, for example, when an orchestra tunes to modern 'concert pitch' defined by the frequency of the note A (440 cycles per second).

Measuring frequency in speech or music is rather like measuring the speed at which a car is travelling. For example, it is possible to travel at 60 miles per hour for less than a minute, and then accelerate to 70 miles per hour. Strictly speaking, the figure of 60 mph displayed on the dashboard is determined by monitoring the revolutions of the wheels; it tells us that if the wheels were to continue to turn at the same rate for an hour, we should expect to cover a distance of 60 miles. However, we usually think of a figure like '60 mph' as a means of quantifying how fast we are going at some particular moment in time. In the same way, the frequency of a sound at any particular moment in time tells us how many cycles of vibration the air particles might execute in a second if they kept going at the same rate. In practice, we usually think of it as a means of quantifying pitch, which might go up or down a few milliseconds later.

Another important aspect of sine waves is *wavelength*. If we think about a sine wave as a pattern in space rather than a pattern in time, we again observe a pattern which repeats itself, this time over equal distances (Figure 2.3). The distance required to execute one cycle is the wavelength. Wavelength is commonly represented by the Greek letter λ (*lambda*).

It is well known that sound travels at a constant velocity. Precisely what this velocity is depends on the medium through which it travels and other factors such as temperature. Here, we shall assume a value of 340 metres per second for sound travelling through air. The velocity of sound is commonly represented by the letter **c**. There is also an important relationship between frequency and wavelength, namely

$c = f \times \lambda$, which implies that
$f = c/\lambda$ and
$\lambda = c/f$.

For example, in the case of the 100 Hz wave of Figure 2.4, the wavelength would be 3.4 metres (340/100 = 3.4). More generally, the shorter the wavelength, the higher the frequency. This particular relationship will become important when we discuss a simple model of vowel production in Section 4.2.2.2.

## 2.3   Types of sound waves

Sound waves may be classified into three basic types:

1 *Periodic.*   A periodic wave is one which is cyclic in nature, and is characterised by a repeating pattern. A sine wave is the simplest example of a periodic wave and, accordingly, is said to be *simple*. *All* other types of periodic waves are *complex*. Among speech sounds, periodic waveforms are characteristic of voiced sonorants, that is, vowels and sonorant consonants ([m], [l], etc.). Each period of the acoustic signal corresponds to a single cycle of vocal fold vibration (Section 8.3.2). The frequency of repetition is the *fundamental frequency*, symbolised by $F_0$ or lower-case $f_0$. We have already said that the pitch of a pure tone is related to its frequency; more generally, the pitch of a sound with a periodic waveform is related to its fundamental frequency.[1]

Figure 2.5 (a) is an example of a periodic waveform from speech.[2] It shows the waveform for a single pronunciation of the vowel [i] (English /i/ of **beat**) by a male speaker. In this example, the period is 8.3 msec (.0083 sec) and the fundamental frequency is 120.5 Hz ($120.5 \times .0083 = 1$).

The opposite of *periodic* is *aperiodic*. Aperiodic waveforms are waveforms which have no repeating pattern. There are two types of aperiodicity, giving two further types of sound.

2 *Aperiodic continuous.*   We shall use the term *noisy* to refer to this type. Variation in air pressure is essentially random, and there is no repeating pattern, although the sound may be continued for a considerable length of time. Among speech sounds, voiceless fricatives are noisy sounds *par excellence*. The aspiration which is typically heard following the release of plosives in English is another good example. An example of a waveform for a voiceless fricative [s] (English /s/) pronounced by a male speaker is shown in Figure 2.5 (b).

Types (1) and (2) may combine to give a compound type, characterised by periodicity with superimposed noise. Prototypical examples of this type of sound are the voiced fricatives, in which noise is superimposed on the regular waveform associated with vocal fold vibration. A good example is shown in Figure 2.5 (c), which is a waveform for the voiced fricative [z] (English /z/) pronounced by a male speaker. This has a discernible pattern of up-and-down movement rather similar to that of (a) but with superimposed noise which resembles the waveform of (b).

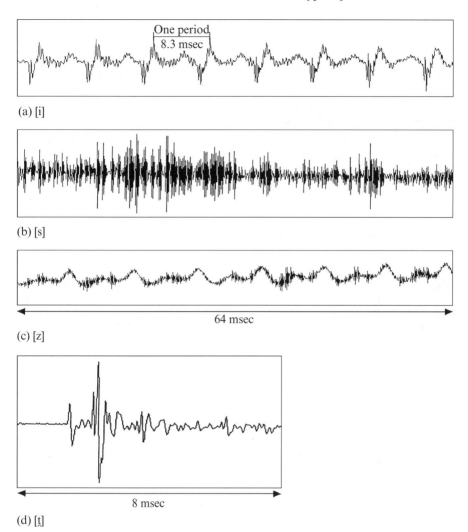

FIGURE 2.5    Four examples of speech waveforms.

3 *Transient*.    Transient sounds are defined by their very brief duration. Although their waveforms may show up-and-down movements which resemble those of periodic waveforms, the movements die away too quickly for any pattern to develop. Transient sounds in speech are exemplified by releases of stop consonants. (The term *stop* here includes voiced and voiceless plosives, ejectives and implosives, but excludes nasals.) Figure 2.5 (d) shows an example of a waveform for the release of a stop – in this case, an unaspirated [t̪] (Thai /t/) pronounced by a male speaker of Standard Thai.

In the case of fully voiced stops, a periodic waveform will be observed during the closure interval, when the vocal folds are vibrating, but this will be followed by a transient, corresponding to the release of the oral closure (Section 7.3.2). Accordingly, the waveforms associated with voiced stops combine periodic and aperiodic elements, but these occur in sequence (periodicity followed by aperiodic transient) rather than simultaneously as in the case of voiced fricatives.

More generally, voiceless obstruents have aperiodic waveforms and voiced obstruents have waveforms which combine periodicity and aperiodicity in some way. However, aperiodicity is not in itself sufficient to distinguish obstruents from sonorants in all cases. Voiceless sonorants (for example, voiceless vowels) have aperiodic, fricative-like waveforms. Sonorants produced with breathy voicing have waveforms in which aperiodicity is superimposed on periodicity (Section 8.3.6.4).

## 2.4    The structure of sound waves

It is remarkable that, although the four waveforms shown in Figure 2.5 are quite diverse in appearance, they are all built up out of the same basic elements. The basic elements – we might say the 'atoms' or 'primes' – of acoustic analysis are sine waves. In other words, it is possible to generate *any* waveform, be it periodic, noisy, transient, or some combination of these, by combining sine waves. The sine waves themselves cannot be broken down into anything simpler. In this section, we shall focus on complex periodic waves.

A second point is that the relationship between a particular complex wave and the set of sine waves which will generate it is one-to-one. Any given set of sine waves will combine to form one, and only one, complex wave, and any given complex wave can be generated by one, and only one, set of sine waves. That having been said, the order in which the sine waves are combined is not crucial. They can be mixed together, as it were, all at once or added in one by one in any order – the final result is the same.

The above statement belongs to the general domain of mathematics rather than acoustics. In the case of a periodic wave (in mathematical terms, a periodic function), it can be shown that all of the component waves will have frequencies which are multiples of the fundamental frequency. For example, a periodic wave with period 10 msec (0.01 sec) and fundamental frequency 100 Hz will be entirely made up of sine waves having frequencies which are multiples of 100. The work of the French mathematician and Egyptologist Joseph Fourier (d. 1830) was of fundamental importance in establishing this property of periodic functions, and for this reason the analysis of a wave into its sine wave components is known as *Fourier analysis*.

The sine wave components of a complex periodic wave are known as *harmonics*. The harmonic which is the lowest in frequency is known as the *fundamental*. The harmonics are named according to their relationship to the fundamental. For example, if the fundamental frequency is 100 Hz, a component with frequency 300 Hz would be called the *third harmonic* and a component with frequency 1000 Hz would be called the *tenth harmonic*; the fundamental itself is the *first harmonic*.

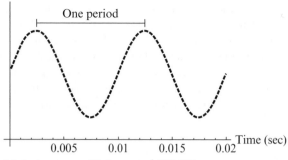

(a) A sine wave with frequency 100 HZ.

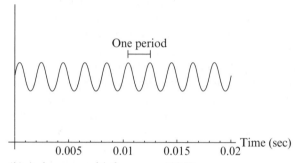

(b) A sine wave with frequency 500 Hz.

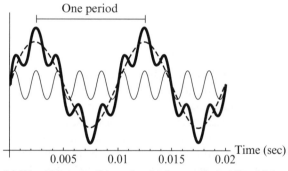

(c) Wave (a), wave (b), and a third wave (in bold), which
was generated by combining (a) and (b). The new wave
looks like the 100 Hz wave with the 500 Hz wave
superimposed. Like wave (a), its period is .01 seconds
and its frequency is 100 Hz.

FIGURE 2.6    A simple example of how a complex periodic wave can be generated by
combining two sine waves.

A simple example showing how two sine waves can be combined to generate
a third, more complex, wave is shown in Figure 2.6. Wave (a) has a frequency
of 100 Hz and wave (b) has a frequency of 500 Hz. In (c), both waves are
shown on the same graph, together with a third wave (in bold) which is their

sum, or combination. It is clear that the sum wave of (c) combines characteristics of both of its components; it looks like the 100 Hz wave with additional up-and-down movements, corresponding to the 500 Hz wave, superimposed on it. In this case, the 100 Hz component is the fundamental while the 500 Hz component is the fifth harmonic. Note that the name 'fifth harmonic' does not imply that there are four other harmonics in the complex wave; it merely indicates that the frequency of the relevant harmonic is five times that of the fundamental.

### 2.4.1   *Specifying sound waves*

Since all sound waves are unique combinations of sine waves, it follows that we can specify any wave uniquely by specifying its sine wave components. Fortunately, for our purposes, any sine wave can be specified adequately – though not uniquely – using only two classificatory dimensions: frequency and amplitude. Only the first (frequency) has been discussed thus far.

The term *amplitude* in this context refers to the maximum height above the baseline achieved by the sine wave, irrespective of frequency. This is distinguished from the *peak-to-peak amplitude*, which is the difference between the highest and lowest points, as illustrated in Figure 2.7 (a). Frequency and amplitude are independent. This is illustrated in Figure 2.7, which shows all four possible ways of combining two different frequencies and amplitudes.

- Same frequency, different amplitudes: (a) and (b) (100 Hz) vs. (c) and (d) (200 Hz).
- Same amplitude, different frequencies: (a) and (c) vs. (b) and (d). The amplitude of waves (b) and (d) is half the amplitude of waves (a) and (c).

In Figure 2.6, the amplitude of wave (a) is three times the amplitude of wave (b), while the frequency of wave (b) is five times that of wave (a).

Whereas frequency is related to our sensation of pitch, amplitude is related to our sensation of loudness. Other things being equal, the larger the amplitude, the louder the sound. We can also regard amplitude as a measure of the strength of a wave. Strictly speaking, amplitude should be measured in the units which physicists use to measure air pressure. However, linguistic phoneticians almost never need to work with such units. This is because what really matters for our purposes is *relative* amplitude. For example, in Figure 2.6, it is crucial that the amplitudes of waves (a) and (b) stand in the proportion 3:1, but we are not really bothered about what the amplitudes are. This is because the perceived quality of a sound depends on what sine waves are present in what proportions, but not on their absolute (actual) amplitudes. It is fortunate for us that this is so. If the perceived quality of a sound depended on absolute amplitude, then our ability to recognise sounds would depend crucially on their having the 'correct' degree of loudness or softness. Among other things, it would not be possible for us to recognise sounds which herald the approach of danger (e.g. the noise of an approaching car) unless they maintained a fixed loudness.

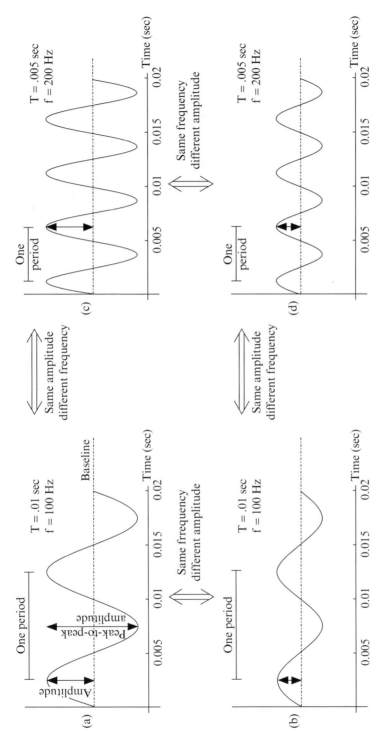

FIGURE 2.7   Four sine waves which illustrate the independence of frequency and amplitude. The *amplitude* of a sine wave is its maximum height above the baseline. This corresponds to the maximum displacement from the rest position of the prong of the tuning fork in Figure 2.1 (position 2). The difference between the highest and lowest levels of a sine wave is the *peak-to-peak amplitude*, as illustrated in (a). The pairs (a)–(b) and (c)–(d) have the same frequency but differ in amplitude; the amplitude of (a) and (c) is twice that of (b) and (d). In contrast, the pairs (a)–(c) and (b)–(d) have the same amplitude but differ in frequency.

From what has just been said, it follows that a complex sound can be specified by giving the frequencies and relative amplitudes of its sine wave components. Such specifications have often been compared to culinary recipes which list ingredients and proportions. For example, a standard recipe for salad dressing calls for oil and vinegar in the proportions 3:1. Whether the cook chooses to use 3 tablespoons of oil to 1 of vinegar or 3 cups of oil to 1 of vinegar, he or she is still making the 'same' recipe. Similarly, whenever we combine a 100 Hz wave and a 500 Hz wave in the proportions 3:1, we generate the 'same' waveform.

To conclude this section, we should note that, in order to specify a sine wave fully, it would also be necessary to include information about *phase*. Figure 2.8 illustrates what is meant by 'phase'. The two sine waves shown have the same amplitude and frequency, but wave (b) is a quarter-cycle ahead of wave (a). It is said that the two waves differ in phase or, more colloquially, that they are 'out of phase'. It should be obvious that, when sine waves are combined together as in Figure 2.6, the relative phases of the individual waves – that is, how the waves are aligned with one another – will affect the shape of the combination. However, this is not considered to have a significant effect

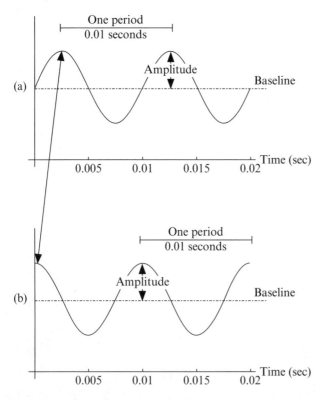

FIGURE 2.8    Two sine waves which have the same frequency and the same amplitude, but which differ in phase. Wave (b) is a quarter-cycle ahead of wave (a).

on the perceived sound. For this reason, information about phase is generally ignored when specifying sounds for phonetic (as well as many other) purposes.

### 2.4.2   *The spectrum*

We have seen that sine waves can be specified sufficiently using only two classificatory dimensions, *frequency* and *relative amplitude*. Accordingly, it is possible to represent the structure of a complex sound using a two-dimensional diagram. Such a diagram is called a *spectrum* (plural *spectra*). Spectra are important for two reasons. Firstly, they are a highly convenient way of visualising the internal structures of complex sounds, which makes it easy to compare one sound with another. Secondly, it is clear that a sort of spectral analysis of incoming sound is performed by the auditory system (Section 5.3). Thus, a spectrum (as compared with a waveform) brings us closer to the way in which the auditory system 'sees' an incoming sound.

Figure 2.9 shows the spectrum of the complex wave of Figure 2.6. It is a two-dimensional graph with the horizontal axis representing frequency and the vertical axis representing relative amplitude. We have seen that the wave contains two sine wave components with frequencies 100 Hz and 500 Hz and relative amplitudes 3 and 1. Accordingly, the first component corresponds to a point with horizontal coordinate 100 and vertical coordinate 3, while the second component corresponds to a point with horizontal coordinate 500 and vertical coordinate 1. It is customary to draw vertical lines connecting each point to the horizontal axis, which makes it easier to identify the frequencies of the components.

As regards the vertical dimension, the fact that we are working with proportions rather than absolute values makes the labelling of the vertical axis somewhat arbitrary. For this reason, the vertical axis is usually left unlabelled on example spectra in introductory textbooks.

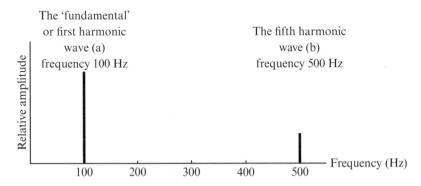

FIGURE 2.9   Spectrum of the complex wave shown in Figure 2.6 (c). Each line corresponds to one of the two sine wave components. The height of the line for the 100 Hz component is three times the height of the line for the 500 Hz component, reflecting the relative amplitudes of the two waves.

Spectra are often referred to as *frequency-domain representations*. By contrast, waveforms are *time-domain representations*.

### 2.4.3  *Generating some vowel-like waveforms*

Figure 2.10 shows three near-periodic waveforms from speech. These represent the vowels (a) [u] (English /u/ in **who'd**),[3] (b) [i] (English /i/ in **beat**) and (c) [ɑ] (English /ɑ/ in **bark**) pronounced by male speakers. In this section, we shall generate waveforms which resemble them by combining small numbers of sine waves.

Of the three vowels, [u] is the simplest to analyse by eye. Each fundamental period contains two major peaks and two major valleys. This suggests that a sine wave which has a frequency twice that of the fundamental – in other words, the second harmonic – is prominent. In fact, we can produce a similar

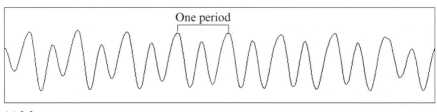

(a) [u]

(b) [i]

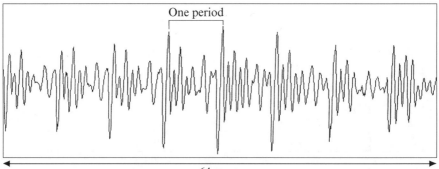

64 msec

(c) [ɑ]

FIGURE 2.10  Waveforms for the vowels [u], [i], and [ɑ], pronounced by male native speakers of English.

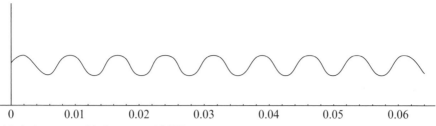

(a) A sine wave with frequency 135 Hz.

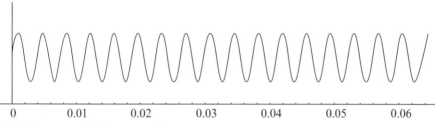

(b) A sine wave with frequency 270 Hz.

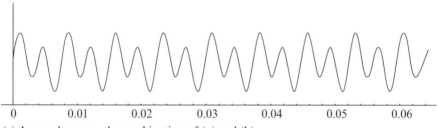

(c) A complex wave, the combination of (a) and (b).

FIGURE 2.11   Combining two sine waves to generate an [u]-like wave.

shape by combining only two sine waves. This is illustrated in Figure 2.11, which shows the two relevant waves individually, together with their combination. The fundamental component has frequency 135 Hz and the second harmonic has frequency 270 Hz. The amplitude ratio is 1:2, in other words, the second harmonic has twice the amplitude of the fundamental.

The second vowel, [i], resembles [u] in that it has two major peaks and valleys in each fundamental period. However, superimposed on this basic pattern is a high-frequency pattern of up-and-down movement. This suggests that a higher-frequency sine wave is superimposed on a more [u]-like pattern. An similar waveform, produced by combining only three sine waves, is shown in Figure 2.12. Part (a), which resembles our /u/-like waveform, represents a combination of a fundamental of 120 Hz and the corresponding second harmonic of 240 Hz. In (b), the eighteenth harmonic, with frequency 2160 Hz,

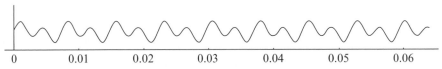

(a) A complex wave, the combination of a sine wave with frequency 120 Hz and a sine wave with frequency 240 Hz.

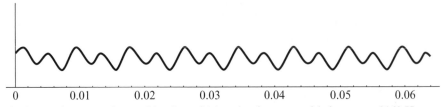

(b) A complex wave, the combination of (a) and a sine wave with frequency 2160 Hz.

FIGURE 2.12    Combining three sine waves to generate an [i]-like wave.

is superimposed to give the high-frequency up-and-down movements. The amplitude ratio of the three components is 3:4:2.

The third vowel, [ɑ], is difficult to analyse by eye, and appears to contain a larger number of components. The second harmonic does not appear to be very prominent (each period does not contain two major peaks and valleys), nor do we see superimposed high-frequency squiggles like those of [i]. To produce a similar waveform, it is necessary to give a prominent role to frequencies in between. An example is given in Figure 2.13, which shows (as (d)) the effect of combining four sine waves: (a) a fundamental of 125 Hz, (b) the seventh harmonic, 875 Hz, (c) the eighth harmonic, 1000 Hz, and also the tenth harmonic, 1250 Hz (not shown). The amplitude ratio of the four components is 5:9:9:9.

Spectra for our three vowel imitations are shown in Figure 2.14. For [u], our two components are at the lower end of the frequency scale. The spectrum of [i] is similar but there is also a somewhat prominent high-frequency component. For [ɑ], the most prominent components lie in the middle, between the low-frequency and high-frequency components of [i]. We shall relate these characteristics to vowel production in Chapter 4. They will also be important in our discussion of the acoustic characteristics of vowels in Chapter 6.

### 2.4.4  *Spectra of aperiodic sounds*

Periodic waveforms are characterised by the regular relationship between their sine wave components. By contrast, in the case of aperiodic waveforms – which by definition *never* repeat themselves – there can be no such regular relationship. Such sounds have an infinite number of sine wave components infinitely close together. Accordingly, it is not possible to draw individual vertical lines for all of the components, and it no longer makes sense to think in terms of discrete individual components. Spectra of aperiodic sounds are continuous

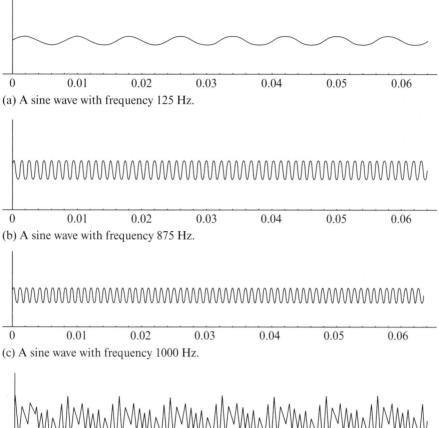

(a) A sine wave with frequency 125 Hz.

(b) A sine wave with frequency 875 Hz.

(c) A sine wave with frequency 1000 Hz.

(d) A complex wave, the combination of (a), (b) and (c) and a fourth wave with frequency 1250 Hz.

FIGURE 2.13   Combining four sine waves to generate an [ɑ]-like wave.

curves, and are called *continuous spectra* in contrast to the *line spectra* of periodic sounds. An example of a continuous spectrum is given in Figure 2.15, which shows a spectrum for a voiceless fricative consonant (English /s/ in **sigh**).

Another way of thinking about a spectrum is as a diagram showing the distribution of energy across a range of frequencies. In the case of periodic sounds, energy falls at discrete frequencies, each of which corresponds to a line. In the case of aperiodic sounds, energy is distributed over a continuous band of frequencies.

There are two types of aperiodic sounds, noisy and transient (Section 2.3), but, for reasons which cannot be gone into here, these do not correspond to

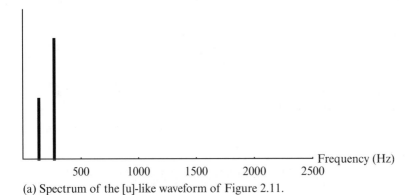

(a) Spectrum of the [u]-like waveform of Figure 2.11.

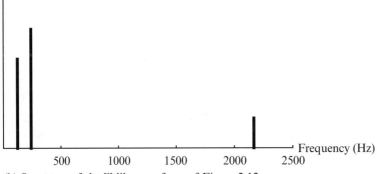

(b) Spectrum of the [i]-like waveform of Figure 2.12.

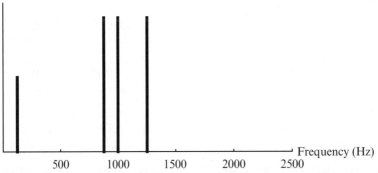

(c) Spectrum of the [ɑ]-like waveform of Figure 2.13.

FIGURE 2.14    Spectra of the three vowel-like waves illustrated in Figures 2.11, 2.12 and 2.13.

two distinct types of spectra. In the case of noisy (continuous) sounds, the overall shape of the spectrum may emerge only when the waveform is averaged over a period of time. This point becomes important in the acoustic analysis of fricative consonants (Section 7.4).

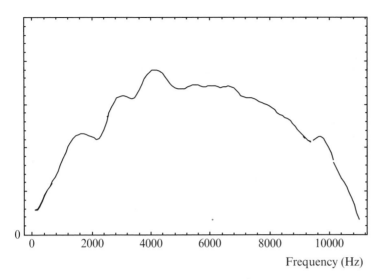

0

0     2000     4000     6000     8000     10000

Frequency (Hz)

FIGURE 2.15   Spectrum of the initial /s/ of English **sigh**, pronounced by a male speaker. As for aperiodic sounds generally, the spectrum is a continuous curve rather than a series of vertical lines, representing a fundamental and higher harmonics.

## 2.5   Scaling and the spectrum

The main point which emerges from Section 2.4 is that sound waves of all types can be generated by combining sine waves. In order to specify a sound wave, it is sufficient to give the frequencies and relative amplitudes of its sine wave components. This information is presented visually in the spectrum.

In the example spectra I have shown so far, the relationship between the component waves, the complex waveform and the spectrum has been straightforward in visual terms. For example, in our imitation [u] of Figures 2.11 and 2.14 (a), it is clear that the amplitude of the second harmonic (Figure 2.11 (b)) is twice that of the fundamental (Figure 2.11 (a)). Correspondingly, the height of the line corresponding to the second harmonic is twice the height of the line corresponding to the fundamental in Figure 2.14 (a). Visually, it all makes good sense. This kind of arrangement, in which relative distance (in this case, along the vertical axis) corresponds to the relative magnitude of the thing being measured (in this case, amplitude) is called *linear scaling*.

Linear scaling is the obvious choice for introductory discussions of spectra, but it is rarely, if at all, found in the spectra of speech sounds which appear in publications on phonetics. Linear scaling works much less well when the range of amplitude values which we need to display is large. Consider, for example, the waveform of Figure 2.16 (a). This waveform will be of particular interest to us in Section 4.2.1 because it is a good approximation to the pattern of air flow through the vocal folds during vocal fold vibration. In this example, the

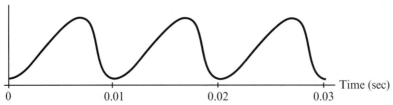

(a) A periodic waveform which approximates the pattern of air flow through the vocal folds during voicing.

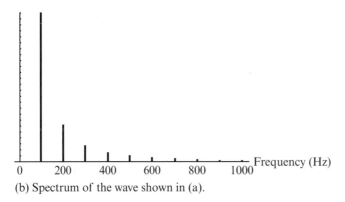

(b) Spectrum of the wave shown in (a).

FIGURE 2.16    An example of a waveform and a spectrum for which it is necessary to display a large range of amplitude values.

fundamental frequency is 100 Hz. The spectrum of the waveform up to 1000 Hz is shown in (b). The amplitude ratio of the fundamental (100 Hz) to the tenth harmonic (1000 Hz) is roughly 100:1. If we were to continue the spectrum up to 4000 Hz (which we shall want to do in Chapter 4), we should find that the amplitude ratio of the fundamental to the 40th harmonic (4000 Hz) was roughly 1600:1. This is not a large ratio from the point of view of the human ear, but it is too large to take in by eye or to represent on a textbook-size piece of paper.

These difficulties appear worse still when we point out that there is, in fact, a patterning in the relative heights of the lines in Figure 2.16 (b). For every doubling along the frequency axis, the amplitude decreases by a factor of 4. Thus, the amplitude of the second harmonic (200 Hz) is one fourth that of the fundamental and the amplitude of the fourth harmonic (400 Hz) is one fourth that of the second harmonic (200 Hz) and one sixteenth that of the fundamental (100 Hz). It is impossible to take in this patterning by eye.

The solution to such problems is to change the scaling of the vertical axis from linear scaling to *logarithmic scaling*. The essence of logarithmic scaling is that equal proportions correspond to equal distances along the scale. This is rather like our use of percentages rather than absolute numbers in talking about matters such as inflation, wages and prices. For example, suppose we read that the price of houses in London went up by 5% last year. This means that a house which would have sold for £20,000 at the beginning of the year has increased in value to £21,000, whereas a house which would have sold for £200,000 has increased in value to £210,000. The first has gone up by £1,000 and the second has gone up by £10,000 – a large difference in absolute terms – but when the values are converted to a percentage scale, each has gone up by exactly the same amount. (This analogy cannot be pushed too far, because a percentage scale does not have all of the properties of a logarithmic scale.)

The logarithmic scale used for comparing amplitudes is known as the *decibel* scale. The **-bel** element of the name honours A. G. Bell (d. 1922), while the **deci-** element refers to a factor of 10, which enters into the calculation. Actually, the decibel scale is defined not with reference to amplitude but with reference to another quantity, *intensity*. It is therefore necessary to digress slightly and to consider intensity and its relation to amplitude.

### 2.5.1  Amplitude, power and intensity

Amplitude, as defined earlier, is a measure of how far a sine wave departs from its baseline value. However, we can also think of amplitude in relation to the amount of energy expended. This notion is relevant whether we conceive of sine waves as movements of air particles, as variations in air pressure, or as variations in electrical voltage. Expending more energy requires greater power, and it is the power of sounds which is, in fact, our chief concern.

'Power' is an abstract concept, which we apply in many everyday situations. For example, the powers of diverse household appliances such as light bulbs, hair dryers and vacuum cleaners are all measured using the same unit, the watt. The power of a sound wave may also be measured in watts. In general, however, we are not interested in the total power generated by the source – which is what we quantify in the case of light bulbs – but the power at the particular position in space where the sound impinges on our ears or our microphones. Thus, acousticians usually refer to *intensity*, which may be loosely defined as power per unit area. Intensity may be measured in watts per square centimetre (or other equivalent units) when a precise value is required.

In the case of sine waves, there is a simple relationship between the waveform's maximum height above the baseline (amplitude) and intensity: the intensity is proportional to the square of the amplitude. In other words, other things being equal, if the height of a sine waveform is doubled, the motion or pressure variation which it represents must require four times as much power.

Unfortunately, however, this simple rule cannot be applied to complex waves. Instead, it is necessary to consider the average deviation from the baseline exhibited by the waveform. This average deviation of a complex waveform from its baseline is known as *root mean square* or RMS amplitude.[4] Just as the square of the amplitude of a sine wave is proportional to its intensity, so the square of the RMS amplitude of a complex wave is proportional to its intensity. Fortunately, phoneticians are never called upon either to calculate RMS amplitudes, or to calculate their squares, and we shall not illustrate such calculations here. The important point is that it is possible to extend the notion of amplitude from sine waves to complex waves, and that, in general, the intensity of a wave is proportional to the square of its amplitude. This has an important implication: relative intensity can be obtained by squaring relative amplitude. For example, if the amplitude ratio of two waves is 2:1, the intensity ratio will be 4:1. If the amplitude ratio is 5:3, the intensity ratio will be 25:9. If the amplitude ratio is 9:7, the intensity ratio will be 81:49. Thus, we (or, rather, our computers) can compare the overall intensity of one complex sound with another as well as making comparisons involving two sine waves. For example, we might wish to compare the intensities of two different vowels or of stressed and unstressed versions of the 'same' vowel.

### 2.5.2  The decibel scale

The decibel scale (abbreviated dB) is defined with reference to intensity, and is so constructed that each tenfold increase of intensity corresponds to adding on 10 decibels. Conversely, each decrease of intensity by a factor of 10 corresponds to subtracting 10 decibels. The reader with memories of logarithms from school mathematics will see that the decibel scale is based on logarithms. The intensity in dB of Sound B relative to Sound A is obtained by finding the logarithm to the base 10 of the intensity ratio $(I_B/I_A)$ and multiplying by 10. For example, if B has twice the intensity of A, the intensity ratio is 2. The logarithm of 2 is 0.3, and multiplying this by 10 gives a value of 3 dB. If the intensity of B is half that of A, the intensity ratio is 1/2. The logarithm of 1/2 is $-0.3$, and multiplying this by 10 gives a value of $-3$ dB.

Since the intensity ratio can be obtained by squaring the amplitude ratio, the decibel scale can also be used for comparisons if relative amplitudes are known. The difference in decibels can also be determined by taking the logarithm of the amplitude ratio and multiplying by 20. For example, if the amplitude ratio is 2:1, the difference in decibels (6 dB) may be obtained either (1) by calculating the intensity ratio (4:1) and converting that value to decibels (6 dB) or (2) by multiplying 0.3 (the logarithm of 2) by 20. Some examples are as follows:

| Amplitude ratio | Intensity ratio | Difference in dB |
| --- | --- | --- |
| 1:1 | 1:1 | 0 |
| 2:1 | 4:1 | 6 |
| 4:1 | 16:1 | 12 |
| 1:2 | 1:4 | −6 |
| 1:4 | 1:16 | −12 |

The effect of using the decibel scale in the example of Figure 2.16 is shown in Figure 2.17 (a). We have said that for each doubling of frequency, the amplitude decreases by a factor of 4. The table above shows that this is equivalent to a decrease of 12 decibels. Between 100 and 800 Hz, the frequency doubles three times ($100 \times 2 = 200$; $200 \times 2 = 400$; $400 \times 2 = 800$). Accordingly, the amplitude will decrease by 36 decibels ($36 = 12 \times 3$). Between 800 and 1000 Hz, there will

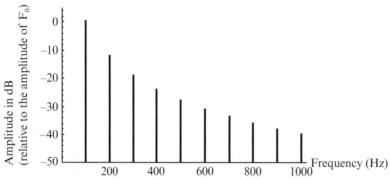

(a) Spectrum of the wave illustrated in Figure 2.16 (a) with logarithmic
scaling applied to the vertical axis. For this example, values in decibels are
relative to the amplitude of the fundamental (100 Hz) component.

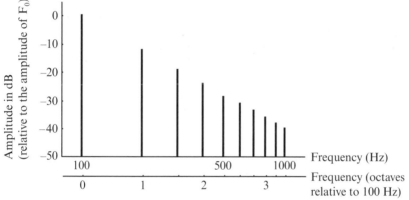

(b) Spectrum of the wave illustrated in Figure 2.16 (a) with logarithmic scaling
applied to both axes. As in (a), values in decibels on the vertical axis are relative
to the amplitude of the fundamental (100 Hz) component. Values in octaves on
the horizontal axis are relative to the frequency of the fundamental component.

FIGURE 2.17    The effects of applying logarithmic scaling to the spectrum of the wave
illustrated in Figure 2.16.

be a further decrease of just under 4 decibels. Consequently, an overall range
of 50 decibels, as in Figure 2.17 (a), is more than sufficient to show the range of
amplitude values of the first ten harmonics.

Figure 2.17 (a) also illustrates an important consequence of using logarithmic
scaling in general and the decibel scale in particular: it is no longer possible to
get away with leaving the vertical axis unlabelled. In the spectra of Figure 2.14,
the relative heights of the lines corresponded to the relative amplitude of the
components. The actual numbers were not important because relative amplitude could, in principle, be determined by comparing the heights of the lines.
When the decibel scale is used, it is the differences in numbers of decibels

rather than proportions which indicate relative amplitude. For example, if the vertical axis in Figure 2.17 (a) were left uncalibrated, we would not be able to work out that the difference in amplitude between the fundamental and the second harmonic was 12 decibels, in other words that the amplitude of the first was four times that of the second.

At the same time, there is a sense in which the numbers used to label the vertical axis in Figure 2.17 are arbitrary. The figure was designed so that the fundamental component would have an amplitude of 0 and the amplitudes of all of the harmonics would be negative. However, we might also have chosen to give the fundamental some other amplitude value. For example, if the fundamental had been assigned an amplitude of 100, the amplitude of the second harmonic would have been 88. It is the differences which matter rather than the absolute values of the numbers. This point will become relevant when we consider the practicalities of analysing sound waves (or, more generally, signals) in Chapter 3.

A common way of expressing the feature of the decibel scale just mentioned is to say that the choice of reference level is arbitrary. Sometimes, however, decibels are used as though they were absolute numbers, as for example when the noise level produced by a pneumatic drill or an antisocial neighbour's loudspeakers is quantified in terms of numbers of decibels. In such cases, the value in decibels is to be understood as relative to the intensity of the faintest sound audible (in the absence of other sounds) to an average human with normal hearing. If a sound level is specified relative to this reference level, it is referred to as a *sound pressure level*, abbreviated SPL. Normal conversational speech typically has a pressure level of 60–70 dB (more fully, dB SPL). Sounds which are loud enough to cause pain have a level of about 130 dB SPL.

### 2.5.3   *The octave scale*

The use of logarithmic scaling for the vertical (amplitude) axis of spectra – in other words, the use of the decibel scale – is very much the norm among acoustic phoneticians. The spectra which are produced by computer workstations and which appear in published articles are typically done in this way. By contrast, it is unusual to see logarithmic scaling applied to the horizontal (frequency) axis. This is probably because the range of frequencies phoneticians need to deal with is not unmanageably large.

When logarithmic scaling of the frequency axis is wanted, the scale used is the *octave* scale. The octave scale is so defined that an increase of one octave corresponds to a doubling of frequency, while a decrease of one octave corresponds to a halving of frequency. For example, 200 Hz is one octave above 100 Hz, and 400 Hz (= 200 Hz × 2) is two octaves above 100 Hz. Similarly, 50 Hz is one octave below 100 Hz (50 = 100 × 1/2). The name *octave* comes from Western music, where, if a player or singer performs a major scale, the 'same' note will re-occur every eight notes. (For example, C̲ D E F G A B C̲ D E F G, etc.) In terms of frequency, the passage from one note to its counterpart an octave above corresponds to a doubling, while the passage from one note to its counterpart an octave below involves a halving. Thus, if we start from A = 440 Hz (the A above middle C on a piano keyboard), the next occurrence of the note A going up the scale has a frequency of 880 Hz. If we go down the scale from A 440, the next A has a frequency of 220 Hz. Like the decibel scale, the octave scale is inherently relative and presupposes a point of reference. For example, we can specify a particular note as 'one octave above A 440' or 'one octave below A 440' but not as simply 'one octave'.

Figure 2.17 (b) shows the advantage of applying the octave scale to horizontal axis of 2.17 (a). The lines corresponding to the individual harmonics now decrease in height in a straight line. This brings out the systematic nature of the relationship between frequency and amplitude in the spectrum: for each octave increase in frequency (doubling), the amplitude decreases by 12 decibels (by a factor of 4). The relationship can be summed up by saying that the slope of the spectrum is −12 dB per octave.

A final point about logarithmic scaling is that it brings us closer to perception. Although decibels and octaves are not, in fact, measures of loudness and pitch (Section 5.4), they bring us closer to loudness and pitch than does straightforward linear scaling. For example, the perceived difference in pitch between 220 Hz and 440 Hz is nearly the same as the perceived difference between 440 Hz and 880 Hz; as we have just seen, both correspond to musical intervals of an octave. By contrast, the perceived difference in pitch between 440 Hz and 660 Hz (660 = 440 + 220) is much less, and corresponds to the musical interval of a fifth. When we reflect on this fact, it seems rather anomalous that spectra are usually drawn with logarithmic scaling (decibels) used for the vertical axis but with linear scaling (Hz) used for the horizontal axis. Nevertheless, this is the most common format.

## 2.6   Summary

We have now gone through all of the essential points about the structure of sound and its visual representation. We have seen that sound is a type of wave motion, usually through the medium of air, in which patterns of movement are transmitted from one layer of air particles to another. These patterns of movement result in small variations of air pressure, which follow the same pattern as the movements which give rise to them. Visually, we can represent a sound wave by means of a two-dimensional graph showing variation through time. Such representations are known as *waveforms*.

In principle, every sound wave is a combination of sine waves and every sound wave can be specified by listing its sine wave components. This is conventionally done visually, using a two-dimensional diagram known as a *spectrum*. The dimensions of a spectrum are frequency (on the horizontal axis) and amplitude (on the vertical axis). A spectrum is a *frequency-domain* representation, in contrast to a waveform which is a *time-domain* representation.

We have classified waveforms into three basic types: periodic, noisy (aperiodic continuous) and transient. Among speech sounds, vowels and sonorant consonants are prototypical examples of periodic waveforms, voiceless fricatives are prototypical examples of noisy waveforms, and the releases of stop consonants are prototypical examples of transient waveforms. There are also composite types, for example, voiced fricatives which have noise superimposed on periodicity. Periodic sounds are composed of a *fundamental* component and higher-frequency components known as *harmonics*. The frequencies of the harmonics are all multiples of the fundamental. By contrast, aperiodic sounds (both noisy and transient) have no 'fundamental' frequency, and their sine wave components are infinitessimally close together.

The chapter concluded with further consideration of scaling and its effect on the visual appearance of the spectrum. We distinguished between *logarithmic* and *linear* scaling, and noted that it was particularly advantageous to use logarithmic scaling for the vertical axis of spectra because of the large range of values which need to be represented. The scale used for logarithmic scaling of amplitude is known as the *decibel* scale. Logarithmic scaling of the horizontal axis is less common, but the octave scale is sometimes used for this purpose. As regards the decibel scale, it is also commonly used outside the context of the spectrum to compare the overall amplitude of one sound with another.

## 2.7  Further reading

There is currently a wide choice of books which provide an introduction to acoustics for phoneticians. The most detailed, but still elementary, treatment is Ladefoged (1996). I shall also mention Borden *et al.* (1994), Clark and Yallop (1995), Denes and Pinson (1993), Fry (1979), Johnson (1997), Lieberman and Blumstein (1988), Pickett (1980) and Rosen and Howell (1991). A personal favourite is Handel (1989).

## Notes

1   It needs to be added here that the perceived pitch of a sound with a complex periodic waveform will be influenced by factors other than fundamental frequency, although fundamental frequency is of primary importance. For a pure tone, frequency and fundamental frequency are the same.

2   Strictly speaking, a waveform is periodic only if the repetitions of the pattern are absolutely identical and if it continues for an infinite amount of time. However, it is useful to treat waveforms like that of Figure 2.5 (a) as if they were periodic.

3   This was a careful production of the word by a speaker with phonetic training, so that the vowel was further back and closer to IPA [u] than most Southern British English pronunciations.

4   To give a formal definition, the RMS amplitude is the square root of the average (mean) of the square of the distance of the curve from the baseline.

**Chapter 3**

# Analysing sound: the spectrograph

## 3.1 Introduction

In Chapter 2, we adopted an abstract way of thinking about and describing sound. Sound waves are, in essence, complex patterns of variation through time, which we can represent as two-dimensional pictures, or *waveforms*, on pieces of paper or computer screens. In principle, any such wave is a combination of sine waves, and any two-dimensional waveform can be re-created by combining sine waveforms. Because of this, it is also possible to describe a wave by specifying its sine wave components. This is the basic idea behind the *spectrum*. A spectrum is a two-dimensional diagram which shows which sine wave components are present and their relative strengths.

Unfortunately, the knowledge that every sound, in principle, has a spectrum does not in itself enable us to determine what that spectrum is. In a few cases – for example, the imitation [u] of Figure 2.11 – it is possible to arrive at a reasonably good approximation by visual analysis and a small amount of trial and error. However, such methods are not really practical for research into speech because, even when they work well, they are too slow. The difficulty is made worse by the fact that the spectrum of speech is constantly changing. Even at slow tempos, segments of very different types, such as stops, fricatives and vowels, alternate with one another in quick succession. In any case, as students of speech, we want to do more than analyse individual segments; we want to see how the spectrum changes as the speaker moves from one segment to another.

A practical solution to the problem is provided by the technique of *sound spectrography*. Spectrography is the most important technique available to the experimental phonetician, and the visual images which it produces – known as *spectrograms* – are the visual images most often associated with experimental phonetic research. The purpose of this chapter is to introduce spectrography and related techniques for analysing sound.

## 3.2 Spectrography

### 3.2.1 Basic principles

The technique of spectrography is based on a different approach to the analysis of sound from that of Chapter 2. It is very difficult to determine the spectra of speech sounds exactly, but it is much easier to test for the presence of sine wave components within particular frequency bands. Devices which do this are known as *filters*, more specifically *bandpass filters*. For example, a bandpass filter with pass band 300–600 Hz could be used to determine whether or not a particular vowel sound contained any sine wave components between 300 and 600 Hz. Another way of expressing this is to say that a filter may be used to detect the presence of acoustic energy within its pass band. More specifically, when the signal to be analysed is input to the filter, the filter will produce an output signal, the amplitude of which is proportional to the amplitude of the combined sine wave components within its pass band. (In fact, *filter* is a more general concept, as we shall see in Section 4.2.2.) It is the amplitude of this output signal which is of interest.

To give a simple example, let us imagine using bandpass filters to analyse our three imitation vowel waves of Figures 2.11–2.13. Obviously, one filter on its own will not be very informative, but if we use a series of filters which cover a sufficiently wide range between them, we can obtain an overall picture of the structure of the three vowel sounds. The result is illustrated in Figure 3.1. We imagine using eight filters, each with a pass band 300 Hz wide, which between them cover the frequency range 0–2400 Hz. Filter 1 has pass band 0–300 Hz, Filter 2 has pass band 301–600 Hz, and so on. In the case of the imitation [u], both of the harmonics (135 Hz and 270 Hz) have frequencies less than 300 Hz, and both will fall within the pass band of the first filter. In the case of the imitation [i], there are two harmonics below 300 Hz, and also one high-frequency harmonic which will fall within the pass band of the eighth filter (2101–2400 Hz). In the case of the imitation [ɑ], each harmonic falls within the pass band of a different filter, giving a wide and broad pattern of filter response in the mid frequencies. The three spectra of Figure 3.1 appear rather crude in comparison with the line spectra of Figure 2.14; for example, in the case of [i] and [u] it is impossible to separate the fundamental (lowest) component from the second harmonic, since both fall within the pass band of the first filter (0–300 Hz). On the other hand, the spectra still bring out the essential characteristics of the three vowels.

The graphs shown in Figure 3.1 are still only two-dimensional and do not show change through time. An illustration of how filters can be used to produce a three-dimensional image is provided in Figure 3.2. This shows the *Direct Translator*, a device developed with the aim of making speech visible to the deaf (Potter *et al.* 1947).

The Direct Translator used twelve analysing filters, each with a bandwidth of 300 Hz, giving a total frequency range of 3600 Hz. Each filter was linked to a small lamp, which in turn produced a trace of light on a moving belt of phosphorescent material. The greater the intensity of the output of a filter, the stronger the light produced by the corresponding lamp, and the brighter the trace on the phosphorescent belt. Thus, the possibility of varying degree of brightness provides for a third dimension in the representation. The lowest band of frequencies is at the bottom and the highest band of frequencies at the

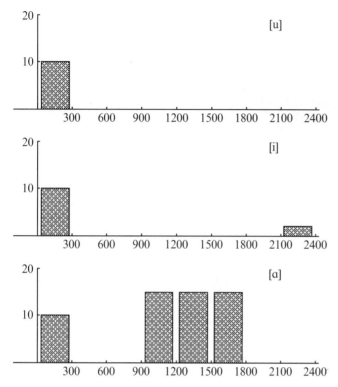

FIGURE 3.1   Using eight hypothetical filters to analyse the [u]-like, [i]-like, and [ɑ]-like waves of Figures 2.11, 2.12, and 2.13. Each filter has a bandwidth of 300 Hz, so that the eight filters span a total range of 0–2400 Hz. Each filter detects the presence of acoustic energy within its frequency band. Notice that, for [i], there is both a low-frequency bar and a high-frequency bar (above 2000 Hz). These correspond roughly to the two lowest of the wide, dark bands running from left to right on the spectrogram of Figure 3.4.

In these diagrams, the relative amplitude of the output of the filters is shown on the vertical axis, and the decibel scale is used. The output of the first (0–300 Hz) filter is set at 10 dB in each case.

top, so that frequency is now represented on the vertical axis. The example illustrates an analysis of the words **one, two, three**.

The capabilities of the Direct Translator are inherently limited by the number of filters. In order to span a frequency range of over 3000 Hz with only twelve filters, it is necessary that each filter should have a wide pass band, and this results in the loss of detail. On the other hand, reducing the bandwidth of some or all of the filters would also reduce the frequency range which could be displayed. The problem was solved by using only one filter and varying the centre frequency (and, accordingly, the pass band) to which it is 'tuned'. This is the principle behind the Sound Spectrograph, developed in the early 1940s

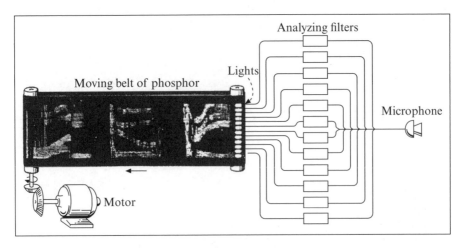

FIGURE 3.2 The *Direct Translator*. This machine made use of twelve analysing filters, each linked to a small lamp. The greater the intensity of the output of each filter, the stronger the light produced by the corresponding lamp, and the brighter the track on the phosphorescent belt. This picture illustrates an analysis of the English words **one, two, three**. From Potter *et al.* (1947).

at Bell Telephone Laboratories. The Direct Translator grew out of the same research and was an attempt to produce spectrograms in 'real time'.

A schematic diagram illustrating how the original Sound Spectrograph worked is shown in Figure 3.3, reproduced from Potter *et al.* (1947). A short utterance to be analysed is recorded onto a tape loop either from a microphone or from a tape recorder. Once the recording has been made, the loop is played back over and over again. The speech is input to the filter, the tuning of which is shifted for each repetition. The centre frequency of the filter is gradually moved up the frequency scale, until the maximum frequency is reached. In this way, it is possible to create what is, in effect, a large bank of filters using only one filter.

The filter output is connected to a stylus, which just touches a piece of electrically sensitive paper, wrapped around a drum. The drum revolves together with the tape loop. The stronger the output of the filter, the darker the mark which is burned onto the paper. As the centre frequency of the filter is shifted upwards, the stylus is shifted along the drum from the bottom to the top of the paper. In this way, the output traces from the series of repetitions are recorded one above the other, in the same way that the outputs of the twelve filters are displayed together in the Direct Translator. In the case of the Sound Spectrograph, the display is a permanent record on paper rather than a temporary display on a belt of phosphorescent material. Intensity is represented on a scale of relative darkness rather than a scale of relative brightness.

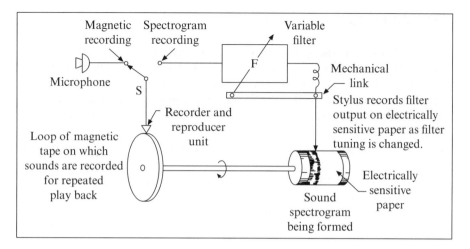

FIGURE 3.3 A schematic diagram of the original Sound Spectrograph. In contrast to the Direct Translator, the Sound Spectrograph makes use of only one bandpass filter with variable frequency band. The utterance to be analysed is recorded onto the tape loop and is played back many times in succession. With each repetition, the centre frequency of the filter is increased until the maximum frequency is reached.

As the centre frequency of the filter moves up the frequency scale, the stylus moves up the paper. The greater the intensity of the output of the filter, the darker the mark produced by the stylus on the paper. From Potter *et al.* (1947).

The Sound Spectrograph was a major breakthrough in the study of acoustic phonetics. Firstly, it greatly speeded up the process of speech analysis, making it possible to study the acoustics of speech on a large scale. Secondly, it was straightforward to use, so that anyone who possessed such an instrument was able to break down speech into component frequencies, whether or not they had an extensive background in acoustics. Thirdly, it provided a means of representing the change of sound through time which can make visual sense to acoustician and non-acoustician alike. Advances in technology have meant that it is possible to use computers to determine the output of the filters by calculation, so that it is no longer necessary to construct actual filters. This has made the technique more flexible, giving the user more choice as to the frequency range and the temporal length of each spectrogram, and also as to the bandwidths of the filters. However, both the basic principles and the nature of the visual display have remained essentially unchanged.

The term *Sonagraph* is sometimes used rather than *spectrograph*; *Sonagraph* is the name of the series of instruments manufactured by Kay Elemetrics Corporation, which have been extremely popular. Computer-based systems are known by a variety of names such as *speech workstations, speech analysis software packages,* and *digital spectrographs.* I shall use the term *computer-based spectrograph* here.

### 3.2.2  *An example spectrogram*

Figure 3.4 shows a spectrogram of the vowel of the English word **be**, pro-nounced by a male speaker on a rising pitch, in the sentence **Did you say 'be'?** This spectrogram was produced on a computer-based spectrograph, using a broad filter bandwidth (Section 3.4.2). The frequency range of this spectrogram is 0–5000 Hz or 5 kHz (*kiloHertz*), and the vertical axis is labelled accordingly. The total duration shown is 319 msec (.319 sec). This speaker also produced the example of [i] for which the waveform appears in Figure 2.10 and is imitated in Figure 2.12.

The release of the /b/ corresponds to the somewhat weak vertical spike on the left of the spectrogram just before the onset of the vowel. It can be seen that there is a brief gap between the release spike and the onset of striations for the vowel. This reflects the fact that the voicing has faded out during the /b/ closure, and a short amount of time (about 7 msec) is necessary for it to get going again. (The nature of voicing in obstruent consonants such as /b/ is a point which we shall return to in Chapters 7 and 8.)

In looking at the vowel itself, a first obvious point is that the shading becomes lighter overall as we move from left to right, indicating that the sound is becoming softer (less intense). A second point is that dark, somewhat broad bars extend from left to right across the vowel's duration. These bars pick out regions in which harmonics are particularly prominent. The lowest is low in frequency (below 500 Hz), while the second rises to just over 2000 Hz. These two bars correspond roughly to the two bars on the bar chart for [i] in Figure 3.1, and also to the regions of prominent harmonics in the line spectra of Figure 2.14.

As we shall see in Chapter 4, the bars correspond to the so-called *formants* of the vowel. The frequencies of the formants are determined by the shape and size of the mouth and pharynx (and in some cases also the nasal) cavities. The fact that higher-frequency bars rise at the onset of the vowel reflects the change in the configuration of the oral cavity as the lips move from the closed position (which is necessary for /b/) to a more open and spread position (Sec-tion 7.3.3.2).

More unexpected – at least on the basis of what we have said so far – is the presence of vertical lines, called *striations* throughout the course of the vowel. To understand why these are present we need to think about how vowel sounds are produced. Vowel sounds are normally produced with vocal fold vibration, and it is the regular opening and closing of the vocal folds which ultimately accounts for the periodic character of vowel waveforms. When the vocal folds vibrate, they open and then snap shut in quick succession. Each snapping shut is like giving a quick tap to the cavities above, making them 'ring' briefly rather as a bottle or glass rings when tapped. As listeners, we are unaware of the individual taps because they are too quick to be perceived as separate events, and our ears smear them together. However, they do show up as separate events on the spectrogram provided that the frequency of the vibration is not

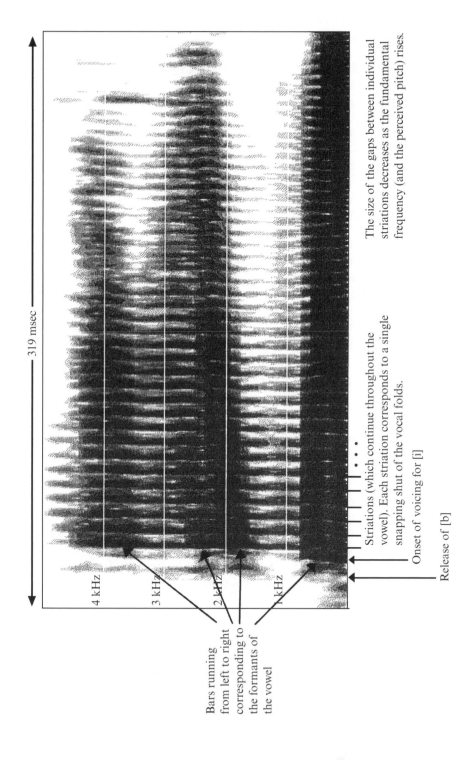

The size of the gaps between individual striations decreases as the fundamental frequency (and the perceived pitch) rises.

Striations (which continue throughout the vowel). Each striation corresponds to a single snapping shut of the vocal folds.

Onset of voicing for [i]

Release of [b]

Bars running from left to right corresponding to the formants of the vowel

4 kHz

3 kHz

2 kHz

1kHz

319 msec

FIGURE 3.4    Spectrogram of the English word **be**, pronounced on a rising pitch.

too high. In practice, this means that the striations are usually visible for male speakers but not always for female or child speakers.

As we move from left to right in the spectrogram, the striations become closer together. This reflects the fact that the vocal folds are speeding up, so that there is less time between taps. In other words, the period of the vocal fold vibration is gradually decreasing, with the result that the fundamental frequency is increasing (Section 2.2.4). The gradual increase in fundamental frequency is perceived as a rise in pitch. Figure 3.4 may be contrasted with the spectrograms of Figure 3.6, which show the word **door** pronounced on a falling pitch, in the sentence **I said 'door'**. In this case, the striations gradually become further apart as the pitch falls. There is also noticeable irregularity, reflecting this speaker's tendency to use creaky voice at low pitches (Section 8.3.2). We should also notice in passing that the formant pattern (as shown in the dark bars) is different for this vowel (/ɔ/) than for the vowel of **be**.

It may seem paradoxical to describe the voiced sounds of speech as successions of separate and discrete taps. We have already said in Chapter 2 that they were combinations of smooth and continuous sine waves. Nevertheless, both conceptions are correct, and it can be shown that they are mathematically equivalent. Phoneticians may choose to adopt one view or the other, depending on which is the more useful for the purpose at hand. Spectrograms like that of Figure 3.4 are more in accord with the 'series of taps' view.

### 3.2.3 Narrow band spectrograms

We have already said that the technique of spectrography is based on the use of bandpass filters to detect the presence of acoustic energy within their individual frequency bands. In the example of Figure 3.4 (and also the hypothetical example of Figure 3.1), the filter bandwidths were too wide to separate out or *resolve* individual sine wave components (harmonics). Another way of expressing this is to say that the *frequency resolution* of the filters is poor. On the other hand, as regards the temporal aspects of the signal, the filters have done quite well in separating out the individual taps of the vocal folds (reflected in the presence of striations). Another way of expressing this is to say that the *temporal resolution* of the filters is good.

The combination of poor frequency resolution and good temporal resolution evident in Figure 3.4 is not accidental. It is part of the nature of filter-based analysis that it is impossible to achieve both good frequency resolution and good temporal resolution simultaneously. The broader the pass band of a filter – that is, the less precise it is as a frequency detector – the better its temporal resolution. Conversely, filters with narrow pass bands will have good frequency resolution because (at least in the case of voiced sounds) only one harmonic will fall within each pass band, but they will have poor temporal resolution. Accordingly, it is common to distinguish between *broad band* and *narrow band* types of analysis. The original spectrographs provided for only two possibilities: a broad band analysis based on a filter bandwidth of 300 Hz and a narrow band analysis based on a filter bandwidth of 45 Hz. Current computer-based spectrography, which does not require the manufacture of actual filters, also offers intermediate possibilities.

The spectrogram of Figure 3.4 is of the broad band type. Figure 3.5 shows a narrow band spectrogram of the same word. In this case, the individual harmonics which make up the vowel appear as relatively narrow lines running from left to right. These lines rise in parallel as the fundamental frequency (and with it, the perceived pitch) of the voice rises. Because of the poor temporal resolution, the vertical spike which corresponds to the release of the /b/ is not sharply defined, and there are no vertical striations. Thus, narrow band analysis is more in accord with the alternative conception of (voiced) speech as combined sine waves.

Although narrow band analysis provides more detail as regards frequency, broad band analysis is the more generally useful. In the first place, spectrograms are frequently used to measure durations of sounds. It is now usual for computer-based spectrographs to include provision for two or more cursors, which can be placed at the boundaries of the sound to be measured; the temporal distance between them can then be determined automatically. For such purposes, the greater temporal precision of broad band spectrograms and their sharper definition of onsets and offsets (beginnings and ends) of sounds is a real advantage. For example, if we wished to measure the temporal distance between the release of the /b/ and the onset of voicing (the *Voice Onset Time*, see Chapters 5 and 7), this could only be done from the broad band spectrogram of Figure 3.4.

A second advantage of broad band spectrograms is that it is usually easier to discern overall patterns. The detail of the narrow band spectrogram may obscure the gross alternations of darker and lighter areas along the vertical axis. This is particularly true if the pattern is changing. The onset of the vowel in Figures 3.4 and 3.5 provides a good example; in Figure 3.4, it is easy to see that the dark bars above 2000 Hz are rising, whereas this point is rather lost in the detail of the harmonics in Figure 3.5.

### 3.2.4  Pre-emphasis

It is characteristic of speech generally that the lower frequencies are stronger than the higher frequencies. The practical consequence of this is that higher-frequency components may be weak or even invisible on a spectrogram. If the phonetician is particularly interested in the higher components, this is a major disadvantage. A solution is to boost the amplitude of the high-frequency components. This is known as *pre-emphasis*. Pre-emphasis is not part of the analysis procedure itself, but is applied beforehand.

Figure 3.6 shows two broad band spectrograms of the English word **door** (/dɔ/), pronounced on a falling pitch, in the sentence **I said 'door'**. Pre-emphasis was not applied in (a), but it was applied in (b). If we compare the two, we can see that the lower frequencies are weaker and the higher frequencies are stronger in (b) as compared with (a).

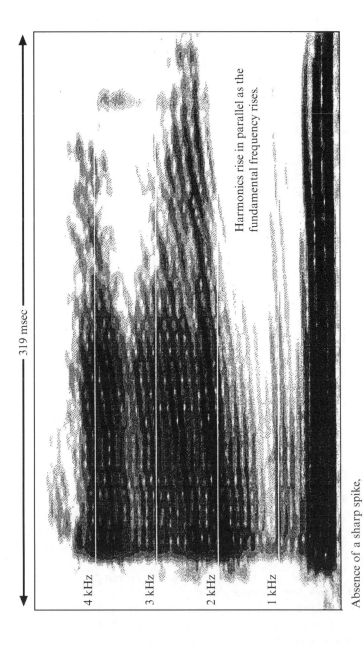

FIGURE 3.5    Narrow band spectrogram of the English word **be**, illustrated in Figure 3.4.

319 msec

Harmonics rise in parallel as the fundamental frequency rises.

Absence of a sharp spike, which would correspond to the release of the [b].

4 kHz

3 kHz

2 kHz

1 kHz

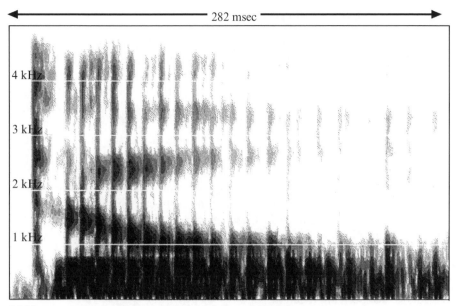

(a) No pre-emphasis. Strong low frequencies, weak high frequencies.

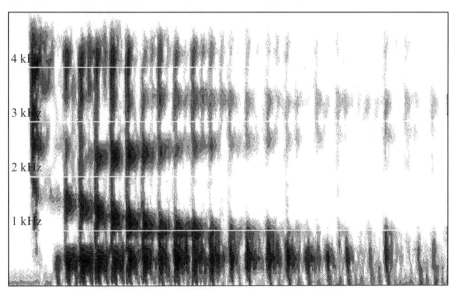

(b) Pre-emphasis. The low frequencies are weaker and the high frequencies stronger than in (a).

FIGURE 3.6    Two broad band spectrograms of the English word **door**, pronounced on a falling pitch. The first was recorded without pre-emphasis, while the second was recorded with pre-emphasis. As a result, the balance between low and high frequencies is different in the two versions.

Note that the striations are further apart than in Figure 3.4, and the size of the gaps between them increases as the fundamental frequency falls.

### 3.2.5  *Two-dimensional spectra*

The great advantage of spectrography is its ability to provide a three-dimensional display on a two-dimensional surface. However, it has to be admitted that the detail of the third dimension (amplitude) is difficult to judge by eye, even when, as in many systems, the scale of dark-to-light shading is replaced by a scale of colours. Furthermore, a scale based on shading or colour does not lend itself to precise measurement.

For many purposes, we wish to make more precise measurements of relative amplitude for a stretch of speech which is relatively steady-state. For example, we might wish to examine in detail the structure of the vowel of **be** at its midpoint. In such cases, it is useful to be able to produce a two-dimensional spectrum from which more precise measurements can be made. A common procedure is to use a broad band spectrogram to locate the time of interest and then to request the two-dimensional display. On computer-based spectrographs, this is typically done by positioning a cursor and then selecting the appropriate instruction from a menu. The cursor, in this case, does not really specify an instant in time but rather the location of the *window* which will be used to calculate the spectrum (Section 3.4.2).

Figure 3.7 shows two spectra, one broad band (a) and one narrow band (b), for our example [i]. In requesting both these spectra, the cursor was placed at a

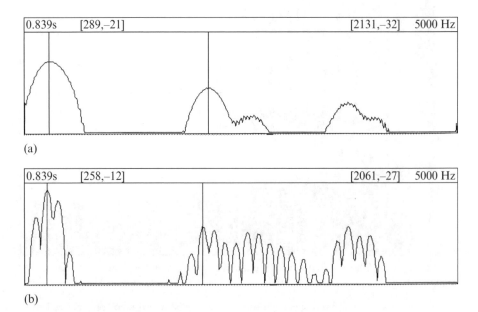

(a)

(b)

FIGURE 3.7  Broad band (a) and narrow band (b) spectra for the vowel [i] of **be**, the spectrogram for which is shown in Figure 3.4. The cursors pick out the lowest two peaks in the spectrum, corresponding to the lowest two formants of the vowel.

point 79 msec after the onset of the striations for the vowel in the broad band spectrogram of Figure 3.4. (The number 0.839s in the upper left-hand corner is the starting time of the window, measured from the beginning of the segment of speech stored in the computer's memory.) As we would expect, the broad band spectrum (for which the filter effective bandwidth was 160 Hz) does not separate the individual harmonics, while the narrow band (for which the filter effective bandwidth was 40 Hz) does.

Each spectrum spans a frequency range of 5000 Hz, which, as we shall see, is determined by the user's choice of sampling rate at the time the speech is input to the computer (Section 3.4.1). The vertical axis is scaled using the decibel scale (Section 2.5.2), and displays a range of 40 decibels. In many systems, as in this one, the range of amplitudes to be displayed is specified by the user. Since the decibel scale is based on relative intensity (power), such spectra are often referred to as *power spectra*. The term *FFT spectra*, which refers to the method used to calculate the outputs of the filters (Section 3.4.2), is also used.

Each spectrum shows two cursors, which have been positioned to coincide with the first and second peaks. It will be seen that, in both cases, the peaks match up in frequency with the broad bars on the broad band spectrogram of Figure 3.4 and the darker harmonics on the narrow band spectrogram of Figure 3.5. At the top, an amplitude value, in decibels, is given for each cursor. On this particular system, amplitudes are measured relative to a 'ceiling' value, and so the values which appear are always negative. They have little meaning in themselves, but they are very useful in making comparisons. For example, on the basis of the narrow band spectrum, we could say that the strongest harmonic in the first, low-frequency peak (250 Hz) is 15 dB more intense than the strongest harmonic in the second peak (2061 Hz); this value is arrived at by subtracting −27 from −12.

Another type of spectrum, which is not based on the use of filters, and which is known as an *LPC spectrum*, will be illustrated in Section 4.5.

### 3.2.6 Supplementary displays: waveform, intensity and fundamental frequency

Spectrographs typically provide for other types of displays as well. Figure 3.8 shows three common possibilities. In (a), we see the waveform of the sound. This shows less detail than the 'close-up' view of the waveform of Figure 2.10 (b). In (b), we see an overall intensity contour (Section 2.5.1), which shows how the overall intensity rises and falls; on computer-based systems, this is determined from the RMS amplitude of the wave (Section 2.5.1). We have already observed (Section 3.2.2) that the intensity of the vowel appears to decrease over the course of its duration. This is confirmed by both the waveform and the intensity displays; the waveform clearly decreases in amplitude in parallel with the decline in intensity. Figure 3.8 (c) shows the fundamental

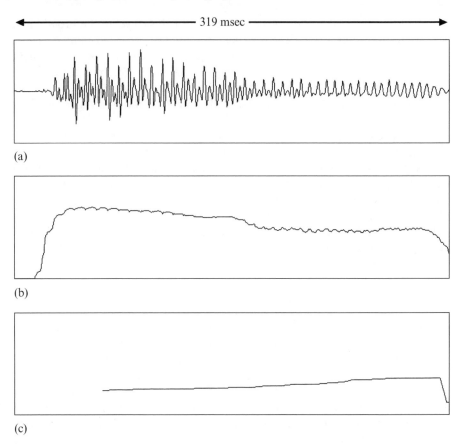

FIGURE 3.8    Waveform (a), relative intensity (b), and fundamental frequency (c) displays for the vowel [i] of **be**, the spectrogram for which is shown in Figure 3.4.

frequency, abstracted from other characteristics of the speech. Fundamental frequency tracking is extremely useful for studying tone and intonation, where the rise and fall of the fundamental frequency of the voice (heard as rising and falling pitch) is the main object of interest.

This concludes our introductory overview of the technique of spectrography. In order to use the technique effectively, it is necessary to have some under-standing of how a spectrograph works. Accordingly, in what follows, we shall look at some of the technicalities of computer-based spectrography. Before we begin, however, it is necessary to give some consideration to the nature of sound recording. In fact, equipment for speech analysis never works with the sound directly. Rather, it deals with electrical signals which are analogous to the sound being analysed. A microphone, and usually also a recording (on tape or compact disk or some other medium), provide the necessary intermediate links.

## 3.3  Recording

From what has been said about the nature of sound, it should be clear that sound is very elusive. The movements of air particles and the resulting variations in air pressure are very small, take place very quickly and cannot, in themselves, be preserved. To record sound, we must record enough information about the small variations in air pressure to enable them to be re-created.

### 3.3.1  *Recording as translation*

The first sound recordings, made by Thomas Edison in 1877, achieved this by what now seems a very simple and primitive system. Edison's recording system was based on a horn, with a diaphragm at the narrow end. A steel needle was attached to the diaphragm. When someone spoke or sang into the horn, the diaphragm, and with it the steel needle, were set into vibration. While this was going on, a cylinder covered with tin foil was rotated under the needle, in such a way that the needle made indentations in the tin foil, going from one end of the cylinder to the other in a spiral pattern. The indentations in the tin foil provided a record of the small variations in air pressure (resulting from the motions of the air particles) in the original sound.

To play back the recording, the process was reversed. The cylinder was turned, causing the needle to vibrate following the pattern recorded in the tin foil. The needle in turn caused the diaphragm to vibrate, which in turn caused the adjacent air particles to vibrate, so that the sound which emerged from the horn was recognisably a reproduction of the original.

The whole process of recording might be described as translating the small variations in air pressure produced by the small movements of air particles into variations in something else. In Edison's case, the 'something else' was the groove drawn by the needle along the surface of the tin foil. The diaphragm and the needle provided the link between the two. In more technical terminology, translation from one medium to another is known as *transduction* (from Latin *transduco* 'lead across'). *Transducers* need to be distinguished from *amplifiers*, which produce a larger-scale copy of an input signal without changing the medium.

Like the early phonograph, modern recording systems are based on translating and re-creating the original acoustic signal, though it is not possible to follow the process by eye. We can distinguish three general stages:

1   Variations in air pressure in the input acoustic signal are translated (transduced) into variations in voltage in an output electrical signal. Whatever the eventual storage medium, this is always the first step. The role of the microphone is to perform this conversion.
2   Variations in voltage in the electrical signal (output from the microphone) are translated into a form suitable for transfer to the storage medium. This may involve several intermediate stages, including amplifying the microphone output. In the case of a tape recorder, the final output of this process is a varying magnetic field in the record head.

3   The third and final step is the transfer to the storage medium itself. In the case of tape recording (cassette or open reel), small particles of metal on the surface of the tape, which are invisible to the naked eye, are magnetised as the tape is wound past the record head. (Before reaching the record head, the tape is wound past an erase head which wipes out any previous recording.) In this way, variations in the magnetic field in the record head are translated into variations in magnetisation on the surface of the tape. Since the variations in the strength of the magnetic field are, ultimately, translations of the variations in air pressure in the original acoustic signal, the surface of the magnetic tape provides a permanent record of the original, just like the surface of the tin foil in Edison's primitive system.

To play back a copy of the original sound, the multi-stage process of translation is reversed. The final stage is always vibration of a diaphragm, inside a speaker or headphone, which brings about vibration of the surrounding air particles – in other words, a sound wave.

### 3.3.2   Fidelity

A good system for recording and reproducing sound is characterised by *high fidelity*. The greater the fidelity, the more closely the reproduction corresponds to the original. Since the recording process involves re-creating the input sound several times, fidelity will be achieved only if the transmission is accurate at every stage. For example, in the case of the early phonograph, it does not matter how well the motion of the diaphragm reproduces the motion of the air particles if the steel needle does not do its job well. An expensive high-quality tape recorder cannot achieve fidelity if it is used with a low-quality microphone. The chain is only as strong as its weakest link.

To evaluate the fidelity of a system as a whole, or of an individual component such as a microphone, two factors stand out as crucial:

1   *Frequency response.* If a particular instrument – for example, a tape recorder – reproduces sound faithfully, the spectrum of the reproduction must be identical to the spectrum of the original. In other words, it will show the same sine wave components in the same proportions. The same general criterion can be applied to an instrument such as a microphone, which translates the original pressure variations into variations in some other medium. The spectrum of the translation must be identical to the spectrum of the original.

   Let us now imagine testing out a tape recorder with a complex sound in which all of the sine wave components are equal in amplitude. In this case, all of the sine wave components in the reproduction should also be equal in amplitude. This possibility is illustrated in Figure 3.9 (a) and (b). If, on the other hand, the spectrum of the reproduction is not 'flat' – that is, if some frequencies are larger in amplitude than others, as in Figure 3.9 (c) – then

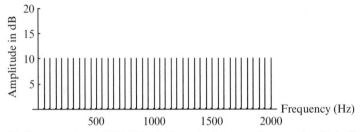

(a) Spectrum (up to 2000 Hz) of a hypothetical complex wave in which all sine wave components are equal in amplitude.

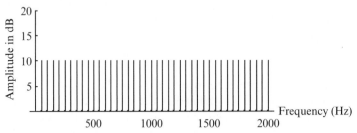

(b) Spectrum of a faithful reproduction of (a).

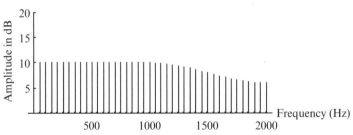

(c) Spectrum of another reproduction of (a), which is not very faithful.

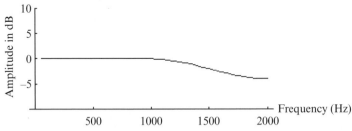

(d) *Frequency response* curve for the recording system which produced (c). For each sine wave component, the amplitude in (a) is subtracted from the amplitude in (c), and the resulting points are joined to form a smooth curve. What is important is not the actual amplitude values (in dB), but the extent to which the curve corresponds to a horizontal line. In this case, the curve is flat up to 1000 Hz but slopes down for frequencies above 1000 Hz.

FIGURE 3.9    An imaginary experiment to determine the frequency response of two recording systems.

the reproduction is not faithful. In practice, this kind of check can be performed by testing the sine wave components one at a time rather than all at once as we have envisaged it.

An experiment like the one just described is said to determine the *frequency response* of the instrument being tested. The ideal is an absolutely flat response across the frequency range perceived by the human ear (roughly 20–22,000 Hz).

2   *Dynamic range.* A faithful system must not only give all frequencies equal treatment – it must be able to do so for both loud and soft sounds. For example, in recording a performance by a large symphony orchestra, the system must be able to reproduce both the quiet passages performed by the solo flute and the loud passages, when all the instruments are playing together at high volume. When recording speech, the system must reproduce both inherently quiet sounds such as [f] and inherently sonorous sounds such as [a].

A common measure of dynamic range is the so-called *signal to noise ratio*, abbreviated *S/N ratio*. This is defined as the ratio of the intensity of the signal to the intensity of any background noise inherent in the system. It is measured in decibels. Since the dynamic range of speech is about 55 dB, recording systems used in speech analysis should have a S/N ratio of 60 to 70 dB.

### 3.3.3   Digital recording

Most, if not all, readers will be aware that a distinction exists between *digital* and *analogue* recording. In an analogue system, what is stored or displayed varies continuously in a manner analogous to the original. For example, all of the drawings of waveforms in this book are analogues of (actual or imagined) waves. In Edison's early phonograph, the continuously changing position of the line traced by the needle on the tin foil is an analogue to the continuously changing air pressure at the diaphragm. In the case of recording on magnetic tape, the magnetic properties of the particles on the tape change continuously. They are analogous to the variations in voltage in the electrical signal which was output from the microphone and, ultimately, to the variations in air pressure in the original sound wave.

In a digital recording, no continuously varying counterpart of the original signal is created. Instead, information about variation in voltage is stored as a series of numbers. These numbers indicate the amplitude (height) of the waveform at equally spaced intervals of time. (Notice that, in this usage, *amplitude* may refer to the height of the waveform at any chosen point in time rather than to the maximum height as in Section 2.3.1.) This method, known as *sampling*, is illustrated in Figure 3.10. Part (a) shows one cycle of a continuous sine wave. This drawing on paper is an analogue of a single cycle of a pure tone with frequency 100 Hz. For the purposes of this illustration, we have

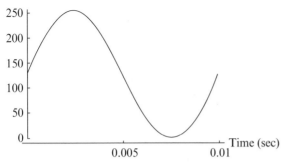

(a) One cycle of a sine wave with frequency 100 Hz.

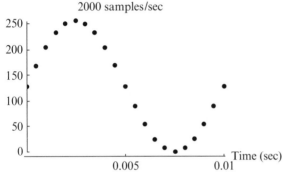

(b) The waveform of (a), presented as a series of 21 sample points, corresponding to a sampling rate of 2000 samples per second (2000 Hz). The interval between successive sample points is .0005 seconds.

| Amplitude values |
| :---: |
| 127, 167, 202, 230, 248, 254, 248, 230, 202, 167, 127, 88, 53, 25, 7, 0, 7, 25, 53, 88, 127 |

(c) Amplitude values (heights) for the 21 dots of (b). Using these numbers, we could redraw the picture of (b). We could then reconstruct the original waveform (a) by connecting the dots.

FIGURE 3.10   Sampling a wave.

imagined that the vertical axis is calibrated in 'voltage units' and that the baseline value is 127 voltage units.

In (b), the same wave is represented as a series of 21 points (including the beginning and end points), separated by intervals of 0.0005 seconds. The values (heights in voltage units) for the individual points are given underneath. These numbers alone are sufficient to enable us to draw an approximation to the waveform – we need only plot them on a graph like that of Figure 3.10 (b) and then connect the dots. Accordingly, in a digital record of the waveform, only the numbers need to be stored. Any storage medium which can cope with large numbers of numbers can be used, the most generally familiar being computers and compact disks.

Sampling the sound wave is the essential step in *analogue to digital conversion*, usually abbreviated as *A-to-D conversion*. A-to-D conversion does not work directly from the sound wave, but from an amplified version of the electrical signal output from the microphone. Thus, the amplitude values are usually measured in volts.

As in the case of analogue recording, the fidelity of a digital system will depend on its frequency response and dynamic range. However, these characteristics are usually quantified in different ways, reflecting the special characteristics of digital recording. Two aspects need to be examined here: *sampling rate* and *quantisation*.

### 3.3.3.1   Sampling rate

Sampling rate refers to the number of times the amplitude of the wave is recorded per second. The higher the sampling rate, the shorter the time interval between individual samples, the closer together the dots in the visual representation, and the greater the resemblance between the sampled version and the original. In the example of Figure 3.10, the sampling rate is 2000 samples per second or 2000 Hz. (The unit Hertz is often applied to sampling rates as well as to frequencies of vibration.)

The choice of sampling rate is important because it sets an upper limit on the frequency range of the recording. This upper limit is half the sampling rate, a value frequently referred to as the *Nyquist frequency*. For example, a sampling rate of 2000 Hz (samples per second) can only be used to record signals for which all the sine wave components are less than 1000 Hz, which is the Nyquist frequency in this case. A sampling rate of 10,000 Hz, providing for a frequency range of 0–5000 Hz, is frequently used in phonetic research. Recordings of music for storage on compact disk commonly use a sampling rate of 44,100 Hz, in order to allow for frequencies of up to 22,050 Hz in the reproduced sound.

### 3.3.3.2   Quantisation

Quantisation refers to the accuracy with which the amplitude values are recorded. This determines the dynamic range of a digital recording.

Storing the actual numbers in a digital recording is like filling in a form, in which a fixed number of slots is allocated to each value. For example, when reporting the reading of a domestic electricity meter in the UK, the customer must write the numbers shown on the meter in a set of boxes on a form provided for the purpose by the supplier. Four boxes are provided, while the meter itself shows five numbers. The rightmost number on the meter must therefore be ignored, with the result that the reported reading is less accurate than it could be. The smallest reading which can be reported is 1 'unit of electricity', while the largest reading which can be reported is 9999 – nearly 10,000 times as great. If, however, five boxes were to be made available on the form, it would be possible to report fractions of a unit of electricity. The smallest reading which could be reported would be 0.1 unit and the largest reading which could be reported would be 9999.9 units – nearly 100,000 times as great. Adding an extra box to the form would increase the range of possible values by a factor of 10 and would, consequently, make reports of electricity consumption more accurate.

We now see how dynamic range may be quantified in a digital recording system. It is sufficient to note how many slots are available to record each amplitude value. The greater the number of slots, the greater the range. For example, a five-box form can record a greater range of values than a four-box form.

Unfortunately, there is an extra complication. Digital recording systems – like computers generally – do not use our familiar decimal numbers, but rather binary numbers. Whereas, for ordinary purposes, we have ten distinct digits (0 to 9) at our disposal, a computer only has two, 0 and 1. This makes the encoding of numbers very simple. For example, the surface of a compact disk is divided into a large number of very small slots. For each slot, *flat* corresponds to 0 and *indentation* to 1.

The restriction of digits used in coding to 0 and 1 has a corresponding disadvantage in that more slots are required to represent each number. In binary notation, 10 corresponds to 2 in decimal notation, 100 corresponds to 4 ($= 2 \times 2$ or $2^2$), 1000 corresponds to 8 ($= 2 \times 2 \times 2$ or $2^3$), 10000 corresponds to 16 ($= 2^4$) and so on. In more general terms, a 1 followed by $n$ 0s represents $2^n$. Other numbers are filled in in between. For example, between 100 ($= 4$) and 1000 ($= 8$), we have 101 ($= 5$), 110 ($= 6$), and 111 ($= 7$).

In accordance with computer usage, the lengths of numbers are measured in *binary digits* or *bits* rather than in decimal digits. A system with two bits per number at its disposal can record four values: 0, 1, 10 ($= 2$), and 11 ($= 3$). A system with three bits can record seven values, from 0 up to (but not including) 8. More generally, a system with n bits can record values from 0 up to (but not including) $2^n$.

The effect of quantisation level on the shape of the stored waveform is shown in Figure 3.11. In (a), we see one cycle of a complex waveform which is the sum of a 100 Hz sine wave and a 500 Hz sine wave (compare Figure 2.6). In (b), the same waveform is represented using only four amplitude levels, 0, 1, 2 and 3 (requiring 2 bits), resulting in considerable distortion. If the wave were played back, it would sound as if noise had been added.

In Figure 3.11 (c), the number of levels is doubled to eight (requiring 3 bits). In (d), the number of levels is again doubled to sixteen (requiring 4 bits). Each doubling produces a waveform more like the original shown in (a). In the case of Figure 3.10, 256 levels (0–255) were allowed for. This would require 8 bits ($256 = 2^8$). Sixteen-bit quantisation is usual in high-fidelity music recording.

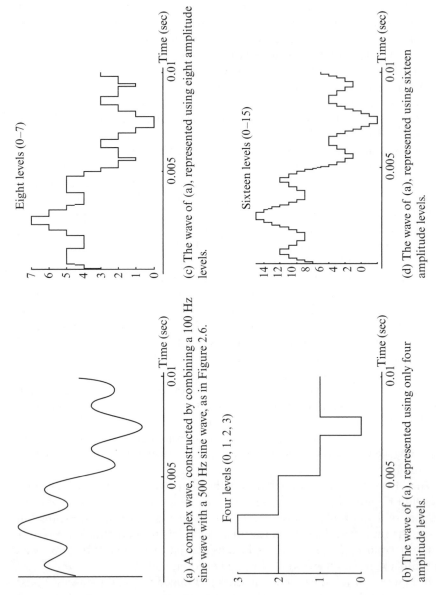

(a) A complex wave, constructed by combining a 100 Hz sine wave with a 500 Hz sine wave, as in Figure 2.6.

(b) The wave of (a), represented using only four amplitude levels.

(c) The wave of (a), represented using eight amplitude levels.

(d) The wave of (a), represented using sixteen amplitude levels.

FIGURE 3.11    The effect of quantisation level on the overall shape of a waveform.

To sum up, in a digital recording system, the dynamic range is determined by the level of quantisation, measured in bits. There is a simple relationship between the number of bits and the range in decibels:

range (in dB) = number of bits × 6.

This follows from the fact that each additional bit approximately doubles the range of amplitude values, and each doubling results in the addition of 6 decibels on the decibel scale (Section 2.5.2).

This concludes our discussion of fidelity in analogue and digital recording systems. For prospective users of computer-based spectrographs, the most important point to remember is the relationship between sampling rate and frequency range in a digital recording: *the upper limit of the frequency range will be half the sampling rate.*

## 3.4 Digital spectrography

Both the Direct Translator of Figure 3.2 and the Sound Spectrograph of Figure 3.3 are analogue devices. The output spectrogram is essentially a series of continuous horizontal traces, one on top of the other, with each trace corresponding to a single filter. Each line varies in intensity – manifested as darkness of marking or brightness on a moving belt of phosphor – according to the strength of its filter's output. In computer-based digital spectrography, a bank of filters is also used, but the output of the various filters is determined not by measurement but by calculation, in most cases by a technique known as the *Fast Fourier Transform* or *FFT*. The result is visually indistinguishable from a spectrogram produced by an analogue spectrograph.

When using such equipment, it is useful to have a basic knowledge of how the calculations are done. In what follows, we shall give a brief account of the steps involved. From the point of view of the user, the two most important specifications for digital spectrograms are the sampling rate and the number of sample points in the FFT.

### *3.4.1  Recording for analysis*

As in the case of the Sound Spectrograph, the first step involves recording. The signal to be analysed (from a microphone, tape, or some other medium) is input and undergoes A-to-D conversion. There will normally be a choice of sampling rates. This is important, because, as we have seen, it is the sampling rate which determines the range of frequencies represented in the recording and, ultimately, in the calculated spectrogram. For most purposes, a sampling rate of 10,000 Hz (giving a frequency range of 5000 Hz) will be sufficient. However, if the intention is to study fricative consonants, a higher sampling rate should be used because these sounds typically show concentrations of energy above 5000 Hz. The user may also need to request pre-emphasis (Section 3.2.4) at this stage. Some systems may offer a choice of quantisation levels.

### 3.4.2  Calculating the power spectrum

After recording, the digital spectrograph has at its disposal a waveform, coded as a series of points as in Figure 3.10 (b). In order to perform its calculations, it must look at the waveform one chunk at a time. For each chunk, referred to as a *window*, the frequency range is divided into bands, corresponding to individual bandpass filters. The output of each filter is calculated, and the values are converted to decibels. The result is a power spectrum like those displayed graphically in Figure 3.7.

The power spectra for the individual windows must then be, as it were, turned on their side so that frequency is on the vertical axis. The amplitude values must be translated into the appropriate shadings or colours. When the resulting vertical spectra are lined up side by side, the result is a spectrogram. From the point of view of the user, the power spectrum is an extra display which supplements the main spectrogram, but in fact calculation of power spectra is logically prior to assembling the spectrogram.

The bandwidth of the filters depends on the duration (in time) of the window selected. *The longer the window, the narrower the filter bandwidth.* This makes intuitive sense, for we can easily imagine that the longer the chunk of waveform the analyser has to work with, the more accuracy it will be able to achieve in its frequency analysis. At the same time, since the analyser can produce only one spectrum per window, longer windows will give less detail about timing (poorer temporal resolution). As with the earlier spectrograph, greater accuracy in the frequency domain (better frequency resolution) must necessarily go with less accuracy in the time domain (poorer temporal resolution).

Figure 3.12 illustrates the steps involved, using a simple example. Part (a) shows a complex wave to be analysed. It was constructed by adding together two sine wave components with frequencies 300 and 1500 Hz. The amplitude of the 300 Hz component is 6 dB above (twice) the amplitude of the 1500 Hz component (Section 2.5.2). We have sampled the wave at a frequency of 5000 Hz, and the sample points are superimposed on the waveform. With our choice of sampling frequency, we have determined the range of the analysis, which will cover frequencies between 0 and 2500 Hz (= 5000/2).

We now select a chunk which is 64 points long. The duration of this chunk (window) is 64/5000 seconds or .0128 seconds. A 32-point window (with length .0064 seconds) is also shown. *The duration in time of a given number of sample points will depend on the sampling rate.* For example, if the sampling rate had been 10,000 Hz, the duration of a 64-point window would be only .0064 (= 64/10000) seconds.

In (b), our selection of 64 points is reshaped, in a process known as *windowing*. The purpose of the windowing is to attenuate the amplitude at the right and left edges. This eliminates the sudden and unnatural transitions to and from silence which would unavoidably occur if the selection in question were simply chopped out. In our example, a type of shaping known as a *Hanning window* has been applied. If no shaping at all is used, it is said that the window is

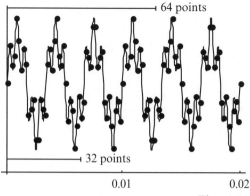

(a) A complex wave was constructed from two sine wave components. The two components have frequencies 300 and 1500 Hz, and the amplitude of the 300 Hz component is 6 dB above that of the 1500 Hz component. The wave has been sampled at a rate of 5000 samples per second (5000 Hz). The range covered in the spectral analysis will extend to half this number.

A *window* consisting of 64 sample points will be .0128 seconds in length (.0128 = 64 ÷ 5000). A 32-point window will be .0064 seconds long.

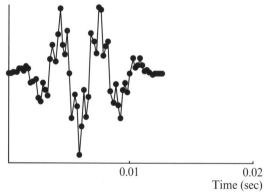

(b) The 64-point window is reshaped by applying a *Hanning window*. This eliminates unnatural transitions to and from silence.

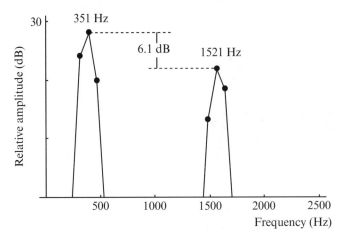

(c) FFT spectrum, calculated from the 64 sample points shown
in (b). Each point represents the calculated output of a single
filter. When the points are connected up, we see two peaks. Each
peak corresponds to one of the sine wave components (harmonics)
of the original wave. The centre frequencies of the peaks are
estimates of the frequencies of the corresponding harmonics.
Notice also that the difference between them in amplitude is
roughly the same as in the wave (a).

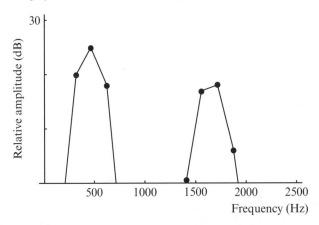

(d) FFT spectrum, calculated from the 32 sample points shown
in (a), after applying a Hanning window, as in (b).

As in (c), we see two peaks, corresponding to the two sine
wave components in the original wave. Notice that the peaks
are much broader. This is because a shorter window results
in a broader bandwidth.

FIGURE 3.12    Calculating an FFT spectrum.

*rectangular*. In general, spectrographs will apply a default type of shaping, chosen by the programmers who put together the necessary software. The user may be able to specify an alternative, but most will probably be content to opt for the default.

After windowing, the spectrum is calculated (c). The technique commonly used is known as the *Fast Fourier Transform* (*FFT*). The FFT is a quick method of calculating the so-called *Discrete Fourier Transform* (*DFT*) and may be used only when the number of sample points is a power of two. This is why possible window lengths are often restricted to numbers which are powers of two (16, 32, 64, 128, etc.). DFT/FFT analysis is an adaptation of the technique of Fourier Analysis (Section 2.4), but it works from a set of individual points rather than from a continuous wave.

As already mentioned, the frequency range is, in effect, divided up into a number of bands, and an amplitude level is calculated for each band. This is like putting a small chunk of signal through a bank of filters. The number of bands in the frequency range covered by the analysis (from 0 to half the sampling rate) will be half the number of points in the window. In the present example, the frequency range is 0–2500 Hz, and it is divided into 32 bands.

If FFT analysis is applied to the windowed points of (b), it is said that a *64-point FFT* is calculated. The result is presented as a graph in (c). The decibel scale has been used for the vertical axis, and a range of just over 30 dB has been allowed for. Each point corresponds to one frequency band. The calculated amplitude for each band (on the vertical axis) is plotted versus the centre frequency (on the horizontal axis). In fact, only six points are shown; the points for the remaining 26 lie below the zero line.

The bands showing the highest amplitudes are the fifth band (312–390 Hz, centre frequency 351 Hz) and the twentieth band (1481–1560 Hz, centre frequency 1521 Hz). The difference in amplitude between the two is 6.1 dB. On the basis of Figure 3.12 (c), we would estimate that our chunk of input signal contains two components with frequencies of about 351 and 1501 Hz and that the first of these is 6.1 dB more intense than the second. In this particular case, we are in the fortunate (though unusual) position of knowing what the answer should be, and we can see that our estimate is quite close to the truth (components at 300 and 1500 Hz, amplitude difference 6 dB), though the estimated frequency of the first component is too high.

It is also necessary to comment on the vertical axis which, in accordance with common practice, shows *relative* amplitude and is on the decibel scale. In such diagrams, the choice of baseline is somewhat arbitrary, and individual systems differ from one another. What is important is the range of values displayed and the difference in height between the various components (Section 2.5.2). For the purposes of our example, we have chosen to display a range of just over 30 dB.

Finally, part (d) of Figure 3.12 shows the effect of decreasing the window length to 32 points. The spikes are thicker and the frequency analysis is correspondingly less accurate. In practice, it is common to smooth out the spectrum in a DFT or FFT analysis. Thus, the broad band spectrum of Figure 3.7 appears considerably smoother than our calculated spectrum in (d).

As already mentioned, from the point of view of the user, the two most important specifications for digital spectrograms are the sampling rate and the number of points in the FFT. *The sampling rate determines the frequency range of the resulting spectrogram. The number of points in the FFT determines the bandwidth of the analysing filters.* The greater the number of points, the narrower the bandwidth, though the precise relationship will depend on the sampling rate. Some computer-based spectrographs make the choice easier by asking the user to choose a filter effective bandwidth rather than to specify a window length.

### 3.4.3  Determining fundamental frequency ($F_0$)

As we have already pointed out (Section 3.2.6), computer-based spectrographs typically include provision for determining and displaying the fundamental frequency contour of the speech signal being analysed. Unfortunately, determining the fundamental frequency of running speech is rather difficult. The nature of the difficulty can be appreciated if we return to the vowel waveforms of Figure 2.10. In theory, the most straightforward way of extracting the fundamental should be based on determining the period (Section 2.2.4). It is fairly easy to divide all three of the waveforms into periods by eye. At the same time, it is not so easy to come up with a cookbook-like set of instructions which a computer could follow and which would work in all cases. In this particular group of three waveforms, particular difficulties are posed by [ɑ], because the shape changes from cycle to cycle.

A number of methods exist for determining fundamental frequency. Some are based on looking for peaks in the waveform ('peak-picking'). In such cases, the input signal will usually be simplified by eliminating higher-frequency harmonics, so that the analyser can work with something more like a sine wave. Sine waves are much easier, because each period has only one peak and one valley, and the period can be defined as the distance between peaks (see Figure 2.4).

Another possibility is to shift the wave forward in time gradually and look for the point at which shifted and unshifted versions match up (or nearly match up); for example, if the waveform for [i] of Figure 2.5 (a) is shifted to the left, it will match up with itself when it has been shifted by 8.3 msec; it follows that 8.3 msec must be the period of the wave. This method is known as *autocorrelation*.

Still another possibility is to start from narrow band spectra. The vertical spikes of a narrow band spectrum are evenly spaced, reflecting the even spacing between harmonics in periodic sounds (Section 2.4.2). This can be seen clearly in the narrow band spectrum of Figure 3.7. A narrow band spectrum is itself like a periodic signal, since it has spikes (corresponding to individual harmonics) at regular intervals. The interval between spikes (which would be the period of the spectrum) is the frequency of the original wave and the frequency of the spectrum (defined as 1 divided by the period, Section 2.2.4) will be the period of the original wave; the term *quefrency* is used for this quantity. Taking the spectrum of the narrow band spectrum will accordingly get us back to the period of the original and enable us to determine the fundamental frequency. The spectrum of the narrow band spectrum is known as the *cepstrum*. (The words *quefrency* and *cepstrum* are derived by rearranging the letters of *frequency* and *spectrum*.) The fundamental frequency contour of Figure 3.8 (c) was determined by the cepstrum method.

Finally, the most accurate method of determining fundamental frequency is to use a system based on monitoring vocal fold vibration, if this is possible. This is because each cycle of vocal fold vibration corresponds to a period in the acoustic signal. Such methods will be discussed briefly in Section 8.3.6.

## 3.5  Summary

We have now come to the end of our overview of spectrographic analysis. The most important points to remember are as follows:

1  The dimensions of a spectrogram are time (on the horizontal axis), frequency (on the vertical axis) and intensity (reflected in the darkness or brightness of the marking).

2  Spectrographic analysis is based on the use of filters as detectors. The signal to be analysed is put through a bank of filters and the strength of the output of each filter is recorded.

3  Spectrographs provide for both broad band and narrow band analysis, so named because the bandwidth of the analysing filters is broad or narrow respectively. Broad band analysis is more precise as regards time but less precise as regards frequency, while for narrow band analysis the opposite is the case. In general, a broad band analysis provides a good general picture, while a narrow band analysis shows more details of harmonic structure.

4  Users of computer-based digital spectrographs will generally have a choice of sampling rate and filter bandwidth. The former relates to the recording of the signal prior to analysis, and determines the frequency range, which will be equal to half the sampling rate. The filter bandwidth is often specified by giving the number of sample points to be used in the FFT analysis, but is sometimes specified more directly.

5  In addition to producing spectrograms, spectrographs normally produce power spectra or FFT spectra. Like the spectra of Chapter 2, these have the dimensions frequency (on the horizontal axis) and relative amplitude (on the vertical axis). Power spectra are a useful supplement to spectrograms, as they give a better view of relative amplitude for a short window of time within the signal being analysed.

## 3.6  Further reading

Sound spectrography is discussed in a number of works, though only the more recent publications include coverage of digital methods. Here, we shall cite Borden *et al.* (1994), Clark and Yallop (1990), Denes and Pinson (1993), Fry (1979), Lieberman and Blumstein (1988), Pickett (1980) and Rosen and Howell (1991). Potter *et al.* (1947), though not widely available, is still to be recommended, and remains one of the most fully and clearly illustrated books on spectrography.

Particular mention should be made of Ladefoged (1996) and Johnson (1997), which provide illustrations of the calculations involved in digital methods, and which do not presuppose any advanced mathematics. Of these two works, Ladefoged's is the more detailed and has somewhat fuller coverage. Baken (1987, Chapter 5) provides a good review of techniques for determining fundamental frequency.

**Chapter 4**

# The acoustics of speech production

## 4.1 Introduction

In Chapters 2 and 3, our main concern was with the description of speech as sound. For phoneticians and linguists, however, this is not an end in itself. As explained in Chapter 1, we need to relate the sound of speech to speech production on the one hand and to speech perception on the other. In this chapter, we shall focus on the relationship between acoustics and production. The crucial link is provided by the *source-filter theory*, also often referred to as the *acoustic theory of speech production*.

More specifically, the source-filter theory is concerned with the final stage of speech production, when sound is actually generated. It addresses the question of why particular articulations should give rise to particular sounds, but is not concerned with how the speaker produces the articulations in the first place. For example, the source-filter theory can explain why a vowel produced with a high front tongue position and spread lips ([i]) will have a spectrum like that of Figure 3.7, but it has nothing to say about how the speaker gets his or her tongue to the high front position.

The basic idea behind the source-filter theory is quite simple. Sound production often involves more than one stage, and so it is necessary to distinguish between the original *source* of sound and later modifications (*filtering*) of that source. For example, in the case of a violin, the original source of sound is a vibrating string, but the vibration of the string is transmitted to a sort of box and it is the vibration of this second object which is responsible for the sound which is transmitted to our ears. At the risk of oversimplification, we may say that the string and the box make separate and independent contributions to the output sound. For example, the pitch and loudness of a note (among other things) depend on what the player does to the string, but the overall 'violin' quality comes from the box.

It is not difficult to see how this general approach might be applied to the description of vowel sounds. In this case, the source is the vibrating vocal folds (more accurately, the air flowing through them). They produce a sound-to-be which is then modified in the oral and pharyngeal (and possibly also the nasal) cavities. The pitch, the loudness and the phonation type are determined at the level of the source, whereas the vowel quality is determined by the filter (that is, by the shaping of the cavities above the vocal folds).

None of what we have said thus far goes beyond the insights of impression-istic phonetics, which recognises the independence of the vocal folds and the cavities above them and incorporates this into its descriptive framework. The source-filter theory represents an advance insofar as it provides a means of relating both vocal fold activity and the positions of the vocal organs to the output sound in a principled way. In impressionistic phonetic description, the sound which corresponds to a particular vocal setting is something to be heard and retained in memory. In the source-filter approach, the sound – which is now conceived of not as an auditory percept but as a visual spectrum – is pre-dicted from the setting by universally valid procedures which apply not only to speech but to the production of sound in general. In the next section, I shall illustrate the basic principles by working through a simple example.

## 4.2   Modelling a simple vowel

Perhaps ironically, the sounds which are easiest to describe in terms of the source-filter theory are those which have posed the greatest problems for im-pressionistic phoneticians, that is, vowels. Of all the vowels, the easiest to describe is a mid-central vowel, often referred to as *schwa* and transcribed as [ə] or, in the context of British English, [ɜ] (used for the vowel in words such as **sir** or **fur**). For this reason, it is the standard textbook example. We shall imagine that we are describing the speech of a male speaker with a low-pitched voice.

A first point to be made is that speech ultimately originates in air flow. The small variations in air pressure which constitute the output sound begin as variations in rate of flow. When the sound-to-be leaves the mouth at the lips, the main bulk of the air flow is absorbed into the vastness of the outside atmosphere, while the small variations set up a pressure wave which is trans-mitted through the air in the same way that any other sound wave would be. This means that, strictly speaking, from the glottis to the lips, a speech sound consists of variations in flow rather than variations in pressure. It is possible to feel the air flow of speech, but it is necessary to place the hand immediately in front of the mouth in order to do so.

Rate of air flow – in more technical terms, *volume velocity* – can be trans-lated into a pattern of varying electrical voltage (Section 8.2.3.2), displayed as a waveform and analysed as a sum of sine wave components. When working in the source-filter framework, it is customary to think simply in terms of modifica-tions of an abstract pattern (Section 2.2.2). Before radiation into the outside atmosphere, this is a pattern of variation in flow; by the final stage, it has been translated into a pattern of variation in pressure.

### 4.2.1   The voice source

For any voiced sound, the source is the *voice source*, produced by the vibrat-ing vocal folds. When the vocal folds vibrate, they peel open and snap shut (Section 8.3.2). Remembering that, at this stage, our concern is flow rather than pressure, we can represent the voice source as a graph showing volume velocity (measured in units such as millilitres per second) vs. time. The waveform already shown in Figure 2.16 (a) is commonly used as an approximation to the typical pattern of flow during normal (*modal*) voice. The more gradually sloping left side and steeper right side of the individual pulses of air reflect the fact that vocal fold opening is gradual but closure is more sudden. The spectrum of this waveform was shown in Figure 2.17 (a) (repeated at the top of Figure 4.3).

### 4.2.2   *The vocal tract filter*

#### 4.2.2.1   The concept of *filter*

At this stage, we must digress slightly, and clarify what is meant by the concept of *filter*. In everyday language, a filter is a device used to 'filter out' something undesirable from a mixture. For example, the function of a coffee filter is to separate out the coffee grounds from a mixture of grounds and coffee-flavoured liquid. Bearing in mind that every sound wave is a mixture of sine waves, we might imagine that 'filtering' a sound wave would involve eliminating undesirable sine wave components. Sometimes this is indeed the case. For example, an unpleasant hiss on a tape recording may often be made less obtrusive or even eliminated altogether by filtering out the high-frequency components. This would be called *low pass filtering*, since all frequencies above a specified cut-off frequency would be eliminated but the frequencies below would be allowed to pass through the filter.

Filters may also be used as detectors. We have already seen (Section 3.2.1) that the technique of spectrography is based on the use of bandpass filters. Because a bandpass filter will only allow frequencies within its band to pass through, it follows that, if anything at all does pass through, there must have been some component(s) within the pass band in the original input sound.

The term *filter* may also be used in a more general way, and applied to devices which simply alter the balance between the various component frequencies of a sound, with no implication that undesirables are being eliminated. For example, it is common for radios, cassette players, and CD players to have a knob which can be used to alter the balance between bass and treble; those which come equipped with 'graphic equalisers' are more sophisticated, allowing the user to make more elaborate adjustments as regards the relative strengths of frequencies within various bands. All such adjustments are examples of 'filtering' in this more general sense.

The behaviour of a filter is conveniently described in terms of a *frequency response curve*. We have already seen an example of one such curve in Figure 3.9 (d). In that example, it was used for the purpose of characterising a poor recording system, which altered the balance between the low and high frequencies in the original sound. In the terminology used here, this is also a sort of filtering, since the low frequencies have been given more prominence and the high frequencies less prominence than in the original. What the frequency response curve tells us is how many decibels will be added to or taken away from each possible input frequency during the filtering process. This is sometimes called the *gain* of the filter.

In Section 3.3.2 and Figure 3.9, we imagined determining such a curve experimentally, by recording a mixture of sine waves of equal amplitude and then seeing if any of these waves showed up as strengthened or weakened in the reproduction. The input was the original wave and the output was the reproduced version (the output of the recording process). When we model the vocal tract filter, our aim is not to determine the curve experimentally, but to predict it from a simplified representation of the vocal tract itself. If the model is successful, the predicted vowel spectrum will match the spectra of naturally produced vowels.

### 4.2.2.2   Formant frequencies

For *schwa*, the vocal tract is essentially unconstricted, as illustrated in Figure 4.1. For the purposes of our model, we shall ignore the bend at the junction of the pharynx and mouth cavities and variations in shape, and think of it as a straight *uniform* tube, with no taperings or bulges. The tube is open at one end, for it is closed at the glottis (that is, the vocal folds) and open at the lips. Fortunately, tubes open at one end have been well studied (for example, open organ pipes fit into this category), and much is known about their frequency response patterns. More accurately, we should say 'the response patterns of the column of air inside such a tube' since it is the vibration of the air inside which will produce the output sound.

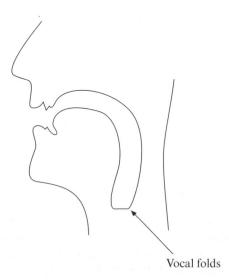

Vocal folds

FIGURE 4.1   Schematic view of the vocal tract tube during the production of a mid-central vowel ([ə]). For the production of this vowel, the shape of the vocal tract is very similar to that of a uniform tube, with no taperings or bulges.

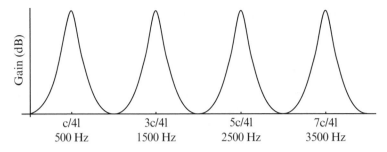

FIGURE 4.2    Frequency response curve for a tube open at one end. The resonant (formant) frequencies are odd multiples of **c/4l**, where **l** is the length of the tube. In the case of a tube which is about the length of a male vocal tract (17 cm), these will be 500 Hz, 1500 Hz, 2500 Hz, etc.

The frequency response curve of a tube open at one end looks like the curve of Figure 4.2. It has peaks which are well-defined, regularly spaced and separated by valleys. The most important part of the specification of the curve is the frequencies of the peaks. These are the frequencies which are most favoured, and they are known as the *resonant frequencies*. In the context of speech research, the term *formant frequencies* is commonly used to refer to the resonant frequencies of the vocal tract. The lowest peak is known as the *first formant*, the second as the *second formant*, and so on. The frequencies of the formants are commonly represented by capital F followed by an appropriate number, so that, for example, the first formant frequency is $F_1$ and the second formant frequency is $F_2$.

The resonant frequencies (formant frequencies) of a tube open at one end are easy to calculate. The wavelength (Section 2.2.4) of the lowest resonant frequency is **4l**, where **l** is the length of the tube. Applying the general formula of Section 2.2.4, we arrive at the more specific formula **f = c/4l** (where **c** is the velocity of sound in air). The higher resonant frequencies are odd multiples of this number, that is, **3c/4l**, **5c/4l**, **7c/4l**, etc. The basic idea behind these calculations is that – for reasons which we shall not go into here – a tube open at one end is ideally suited to accommodate a quarter-wavelength (and, by extension, $\frac{3}{4}$ wavelength, $1\frac{1}{4}$ wavelengths, etc.) of a sine wave.

A commonly used estimate of the length of the average male vocal tract is 17 cm. Using c = 340 metres/second (34,000 cm/sec), we only need divide 34,000 by 68 cm (68 = 17 × 4) to obtain a value of 500 Hz for the lowest resonance; in other words, $F_1$ = 500 Hz. The higher resonances will be odd multiples of this number, that is, 1500 Hz, 2500 Hz, 3500 Hz, etc. Thus, the frequency response curve of Figure 4.2, which has peaks at these frequencies, is in fact our predicted curve for *schwa*.

Another term sometimes used to refer to the frequency response curve of the vocal tract is the *transfer function*. Within this terminological framework, the formant frequencies are called *poles of the transfer function* or simply *poles*.

These terms are taken from the vocabulary of electrical engineering, and reflect the crucial role played by engineers in developing models of the vocal tract.

### 4.2.3  Combining source and filter

We must now combine the spectrum of the source with the frequency response curve of the filter. This is very straightforward. The spectrum shows the harmonics which are present in the source and their relative amplitudes in decibels; the frequency response curve tells us how many decibels will be added to or taken away from each harmonic by the filter. The process is illustrated in Figure 4.3 (a)–(c). It will be seen that the output spectrum has the general downward slope of the source but with the peaks (formants) of the filter superimposed. These coincide with the fifth harmonic (500 Hz), the fifteenth harmonic (1500 Hz), the twenty-fifth harmonic (2500 Hz) and the thirty-fifth harmonic (3500 Hz). In principle, we could extend the model to higher frequencies as well.

### 4.2.4  The radiation function

Strictly speaking, we have not quite finished. The spectrum derived by combining source and filter is the spectrum of flow at the lips; this must still be transformed into a pressure wave, via *radiation* into the outside atmosphere. Radiation will not affect the overall pattern of peaks and valleys, but it will boost the amplitude of the high-frequency components. More precisely, according to the model for each doubling along the frequency (horizontal) axis, there will be an increase of 6 dB along the vertical axis, in other words there will be an increase of 6 dB per octave. The effects of radiation can be represented by means of a frequency response curve – the *radiation function* – which gradually slopes upwards. The effects of adding in radiation are shown in Figure 4.3 (d) and (e).

In practice, radiation is of little interest, since its effects are assumed to be constant and are totally outside the speaker's control. The overall effect of the high-frequency boost of 6 dB per octave is to cancel out −6 dB of the slope of the original source spectrum (which was −12 dB per octave). Accordingly, some accounts of the source-filter theory simplify matters by eliminating the radiation stage altogether and using a source spectrum with a slope of −6 dB (= −12 dB − (−6 dB)).

### 4.2.5  Comparison with a spoken vowel

The ultimate test of our model lies in comparing the output spectrum which we have predicted with the spectrum of an actual spoken vowel. Figure 4.4 shows an FFT spectrum for the vowel of **heard**, pronounced by a male speaker on a fundamental frequency of 187 Hz. When comparing this with the output spectrum of Figure 4.3, it should be borne in mind that the range of amplitudes shown in Figure 4.4 is only 50 dB, whereas in Figure 4.3 it is 100 dB.

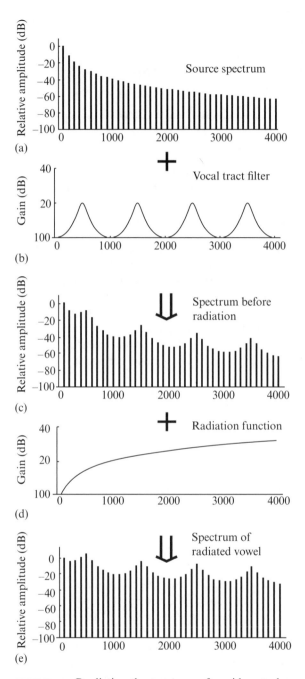

FIGURE 4.3   Predicting the spectrum of a mid-central vowel. The source spectrum (a) is modified by the vocal tract filter (b) to give the spectrum of air flow at the lips (c). This spectrum is, in turn, modified as part of the process of radiation (d) to give the spectrum of the resulting sound wave (e).

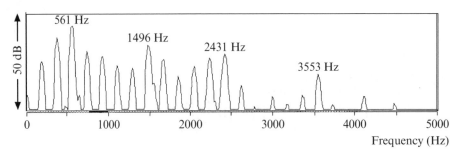

FIGURE 4.4   Narrow band power spectrum of the vowel /ɜ/ of English **heard** pronounced by a male speaker. This should be compared with the predicted output spectrum of Figure 4.3 (e).

It will be seen that the strongest harmonics are the third harmonic (561 Hz), the eighth harmonic (1496 Hz), the thirteenth harmonic (2431 Hz), and the nineteenth harmonic (3553 Hz). These are very close to the first four predicted peaks of the vocal tract filter function (500 Hz, 1500 Hz, 2500 Hz, 3500 Hz).

The resemblance between the predicted spectrum and the actual spectrum appears remarkably good. This is despite the fact that our representations were really rather crude. Furthermore, we have not done a single measurement of the speaker's mouth or pharynx and have not examined the vibration of his vocal folds.

## 4.3   Varying the voice source

As mentioned above, the source-filter theory agrees with traditional impressionistic phonetic description in its assumption that source and filter are independent – in other words, that the vocal folds and the shaping of the vocal tract are controlled separately. Training in impressionistic phonetics helps us to recognise in a vowel, perceived via the ear, characteristics due to the vocal folds (pitch and phonation type) and characteristics due to the shaping of the vocal tract (vowel quality). Similarly, the source-filter approach to vowel production helps us to recognise in the spectrum of a vowel, perceived via the eye, characteristics due to the source and characteristics due to the filter.

Our theoretical spectrum of the voice source, as shown in Figures 2.17 and 4.3 (a), is based on a very simplified *two-parameter model* of the source spectrum. What this means is that the source spectrum is uniquely specified by two numbers (parameters): the fundamental frequency (in Hz) and the overall slope (expressed in dB per octave). Accordingly, if we are to reflect modifications to what the vocal folds are doing, we must make appropriate modifications to one or both of these numbers.

The fundamental frequency of the source spectrum, and accordingly the fundamental frequency of the output sound, is the same as the frequency of vocal fold vibration. When we look at the spectrum of a vowel (or any other voiced sound), the most obvious manifestation of fundamental frequency lies in the spacing between the individual harmonics. The higher the fundamental frequency, the greater the spacing. This follows from the fact that all of the harmonics are multiples of the fundamental (Section 2.4).

In constructing the source spectrum of Figures 2.17 and 4.3, we used a fundamental frequency of 100 Hz, which would correspond to a low-pitched male voice relatively low in its range. If we double the fundamental frequency, the spacing between the individual harmonics will also double, with the result that the frequency range 0–4000 Hz will contain only 20 harmonics rather than 40. The effect of losing so many harmonics is that the shape of the vocal tract frequency response curve shows up much less clearly in the output spectrum. This is illustrated in Figure 4.5, which shows the effect of doubling the fundamental frequency on both the source spectrum and the spectrum of the output vowel. The peaks in the output vowel spectrum are much less clearly delineated than in the output spectrum of Figure 4.3 (e), and accordingly it is not so obvious exactly where the peaks (formants) were in the original frequency-response curve for the filter. The situation will become worse if we raise the fundamental frequency still further, particularly if no harmonics happen to coincide with the formant frequencies.

As regards the slope of the spectrum, this can be related to phonation type. It is common to operate with a three-way division of phonation types into *normal* or *modal*, *breathy*, and *creaky* or *pressed* (Section 8.3.2), depending on the spacing between the vocal folds and the amount of air passing through them. What is not so obvious from this description is that, in breathy voice, the flow waveform (Figure 2.16) will be more symmetrical, while in pressed (creaky) voice, it will be more asymmetrical with more gradual opening and sharper closing. In terms of the spectrum, this involves a difference in slope. For breathy voice, the fundamental component is more dominant and the slope is steeper, whereas for creaky voice, the fundamental component is less dominant and the slope is less steep. Figure 4.6 shows theoretical source waveforms and spectra and output vowel spectra for more breathy and more creaky versions of the *schwa* of Figure 4.3. It is clear the overall slope is the steepest in the breathy version and least steep in the creaky version; the version of Figure 4.3 lies in between.

The relative steepness of the source spectrum may also be related to loudness or 'vocal effort'. The source spectrum for voicing with less vocal effort is similar to the spectrum of Figure 4.6 (a) (breathy) while the spectrum for voicing with more vocal effort is like the spectrum of Figure 4.6 (b) (creaky). This is because louder speech typically has sharper closure of the vocal folds and consequently a less steep spectrum.

The vowel spectra of Figures 4.3, 4.5 and 4.6 were all constructed using exactly the same vocal tract filter, so any differences between them are due to differences in the source brought about by differences in our representation of vocal fold activity. The spacing between the harmonics is entirely determined

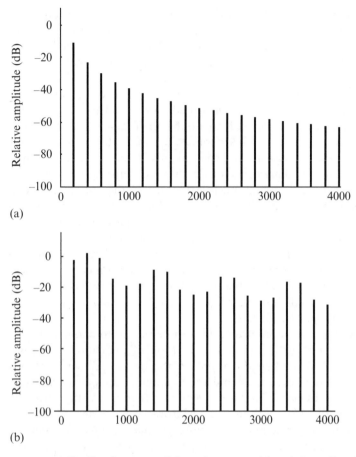

(a)

(b)

FIGURE 4.5   Predicted spectra of the voice source (a) and the radiated vowel (b) for a mid-central vowel [ə] as in Figure 4.3, but with the fundamental frequency increased to 200 Hz. The overall slope of the spectrum in (a) is the same as in the source spectrum of Figure 4.3 (a), but the harmonics are twice as far apart. In the spectrum in (b), the peaks are less well-defined than in the corresponding spectrum of Figure 4.3 (e).

by the fundamental frequency. The slope – that is, the balance between high and low frequencies – is determined by the phonation type and/or vocal effort. Here, however, we must add that the overall slope of the output spectrum will also be affected by the vocal tract filter, as will be explained below.

## 4.4   Varying the vocal tract filter

The vowel *schwa* is the example of choice in introductions to the source-filter theory because, for this vowel, the vocal tract most closely approximates a

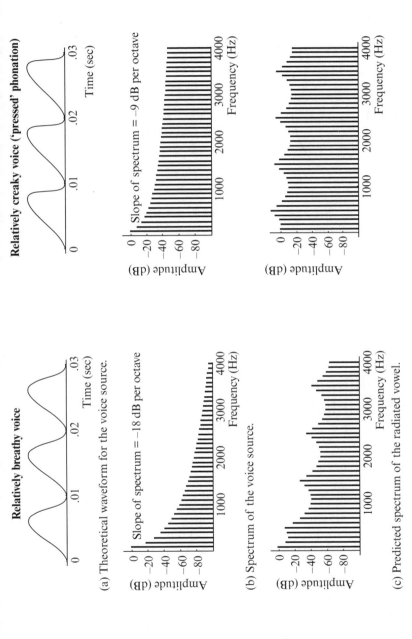

FIGURE 4.6 Theoretical source waveforms, spectra for the voice source, and spectra for the radiated vowel for relatively breathy and relatively creaky (or 'pressed') phonation. The waveforms should be compared with Figure 2.16 (a). It will be seen that the waveform for relatively breathy voice is more symmetrical while the waveform for relatively creaky voice is somewhat more skewed. The spectra of (b) and (c) should be compared with the spectra of Figure 4.3 (a) and (e). The fundamental frequency (and thus the spacing between harmonics) is the same as in the example of Figure 4.3, but the overall slope of the spectrum is altered. For relatively breathy voice, the slope is more steep, whilst for relatively creaky voice it is more shallow.

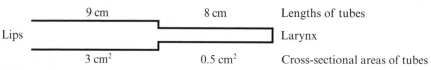

(a) Two-tube model for [a].

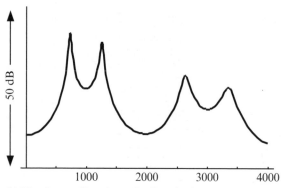

(b) Vocal tract filter (transfer function).

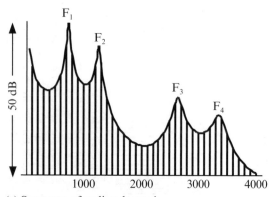

(c) Spectrum of radiated vowel.

FIGURE 4.7    A two-tube model for [a].

simple uniform tube and the formant frequencies are easy to calculate. To extend this type of approach to other shapes – that is, to other vowels – it is necessary to use a slightly more complex representation of the vocal tract.

For example, in Figure 4.7 (a), two tubes are joined together to approximate the shape of the vocal tract during the production of a low central vowel ([a]). Although this two-tube representation is very simple and crude, it presents some complications which do not arise in the case of the single tube. This is because the two tubes are not independent of one another, and the coupling between them causes the resonant frequencies (formant frequencies) to shift away from the values for the corresponding single, uncoupled tubes. Accordingly, the effects of coupling must be taken into account when determining the formant frequencies. The calculations are too complicated to be done by hand.

In fact, the crucial step in going from a representation like that of Figure 4.7 (a) to the corresponding frequency-response curve (transfer function) is to determine the formant frequencies of the system. This may be done by calculation, or by estimating from graphs known as *nomograms* (Section 4.4.3). As we shall see (Chapter 6), the fact that vowel spectra can be predicted from their formant frequencies has lent support to the view that vowel quality should be specified in terms of formant frequencies.

Strictly speaking, it is not entirely true that the formant frequencies alone determine the shape of the frequency-response curve (transfer function). We need to know not only where the peaks are but also how wide and how high they are – in technical terms, their *bandwidths* and their relative levels. However, these can be estimated provided that the formant frequencies are known and certain standard assumptions hold. In this regard, the theoretical work of Gunnar Fant (1956, 1960) has been of crucial importance. In the examples of Figures 4.7, 4.8 and 4.9, bandwidths were estimated from frequencies using an equation suggested by Fant (1985). If the bandwidths are known, the levels are determined automatically.

Once the transfer function has been determined, it only remains to combine it with the source spectrum and radiation function. This proceeds as in the case of our *schwa* example, illustrated in Figure 4.3.

### 4.4.1 Simple models for three vowels

Figures 4.7, 4.8 and 4.9 illustrate simple models for three vowels: a low central unrounded vowel ([a]), a high front unrounded vowel ([i]) and a high back rounded vowel ([u]). In each case, we give (a) a configuration of tubes approximating the vocal tract shape, (b) the calculated vocal tract transfer function and (c) the calculated output spectrum. For the output spectrum (c) in all three cases, we have used the same representation of the voice source as in Figure 4.3 ($F_0 = 100$ Hz, slope of $-12$ dB per octave as expected for modal phonation).[1]

For [a], the mouth passage is wide but the pharynx is somewhat constricted. In Figure 4.7, the articulation is represented by a pair of interconnected tubes, the narrower tube representing the pharynx and the wider tube the oral cavity. For [i], the mouth passage is narrow, due to the raised position of the tongue body, while the pharynx is wide. In Figure 4.8, we have used three tubes, a wide one for the pharynx, a narrow one for the constriction along the hard palate, and one of intermediate diameter for the oral cavity in front of the constriction. For [u], the vocal tract tube is divided into two at the velum and there is an additional constriction at the lips (lip rounding). In Figure 4.9, we have used four tubes, two wide and two narrow – the wide ones correspond to the pharyngeal and oral cavities and the narrow ones to the constrictions at the velum and at the lips. It should be noted that adding on a constriction at the lips has the effect of lengthening the vocal tract as a whole.

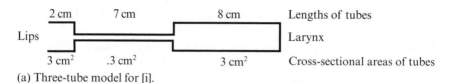

(a) Three-tube model for [i].

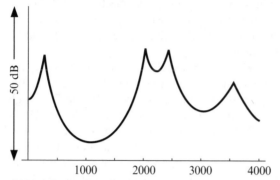

(b) Vocal tract filter (transfer function).

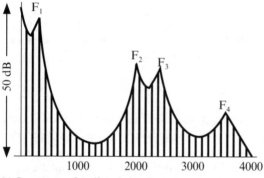

(c) Spectrum of radiated vowel.

FIGURE 4.8    A three-tube model for [i].

The three calculated vowel spectra are visually distinct from each other and also from the calculated spectrum for schwa. Notice that not only the position of the peaks, but also the overall slope, differs from vowel to vowel. This reflects the influence of the vocal tract filter on the overall slope of the spectrum. If two formants are close in frequency (as $F_1$ and $F_2$ for [a] and [u] or $F_2$ and $F_3$ for [i]), they reinforce each other, resulting in a particularly prominent region in the output spectrum. If, on the other hand, $F_1$ and $F_2$ are both low in frequency, as for [u], $F_3$ and $F_4$ will have no reinforcement, and will remain rather weak.

For [a], $F_1$ (the leftmost peak) is higher in frequency than $F_1$ for [i] or [u]. $F_2$ is not far from $F_1$ and, taken together, the two form a double peak centred at about 1000 Hz. For [i], $F_1$ is low and is separated from $F_2$ by a pronounced

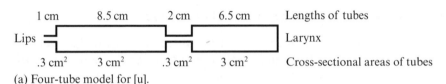

(a) Four-tube model for [u].

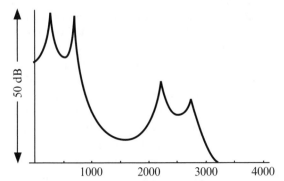

(b) Vocal tract filter (transfer function).

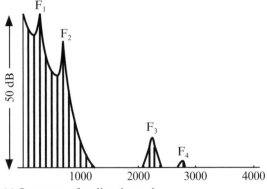

(c) Spectrum of radiated vowel.

FIGURE 4.9   A four-tube model for [u].

valley. In more general terms, it appears that [u] has prominent low frequencies and weak high frequencies, [i] has prominent high frequencies balancing a strong $F_1$, and [a] has marked prominence in the middle region. These same characteristics emerged from our analysis of the same three vowels in Chapters 2 (Figure 2.14) and 3 (Figure 3.1), which was based on picking out prominent harmonics in the output sound. We now see that these are the harmonics which are closest to the formant frequencies. What the models have done for us is to enable us to go beyond simply observing differences between the vowels; we are now able to predict such differences, and to relate them to the shape of the oral and pharyngeal cavities.

### 4.4.2   *More realistic models of vowel articulation*

The use of one, two, three or four tubes to approximate the shape of the vocal tract is really rather crude. What is impressive – even surprising – about the models we have been describing is just how close it is possible to get to the spectra of naturally produced speech using such simple representations. Nevertheless, one purpose of such models is to provide a link between realistic models of tongue and jaw activity and the sound which eventually emerges from the lips, and it is clear that our crude assemblies of tubes will not do for such purposes.

Greater accuracy can be achieved, however, by using a larger number of tubes. For example, Fant (1960), modelling the vowels of a single native speaker of Russian, used a representation of his subject's vocal tract involving about forty tubes (the precise number varied from vowel to vowel). Each tube in the assembly was only five millimetres long. With such a large number of tubes, it is possible to vary the cross-sectional area of the model in small steps, replicating the changing cross-sectional area of the vocal tract. It should also be mentioned here that in studies which, like Fant's, seek to model the vowel production of a specific speaker, much will depend on how accurately the cross-sectional area of the vocal tract can be estimated along the whole of its length, from the glottis to the lips.

Obviously, calculating the formant frequencies is considerably more complicated if one has forty tubes rather than just three or four, though, with the availability of increasingly powerful computers, this is no longer an obstacle. An alternative is to construct an analogous electrical circuit and to use this 'electrical vocal tract' to determine formant frequencies experimentally. The electrical analogues developed at MIT (Stevens *et al.* 1953) and at the Royal Institute of Technology in Stockholm (Fant 1960) played an important role in advancing our understanding of the relationship between articulation and acoustics.

To conclude this section, we should point out that other factors, apart from accuracy in the representation of the shape of the vocal tract, need to be taken into consideration in order to achieve more accurate models. For example, the elastic properties of the walls (soft and compliant or stiff) will also play a role in determining the character of the output spectrum. It has also come to be realised that the assumptions of the source-filter theory may be too strong, and that the source and filter are not entirely independent. As understanding of these matters progresses, it is becoming possible to achieve ever more realistic models which relate the vocal tract configuration to the output sound.

### 4.4.3   *A general model of vowel production*

In the preceding section, we were concerned with getting as close as possible to the shape of a specific person's vocal tract during the pronunciation of a specific vowel. However, linguists are usually more interested in thinking about vowels in a more general way. If we try to think about vowels in the most general way possible, even the crude representations of Figures 4.7, 4.8 and 4.9 are too specific.

A very general way of thinking about vowels is to start from *schwa*, for which, as we have seen, the vocal tract most nearly approximates a uniform tube (Figure 4.1). For other vowels, this basic tube is constricted somewhere along its length. In Figure 4.7 ([a]), the constriction is at the larynx end; in Figure 4.8 ([i]), it is towards the lip end; in Figure 4.9 ([u]), it is in the middle. The three vowels thus differ in constriction location. There is a further discrepancy as regards the length of the tube corresponding to the constriction, which is longest for [a] and shortest for [u]. Finally, the cross-sectional area of the constriction is greater for [a] than for [i] or [u].

If we standardise the constriction length and cross-sectional area, we shall have a very general model, which allows us to examine the relationship between constriction location and formant frequencies. In addition, we can model the effects of rounding the lips by adding on a small fourth tube at the front end, as in Figure 4.9. This would be called a *two-parameter model* because two parameters (constriction location and presence/absence of lip rounding) are allowed to vary while everything else (cross-sectional areas, total overall length) is held constant. We can also imagine a slightly more sophisticated two-parameter model in which lip rounding was not simply present or absent but varied in degree. This would correspond to varying the cross-sectional area of the fourth tube.

Figure 4.10 (a) illustrates a very simple model. It is based on three tubes, with the possibility of adding a fourth to represent lip rounding. The middle tube, which represents the constriction, has a length of 2 cm and a cross-sectional area of .3 cm². The total length of the three main tubes is fixed at 17 cm. For any given constriction location, it is possible to calculate formant frequencies, both with and without adding a separate tube representing the lips.

The results of these calculations are presented in the graph of Figure 4.10 (b), which is known as a *nomogram*. Constriction location is specified by giving the length of the back cavity. (For example, if the back cavity is 10 cm long, the 2 cm constriction begins 10 cm from the larynx end.) The solid lines show how the frequencies of the first four formants – $F_1$, $F_2$, $F_3$ and $F_4$ – change as the constriction location varies from back (on the left) to front (on the right). The dashed lines show the results of similar calculations, carried out when the fourth tube (representing lip rounding) is added. All four dashed lines lie below their corresponding solid lines. This reflects the fact that, if the fourth (lip) tube is added to the three basic tubes for any particular constriction location, the formant frequencies will be lowered. At the same time, the extent of the lowering will differ from one location to another. For example, when the back cavity length is 2 cm, the dashed line for $F_2$ is only slightly lower than the corresponding solid line. By contrast, when the back cavity length is 11 cm, the gap between the two lines for $F_2$ is much greater.

It remains to say something about the phonetic quality of the vowels which would correspond to the various constriction locations in this model. Here, we

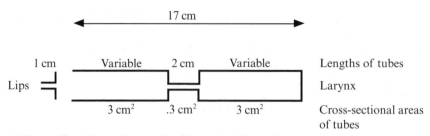

(a) Generalised three-tube model with optional lip section.

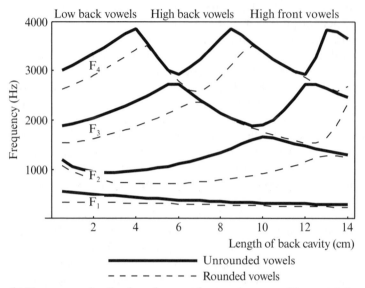

(b) Nomogram showing how formant frequencies vary with constriction location.

FIGURE 4.10    In this general model of vowel articulation (a), the supralaryngeal vocal tract is represented as a series of three tubes with an optional fourth tube representing the lips. The total length is fixed at 17 cm and the constriction length is fixed at 2 cm. However, the lengths of the front and back tubes may be varied. The location of the constriction can be specified by giving the length of one of these cavities, in this case, the length of the back cavity.

The nomogram based on the model (b) shows how formant frequencies vary with constriction location and also the effects of adding lip rounding. Nomograms can be used to estimate formant frequencies. For example, if the back cavity length is 2 cm and there is no lip rounding, $F_1$ will be about 500 Hz and $F_2$ will be about 1000 Hz. These numbers are arrived at by estimating the height of the solid lines corresponding to $F_1$ and $F_2$ at the points corresponding to 2 on the horizontal axis.

must take the cross-sectional area of the constriction into account. In fact, the value which I have chosen is rather small, and corresponds to the situation where the relevant part of the tongue is close to the outer wall of the vocal tract. In terms of impressionistic phonetic classification, this includes all high vowels (which would be placed at the top of the vowel quadrilateral) and all fully back vowels. For the high vowels, the front of the tongue is close to the roof of the mouth; for fully back vowels, the back of the tongue is close to the back wall of the pharynx.

To represent mid and low front and central vowels, it would be necessary to allow for the possibility of widening the cross-sectional area of the middle tube. Of course, it would be possible to redo all of the calculations using a larger value for the cross-sectional area, and to produce a new graph to display the results. In this case, we should have extended our two-parameter model to a three-parameter model by allowing a third parameter (cross-sectional area) to vary in addition to the other two (constriction location and presence or absence of lip rounding). The models described by Stevens and House (1955) and Fant (1960) are three-parameter models.

### 4.4.4 Phonological implications of modelling

Although it might seem that nomograms are of little general interest, it is possible that they may help us to understand why languages prefer particular vowel articulations. This point has been discussed at some length in two classic papers by Stevens (1972, 1989), which present an approach to studying articulatory-acoustic relations known as the *Quantal Theory*. The Quantal Theory begins from the observation that, if we vary a single articulatory parameter along a continuum, the acoustic consequences will be more dramatic at some points along the continuum than at others. For example, suppose that we use the nomogram to study the effects of changing the back cavity length (and with it the constriction location) on $F_2$ in the absence of lip rounding. To do this, we must focus our attention on the solid line labelled $F_2$. For lengths between 2 and 4 cm, and lengths of 10–12 cm, $F_2$ is relatively stable. In contrast, for lengths between 5 and 9 cm, $F_2$ rises rapidly. We might say that changing the constriction location involves a rapid transition between two regions of relative stability. This is the meaning conveyed by the adjective *quantal*. Stevens further argues that languages should prefer articulations in regions of stability. This is because they do not demand too much precision on the part of the speaker as regards the positioning of the articulators.

For example, in the case of vowels pronounced without lip rounding, we have just seen that when the back cavity length is just over 10 cm, $F_2$ is relatively stable as it reaches its maximum; furthermore, $F_3$ reaches its minimum, and $F_1$ is relatively stable. If the constriction location is moved to slightly forward of or slightly behind this point, the formant frequencies will not change very much. In other words, the output sound will not be very different. Speakers can therefore afford to be a bit sloppy with their tongues if they wish to produce a vowel with a low $F_1$ and a high $F_2$ which is close to the $F_3$. The vowel which has these characteristics is [i] (Figures 3.1, 3.7, 4.8). Accordingly, [i] should be a 'good' speech sound.

Taking this kind of reasoning further, we can see that when the constriction is in the lower pharynx (with back cavity length around 2–4 cm) – corresponding to a low back [ɑ]-like vowel – the acoustic output will also be relatively stable. Finally, when lip rounding is added (corresponding to the dashed curves in Figure 4.10), there is a region of stability when the back cavity length is 7–8 cm, since $F_2$ has a very broad minimum, $F_1$ is relatively stable, and $F_3$ is high and well-separated from both (and is bound to be quite weak). This corresponds to an [u]-like vowel. Our examination of the nomogram thus suggests that [i]-like vowels, [ɑ]-like vowels and [u]-like vowels should be particularly common speech sounds in the languages of the world, and the experience of phoneticians and phonologists confirms that this is, in fact, the case. Following Stevens, these three vowels are sometimes referred to as *quantal vowels*.

The Quantal Theory remains controversial among phoneticians. A variety of views are presented in a special issue of *Journal of Phonetics* (volume 17 number 1/2, 1989) which was devoted to discussion of the theory. This issue also contains Stevens' definitive presentation cited above.

## 4.5    Estimating filter characteristics: linear predictive coding

As we have seen, the spectrum of any vowel sound is determined partly by the source and partly by the filter. In many situations – particularly if we wish to relate acoustic data to the categories of impressionistic phonetics – we need to focus on characteristics of the filter only. In particular, we have seen that it is the filter (the shaping of the vocal tract) rather than the source which is responsible for distinguishing between various vowel qualities. If we wish to describe vowel quality in acoustic terms, it is useful to be able to get at the filter on its own, without taking the source into account.

The technique known as *linear predictive coding* (*LPC*) is frequently used to estimate the filter from the output speech. As its name implies, LPC is, in origin, a technique for encoding the speech signal. It was developed as a means of digital recording which would require storing fewer numbers than conventional sampling. It is based on determining equations which will predict the amplitude (height) of the waveform at any particular moment in time on the basis of what has just gone before. Ladefoged (1996) provides a thorough introduction to the calculations involved which does not assume any background in advanced mathematics.

On the face of it, encoding the signal in this way might seem to have little to do with determining formant frequencies. However, the equations which emerge from LPC analysis are remarkably similar to the equations which would be used to define the vocal tract filter. LPC can therefore be used to estimate the formant frequencies and, more generally, to derive a smooth spectrum in which the formant peaks (that is, peaks of the vocal tract filter function) stand out clearly. Figure 4.11 shows an *LPC spectrum* for the vowel of **heard** ([ɜ]), which may be compared with the FFT spectrum of the same vowel which was shown in Figure 4.4.[2]

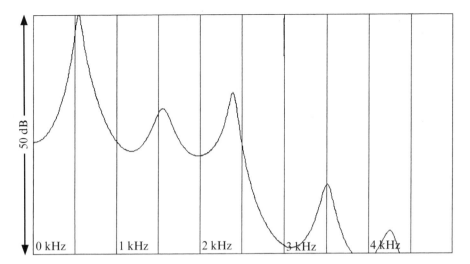

FIGURE 4.11    LPC spectrum for the vowel of English **heard**. The FFT spectrum for
this vowel was shown in Figure 4.4. The frequencies of the peaks are: 550 Hz,
1540 Hz, 2380 Hz, 3500 Hz and 4240 Hz.

LPC analysis produces precise values for the formant frequencies and eliminates the necessity of estimating them by moving a cursor on a spectrogram or
FFT spectrum. This is particularly useful in cases where the formant peaks are
not very clearly defined, as in Figure 4.4 or the hypothetical example of Figure 4.5. Not surprisingly, the technique has proved very popular in studies of
vowel quality, which are typically based on determining formant frequencies
(Chapter 6). Unfortunately, however, LPC analysis is not without limitations.
Chief among these is the assumption that the filter does not contain any negative peaks or *zero*, as will be explained in Section 4.6.

## 4.6    Extending the source-filter approach to other classes of speech sounds

### 4.6.1    *Nasals, laterals and nasalised vowels*

Of all classes of speech sounds, oral vowels – and also semivowels such as [j]
or [w] and some types of R-sound – are the most straightforward from the point
of view of the source-filter theory. Second in terms of level of complication are
the other sonorant consonants, namely nasals and laterals, and also nasalised
vowels. All of these share the characteristic that the vocal tract branches in some
way. In the case of nasals and nasalised vowels, the split is at the soft palate,
where the tract divides into a nasal branch and an oral branch. In the case of
laterals, the split is further forward, at the place of articulation, and there is a
small cavity behind the tongue constriction.

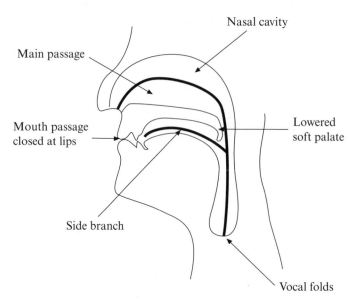

FIGURE 4.12    Schematic view of the vocal tract tube during the production of a bilabial nasal ([m]). The tube branches into a main passage (through the nose) and a side branch (in the mouth).

To illustrate the effects of branching, we may consider Figure 4.12, which shows the vocal tract in position for a bilabial nasal consonant [m]. The main passage for the airstream is now through the nose, and the mouth cavity is a cul-de-sac which, as it were, turns off from the main route. Under these circumstances, the mouth cavity plays a dual role. On the one hand, it is part of a complex system of tubes, and will contribute its own formants to the ensemble. On the other hand, it is competing in a selfish way with the pharynx and nose for the energy which is being put into the system as the vocal folds vibrate. At some frequencies, most or all of the available energy will be diverted from the main route and will remain trapped, with the result that there will be gaps in the output spectrum. This blocking – or at least marked reduction – of energy transmission at particular frequencies is expressed in the frequency-response curve for the vocal tract filter by the introduction of negative peaks, known as *antiformants* or *zeros*. The curve for the filter thus exhibits both extra formants (or poles) and also antiformants (or zeros). Each extra formant has a corresponding antiformant, so that the two occur in pairs.

Figure 4.13 shows an FFT spectrum for the [m] of English **simmer**, together with an LPC spectrum. LPC is not usually used for the analysis of sounds with zeros in their spectra because it is not able to detect zeros. However, something of the nature of the effects of the branching vocal tract can be seen in a comparison of the two. Most obviously, the FFT spectrum dips sharply at around 760 Hz, reflecting the presence of a zero. The low-frequency peak is also broader than in the LPC version.

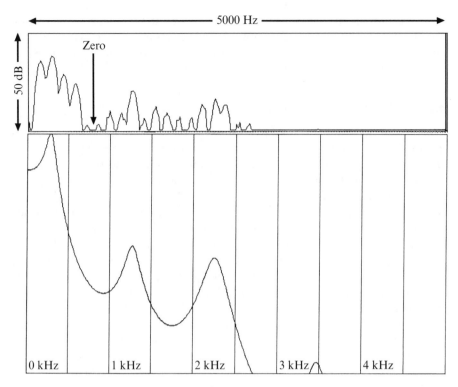

FIGURE 4.13    FFT (a) and LPC (b) spectra for the [m] of English **simmer**. The FFT spectrum shows a broader low-frequency peak and a zero at about 760 Hz. The LPC analysis does not take the possibility of zeros into account.

The case of nasalised vowels is slightly more complicated because of the possibility of different degrees of nasalisation: the soft palate may be in a fully lowered position, resulting in heavy nasalisation, or it may be only slightly lowered, resulting in only slight nasalisation. The lower the soft palate, the wider the passage into the the nasal cavity, and the more strongly the oral and nasal cavities are coupled together. For reasons which cannot be gone into here, stronger coupling results in greater separation between the extra formants and their corresponding antiformants, making both more prominent in the output spectrum. At the other extreme, if the soft palate is only slightly lowered and the passage into the nasal cavity is narrow, the formants and antiformants will be close together and will nearly cancel each other out, so the effects on the output spectrum will be relatively minor. Accordingly, when acoustic phoneticians have sought to produce nasalised vowels in artificial (synthetic) speech, they have been able to vary degree of nasalisation by varying the separation between the formants (poles) and antiformants (zeros). A spectrogram of a nasalised vowel, together with its FFT spectrum, is shown in Figure 6.9.

To sum up, nasals, laterals and nasalised vowels use the same source as oral vowels, but the filter is more complicated. The frequency-response curve can no longer be specified using the formant frequencies alone; it is also necessary to take into account the position of various zeros.

### 4.6.2 Obstruent consonants

While sonorant consonants and nasalised vowels require more care in the specification of the filter, they pose no extra complications with regard to the source. Obstruent consonants, on the other hand, are distinguished by their use of a source other than the vibrating vocal folds. For fricatives, the source will be continuous and noisy, while for stops it will be of the transient type (Section 2.3). It is also necessary to give some thought to the location of the source, which will be at or near the place of articulation rather than at the larynx.

Within the class of obstruents, fricatives have been considered the most challenging. The rasping sound associated with these consonants is due to the turbulent air flow which results from forcing the airstream through a narrow constriction. Since the flow becomes turbulent as the airstream emerges from the constriction, it seems clear that the actual source of the sound must be located in front of the constriction itself. In fact, there are two possibilities. Firstly, if a jet of air emerges from the constriction and is directed at an obstacle (in practice, the upper or lower teeth), sound will be generated at the obstacle. This is the case for the so-called *sibilant* fricatives, including [s] (as in English **sip**) and [ʃ] (as in English **ship**). Secondly, at least for fricatives with places of articulation along the roof of the mouth such as palatal [ç] (as in English **huge**) and velar [x] (as in Scottish English **lo<u>ch</u>**), no obstacle interrupts the flow, and the sound will be generated along a relatively rigid surface (in this case, the hard palate) running parallel to the direction of flow. Accordingly, Shadle (1990), whose work has been of crucial importance in this area, distinguishes between an *obstacle source* and a *wall source*. Other things being equal, obstacle-source fricatives have higher intensity than their non-obstacle counterparts. It has been suggested by Ladefoged and Maddieson (1996) that the traditional class of sibilant fricatives should be equated with the class of obstacle fricatives.

As regards the filter, it is clear that the cavity in front of the constriction is of primary importance for all obstruent consonants. (Labials, which have a constriction at the lips, are an exception to this generalisation; in effect, no filtering takes place in this case.) The importance of the front cavity may be illustrated by means of a comparison between the fricatives [s] and [ʃ]. Although neither of these sounds has a musical pitch, it is nevertheless the case that [s] sounds higher in some sense. The high-frequency character of [s] as compared with [ʃ] can be related to the fact that the cavity in front of the constriction for [s] is smaller than the cavity for [ʃ]. (Other things being equal, smaller tubes have higher resonant frequencies.) It is also possible, however, that cavities behind the obstruent constriction may introduce zeros (antiformants) into the frequency-response curve. In this matter, their role may be compared to the role of the mouth cavity in the production of nasal consonants (Section 4.6.1). We shall not discuss these complications here.

## 4.7  Summary

The main concern of this chapter has been the *source-filter theory* of speech production. The source-filter theory is a model of the final stage of speech production, when the airstream from the lungs is converted into sound. It has two major underlying assumptions. The first of these is that it is possible to make a division between the original source of a sound and subsequent modifications (filtering) of that source. The second is that the source and the filter are independent so that possible interactions between them do not need to be taken into account.

Applying the source-filter theory in any particular case involves predicting the spectrum of the output sound. There are two main steps: firstly, determining the spectrum of the source and, secondly, determining the frequency-response curve (or, in alternative terminology, the transfer function) of the vocal tract filter. Source and filter are combined following standard universally valid procedures. Finally, the effects of radiation – the process whereby a pattern of air flow at the lips is transformed into a pattern of variation in air pressure – must be taken into account. These are assumed to be the same for all speech sounds and are outside the speaker's control.

In the case of voiced sounds, the source spectrum is relatively straightforward, since we know that it must be periodic and will, therefore, have harmonics at regularly spaced intervals. The spacing between harmonics depends on the fundamental frequency. It is also expected that the spectrum will slope downwards to the right and that the slope will depend on the phonation type and/or vocal effort. The breathier the phonation, the steeper the slope and the more the spectrum is dominated by the fundamental; the more creaky (or pressed) the phonation, the shallower the slope, and the more prominent the high-frequency components. The slope of the spectrum can also be related to vocal effort, higher effort being associated with a more shallow slope.

As regards the vocal tract filter, the frequency-response curve will consist of a series of peaks and valleys. The most straightforward sounds are voiced vowels. Here, the most important step is to determine the frequencies of the peaks, or *formants*. Provided that standard assumptions hold concerning the relationship between the frequencies of the formants, their relative heights and their relative widths, the shape of the curve is determined by the formant frequencies alone.

Calculations to determine the formant frequencies are based on simplified representations of the supralaryngeal vocal tract as a series of tubes. The simplest case is that of a mid-central vowel (*schwa*), for which the vocal tract is very like a single tube, closed at one end (the glottis). For other vowels, it is necessary to use two or more tubes, and this makes the calculations more complicated because the effects of the coupling between the tubes must be taken into account. Surprisingly good approximations to actual vowel spectra can be obtained using only a small number of tubes, though more elaborate representations involving larger numbers of tubes will obviously lead to greater accuracy. It is also possible to construct a very general model of vowel articulation, which can be used to study how changes in constriction location and constriction cross-sectional area, and also the presence or absence of lip rounding, affect the formant frequencies of the output vowel sound.

Applying the source-filter theory to other classes of speech sounds presents additional complications. For nasals, laterals and nasalised vowels, it is necessary to take into account the presence of *zeros* – frequencies where acoustic energy is, as it were, held back inside the vocal tract. For these sounds, the source is air flow through the vibrating vocal folds, as for vowels. By contrast, obstruent consonants are distinguished by their use of another type of source located at or near the point of constriction, with the result that determining the precise nature of the source can be problematic.

## 4.8   Further reading

Most works on acoustic aspects of speech include an account of the acoustics of speech production. Of the works cited in Section 3.6, Borden *et al.* (1994), Clark and Yallop (1990), Denes and Pinson (1993), Fry (1979), Johnson (1997), Ladefoged (1996), Lieberman and Blumstein (1988), Pickett (1980) and Rosen and Howell (1991) are also relevant here. Kent and Read (1992) also provides a good introduction. At present, the most thorough account of the acoustics of speech production is Stevens (1998), which is extremely well-written and which promises to become a classic work in the field.

## Notes

1   Formant frequencies and bandwidths were calculated using an adapted version of a calculator programme published by Fant (1985), and the curves for the transfer function were calculated according to the procedure described in Fant (1960). The dimensions chosen for the tubes are similar to those of Stevens (1989).
2   The LPC spectra of Figures 4.11 and 4.13 were computed using a programme written by Geoff Williams. The analysis uses a 25 msec window and 14 LPC coefficients.

**Chapter 5**

# Perception and hearing

## 5.1 Introduction

The first difficulty confronting any would-be researcher into speech perception is deciding just what speech perception is. Does it mean recognising that sound which has impinged on our ears is human speech? Does it mean being able to interpret human speech as a sequence of individual sound segments, whether or not we can assign a meaning to them? Or does it mean being able to recognise the words which the speaker has uttered, whether or not we were able to catch all of the individual sounds? Does a phonetician, using the IPA to transcribe words in a language which he doesn't know, provide an example of speech perception? What about someone with a slight hearing loss, who relies on lip reading to supplement the information which he receives from his ears?

The term *speech perception* has most commonly been used in connection with the recognition and identification of individual phonetic segments. It thus presupposes an ability to identify incoming sound as speech in a particular language. More specifically, the study of speech perception has focussed on the ability of the monolingual native listener with normal hearing to identify and distinguish between the individual sounds (phonemes) of his native language. The recognition of words is usually treated as a separate area of research (*lexical access* or *spoken word recognition*). However, the term *speech perception* is sometimes applied to the study of word recognition, in which case the recognition of individual segments is called *phonetic perception* (though *phonemic perception* would be more appropriate). There has also been considerable interest in relating the two types of perception. Here, we shall concentrate exclusively on speech perception as the recognition of phonetic segments.

Two major issues dominate research into speech perception. The first of these is: what exactly does the perceiver perceive? Here, it is useful to invoke a distinction, made by many psychologists, between *proximal stimulus* and *distal object*. The proximal stimulus is always a kind of energy – such as light rays reflected from objects, sound waves, or pressure on the skin – which is picked up by a human sensory receptor. The distal object is the object in the surrounding environment of which the perceiver gains awareness via his or her senses. For example, when I see the plant on my desk, the proximal stimulus is the light rays being reflected from the plant which impinge on my eyes, and the distal object is the plant itself. In the case of speech perception, the proximal stimulus is a sound wave which impinges on the ears, but the identity of the distal object is far from clear.

There are three general possibilities to consider. Firstly, the distal objects of speech perception might be the articulatory movements which are directly responsible for the sound. Secondly, the objects might be abstract auditory images or prototypes. Thirdly, the objects might be still more abstract linguistic representations, similar to those visualised in Figure 1.3. To give a concrete example, when the native English listener perceives the nonsense syllable **pa**, he or she might be perceiving a human vocal tract performing a coordinated set of movements involving (among other things) a change in the posture of the lips from fully closed to fully open. A second possibility is that he or she perceives a sound **pa** or a sound **p** followed by a sound **a**. A third possibility is that he or she perceives two constellations of abstract phonological features (one for **p** and one for **a**). Since the **p** of **pa** will typically be aspirated in English, the list of features associated with **p** might match up with one of the representations of Figure 1.3.

The second major issue concerns the specialness of speech. Is the perception of speech fundamentally different from the perception of other sounds? Are there special mechanisms – catered for by specialised neural circuitry – which are dedicated to speech perception and nothing else? This issue has come to be seen as part of a larger debate about the possible 'modular' organisation of human mental capacity (Fodor 1983).

According to the modularity hypothesis, the human mind is organised around a central processor, responsible for general capabilities such as thought, reasoning and belief. This central processor obtains information about the outside environment via a number of input systems. Between them, the input systems cover the domains of the traditional five senses (seeing, hearing, touch, smell, taste) plus language. However, the domains of individual input systems are more specialised. For example, in the case of vision, there might be separate input systems for colour perception and for the analysis of shape. Each input system is associated with a specialised task, has its own specialised neural architecture, operates automatically without having to be consciously turned on, and is not subject to central control. For example, if I look out of the window during the daytime, I can't help but see the trees in the garden.

Theoretical linguists working within the Chomskyan tradition have been enthusiastic in their support for the modularity hypothesis. An important part of this view is the idea that human beings have an innate predisposition (via a language module) to learn a language. The complexities of syntax, it is argued, are so great that children could not possibly acquire grammars if they were not pre-programmed to do so. Within this general context, any evidence that phonetic categories (such as /p/ vs. /t/ vs. /k/) should be inherently difficult to learn, or evidence that there is a distinction between *auditory perception* (of sounds in general) and *phonetic perception*, is particularly welcome. For example, in his popular book *The Language Instinct* (1994), Steven Pinker writes: 'phonetic perception is like a sixth sense. When we listen to speech the actual sounds go in one ear and out the other; what we perceive is *language*' (p. 159). However, as we shall see (Section 5.2.3.5), the evidence as regards speech is less than clear and the issues involved are difficult ones.

There have been two main lines of enquiry into speech perception. The first involves attempting to relate characteristics of the acoustic signal directly to perceptual objects. The second involves attempting to understand how the ear deals with incoming sound and how information about sound is transmitted to the brain. This second line of enquiry, in turn, is divided into two main approaches. Firstly, neural responses to speech sounds can be monitored directly in experimental animals. Secondly, human listeners can be asked to make judgements about very simple, basic sounds, revealing much about the basic dimensions of human perceptions.

We shall now consider each of these lines of enquiry in turn.

## 5.2    From acoustic signals to perceptual objects: the search for acoustic cues

From what has just been said, it might appear that the task of relating acoustic signals to perceptual objects is an impossible one, since we do not know what the objects are in the first place. In practice, however, it has been possible to tackle the problem experimentally by investigating listener responses to carefully controlled acoustic *stimuli*. In the most common type of experiment, listeners are asked to classify individual stimuli into a limited number of categories, each of which has a distinct written representation. For example, English native listeners might be asked to classify nonsense-syllable stimuli as **ta** or **da** by ticking boxes on an answer sheet. It is assumed that the distinct written representations correspond to distinct perceptual objects.

It is to be expected that the acoustic-phonetic classification of sounds will match up with the articulatory-phonetic classification of sounds, familiar from impressionistic phonetics. Thus, experiments are usually designed with a particular impressionistic-phonetic dimension in mind such as the voicing dimension or place of articulation. It is further assumed that listeners classify sounds into categories by attending to particular acoustic dimensions which, accordingly, serve as *cues* for the impressionistic-phonetic dimension being investigated.

In the next section, we shall work through a specific example relating to the voicing contrast in stop consonants. In order to avoid confusion, we shall use [+ voiced] and [− voiced] to refer to phonemic categories, for example to English /p t k/ and /b d g/. The terms *voiced* and *voiceless* will be used in their more strictly phonetic sense; voiced sounds are those produced with vocal fold vibration whereas voiceless sounds are not.

### 5.2.1   *An example: Voice Onset Time*

The search for acoustic cues usually has its beginnings in inspection of spectrograms. This will typically suggest a hypothesis as to what acoustic dimension(s) may serve as cues for the listener. The hypothesis must then be tested by means of controlled perceptual experiments. If listeners respond as predicted, the hypothesis is confirmed.

Consider, for example, the spectrograms of Figure 5.1, which illustrate the English words **tore** (/tɔ/) and **door** (/dɔ/), pronounced by a male native speaker of Southern British English. As these two words are a minimal pair, any differences which we observe between them will be associated with differences in their initial consonants. One obvious difference concerns the timing of the onset of the vowel. The striations, associated with voicing, begin immediately after the release of the consonant in **door** (there is no evidence of voicing during the /d/ closure itself). In **tore**, however, there is a considerable gap between the consonantal release and the onset of the voiced vowel. The gap is not blank, but is filled with noise. It corresponds to the aspiration, or **h**-like sound, which is characteristic of English /p/, /t/ and /k/ when they occur initially in stressed syllables.

We have now found two acoustic landmarks, which are easy to identify in both spectrograms, namely the release of the stop consonant and the beginning of the striations which mark the onset of voicing. We shall refer to these as R and O respectively. In **door**, the gap between R and O is short, while in **tore**, the gap between R and O is long. To be more precise, we can measure the duration of the gap in both words: in **door** it is 17 msec, while in **tore** it is 91 msec. This measurement is known as the *Voice Onset Time*, or *VOT*.

It is also possible for voicing to occur during the closure. Although voiced initial stops may occur in English, we shall illustrate this possibility from Spanish, where they are very much more the norm. Figure 5.2 shows spectrograms of the minimal pair **tos** (/tɔs/) 'cough' and **dos** 'two' (/dɔs/) in Spanish, pronounced by a male native speaker from Ecuador. In **tos**, the striations which indicate voicing onset begin almost immediately after the release, as was the case in English **door**. In **dos**, they are already in evidence before the release, during the closure for the /d/. In an impressionistic description, we should say that /t/ is unaspirated and /d/ is fully voiced.

The measurement of VOT for **tos** is straightforward; the gap is, in fact, 13 msec in duration. **Dos** is different in that O (onset of voicing) precedes R (the consonantal release), resulting in a low-frequency *voice bar* which is clearly visible on the spectrogram. In order to give expression to this, we say that VOT for **dos** is negative. In fact, the voice bar is 74 msec long, so that **dos** has a VOT of −74 msec.

Although we have chosen to illustrate VOT using coronal stops (/t/ and /d/), it can be applied to stop consonants at any place of articulation. This single acoustic dimension may be used to quantify differences between true voiced stops (as in Spanish **dos**), voiceless unaspirated stops (as in Spanish **tos**), or voiceless aspirated stops (as in English **tore**). (When the /d/ of English **door** is produced without voicing, as in our example, it is usually described as a 'devoiced' voiced stop.) In a real-life experimental situation, the definition of VOT and the observations regarding differences between English and Spanish would, of course, be based on more than just four tokens.

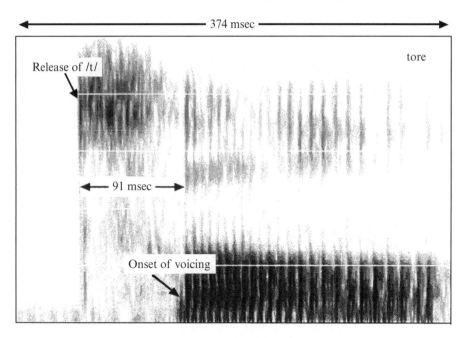

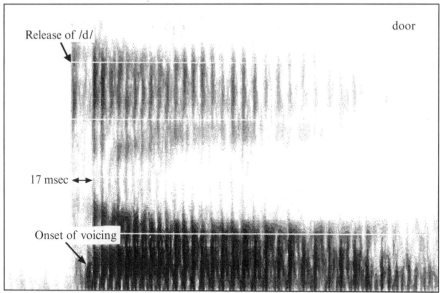

FIGURE 5.1    Broad band spectrograms for the English words **tore** /tɔ/ and **door** /dɔ/, pronounced by a male speaker. The initial consonants are voiceless in both words, but in **tore** there is a much longer gap between the release of the stop closure and the onset of voicing for the following vowel.

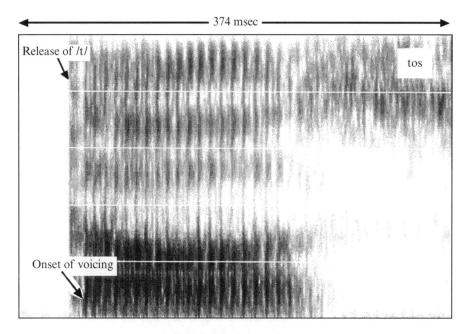

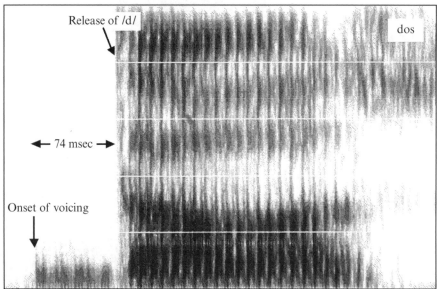

FIGURE 5.2   Broad band spectrograms for the Spanish words **tos** (/tɔs/) 'cough' and **dos** (/dɔs/) 'two'. In **tos**, there is a short gap between the release of the stop closure and the onset of the voicing for the following vowel. In **dos**, a low-frequency *voice bar* is seen before the release of the stop closure. The voice bar is 74 msec long.

VOT is very much associated with the names of Leigh Lisker and Arthur Abramson, and arose out of their efforts 'to determine experimentally the acoustic cues by which listeners distinguish between English /b d g/ and /p t k/' (Lisker and Abramson 1964). Since English /p t k/ and /b d g/ are sometimes distinguished by aspiration (as in our example of **tore** vs. **door**) and sometimes by voicing (as in **ra̱pid** vs. **ra̱bid**, where the preceding vowel is stressed), the idea of combining the two articulatory categories into a single acoustic dimension was a particularly attractive one. However, Lisker and Abramson were also concerned to show that the same single dimension would be useful for distinguishing between categories of stops in other languages.

In any case, having defined VOT, we may formulate a hypothesis as follows: both English and Spanish listeners utilise VOT as a cue for distinguishing between classes of stop consonants, at least in initial position. Negative VOTs and small positive VOTs will give a [+ voiced] (/b d g/) percept while sufficiently high positive VOTs will give a [− voiced] (/p t k/) percept. We might also suspect that, in order to identify a stop consonant as /p/, /t/ or /k/, English listeners will need to hear longer VOT than will Spanish listeners. If, on the other hand, our basic hypothesis is incorrect, we should expect to observe random responses, with no particular preference for /p t k/ or /b d g/ whatever the VOT.

To test the hypothesis properly, it is necessary to conduct an experiment in which subjects are presented with a continuum of possible VOTs, for example a continuum from fully voiced [da] to fully aspirated [tʰa], produced by varying VOT in small steps but keeping everything else the same. The syllables – or *stimuli* – can be arranged on a tape, leaving suitable gaps for subjects to respond between successive stimuli. Subjects can then be asked to classify each syllable they hear as **da** or **ta**, for example by writing down the syllables, ticking boxes on an answer sheet, or pushing buttons labelled **da** and **ta**. Good experimental practice would require random ordering, and also more than one repetition of each stimulus.

In order to create such a continuum of stimuli, it is necessary to use artificially produced synthetic speech. Only in this way can we be assured that the individual stimuli will differ *only* in VOT and nothing else. No one, not even the most accomplished practical phonetician, could be relied on to change VOT systematically in 10 msec steps keeping everything else absolutely constant. With synthetic speech, it is possible to exert precise control over where voicing begins.

Such an experiment was, in fact, carried out by Lisker and Abramson for both American English speakers (Abramson and Lisker 1970) and Latin American Spanish speakers (Abramson and Lisker 1973). The results for the English speakers are presented graphically in Figure 5.3. The horizontal axis represents the VOT continuum, from −150 msec on the left to +150 msec on the right. Each stimulus corresponds to a point along this continuum. In most cases, the interval between successive VOT steps was 10 msec, but extra intermediate steps were added between −10 msec and +50 msec, giving a total of 37 stimuli in all.

The vertical axis represents listener responses, reported as percentages. Each graph has two crossing curves, one for **pa** (or **ta** or **ka**) responses and one for **ba** (or **da** or **ga**) responses. When, as in this case, **pa** and **ba** are the only

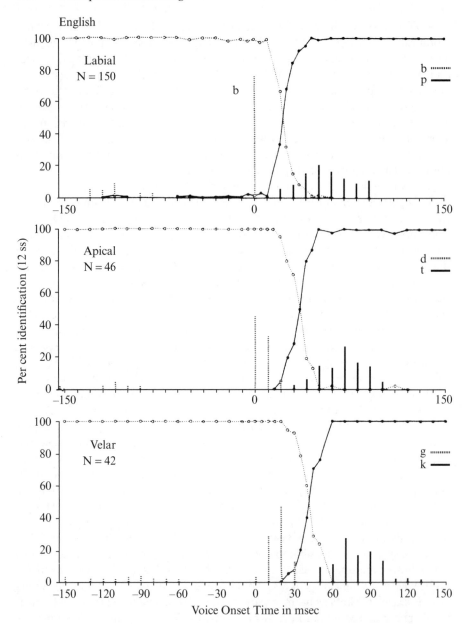

FIGURE 5.3    Classification of synthetic CV syllables with varying VOT by native English listeners. If VOT is negative, the initial consonant is unanimously classified as [+ voiced] (/b/, /d/ or /g/). If VOT is positive and is sufficiently large, the initial consonant is unanimously classified as [− voiced] (/p/, /t/ or /k/). Between these two extremes, there is a transitional region, in which the [+ voiced] and [− voiced] curves cross.

*continued at bottom of next page*

possible responses, the two values will add up to 100% at any point along the horizontal VOT continuum. Thus, where **pa** responses are near 100%, **ba** responses are near 0 and vice versa. As predicted, the results show that syllables with a large positive VOT are unanimously perceived as **pa** and syllables with large negative values of VOT are unanimously perceived as **ba**. There is also a middle ground, where both **pa** and **ba** responses are obtained. If the basic hypothesis had been incorrect, and listeners were not attending to VOT, we should have observed no particular preference for **pa** or **ba** at either end of the continuum.

In an experiment of this nature, particular interest attaches to the *crossover point*, where the two curves cross at height 50%. This is be taken as the boundary between the [+ voice] and [– voice] sections of the continuum of possible VOTs. In the case of **ba** and **pa**, the crossover point obtained for English in Abramson and Lisker's experiment was approximately 25 msec; for Spanish speakers (data not shown), it was somewhat lower, approximately (14 msec.

In order to facilitate comparison between production and perception, the graphs also display the results of another experiment in which native speakers were recorded producing initial voiced and voiceless stops. This is the meaning of the vertical lines at the baseline. Each line indicates the percentage of examples which showed particular VOTs (following rounding off of the actual measured values). For example, in the top graph, the solid vertical lines indicate that English speakers produced /p/ with VOTs ranging from +20 msec (represented by the leftmost line) to +90 msec (represented by the rightmost line). The most commonly recorded value was VOT = +50 msec (for which the line is the tallest), accounting for just over 20% of the cases. For /b/, there was a strong preponderance of values close to 0 (as shown by the positioning of the dotted lines).

The experimental results provide evidence in favour of the hypothesis that VOT serves as a cue for the distinction between [± voiced] pairs. Both Spanish and English listeners divided the VOT continuum into two parts, a [+ voiced] part and a [– voiced] part. It is also interesting that the results are at least to some extent language-specific. English speakers, who produce their /p/s with longer VOT than Spanish speakers, also need longer VOTs if they are to identify an initial stop consonant as /p/. The language-specific character of the results also received support from a similar experiment with Thai subjects, also described in Lisker and Abramson (1970). They were asked to classify the same stimuli into three categories, corresponding to the three types of stop consonants ([+ voiced],

FIGURE 5.3    (*cont'd*)
The vertical lines on each graph provide data relating to a separate and complementary experiment in which VOT values were measured for native English speakers producing initial [+ voiced] and [– voiced] consonants. Each line indicates the percentage of examples which showed particular VOTs (following rounding off of the actual measured values). Notice that English speakers generally produce /p/, /t/ and /k/ with VOTs to the right of the crossover point, while /b/, /d/ and /g/ show VOTs to the left of the crossover point. From Lisker and Abramson (1970).

[– voiced] unaspirated, and [– voice] aspirated) in their native language. For example, for labials, the category labels were symbols for /ba/, /pa/ and /pʰa/ in the Thai script.

To sum up, we have defined a simple methodology which can be used to gain insight into what native listeners utilise when they recognise and distinguish between the sounds of their own language. Firstly, the researcher looks for a single acoustic dimension which serves to distinguish between the sounds of interest when they are produced by native speakers. Secondly, a continuum of stimuli, varying along this single acoustic dimension, is synthesized. Thirdly, subjects are asked to listen to the stimuli as if they were listening to speech and classify them into the appropriate categories (for example, as **pa** or **ba**).

We should conclude this section on a historical note. Experiments of the type I have just been describing, in which listeners' responses are elicited to variation in a single cue, are based on the application to speech of methodology originally developed for research in psychophysics (Section 5.4). This type of research into speech perception was pioneered in the 1950s at Haskins Laboratories in New York. Many of the experiments conducted at Haskins – including those of Lisker and Abramson – have laid the foundation for our current understanding of the nature of speech perception, and Haskins (now in New Haven, Connecticut) remains a leading centre for speech research.

### 5.2.2 *The problem of lack of invariance*

Unfortunately, the interpretation of acoustic cues is not so straightforward as Section 5.2.1 might suggest. The major problem is variability or, as it is more commonly put, *lack of invariance*. It would be nice to think that, for every classificatory dimension of impressionistic phonetics, we could find one or more acoustic dimensions which serve as consistent cues. For example, at least for English native listeners, we might like to suppose that if a stop consonant had a VOT greater than 25 msec, listeners would report a [– voiced] percept while if the VOT was less than 25 msec they would report a [+ voiced] percept. (Recall that, in the experiment described above, 25 msec was said to be the boundary between /p/ and /b/.)

In the case of VOT and the [± voiced] distinction, a first difficulty is that the boundary between [+ voiced] and [– voiced] categories varies with place of articulation. Other things being equal, VOT will be greatest for velar stops and smallest for labial stops, with coronals occupying an intermediate position. Lisker and Abramson (1973) give the following average crossover values for English subjects:

| Labial | 25 msec |
|--------|---------|
| Coronal | 35 msec |
| Velar | 42 msec |

This means that, for English listeners, a VOT of 35 msec is likely to be interpreted as [– voiced] (**pa**) if the stop in question is labial but as [+ voiced] (**ga**) if it is velar; it could be ambiguous (**ta/da**) if the stop is coronal.

The situation becomes more complicated when we come to consider a wider variety of contexts. A good example is the interaction between VOT and stress. The classic VOT experiments involved stops in initial position in isolated monosyllabic words. In such cases, the stop consonant is not only word-initial but initial in a stressed syllable. However, at least for the [– voiced] series (p, t, k), VOT is shorter in the absence of stress. For example, Lisker and Abramson (1967) report an average VOT for /p/ of 59 msec in stressed syllables but of only 38 msec in unstressed syllables (based on data for three speakers pronouncing isolated words). This latter value is within the [+ voiced] range for velar stops (i.e. for /g/ as opposed to /k/). VOT is also influenced by the identity of the following vowel (it is longer before high vowels than before low vowels).

Finally, there are some cases in which VOT cannot be defined. Obvious examples are syllable-final unreleased stops (where there is neither a release nor a following voiced vowel) and pre-pausal stops of any sort (where there may be a release but no vowel follows). The case of intervocalic [+ voiced] stops (b, d, g) is also problematic because voicing tends to carry over from a preceding vowel, resulting in full voicing during the closure interval or, worse still, partial voicing at the beginning of the closure interval.

The problem of lack of invariance has arisen time and again in the search for acoustic cues corresponding to impressionistic-phonetic dimensions. Some of this variability is due to the immediate phonetic context, as in the examples relating to VOT which we have just been discussing. Variability can also arise from a change in the overall context, relating to such factors as speaking rate or whether the speaker is male or female (Section 6.9). The problem of how listeners relate highly variable acoustic signals to more abstract and invariant units of linguistic representation appears to be much more difficult than could ever have been imagined 50 years ago, when research into acoustic cues was only just beginning.

### 5.2.3  Is speech special?

As already mentioned (Section 5.1), a major issue in the study of speech perception has been whether or not, and to what extent, speech perception might constitute a special module – possibly a sub-module of a language module – within mental organisation. In other words, does the perception of speech require special types of processing which are not involved in the case of non-speech sounds? The debate has centred around certain specific phenomena which have come to light in the course of research into acoustic cues. Some researchers have claimed that these phenomena are unique to speech perception, and this has inspired others to look for evidence to show that they are not unique to speech perception. Whatever the final resolution of the debate, the phenomena are not without interest in themselves and provide further examples of the lack of invariance in speech.

### 5.2.3.1    Categorical perception

Probably the most-discussed evidence in the debate about the specialness of speech is that concerning *categorical perception*. In categorical perception, the listener 'hears' a continuum of sounds not as a continuum but as a small number of discrete categories. In the ideal case, this is manifested in two ways. Firstly, when asked to identify stimuli varying along the continuum, listeners switch suddenly, rather than gradually, between categories. Secondly, and more importantly, listeners are better at discriminating between stimuli which belong to different categories than they are between stimuli which belong to the same category.

Abramson and Lisker's experiments concerning VOT provide an example of categorical perception. In the graph of Figure 5.3, it can be seen that most of the stimuli are categorised unanimously as **pa** or **ba**; the transition region is really very small. By contrast, if perception were 'continuous', we should expect a much more gradual transition from definite **ba**s to definite **pa**s.

In other, complementary studies, Lisker and Abramson tested listeners' ability to discriminate between the stimuli. For example, could listeners hear that two CV (consonant–vowel) syllables were different when they were only one step apart along the continuum (that is, when they differed in VOT by only 10 msec)? What about syllables which were two or three steps apart?

A general expectation in such experiments is that listeners should do better overall when the degree of separation is greater. In other words, it should be easier to tell that two CV syllables are different when the VOTs differ by 40 msec than when the VOTs differ by only 20 msec. If listeners are using categorical perception, however, then they should also do much better when the two CV syllables are on opposite sides of a boundary. In the case of English listeners classifying labial stops before low vowels (**pa** vs. **ba**), we have seen that the boundary between categories is about VOT = +25 msec. Accordingly, listeners should find it easier to distinguish between syllables with VOT = +20 and VOT = +40 than between syllables with VOT = +50 and VOT = +70 because both members of the second pair are firmly in the **pa** category. Figure 5.4, taken from Abramson and Lisker (1970), illustrates a *discrimination function* for a group of five English listeners. The percent correct discrimination for each pair of CV syllables is plotted as a function of their average VOT (on the horizontal axis). For example, for a pair of syllables with VOT = +10 and VOT = +30, the average VOT would be +20.

On this figure, the vertical line corresponds to the 50% crossover point determined in the identification experiment (Figure 5.3). The three plots correspond to two-step, three-step and four-step discrimination. 'Step' here refers to the number of steps along the continuum, so that for example two-step discrimination involves discriminating between two CV syllables which differ in VOT by 20 msec. As expected, the subjects performed best in four-step

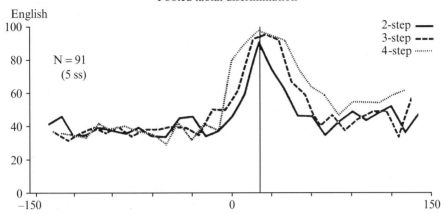

FIGURE 5.4    Discrimination function for CV stimuli along a **pa–ba** continuum for native English listeners. The percent correct discrimination for each pair of CV syllables is plotted as a function of the average of the two VOTs. The three plots correspond to two-step, three-step and four-step discrimination. 'Step' here refers to the number of 10 msec steps along the continuum, so that for example two-step discrimination involves discriminating between two CV syllables which differ in VOT by 20 msec.

The vertical line corresponds to the 50% crossover point determined in the identification experiment (Figure 5.3). All three graphs peak at the 50% crossover point, confirming that discrimination is easiest when the two stimuli being compared belong to different categories (in this case, /pa/ or /ba/). From Abramson and Lisker (1970).

discrimination. (This is shown by the fact that the four-step curve is broader than the other two.) However, even the four-step discrimination is not good when the VOTs of the stimuli are either negative or high and positive. This confirms that discrimination is easiest when the two stimuli belong to different categories, even when the VOT values differ by 4 steps (40 msec).

The main point about categorical perception is that listeners perceive the test stimuli not as sounds pure and simple, but rather as members of categories. If they were listening to the stimuli (in this case CV syllables) as sounds, then the ability to discriminate should not depend on the position of the category boundary.

### 5.2.3.2   Multiple cues and trading relations

Experiments in speech perception have commonly focussed on a single acoustic cue and a single impressionistic-phonetic dimension. Nevertheless, it would be highly exceptional for a single cue to be solely responsible for signalling a simple phonetic contrast. In other words, speech is highly redundant. This is, of course, beneficial from the listener's point of view, since the use of multiple cues will serve to heighten the contrast between distinct segments.

The distinction between [+ voiced] and [− voiced] stop consonants in English is a good example. The contrast between [− voiced] /p/ (or /t/ or /k/) and [+ voiced] /b/ (or /d/ or /g/) is associated with a number of other cues in addition to VOT. These include the fundamental frequency ($F_0$) of the onset of the following vowel (higher for /p/, lower for /b/), the frequency of the first formant at the onset of the following vowel (higher for /p/ lower for /b/), and, in the case of intervocalic stops, the closure duration (longer for /p/, shorter for /b/). Indeed, Lisker (1986) lists sixteen such cues. Not all potential cues will be relevant in any single example of /p/ or /b/, but there will usually be more than one to go on.

If listeners are asked to classify stimuli which vary with regard to two or more cues, then there is typically a *trading relation* between the cues. 'Trading relation' is used here in the sense in which 'trade-off' is used in everyday situations. For example, in deciding whether to travel by train or by bus, there is a trade-off between cost and journey time. The bus is cheaper but the train is quicker. If the difference in price becomes very large, nearly everyone will opt for the bus; if difference in price is reduced to a few pennies, nearly everyone will opt for the train. However, there is a large middle ground where a change in one factor can be compensated for by a change in the other. If the bus becomes just a bit cheaper, the train can retain its share of the market by becoming a bit quicker.

A well-known example of a trading relation in speech involves the VOT and the first formant ($F_1$) of the following vowel. We start with the observation that naturally produced CV sequences show that VOT tends to vary with the onset frequency of $F_1$. For low vowels (which have high $F_1$, see Section 6.2), $F_1$s which rise from a low onset frequency are associated with [+ voiced] consonants, while $F_1$s which are more nearly flat are associated with [− voiced] consonants. An example is shown in Figure 5.5, which presents contrasting spectrograms for the English words **tart** and **dart**.

Let us now return to VOT. Figure 5.3 suggests that, at least for English native listeners, VOTs above about +60 msec will give a 'voiceless' percept (/p/, /t/ or /k/) while VOTs below about +10 msec will give a 'voiced' percept (/b/, /d/ or /g/). Within the middle ground of +10−+60 msec, the precise location of the VOT boundary varies with the place of articulation of the consonant. An obvious next step is to investigate the effect of varying $F_1$ onset frequency within the middle ground.

In a well-known series of experiments, Summerfield and Haggard (1977) showed that $F_1$ onset frequency could be traded for VOT. Their stimuli were synthetic CV syllables in which the C was a velar consonant (/k/ or /g/). The experimental designs were rather complicated because the experimenters were keen to show that it was the onset frequency of $F_1$ which was the decisive cue, rather than rising (as opposed to flat) $F_1$ or other factors related to the second formant ($F_2$). Figure 5.6 shows one set of results. In this experiment, there were three possible $F_1$ onsets (208 Hz, 311 Hz and 412 Hz), each corresponding to one graph in the figure. For each onset value, $F_1$ could be flat (solid lines) or

←——————————— 267 msec ——————————→

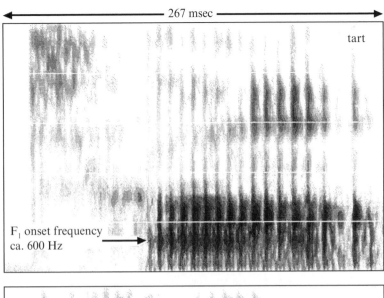

tart

F$_1$ onset frequency
ca. 600 Hz →

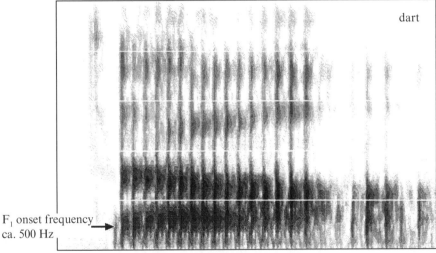

dart

F$_1$ onset frequency
ca. 500 Hz →

FIGURE 5.5   Spectrograms of the English words **tart** (/tɑt/) and **dart** (/dɑt/), pronounced by a male speaker. In **tart**, the bar corresponding to F$_1$ begins high and remains flat. In **dart**, the bar corresponding to F$_1$ can be seen to rise following the onset of voicing, though it quickly flattens out. Accordingly, the F$_1$ onset frequency is higher in **tart**.

rising (dashed lines); furthermore, a smaller rise was contrasted with a larger rise (represented by two types of dashing). VOT was varied between +15 msec and +50 msec, corresponding to the middle ground of Lisker and Abramson's continuum. In all three graphs, all three curves slope downwards, indicating a shift toward /k/ as VOT increases. At the same time, the effect of varying F$_1$

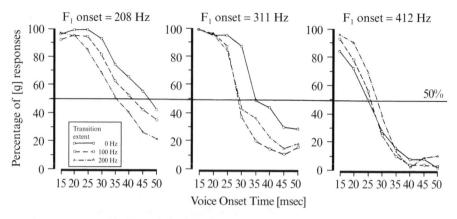

FIGURE 5.6  Evidence for a trading relation between VOT and $F_1$ onset frequency. In this experiment, three $F_1$ onsets were combined with a continuum of VOT values to give a series of CV syllables. C was a velar stop (/k/-like or /g/-like) in all cases. There was also a contrast between flat $F_1$ (solid lines) and rising $F_1$ (dashed lines).

Listeners were asked to classify the initial consonant as /k/ or /g/, and each graph shows percent /g/ responses. In all three graphs, all three curves slope downwards, indicating a shift toward /k/ as VOT increases. The effect of varying $F_1$ onset frequency can be seen in a comparison of the three graphs. In the rightmost graph, the greater part of all three curves lies below the 50% line, indicating that /k/ responses predominate, although listeners identify stimuli with low VOTs as /g/ more than 50% of the time. In the leftmost graph, nearly all of the curves lie above the 50% line, indicating that /g/ responses predominate, although listeners identify stimuli with high VOTs as /k/ more than 50% of the time. Taken together, the graphs suggest that a low $F_1$ onset (suggesting [+ voiced] /g/) can be compensated for by a high VOT (suggesting [- voiced] /k/). Adapted from Summerfield and Haggard (1977).

onset frequency can be seen in a comparison of the three graphs. In the rightmost graph, the greater part of the curves lies below the 50% line, indicating that /k/ responses predominate. In the leftmost graph, nearly all of the curves lie above the 50% line, indicating that /g/ responses predominate. The situation in the middle graph is between these two extremes.

The overall results of Summerfield and Haggard's study can be summed up as follows: the lower the $F_1$ onset frequency, the more likely a [+ voiced] percept. However, a low $F_1$ onset (which will incline the listener towards a [+ voiced] percept) can be offset by increasing the VOT (which will incline the listener towards a [- voiced] percept). In other words, there is a 'trade off' between VOT and $F_1$ onset frequency. The main point here is that listeners automatically arrive at the same phonetic percept (/k/) for stimuli which are actually quite different. Higher onset $F_1$ + lower VOT is equivalent to lower onset $F_1$ + higher VOT. Trading relations are also examples of lack of invariance in that the same acoustic cue (for example VOT = +35 msec) is interpreted differently (in this case, as /g/ or /k/) in different contexts (when combined with different $F_1$ frequencies).

### 5.2.3.3  Duplex perception

One striking characteristic of speech is that it contains a number of sounds which do not sound like speech at all if they are taken out of context. This is easy to illustrate in a crude way on a computer-based spectrograph which makes it possible to cut out bits of sound and listen to them in isolation. For example, the **thr-** (/θr/) cluster of English words such as **threw** or **three** (commonly pronounced [θɹ̥] with devoicing of the /r/) may sound like a descending whistle when it is cut out and played on its own.[1] However, when it is joined to the rest of its source word, its whistle-like character disappears, and it sounds like a sequence of /θ/ and /r/.

More sophisticated experiments have shown that it is possible to elicit a 'normal CV sequence' percept and a 'whistle' percept simultaneously, a phenomenon known as *duplex perception*. In one well-known experiment described in Whalen and Liberman (1987), the focus of attention was the third formant ($F_3$) transition in CV syllables. The third formant transition is the rapid change of $F_3$ at the onset of a vowel as the articulators move from the consonant position to the vowel position; furthermore, the direction of the $F_3$ transition can be crucial in distinguishing **da** from **ga** (Section 7.3.3.2). When an $F_3$ transition is synthesised and played in isolation, it sounds like a sort of whistle: **da** transitions fall in pitch whilst **ga** transitions rise in pitch. In the crucial experiments, synthetic CV syllables were constructed without a third formant transition and were presented to one ear; on their own, these syllables sounded like CV syllables with an indeterminate initial consonant. A possible formant transition was then simultaneously presented to the other ear: In these circumstances, listeners reported hearing **da** or **ga** as appropriate to the transition. Provided that the transition was sufficiently intense, they also heard the high-frequency whistle. The fact that they could identify the syllable as **da** or **ga** showed that they must be combining the whistle and the basic CV syllable into a perceptual whole but, on the other hand, the fact that they continued to hear the whistle showed that they must also be perceiving it as a separate event. Since the transition-whistle is perceived in two distinct ways simultaneously, the percept is said to be *duplex*.

It has been claimed that duplex perception points to a divergence between the perception of sound in general and phonetic perception. A single whistle or chirp ceases to be perceived as a whistle or chirp when it is integrated into a suitable phonetic whole. More generally, duplex perception provides another example of lack of invariance, since the same sound can be heard as (a component of) speech or as something which is not speech at all.

### 5.2.3.4  Bimodal perception

Although we think of speech as primarily something to be heard, there are many situations – such as trying to carry on a conversation through the window of a train carriage – in which lip reading can provide a valuable supplement to sound. Furthermore, a mismatch between lip movements and sound, such as occurs when films are dubbed into a second language, is usually noticeable, and can be very annoying if the mismatch is too great. Other things being equal, we expect that what we see will be consistent with what we hear. In more technical language, speech perception is often *bimodal* and involves combining (*integrating*) visual and auditory information.

The best-known work on the role of visual information in speech perception is that of McGurk and MacDonald (McGurk and MacDonald 1976; also MacDonald and McGurk 1978). For their 1976 study, a woman was filmed as she pronounced the simple CVCV nonsense words **ba-ba**, **ga-ga**, **pa-pa** and **ka-ka**. When subjects watched the film, or listened to the sound track alone, they identified all four words correctly. A new film was prepared by dubbing the original in such a way that visual labials (**ba-ba** and **pa-pa**) were combined with audio velars (**ga-ga** and **ka-ka**) and vice versa. When they watched this material, subjects' identifications were very different. When audio labials were combined with visual velars (**ba-ba** with **ga-ga** and **pa-pa** with **ka-ka**), they reported hearing **da-da** or **ta-ta**. In the reverse case (audio velars with visual labials), they tended to hear words which included both types of consonant, such as **bagba** or **paka**. In general terms, what the subjects 'heard' was very much affected by what they saw.

The phenomenon of visual information influencing what listeners 'hear' is known as the *McGurk effect*. The McGurk effect is yet another example of lack of invariance, insofar as the same sound is interpreted differently in different visual contexts. Cross-linguistic aspects of the McGurk effect are discussed by Massaro *et al.* (1993) and Sekiyama and Tohkura (1993).

### 5.2.3.5   Arguments against the specialness of speech

Although the perceptual effects described above are well-established, their significance for speech perception remains controversial. The main point at issue has been whether or not they are unique to speech. If they are indeed unique to speech, then they would constitute evidence for a special speech modality involving special neural circuitry. If, however, the same phenomena can also be observed outside of speech, then they must belong to auditory perception generally and cannot be taken as evidence for a speech mode.

In any case, there is now a large body of work which has sought to demonstrate that categorical perception, trading relations, bimodal perception and duplex perception are not, after all, confined to the perception of speech by human beings. There have been three lines of attack. Firstly, it has been shown that the same phenomena can be observed in the perception of other, non-speech, objects by human beings. The non-speech objects most commonly investigated have been simple stimuli, in which tones and buzzes are put together in speech-like patterns, and music. An example of a particularly ingenious experiment is Fowler and Rosenbaum's study of duplex perception using stimuli derived from a recording of a slamming metal door (Fowler and Rosenbaum 1990, 1991).

The second line of attack has involved investigating animal perception. Since speech is confined to human beings, any evidence that animals can learn to categorise speech sounds in the same way that humans do must argue against the proposal that speech is special and in favour of the view that general auditory mechanisms are involved. As an example, we may mention Kuhl and Miller's demonstration that chinchillas perform in a way remarkably similar to humans when they are made to categorise stimuli varying in VOT (Kuhl and Miller 1978; Kuhl 1981). To quote Ehret (1992: 108), 'Fundamental differences between human and mammalian speech and complex sound perception may first occur at the recognition or language level, that is, in the *interpretation* of the semantic content of speech sounds. Animals can perceive and analyse speech, but they do not know what we mean.'

The third line of attack has involved arguing that, at least in the case of categorical perception, the phenomena are a by-product of particular experimental designs, and may not exist in real-life perception (Massaro 1994). Taken together, then, all of this work has cast serious doubt upon, if not eliminated altogether, the positive evidence in favour of a special speech module. At the same time, it does not prove that a special speech mode does not or could not exist, and so the possibility remains open.

If a special speech module did exist, this would imply that the evolution of the human capacity for speech included the development of special perceptual capabilities. The opposite position must also be considered. This would be that, as the human capacity for speech evolved, it took advantage of a number of special capabilities and sensitivities which existed already.

To give a concrete example: data from both studies of production and studies of perception show that the VOT boundaries between unaspirated (= English [+ voiced]) and aspirated (= English [– voiced]) categories are remarkably similar across languages. Despite variation between languages, they typically fall within a range of +20–+40 msec (as for example in Figure 5.3). There is also some evidence from perceptual studies to indicate that discrimination is easier across this 20–40 msec boundary (Section 5.2.3.1). It seems likely that this preference for a boundary in the 20–40 msec range is neither accidental nor a special characteristic of speech. It may reflect a natural auditory sensitivity (Section 5.3.3). If so, then speech has, as it were, 'latched on' to this sensitivity and put it to work for the purposes of distinguishing phonetic categories.

For a strong statement of this view, we may quote Stevens (1981: 74): 'the auditory system discriminates physical differences in speechlike sounds organised along various continua. Our point of view is that the auditory system is predisposed to provide some kind of distinctive pattern of response when the sounds have these attributes. This predisposition in fact may impose constraints on the kinds of acoustic distinctions that are used in language to form phonetic contrasts.' Whether or not such a position is totally incompatible with the modularity hypothesis remains to be seen.

### 5.2.4   *Theories of speech perception*

The considerable difficulties involved in the study of speech perception have not discouraged researchers from theorising about it, and a great variety of views have been put forward. In this section, we shall give a brief overview of five contrasting theories, which represent very different views as to both what is perceived and how it is perceived. This is far from a complete treatment, but it will give some idea of how various theoretical approaches have dealt with the problem of lack of invariance, and how they differ from one another.

#### 5.2.4.1   The Motor Theory

The Motor Theory, which is particularly associated with Alvin Liberman, is one of the best-known theories of speech perception. It is also the theory most closely associated with the modularity hypothesis. The theory has its roots in primary research into acoustic cues at Haskins Laboratories. It was first proposed as a solution to the problem of lack of invariance, especially with regard to cues for place of articulation (Section 7.3.3). Given the disappointing lack of invariance in the acoustic domain, an obvious solution is to look for invariance in the articulatory domain. For example, an English /t/ is always associated with contact between the tip and/or blade of the tongue and the roof of the mouth somewhere between the teeth and the back of the alveolar ridge, however that is manifested acoustically.

In practice, articulatory movements – and the motor commands which initiate them – are not so invariant as might be supposed. For example, what actual movements are involved in producing an English /t/ will depend crucially on what other sounds precede or follow. Accordingly, in the definitive account of the current theory published by Liberman and Mattingly (1985), it is supposed that the listener perceives not the actual articulatory movements but abstract intended gestures which exist in the mind of the speaker. More specifically (*ibid.*, p. 30), 'the neural representation of the utterance that determines the speaker's production is the distal object that the listener perceives; accordingly; speaking and listening are both regulated by the same structural constraints and the same grammar'. Presumably, in recovering the neural representation, the listener also recovers the intended utterance.

One criticism of the Motor Theory has been that it does not provide an account of just how acoustic signals are translated into intended gestures. Proponents of the theory appeal to the modularity hypothesis, and argue that this must be handled by the relevant module. In other words, specialised neural structures must exist which are able to translate acoustic information into intended gestures directly. These structures are innate, so that the relationships between acoustics and intended gestures do not need to be learned. Accordingly, the mechanisms can be fully understood only when these neural structures are identified and investigated. Liberman and Mattingly (1985: 8) suggest a parallel with auditory localisation (the ability to locate sounds in space), for which such specialised mechanisms exist. However, an important difference is that, whereas neural mechanisms for localisation are similar across species, neural mechanisms for processing speech could exist only in humans. Thus, they could not be investigated by studying the neurophysiology of hearing in other species, a limitation which makes the Motor Theory untestable at present.

Liberman's papers are collected and published together in Liberman (1996), and this volume provides an excellent introduction to Motor Theory. The volume *Modularity and the Motor Theory of Speech Perception* (Mattingly and Studdert-Kennedy 1991), which includes papers by both proponents and critics of the theory, is also of great interest.

### 5.2.4.2  Direct Realism

The Direct Realist theory, which is particularly associated with Carol Fowler, is sometimes considered to be a variant of the Motor Theory. This is because, like the Motor Theory, it holds that the distal objects of perception are articulatory gestures. However, the philosophical view of perception which underlies it is quite different.

The Direct Realist position takes as its starting point the general theory of *direct perception* put forward by the psychologist James Gibson. The essence of the Gibsonian approach is that perception is best studied from outside the perceiver. As observers, we should study the nature of the stimulus which impinges on an organism's senses and the way in which the organism reacts to the stimulus. It is argued that the organism recovers information about the distal objects in the environment directly, making use of information from the proximal stimulus to this end; it perceives an object, not an image of an object. For example, suppose that, when I am crossing a road, light rays impinge on my eyes which are reflected from a bicycle headed towards me at full tilt. What is important is not that the size of the reflected image is getting larger as the bicycle approaches, but that I can use that information to see that a bicycle is about to hit me and take appropriate action. I perceive the bicycle itself, not an image of the bicycle.

In the case of speech perception, the distal objects in the environment are the moving vocal tracts which produce speech. Accordingly, the listener is said to use information in the acoustic signal to recover the actual vocal tract gestures. Furthermore, recovery of the gestures is an end in itself, not merely the first stage in recovering some more abstract representation. If different individual pronunciations (tokens) are regarded as instances of the same thing, this is because of their inherent similarity in the real world, not because they are related to a common abstract mental representation. For example, pronunciations of the English word **cup** have in common that the back of the tongue is raised to touch the velum at the beginning, that the lips are brought together at the end, and that between these two movements there is some opening and closing of the jaw; this commonality is inherent in the gestures themselves and does not need to be explained in terms of a more abstract representation such as /kʌp/. In this sense, my recognition of this particular set of gestures as the lexical item **cup** is no different from my recognition that an object which I see on the table is a cup. Accordingly, the perception of speech makes use of the same kind of mechanisms as other types of perception. Fowler also allows for the possibility of *mirages*. For example, human beings may perceive the 'utterances' of parrots or speech synthesizers as speech because they structure the acoustic signal in ways that mimic structuring by human vocal tracts.

Lack of invariance is not a problem for the Direct Realist approach because it arises naturally from the gestural pattern. For example, the fact that VOT is longer in /gi/ than in /pa/ in English is simply a 'lawful' result arising from particular combinations of movements involving the mouth and larynx. Listeners unconsciously know that this is so and take it into account when they perceive speech. Indeed, experimental evidence cited in support of the Direct Realist approach indicates that this is, in fact, what listeners do.

In practice, the Direct Realist theory has been closely linked with the approach to defining articulatory gestures known as *task dynamics*. A very brief account of task dynamics will be given in Section 8.5.

The first number of Volume 14 of the *Journal of Phonetics* (1986) is entirely devoted to papers on Direct Perception and Task Dynamics, and includes a paper by Fowler herself, papers by critics of the theory, and Fowler's replies to the critics.

### 5.2.4.3   The Fuzzy Logical Model

The Fuzzy Logical Model of Perception, proposed by Dominic Massaro, is very different from the two approaches just outlined. According to this model, the listener is equipped with a set of prototypes, stored in memory, corresponding to the various V, CV and VC syllables of his or her language. Each prototype is defined in terms of a number of characteristics. For example, the prototype for English /ba/ would include initial closure of the lips.

In order to decide whether or not a particular CV syllable is or is not /ba/, the perceiver may combine information from a variety of sources. For example, judgements about labiality could take visual as well as auditory information into account. Each potential source of information might or might not provide a clear answer, and this is where the fuzzy logic comes in. Answers can be not only 'yes' or 'no' but also 'possibly'. For example, definite closure of the lips would indicate 'definitely labial' and a wide mouth opening would indicate 'definitely not labial', but if the perceiver cannot quite see whether the lips completely close or not, this would indicate 'possibly labial'. What we have just called the 'possibly' category would be expressed mathematically in terms of a 'fuzzy' truth value somewhere between 0 (false) and 1 (true). By combining the definite and fuzzy truth values from as many sources of information as are available, the perceiver arrives at a judgement as to whether or not the consonant is in fact labial.

Lack of invariance is not a problem for the Fuzzy Logical Model because it allows for a large number of prototypes; for example, the prototype for /ba/ would incorporate a different ideal VOT value than the prototype for /gi/. The particular strength of this theory is its ability to account for integration of information from different sources.

Massaro's contribution to the *Handbook of Psycholinguistics* (Gernsbacher 1994) contains a succinct account of the Fuzzy Logical Model, in the context of a more general account of psychological aspects of speech perception. Massaro (1987) is a full-length work which presents the model in more detail.

### 5.2.4.4   Strong theories relating the acoustic signal to phonological features

Very different still are the views put forward by Kenneth Stevens and his colleagues, according to which the listener identifies individual segments by extracting abstract phonological features (Section 1.4.2) from an auditory representation.

According to Stevens, it is possible to find straightforward, robust and invariant correlates for all phonological features in both the acoustic signal and the auditory spectrum, provided that one looks for them in the right place. For example, the feature [+ spread glottis] which characterises aspirated stop consonants (Figure 1.3) would be signalled by a VOT greater than about +25 msec. The feature [− sonorant] would be signalled by a reduction in the amplitude of the spectrum at low frequencies. Since acoustic and auditory correlates of the features can be defined in a straightforward way, the problem of lack of invariance simply does not exist (though it is not clear how the theory would account for bimodal perception). Such proposals have been particularly controversial as regards features for place of articulation, a matter to which we shall return in Section 7.3.3.

In fact, Stevens' approach is much more than a theory of how speech sounds are perceived. Rather, it is part of a more ambitious account of articulatory-acoustic-auditory relations which attempts to elucidate the structure of linguistic sound systems as well as the activities of individual speaker-hearers. Stevens argues that some segment types are particularly common among the world's languages precisely because these segments are well-suited to human capacities for perception and production. For example, it is natural that languages should define a category of stop consonants with reference to a VOT category boundary of around +25 msec because there is a natural auditory sensitivity in this region. This is very much in line with his views on the evolution of speech, already quoted in Section 5.2.3.5. As regards speech production, an example regarding the production of vowels was discussed in Section 4.4.4.

Stevens' position has been characterised as 'double strong' by Neary (1995) because it posits two types of simple, robust and transparent relationships: (1) between phonological features and auditory properties and (2) between phonological features and articulatory gestures. This contrasts with 'strong gestural' approaches such as the Motor Theory and Direct Realism, which argue for relationships of type (2) but see relationships of type (1) as more complex and indirect.

We have not yet mentioned the possibility of a 'strong auditory' theory which would posit relationships of type (1) but see relationships of type (2) (between features and gestures) as more complex and indirect. Strong arguments for such a position have been put forward by Randy Diehl together with colleagues. As regards perception, their general claims are very similar to those of Stevens. Diehl and Stevens and their co-researchers have also shared an interest in *auditory enhancement*, that is, in the possibility that various acoustic properties may, as it were, work together to increase the auditory salience of phonological contrasts. We shall consider some specific proposals concerning auditory enhancement in Sections 7.7 and 7.9.

As regards the modularity hypothesis, it has received little explicit attention in discussions of perception from a 'double-strong' or 'strong auditory' perspective. Although specialised neural circuitry is not required to solve the problem of lack of invariance (as in the case of the Motor Theory), the possibility remains open that some specialised mechanisms might exist to link the information extracted from the incoming acoustic signal with abstract phonological features.

A good introduction to the views of Stevens and his colleagues is Stevens and Blumstein (1981). The second number of Volume 1 of the journal *Ecological Psychology* (1989) is devoted to papers discussing the position of Diehl and his colleagues from a variety of perspectives. It begins with a paper by Diehl and Kluender, setting out their views on the objects of speech perception.

### 5.2.4.5   Non-analytic approaches

When we listen to speech, we can recognise both what is said and (at least in many cases) who is saying it. For example, if I pick up the telephone and hear the voice of a good friend saying the single word **hello**, I can identify both the word and the talker. Is there any connection between these two types of recognition? Most theoretical accounts of speech perception (including all four considered thus far) have taken for granted that there is not. Indeed, concepts such as *invariant cue* carry with them the implication of invariance across talkers (and other aspects of the environment) as well as invariance across phonetic-phonological contexts. If, for example, a reduction in the spectral amplitude at low frequencies enables a listener to identify a segment as [− sonorant], this applies not only to all [− sonorant] segments produced by a single talker but also to all such segments produced by all talkers, whether they speak slowly or quickly, in a noisy or a quiet environment.

From this basic assumption, it follows that any variability which does exist must make speech perception more difficult for the listener rather than facilitating it. Furthermore, since information about specific instances of a particular word is, as it were, discarded by the listener in the process of speech perception, such information can play no role in the representation of words in memory. This fits in well with, and indeed has been influenced by, theories put forward by linguists about the abstract and invariant character of representations within the mental lexicon (Section 1.4). To quote Halle (1985: 101), writing about the representation of words in memory: 'voice quality, speed of utterance, and other properties directly linked to the unique circumstances surrounding every utterance are discarded in the course of learning a new word'.

In recent years, this major assumption has come to be questioned by researchers working within a *non-analytic* or *exemplar-based* approach to speech perception and word recognition. Like the Direct Realist approach, the non-analytic approach starts from a very general psychological theory (Jacoby and Brooks 1984), and regards speech perception and categorisation as basically similar to other types of perception and categorisation. The basic premise is opposite to Halle's: information about particular instances (episodic information) is not discarded, but is retained in memory and continues to be utilised by the listener in perception. Mental representations need not be highly abstract, and they do not necessarily lack redundancy.

The non-analytic approach *par excellence* is found in exemplar models of perception. In exemplar models, categorisation of an incoming stimulus (such as a word) is accomplished not by comparison with an abstract, prototypical representation (as in the linguist's mental lexicon) but instead by comparison with all remembered instances of each category. For example, if each time I hear the word **hello** I store a detailed trace in memory, I can recognise a new instance of the word **hello** because it will have much in common with all the stored instances of **hello**. Similarly, I can compare an incoming **hello** with all stored instances of a particular talker's voice. Thus, my simultaneous recognition of the word **hello** and of the voice which produced it are both based on comparison with memory traces. More specifically, exemplars stored in memory will be *activated* to a greater or lesser extent according to their degree of similarity to an incoming stimulus, and activation levels will determine the eventual categorisation. The lexicon itself is basically *episodic* (based on memories of specific instances) rather than abstract and general.

Two obvious problems would seem to exist for exemplar models of speech perception. The first is lack of sufficient memory capacity (even though humans can remember a surprising amount, it is doubtful that we can retain a unique trace in memory of every utterance we have ever heard). For this reason, there must be some allowance for more general memories, especially of very frequent words, even in models which take the idea of exemplar-based recognition to its logical extreme (Goldinger 1997). The second problem is accounting for human abilities to produce speech as well as understand it. This might be overcome by assuming that a talker's memory of his or her own utterances includes information about the articulatory gestures involved in producing them, as suggested by Johnson (1997). Another possibility, suggested by Coleman (1998), is that talkers are able to compute articulatory plans as needed to produce utterances that will sound like their auditory memories.

If we propose that the lexicon is based on unanalysed auditory memories, we are, in effect, suggesting that unanalysed auditory representations exist at the very highest levels of the speech chain (Section 1.3). In this respect, exemplar models might be compared to the theory of *Articulatory Phonology* (Section 8.5), according to which high-level mental representations are in terms of articulatory gestures. In both cases, representations usually said to belong to the domain of phonetics (articulatory or auditory) are projected upwards to the brain end of the speech chain (Section 1.3), into territory traditionally said to be the domain of phonology. However, in either case, it is unclear that more abstract phonological representations can be, or should be, eliminated altogether from models of linguistic knowledge. An interesting contribution to the debate is Beckman and Pierrehumbert (1999), who argue that phonological categories must emerge in acquisition, as children remember and come to categorise newly encountered linguistic forms.

A good introduction to non-analytic approaches is the volume *Talker Variability in Speech Processing*, edited by Johnson and Mullennix (1997).

This brings to an end our brief overview of five contrasting approaches to perception. Of the proposals considered, Stevens' and Fowler's are the most comprehensive, since they incorporate views about phonological representation and also provide a basis for accounting for speech production in a straightforward way (see further Section 8.5). However, much testing remains to be done before a definitive account emerges. We shall now turn our attention to the second general approach to perception, namely, that which starts from the processing of sound in the ear.

## 5.3  Hearing

It seems obvious that a full understanding of speech perception will be possible only when we are able to follow the progress of an incoming sound up the neural pathways which link the ear with the areas concerned with speech in the brain. At present, for obvious reasons, recordings of neural responses to sound must be done using experimental animals, rather than human beings, as subjects. Since the organisation of the auditory system, particularly at the periphery, is very similar across mammalian species, it seems likely that results of studies on animals can be applied to humans as well.

Neurophysiological studies of animals, however revealing, tell us nothing about matters such as the limits of human perception, human abilities to discriminate between sounds which are only slightly different, or human judgements concerning the perceptual distance between sounds. Accordingly, such studies are complemented by other methods which probe into the workings of the human auditory system by determining how human listeners respond to very simple acoustic stimuli. These belong to the field of *psychophysics*, more specifically *psychoacoustics*. The results of both neurophysiological and psychophysical investigations apply to sound in general rather than to speech in particular.

It is generally agreed that a spectral analysis of *all* incoming sound is performed in the ear and that the information about sound which is transmitted to the brain starts out as a kind of spectrogram. Accordingly, a major research goal has been to describe the workings of the 'auditory spectrograph' and to develop computer programs which will transform narrow band FFT spectra or spectrograms (Sections 3.2 and 3.4) into visualisations of 'auditory spectra'.

It would be nice to think that auditory processing of speech could be divided into a purely mechanical stage, over which the brain exerts no control, followed by later stages which are subject to management from the centre. This would mirror the division of speech production into articulation and actual sound production (Section 4.1). If such a division does exist, it is likely to correspond to the division between the *peripheral* and *central* parts of the auditory system (Section 5.3.1). However, it is also possible that the brain exerts some control over the earliest stages, as suggested by Greenberg (1996). If it could indeed be shown that a special kind of intervention occurs when humans listen to speech, this might provide some support for the existence of a speech module.

### 5.3.1 Structure of the auditory system

An overview of the structure of the auditory system is shown in Figure 5.7 (a). From the inner ear (cochlea), nerve impulses are transmitted by the auditory nerve to the *cochlear nucleus*, which is part of the brain stem. A complicated system of neural pathways links the cochlear nucleus with the auditory cortex and, ultimately, with those areas of the brain involved in speech recognition. Special neural pathways, represented by dashed lines, are devoted to the localisation of sound in space. It is common to make a major division between the *auditory periphery* and the remaining *central* parts of the system, and this is also shown on the diagram.

Figure 5.7 (b) shows a simplified representation of the auditory periphery, which consists of the ear itself and the auditory nerve. Incoming sound is channelled into the ear canal (outer ear). The ear-drum – which might be compared to the diaphragm of the early phonograph (Section 3.3.1) – is set into vibration and transmits its vibration to a bone chain in the middle ear. The bone chain in turn transmits the vibration to a small membrane at the end of the inner ear, and this, in turn, causes the fluid inside the inner ear to vibrate.

The inner ear is essentially a thin tube, about 32 mm long, which is rolled up into a coil. This makes it resemble a snail shell, and because of this resemblance it is called the *cochlea* (which means 'snail' in Latin). Inside, the tube is filled with fluid. It is divided in half lengthwise by a partition which runs nearly the whole of its length (a small gap at the end allows fluid to pass between upper and lower parts). The partition has a complicated structure which we shall not discuss here, beyond noting that the membrane which forms its base – called, appropriately, the *basilar membrane* – is set into vibration when the surrounding fluid vibrates. The fibres of the auditory nerve are attached to the partition.

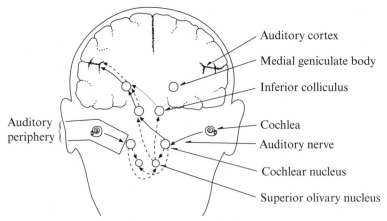

(a) The structure of the auditory system. Adapted from Handel (1989).

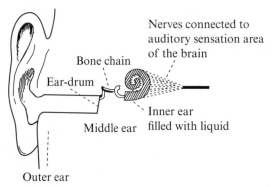

(b) A schematic diagram of the auditory periphery. From Ladefoged (1996).

FIGURE 5.7    The structure of the auditory system and of the auditory periphery.

Although the auditory periphery is many stages removed from the areas of the brain concerned with speech, it is still of crucial importance in the perception of speech as well as of other sounds. It is here that mechanical vibrations are converted into nerve impulses, and a basic spectral analysis is performed. Also, because the auditory periphery is peripheral, it is more accessible, and more is known about it than about higher parts of the system. In what follows, we shall consider a few aspects of the representation of sound at the level of the auditory nerve which are of particular interest for students of speech.

### 5.3.2   Spectra in the auditory nerve

The auditory nerve is made up of a large number of individual nerve fibres. These individual fibres are attached to the cochlear partition all along its length. When the basilar membrane vibrates, its motion will bring about stimulation of at least some of the nerve fibres, causing them to *fire*. The resulting impulses will then provide stimulation for other nerve fibres further up the chain of neural pathways. Which fibres are stimulated, and how strongly, depends on the nature of the vibration, which ultimately depends on the nature of the stimulus presented to the ear.

The firing of a nerve fibre is essentially a chemical reaction accompanied by electrical discharge. It is important to understand that it is a simple, all-or-nothing event. A single nerve fibre cannot fire with different strengths. Furthermore, individual fibres fire from time to time in the absence of stimulation, so that each has a characteristic *spontaneous rate* (SR). When a fibre responds to stimulation, an increase in the rate of firing is observed above the spontaneous rate. Firing rates are usually measured in *spikes per second.*

How is it possible for the auditory nerve fibres (ANFs) to transmit information about spectral structure? When we say 'information about spectral structure', we mean information about which sine wave components are present, and in what strengths, in a complex sound. Accordingly, the ANFs must be able to convey information about frequency and intensity for a number of component frequencies all at the same time. Although the encoding of frequency and intensity in the auditory nerve is not yet fully understood, three basic mechanisms have been identified by which this could be accomplished.

Firstly, individual fibres are tuned to particular frequencies. Each has a preferred frequency, known as its *characteristic frequency* (*CF*), to which it is most sensitive. This tuning is particularly manifest when the stimulus is of low intensity (soft). In such a case, for example, an ANF with CF = 2000 Hz will respond only to tones with frequencies at or close to 2000 Hz. At higher levels of processing, impulses from an ANF with CF = 2000 Hz would signal the presence of a sine wave component of around 2000 Hz in the original stimulus. The characteristic frequency of any particular ANF is determined by the place at which it is attached to the cochlear partition in the inner ear, and an association between location and frequency is also found at higher levels along the neural pathways. For this reason, it is often said that the organisation of the auditory system is *tonotopic* (from Greek *tonos* 'tone, note' and *topos* 'place').

Secondly, as the intensity of stimulation increases, the firing rate of individual ANFs increases. Thus, a higher firing rate would signal a higher-intensity stimulus. However, there are some complicating factors. The association between stimulus intensity and firing rate breaks down at high intensities because the ANFs reach their maximum firing rates (saturation) at intensities lower than the upper end of the audible range. Also, at higher intensities, more ANFs, representing a broader band of CFs, will be stimulated to fire, so the association between particular fibres and particular frequencies is weakened.

Thirdly, ANFs show a tendency to fire 'in step' with the waveform of the stimulus. This tendency is known as *phase-locking*. A hypothetical example of perfect phase-locking is shown in Figure 5.8. In this case, the nerve fibre fires only when the sine wave stimulus is at the lowest point of its cycle. What

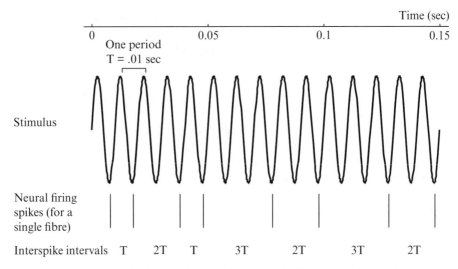

FIGURE 5.8    A hypothetical example of perfect phase locking. The stimulus is a sine wave with frequency 100 Hz and a period of 0.01 seconds. The nerve fibre fires only at the lowest point of the cycle, though it skips over some cycles. Accordingly, the intervals between firings are multiples of 0.01 seconds.

is important here is that the firing always takes place at the same point in the cycle; there need not be one firing per cycle. Accordingly, information about frequency could be derived by monitoring the intervals between firings (spikes), which will be multiples (at least approximately) of the fundamental period of the stimulus. The tendency to phase-locking becomes more marked when the intensity of the stimulus is high.

To illustrate how these mechanisms may encode spectral structure, we shall look briefly at some data concerning voiceless fricatives and vowels.

### 5.3.2.1   Voiceless fricatives

Voiceless fricatives provide an example of a class of speech sounds where CF and firing rate may work together to convey information about spectral structure. Figure 5.9 shows some results from a set of experiments carried out by Delgutte and Kiang (1984b) which involved monitoring the response of ANFs of cats to synthetic fricative stimuli. In the graphs of (b), discharge rates are plotted versus characteristic frequency. Each circle represents the discharge rate for a single ANF at the onset of the stimulus, and the continuous lines represent average discharge rates computed for a series of frequency bands. There is a marked similarity between the graphs of (b) and the spectra of the original stimuli, shown in (a).

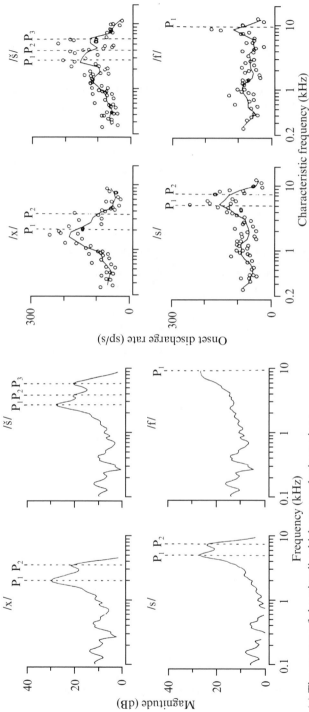

(a) The spectra of the stimuli, which are synthetic versions of the fricatives [x], [s], [ʃ] (symbolised as /š/) and [f]. The dotted lines labelled $P_1$, $P_2$ and $P_3$ pick out the peaks (formants) in the spectra.

(b) The responses recorded at the onset of the stimuli for stimuli presented at a low intensity level. The horizontal axis represents the characteristic frequency (CF) of the nerve fibres which were monitored. Each circle represents the average discharge rate for a single ANF. The continuous lines represent average discharge rate, calculated for a series of frequency bands.

The graphs of (b) provide evidence of relatively high discharge rates for ANFs with characteristic frequencies close to the frequencies of the spectral peaks ($P_1$, $P_2$, $P_3$). Thus, there is a striking similarity between the graphs and the spectra of the original stimuli. From Delgutte and Kiang (1984b).

FIGURE 5.9    Some results from a set of experiments which involved monitoring the response of ANFs of cats to synthetic fricative stimuli.

### 5.3.2.2 Vowels

Vowels are the most intense of speech sounds. Accordingly, it might be expected that phase-locking should be important for conveying information about the spectral structure of vowels. Experimental studies have confirmed this expectation.

Figure 5.10 shows a *neurogram* for auditory nerve activity in response to a synthetic [æ], presented at a medium intensity level (60 dB SPL, roughly that of

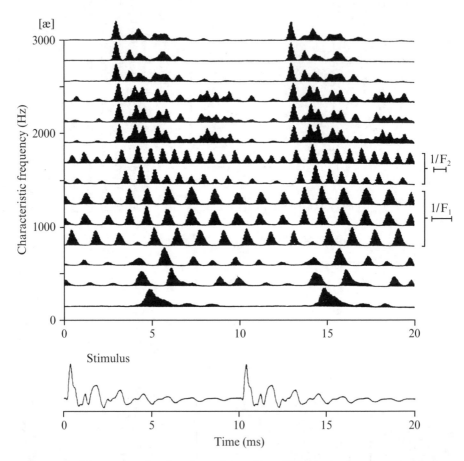

FIGURE 5.10 Neurogram showing the activity of cat ANFs in response to a synthetic [æ], presented at a medium intensity level (60 dB SPL, roughly that of conversational speech). The neurogram shows response patterns for fourteen ANFs, with chracteristic frequencies (CFs) spanning the frequency range from 0 to 3000 Hz. Each horizontal line corresponds to a single ANF. The vertical arrangement of the CFs gives the neurogram some resemblance to a conventional spectrogram. Two periods from the vowel's waveform are shown below the neurogram. See text for further explanation. From Delgutte (1997).

conversational speech). The vowel stimulus had a fundamental frequency of 100 Hz, with $F_1 = 750$ Hz, $F_2 = 1450$ Hz, and $F_3 = 2450$ Hz. The neurogram shows response patterns for fourteen ANFs, with CFs spanning the frequency range from 0 to 3000 Hz. Each trace corresponds to a single ANF.

The neurogram is constructed by analysing the firings for each ANF in 20-msec 'chunks', corresponding to two periods of the original vowel. The height of the trace at each point corresponds to the number of times the ANF fired at the corresponding point in the ensemble of 20-msec chunks. For example, the peaks at 5 msec and 15 msec in the lowest trace indicate that the ANF showed a strong tendency to fire at time intervals 5 msec and 15 msec after the start of each chunk. This is evidence of phase-locking to $F_0$, since the interval between the peaks (10 msec) is equal to the fundamental period (10 msec = 1/100 sec). Fibres with CFs near to the first formant frequency ($F_1$) phase-lock to $F_1$ and fibres with CFs near to the second formant frequency ($F_2$) phase-lock to $F_2$. The higher-frequency fibres show patterns which can be related to the periods of $F_0$, $F_1$ and $F_2$. Data such as this provide evidence that the auditory system is able to extract information about the formant frequencies of vowels, particularly $F_1$ and $F_2$. This, in turn, has provided support for formant-based theories of vowel quality (Section 6.3).

### 5.3.3 The VOT boundary

One of the most discussed proposals regarding natural sensitivities in the auditory system is that concerning the possible VOT boundary in the region of +20 − +40 msec. In more general terms, this involves, firstly, a sensitivity to whether or not two particular events (stop release and onset of voicing) occur simultaneously and, secondly, a sensitivity to the relative length of time separating them. For example, distinguishing between CV syllables with VOT = +20 msec and VOT = +30 msec involves a duration ratio of 1.5 (= 30/20). Distinguishing between CV syllables with VOT = +60 msec and VOT = +70 msec involves a smaller duration ratio of 1.17 and should therefore be more difficult. One might expect that such sensitivities would be very general and that they would be found outside the human species.

The animal most frequently used in studies relating to VOT has been the chinchilla (a small rodent), which shows a remarkable similarity to native English listeners in its categorisation of VOT continua (Kuhl and Miller 1978). Interestingly, a study of the responses of chinchilla ANFs with low characteristic frequencies revealed temporal response patterns which were clearly distinct for stimuli categorised by humans as **ta** and **da** and differing in VOT by 10 msec. In contrast, there was less difference between the patterns for pairs of **da**s and still less between the patterns for pairs of **ta**s. (Sinex *et al.* 1991). This provides some support for the existence of a natural boundary. It further raises the possibility that neural correlates may be found for other phonetic categories which appear to be perceived categorically.

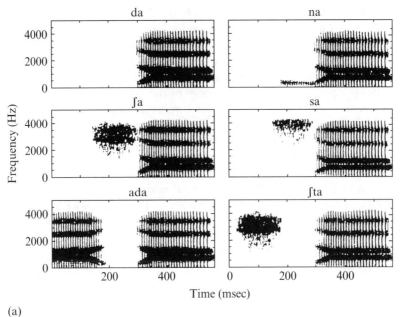

(a)

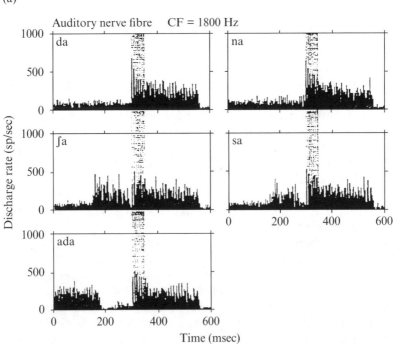

(b)

*Details of this figure at bottom of next page*

### 5.3.4 Adaptation

Another aspect of ANF behaviour which is of particular interest to phoneticians is *adaptation*. Everyone is familiar with the fact that the same sound becomes less obtrusive as one gets used to it. For example, on returning to a busy city from a visit to the countryside, the noise level from traffic seems very loud, but one soon adapts to it and 'tunes it out'. Similar phenomena can be observed on a much smaller scale for individual ANFs. When an ANF is first stimulated at its CF, its firing rate is high, but this soon levels off to a more moderate rate.

The effects of adaptation on neural response to particular speech sounds depend on what sounds have preceded. This is well-illustrated in Figure 5.11, which shows a plot of firing rate vs. time for a single ANF with CF = 1800 Hz, responding to five different synthetic syllables. The shaded area corresponds to the onset of the vowel and the formant transitions (Section 7.2.1). Strong peaks, called *adaptation peaks*, occur at vowel onset for **da** and **na**, because there has been at best weak stimulation at 1800 Hz prior to the vowel onset. The situation is different for ʃa and **ada**, since both the [ʃ] and the [a] preceding the closure interval of **ada** have considerable energy close to 1800 Hz, resulting in adaptation. Thus, the contrast in ANF response is greater than is suggested by the visual appearance of the spectrograms. More generally, the effect of adaptation will be to give greater prominence to onsets (i.e., the beginnings of certain sounds) under certain conditions. This could conceivably have implications as regards preferred linguistic structures.

The main concern of this brief account of the auditory nerve has been to demonstrate that various mechanisms exist for encoding the structure of incoming sound at this very low level of auditory processing. However, recordings of neural activity are not, in themselves, sufficient to enable us to visualise how the auditory system 'sees' incoming sound. To this end, neurophysiological studies must be complemented by other research based on the techniques of psychophysics.

FIGURE 5.11 (*opposite*) Experimental data illustrating the phenomenon of *adaptation*. The illustration shows response patterns of a single cat ANF to five synthetic stimuli. The ANF in question has a CF of 1800 Hz and a high spontaneous rate.

Broad band spectrograms of the stimuli are shown in (a). All incorporate a /da/-like element (appropriate transitions followed by steady-state vowel formants, beginning at about 300 msec on the time axis). However, they differ as regards what precedes. Accordingly, they are perceived by humans as different CV or VCV sequences.

In (b), which shows the response patterns, discharge (firing) rate is plotted vs. time. Shading is used to pick out the time interval corresponding to the formant transition and the onset of the vowel (from 300 msec to 350 msec on the time axis). Although this part of the stimulus is the same in all five of the (V)CV sequences, the neural response patterns are noticeably different. In particular, strong peaks occur at the vowel onset for /da/ and /na/ because there has been little or no stimulation at 1800 Hz prior to the vowel onset. From Delgutte (1997).

## 5.4    Psychophysics and the auditory spectrograph

Psychophysics investigates the relationship between physical and perceptual quantities by eliciting judgements about very simple stimuli. A good example of a psychophysical investigation is the set of experiments, carried out in the 1930s (Stevens and Volkmann 1940), in order to investigate the relationship between frequency and the psychological quantity of pitch. These experiments made it possible to develop a scale of pitch, known as the *mel scale*. Subjects were presented with a reference tone of known frequency and loudness. They were then asked to adjust the frequency of a second tone of equal loudness so that its pitch was twice or half that of the reference tone. In this way, for any reference frequency, the frequency corresponding to a doubling (or halving) of pitch could be determined. In a complementary set of experiments, subjects used a similar technique to divide ranges of frequency (for example 3000 Hz to 12,000 Hz) into four equal intervals.

Taken together, the experimental results made it possible to develop a psychologically realistic scale of pitch. The pitch of a 1000 Hz pure tone was set at 1000 mels. The frequency which was judged to correspond to a doubling of pitch was, accordingly, given a value of 2000 mels, and so on.

A formula which converts frequency, $\mathbf{f}$ (in Hz), to mels is given by Fant (1973: 48):

$$M = (1000/\log_{10}2) \times \log(1+f/1000)$$

The relationship is shown graphically in Figure 5.12 (middle curve). It is obvious that frequency in Hz increases faster than pitch in mels. This is especially true for frequencies above 1000 Hz, above which the curve flattens out noticeably. In addition to the mel scale, two other scales (the Bark and the ERB-rate scales) are illustrated in Figure 5.12. These will be discussed in Section 5.4.1.

More sophisticated psychophysical techniques have been employed to investigate the nature of the auditory spectrograph. The essential characteristic of any spectrograph is that it uses a bank of filters to analyse complex input sounds. Accordingly, much psychophysical research has focussed on the 'filters' of the inner ear. For linguistic phoneticians, the best-known and most influential aspect of this work has concerned the frequency dimension of spectra and spectrograms. It is on this aspect that we shall concentrate here.

### 5.4.1    Scales of frequency based on auditory filters

An important defining characteristic of a spectrographic analysing filter is its bandwidth. The phonetician's spectrograph usually offers a choice of narrow band or broad band filters (Section 3.2.3), and we have seen that this choice is crucial in determining the appearance of the output spectrum. In contrast, the auditory system offers no choice, but operates, as it were, with a fixed set of filters. The filters increase in bandwidth with increasing frequency, so that there

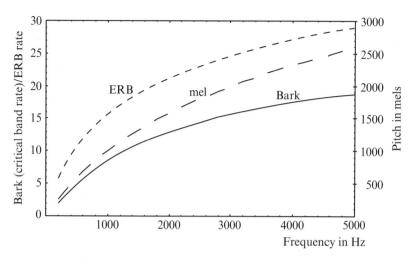

FIGURE 5.12    The relationship between frequencies (in Hz), the mel scale, the ERB-rate scale and the Bark scale. The mel scale is derived from subjects' judgements about the relative pitch of pure tones and is so devised that a pure tone with frequency 1000 Hz has a pitch of 1000 mels. By contrast, the Bark and ERB-rate scales are derived from data on auditory filter bandwidth and, as it were, recast the frequency dimension in terms of numbers of filter bandwidths.

It may be seen that the ERB-rate scale rises more rapidly at low frequencies than do the others. A comparison of the curves for the ERB-rate and Bark scales also shows that ERB-rate values are higher overall. In the right-hand part of the graph (above about 3000 Hz), the curves for the ERB-rate scale and the Bark scale are nearly parallel, and the ERB-rate value is about 1.5 times the Bark-scale value.

Finally, it is necessary to point out that the visual impression as regards the mel scale is influenced by the scaling used to draw the curve (see the right-hand vertical axis). An alternative scaling would make the mel and Bark scales look more similar. An example may be found in Ladefoged (1996: 81).

is a gradual transition from relatively narrow band analysis at low frequencies to extremely broad band analysis at high frequencies. In this way, the listener gets the best of both worlds. At low frequencies, the filters will be able to 'see' individual harmonics, and so the harmonics will be perceived individually (*resolved*). In contrast, at high frequencies, harmonics will be smeared together. The filters are referred to as *auditory filters* or simply *the auditory filter*. The number of filters is large, and their ranges overlap.

The relationship between auditory filter bandwidth and frequency must be determined experimentally, but it has also been possible to work out equations which estimate filter bandwidths for particular frequencies. A further possibility is to recast the frequency dimension so that it becomes a scale based on filter bandwidth. To give a simple example, suppose that on a conventional spectrograph, we use a filter bandwidth of 40 Hz. In this case, 40 Hz is equivalent to one filter bandwidth, 400 Hz is equivalent to 10 filter bandwidths and

1000 Hz is equivalent to 25 filter bandwidths. For any particular frequency (in Hz) we can determine the corresponding number of filter bandwidths if we divide by 40.

Devising a scale based on filter bandwidth becomes more complicated if the filters overlap with one another and more complicated still if the bandwidth increases as frequency increases. As we have just said, this is the case for the filters of the inner ear. Two well-known scales, based on two somewhat different views of the nature of auditory filters, have been proposed. The earlier, which has come to be widely used by phoneticians, is known as the *Bark scale* (after the German engineer H. G. Barkhausen, who devised a scale of loudness). The Bark scale has its roots in the fundamental research into the auditory filter carried out by Zwicker and his colleagues. In their approach, the bandwidth of the auditory filter is referred to as the *critical band* and the Bark-scale value is the *critical band rate*, symbolised by the letter **z**. Conversion from frequency, **f** (in Hz), to Bark can be accomplished by means of a simple formula, which is valid for frequencies above 200 Hz (Traunmüller 1990):

$$z = (26.18 \times f) / (1960 + f) - 0.53$$

A graph relating the Bark scale to frequency in Hz is shown in Figure 5.12 (solid curve).

The second of the two scales is known as the ERB-rate scale (ERB stands for *equivalent rectangular bandwidth*). It is based on more recent research into the auditory filter, and is likely to become more widely used, displacing the Bark scale, in the future. The ERB-rate scale differs from the Bark scale in that the filter bandwidth is considerably smaller at low frequencies and rises rapidly in the lower part of the frequency scale. A simple equation relating ERB-rate, symbolised by E, to frequency (in Hz) is given by Moore (1997):

$$E = 21.4 \times \log_{10}[.00437*f+1]$$

A graph relating the ERB-rate scale to frequency in Hz is also shown in Figure 5.12 (upper curve).

For frequencies above 1000 Hz, the shape of the curve for the ERB-rate scale is similar to that for the mel and Bark scales, but its slope is steeper at low frequencies. At higher frequencies (above about 2500 Hz), the ERB-rate, Bark and mel scales increase at about the same rate. More generally, the correspondence between the mel, Bark, and ERB scales suggests that the basis of our sensation of pitch lies in the way incoming sound is dealt with in the auditory periphery (rather than at some higher level of processing).

It would be misleading to suggest that the only difference between the ERB-rate scale and the Bark scale is the bandwidth of the auditory filters at low frequencies. The two scales are based on rather different views concerning the frequency-response curves which are associated with the filters. The differences cannot be discussed here, and the interested reader is referred to the references in Section 5.6.

### 5.4.2  *Auditory spectra*

Research into auditory filters is part of a larger programme of research into the representation of sound in the auditory periphery. One goal of such research is to produce models of auditory processing. Models make it possible to see sounds as they are 'seen' by the auditory system. In practice, a full model of the auditory periphery involves several stages of calculation, taking into account the effects of the outer ear, the middle ear, the inner ear, and the way in which the motion of the basilar membrane in the inner ear (Section 5.3.1) is translated into neural impulses. However, the most important stage is the spectral analysis by auditory filters which takes place in the inner ear. By focussing on this stage, it is possible to gain some idea of how an 'auditory spectrum' differs from the spectrum produced by a conventional spectrograph. More accurately, this type of spectrum is known as an *excitation pattern* since it reflects the motion along the length of the basilar membrane in the inner ear.

Figure 5.13 shows the [i]-like spectrum of Figure 4.8 and a calculated excitation pattern. The excitation pattern is arrived at by plotting the output level of individual auditory filters (on the vertical axis) vs. their centre frequencies (on the horizontal axis). The horizontal axis of the excitation pattern is on the ERB-rate scale. One effect of the change from Hz to E-units is to increase the spacing between the lower harmonics, giving particular prominence to the lowest three. (Compare the position of the lowest harmonic, $H_1$, on both diagrams.) At the same time, the peaks corresponding to the upper formants $F_2$, $F_3$ and $F_4$ are much closer together. This kind of diagram has been of particular interest to linguistic phoneticians engaged in the description and classification of vowels.

Because of the increasing bandwidth of the auditory filter, the frequency resolution becomes poorer as frequency increases from left to right. Individual harmonics become less and less distinct. For example, the thirteenth harmonic ($H_{13}$) only corresponds to a ripple on the excitation pattern.

As we have just said, excitation patterns represent only one stage of processing in the auditory periphery. As research progresses, models are being developed which are able to arrive at visual representations of speech sounds which bear a closer resemblance to neural patterns and, at the same time, can provide the basis for a three-dimensional representation which resembles a conventional spectrogram. A good example of such a model is Auditory Image Model (AIM) of Patterson and his colleagues (Patterson *et al.* 1992).

## 5.5  Conclusion

This chapter has covered a number of seemingly disparate topics, all relating to the perception of speech. However, all are important for piecing together an account of speech perception. As we have seen, a major handicap in the study of perception is the lack of access to intermediate stages. Early studies had no

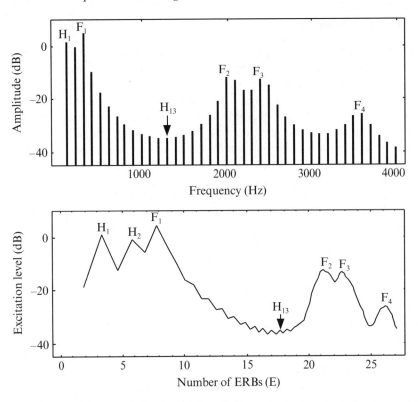

FIGURE 5.13    Spectrum and calculated excitation pattern for a high front vowel ([i]). The spectrum is identical to that of Figure 4.8 (c). The excitation pattern was calculated using the method described by Moore and Glasberg (1983). The horizontal axis of the excitation is on the ERB-rate (E) scale. $F_1$, $F_2$, $F_3$ and $F_4$ are the four formants of the vowel. $H_1$ and $H_2$ are the first two harmonics with frequencies 100 Hz and 200 Hz respectively. $H_{13}$ is the thirteenth harmonic (1300 Hz, 17.65 E), which is only barely visible as a distinct ripple on the overall pattern.

Note that, on the excitation pattern, the first three harmonics stand out as separate peaks, well separated from one another. By contrast, the high-frequency harmonics are, as it were, fused together to give a smooth contour. The peaks corresponding to $F_2$, $F_3$ and $F_4$ are closer together than they are in the spectrum. This is because the frequency resolution of the auditory filter becomes poorer with increasing frequency.

choice but to try to link the lowest stage (the acoustic signal) directly with the final stage (the identification of a linguistic object), and it is hardly surprising that such a disparate range of theories has emerged from that enterprise. As both knowledge and experimental techniques have progressed, it is becoming possible to model various stages in the processing of speech in the ear and neural pathways, and to piece together an account of perception which takes the workings of the auditory system into account. A particularly exciting aspect of this enterprise is the possibility of determining how auditory capabilities and constraints have influenced the selection of sounds used in human language. For theoretical linguists, another area of particular interest is the question of modularity, and one task which remains to be undertaken is that of elucidating the role of both speech perception and speech production within a modular view of language.

## 5.6  Further reading

Good overviews of research on speech perception are provided by Borden *et al.* (1994), Goldinger *et al.* (1996), Handel (1989) and the relevant chapters by Kluender, Massaro and Remez in the *Handbook of Psycholinguistics* (Gernsbacher 1994). Klatt (1989), though not so comprehensive, is also to be recommended. Sawusch (1996) concentrates on the methodology of speech perception studies.

Denes and Pinson (1993) and Borden *et al.* (1994) are good starting points for reading about the auditory system and auditory processing. Also to be recommended are Handel (1989), Johnson (1997) and Rosen and Howell (1991). Delgutte (1997) and Moore (1997), already referred to, are somewhat more specialised. Greenberg (1996) is general but less elementary. Moore (1989) is particularly to be recommended as a full-length work.

The ability to produce synthetic speech, which has not been touched on here, is of crucial importance in experimental work on speech perception. An elementary introduction is provided by Denes and Pinson (1993). Kent and Read (1992) also include a discussion of synthesis. Javkin (1996) is a more thorough introduction.

## Note

1  It needs to be added here that the 'whistling' character of /θr/ is not so striking if the /r/ is not fully devoiced.

# Chapter 6

# The acoustic description of vowels

## 6.1   Introduction

In this chapter, we shall be concerned with the acoustic description of vowels. With regard to the source-filter theory, these sounds are the most straightforward, since it is not necessary to take into account any source other than air flow through the vibrating vocal folds. Their spectra show peaks and valleys, defined by the increasing and decreasing amplitude of their harmonics, as one moves up or down the frequency scale. We have seen that particular importance attaches to the frequencies of the peaks. These correspond to the *formants*, that is, the resonant frequencies of the vocal tract (Section 4.2.2.2). We have seen that, given a set of formant frequencies for a (non-nasal) vowel, it is possible to predict the output spectrum for that vowel (provided that the spectrum of the source is known, Section 4.4).

In Chapter 4, formants were treated as part of the realm of speech production, and we concentrated on their role in generating vowel spectra. However, we may also think of formants in purely acoustic terms, that is, as peaks in the spectrum which will be heard by the listener. On this view, the primary role of formants is to characterise the input to speech perception rather than to determine the output of speech production.

In acoustic studies of vowel quality, the focus of attention is typically on the steady state of the vowel. In natural speech, vowels are rarely pronounced in isolation. In pronouncing a CV, VC or CVC sequence, the organs of speech must move from the consonantal position to the vocalic position and/or from the vocalic position to the consonantal position. These transitional movements are reflected in so-called *transitions* in the vowel's formant pattern. A good example is the spectrogram of the word **door**, shown in Figure 3.6. The dark band running from left to right which corresponds to the second formant ($F_2$) begins at the spike which corresponds to the release of the [d], at a frequency just under 2000 Hz (2 kHz). It shows continuous downward movement until, by the time the midpoint of the vowel is reached, it has almost completely merged with the lowest dark band which corresponds to the first formant ($F_1$). Similarly, the third formant ($F_3$) moves upward from just above 2000 Hz to around 2750 Hz. These downward and upward movements are the transitions (see also Section 7.2.1). The steady state is to the right, where $F_2$ is low and stable and $F_3$ is high and stable. It is often assumed that the steady state is what the speaker aims for and what the listener attends to in identifying vowels, while the transitions are more important for the identification of consonants (though this is an oversimplification).

## 6.2   Formant frequencies and the vowel quadrilateral

For linguistic phoneticians, the most striking characteristic of vowel formants is the remarkable correspondence between plots of the frequencies of the first and second formants ($F_1$ and $F_2$) and the traditional vowel quadrilateral. If we recall our crude models of vowel production (Section 4.4), we remember that a prototypical [i] has low $F_1$ frequency and high $F_2$ frequency, a prototypical [u] has low $F_1$ frequency and low $F_2$ frequency, and a prototypical central [a] has high $F_1$ frequency and mid $F_2$ frequency. If we set up our plot so that $F_1$ frequency is on the vertical axis, increasing from top to bottom, and $F_2$ frequency is on the horizontal axis, increasing from right to left, we obtain:

An example showing frequencies of $F_1$ and $F_2$ for the five vowels of KiMvita Swahili, pronounced by a single male speaker, is shown in Figure 6.1. In (a), each point corresponds to a single vowel token, while in (b), $F_1$ and $F_2$ values for each vowel quality have been averaged together, so that each point represents an average value. Figure 6.2 shows average frequencies of $F_1$ and $F_2$ for ten vowels of American English as pronounced by 33 male speakers. This data is taken from a well-known study of vowels by Peterson and Barney (1951). Such $F_1$–$F_2$ plots can be an extremely useful tool for the descriptive linguist, since they provide an objective means of diagramming vowel qualities which does not depend on the individual researcher's judgement concerning his or her own or the informant's tongue position.

Although it is possible to regard $F_1$–$F_2$ plots as simply a useful tool for descriptive purposes, they may also have a deeper significance. Since formant frequencies are derived from acoustic signals, and since acoustic signals are the input to all human speech perception, it has seemed natural to suppose that formant charts must, in some way, reveal a universal perceptual vowel space. On this view, drawing a formant chart for a particular speaker or a particular language is like producing a map of that speaker's (or language's) vowels in the universal vowel space. If such a vowel space does exist, it might also provide a means of accounting for the perception of vowels. For example, if I hear a word of the form **sVt** in isolation and have to decide between **sit**, **set** and **sat**,

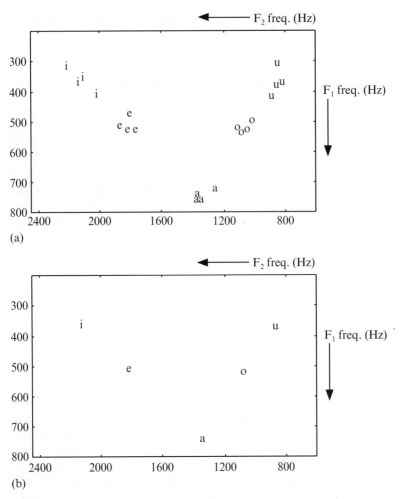

FIGURE 6.1   Formant frequencies for the five distinctive vowels of KiMvita Swahili, pronounced by a male speaker from Mombasa. All of the vowels were pronounced in stressed penultimate syllables of disyllabic words. In (a), each point represents a single token. In (b), the four $F_1$ and $F_2$ values have been averaged for each vowel, giving a single point for each vowel.

I might, as it were, locate the vowel on my mental vowel map. I could then decide to assign the vowel to the /ɪ/ category (**sit**), the /ɛ/ category (**set**) or the /æ/ category (**sat**) on the basis of its location on the map. (Such proposals remain highly controversial however.)

If we accept the idea that a universal perceptual vowel space exists, then there are two types of questions that need to be asked. The first concerns how to define the space in acoustic terms. The second concerns the relationship between the familiar articulatory dimensions of vowel classification and the proposed perceptual dimensions. Both of these will concern us in this chapter.

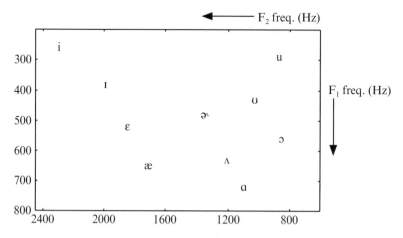

FIGURE 6.2  Average formant frequencies for the distinct monophthongal vowels of American English. Each point represents an average of 33 tokens (produced by 33 male speakers). All of the vowels were pronounced in words of the form /hVd/ (**heed, hid, head**, etc.). The data are taken from Peterson and Barney (1952).

### 6.2.1  The rounding dimension

The correspondence between $F_1$–$F_2$ plots and the vowel quadrilateral is closest for front unrounded vowels, low unrounded vowels and back rounded vowels. Nevertheless, vowels with a front tongue position may be produced with lip rounding, while vowels with a back tongue position may be produced without lip rounding. There can be no doubt that lip rounding is an independent articulatory dimension, but it is much less clear that it has a corresponding independent acoustic dimension.

We must first consider the effect of lip rounding (or the lack of it) on a vowel's formant frequencies. As can be seen from the nomogram of Figure 4.10, rounding generally results in lower formant frequencies, most commonly $F_2$ frequencies. This means that, in general, back unrounded vowels will have higher $F_2$ than their rounded counterparts and front rounded vowels will have lower $F_2$ than their unrounded counterparts. On an $F_1$–$F_2$ plot, such vowels will be located in the middle part of the chart. This is illustrated in Figure 6.3, which plots $F_1$ and $F_2$ values in Hz for the vowels of (a) French (which distinguishes rounded and unrounded front vowels) and (b) Thai (which distinguishes rounded and unrounded back vowels).

In placing front rounded and back unrounded vowels on a two-dimensional vowel chart, we have kept to our original two acoustic dimensions ($F_1$ frequency and $F_2$ frequency) and simply filled in areas which were previously blank. Is there any other characteristic of rounded vowels, any independent third acoustic dimension, which sets them apart from their unrounded counterparts? To put the question in a more abstract way: can we define rounded vowels in terms of intrinsic characteristics of their spectra rather than in terms of their formant frequencies relative to those of unrounded vowels? This problem remains

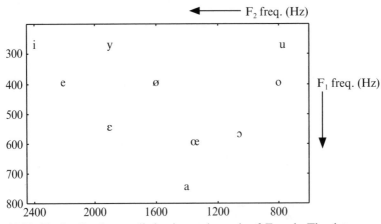

(a) $F_1$–$F_2$ plot for the ten distinctive oral vowels of French. The data are taken from Delattre (1981). Each point represents an average of ten tokens pronounced by five male speakers (two tokens per speaker). All of the vowels were stressed.

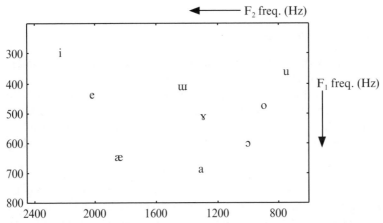

(b) $F_1$–$F_2$ plot for the nine distinctive long vowels of Standard Thai. The data are taken from Abramson (1962). Each point represents an average of ten tokens pronounced by two male speakers (five tokens per speaker, representing the five distinctive tones).

FIGURE 6.3   $F_1$–$F_2$ plots for (a) a vowel system with front rounded vowels (French) and (b) a vowel system with back unrounded vowels (Thai).

unresolved. Stevens (1985a) suggests that rounded vowels might be character-ised by a greater degree of prominence of a single spectral peak (which will be relatively low in frequency for back vowels but relatively high in frequency for front vowels), but this proposal needs to be formulated in more precise terms and tested.

It appears that, while $F_1$ frequency corresponds fairly closely to the articu-latory dimension of vowel height, $F_2$ frequency depends both on backness and

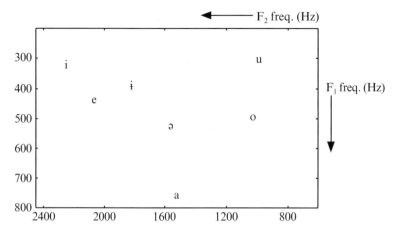

FIGURE 6.4    $F_1$–$F_2$ plot for the seven distinctive vowels of Amharic, pronounced by a male speaker from Gondar. All of the vowels were pronounced in monosyllabic words. Each point represents an average of four tokens.

rounding. The three primary dimensions of articulatory vowel classification are, as it were, collapsed into two acoustic dimensions.

### 6.2.2   Central vowels

Another type of vowel occupying the central area of the chart is the class of so-called 'central vowels', that is, vowels for which the tongue position is, in traditional terms, neither front nor back. The full set of Cardinal Vowels includes high central unrounded [ɨ] and rounded [ʉ], but no mid-central [ə]. Figure 6.4 shows an $F_1$–$F_2$ plot of the vowels of Amharic, which has both high central /ɨ/ (impressionistically somewhat lower than the top line of the chart) and mid-central /ə/ as distinct phonemes.

Many linguists do not distinguish between central and back unrounded vowels, but use the symbol ɨ for vowels of both categories. For example, the high back unrounded vowel of Thai, which we have represented with ɯ is often transcribed as ɨ. A comparison of the Amharic and Thai charts suggests that the two can easily be distinguished acoustically, since the Amharic central vowels are closer to the front vowels (because of their higher $F_2$ frequency) than their Thai counterparts.

### 6.3   Formant frequencies and vowel charts: the problem of psychological reality

The correspondence between $F_1$–$F_2$ plots and the traditional vowel quadrilateral does not, in itself, prove that frequencies of the formants – and especially the first two formants – play a primary role in the perception of vowels. Two other types of evidence may be given greater weight. The first of these is the practical experience of producing synthetic speech. When synthetic vowels have the formant frequencies of their corresponding target vowels (with appropriate bandwidths and relative amplitudes), listeners will generally hear them as expected. Two formants are sufficient to enable subjects to recognise vowels, though two-formant synthetic vowels do not sound like natural vowels. At least, two formants appear to be sufficient for vowels which can be specified in terms of height, backness and rounding, but which lack secondary features such as nasalisation or rhoticity.

The second type of evidence comes from studies of how the auditory system responds to vowel-like stimuli. If we look again at the excitation pattern of Figure 5.13, we see that, at the upper end of the frequency scale, individual harmonics are fused together (*integrated*) to give a smooth pattern of peaks and valleys. At the lower end, individual harmonics are *resolved* and appear as separate peaks. The frequencies of spectral peaks are encoded in the auditory nerve by means of firing patterns of individual nerve fibres (Sections 5.3.2, 5.4.2). Thus, it seems clear that the brain has access to information about the location of spectral peaks. It should be possible to make use of such information when deciding what phonological category any particular vowel belongs to, however this is done. Some special mechanisms might have to be invoked for identifying $F_1$ since the constituent harmonics will normally not be fused together into a smooth peak.

In any case, if we take the two-dimensional $F_1$–$F_2$ plot as our starting point in our quest for a universal perceptual vowel space, we should first try to ensure that the spacing of the vowels on such plots is 'psychologically real'. An obvious first step toward greater psychological reality is to redraw the horizontal and vertical axes so that they correspond to *pitch* rather than to *frequency*. Many early studies of vowel quality used logarithmic scaling, which, as we have seen, is like using a musical scale of tones and semitones (Section 2.5.3). However, in recent years, use of the mel Scale, the Bark scale and the ERB-rate scale (Section 5.4.1), which correspond more closely to perceived pitch, has become more common.

Figure 6.5 shows two $F_1$–$F_2$ plots for the Cardinal Vowels, based on the Hz scale (a) and the Bark scale (b). It will be seen that the change in scale from Hz to Bark has little effect on the spacing between vowels in the height ($F_1$) dimension but does affect the spacing between vowels in the backness ($F_2$) dimension. The effect is greatest for the front vowels (with high $F_2$), which are, as it were, shifted towards the centre of the chart when the Bark scale is used.

## 6.4   The spectral integration hypothesis

We must now address two other potential difficulties inherent in the $F_1$–$F_2$ plot. The first of these is that it assumes that $F_1$ and $F_2$ will always be perceived as distinct peaks. The second, and related, difficulty is that it ignores $F_3$ and the higher formants.

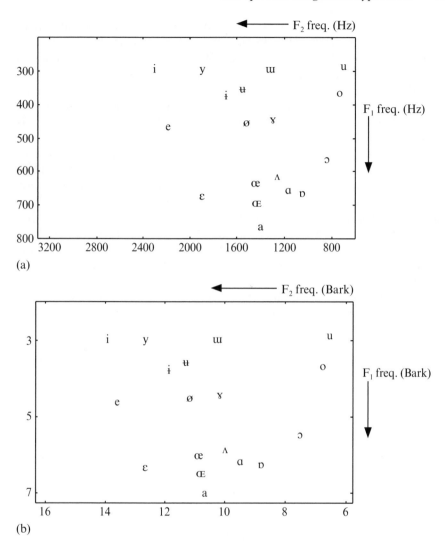

FIGURE 6.5   $F_1$–$F_2$ plots for a set of synthetic Cardinal Vowels, based on natural productions by a male speaker. The data are taken from Bladon (1983). In (a), formant frequency values are plotted in Hz, while in (b), the Bark scale is used.

In these plots, the horizontal ($F_2$ frequency) axis extends over a wider range than in the plots of Figures 6.1–6.4. This makes it easier to compare them with Figure 6.7. Note that the same range of frequencies is used for both the horizontal and vertical axes in (a) and (b); the differences in the positioning of individual vowels and in the spacing between them are due to the use of the Bark, rather than the Hz, scale.

When two formants are close together in frequency, they may combine to give a single perceived peak. This possibility was first discussed by Delattre and his colleagues (Delattre *et al.* 1952), reporting the results of their efforts to synthesise recognisable one- and two-formant versions of all eight primary and eight of the ten secondary Cardinal Vowels. Two aspects of their results stood out as particularly important. Firstly, for vowels in which $F_1$ and $F_2$ are typically close together (that is, back rounded vowels and low vowels), it was possible to produce recognisable synthetic versions which had only one formant. Otherwise, two formants were required. This suggested that, when $F_1$ and $F_2$ are close together, listeners averaged them together, so that they heard only a single formant peak. Consequently, only one peak was necessary in a synthetic version. Secondly, efforts to synthesise vowels which typically have high $F_2$ (particularly [i] and [e], but also [ɛ]) were most successful when $F_2$ was higher than would be expected from natural speech. Since, for these vowels, $F_2$ is typically close to $F_3$, it was suggested that the perceived $F_2$ was, in fact, a sort of fusion of $F_2$ and $F_3$. In other words, $F_2$ and $F_3$ might be *integrated* into a single perceived peak.

If such integration (fusion) does occur, then it cannot take place at the first level of auditory processing where individual formant peaks may be, as it were, moved closer together but are usually not completely fused (Figure 5.13). Accordingly, a number of researchers have argued that a *large scale integration*, resulting in fusion of the individual formants, takes place as part of central auditory processing. If this view is correct, it raises two important questions. Firstly, how close in frequency must two formants be for integration to occur? Secondly, when integration does take place, combining two formants into a single perceived peak, what is the frequency of this new peak?

Some classic experiments which suggested answers to these questions were carried out by the Russian phonetician Ludmilla Chistovich and her colleagues in Leningrad in the 1970s (reviewed in Chistovich 1985). The crucial experiments involved matching vowels with different numbers of formants. For example, subjects might be presented with a single reference vowel, with two formants $F_1$ and $F_2$, and a one-formant vowel, for which the single formant was referred to as $F^*$. The frequency of $F^*$ was variable and could be adjusted by the subjects. Accordingly, they would be asked to manipulate the frequency of $F^*$ and find the frequency at which the one-formant vowel was closest to the two-formant reference. If they consistently agreed on a one-formant vowel with $F^*$ between $F_1$ and $F_2$, the experimenters concluded that integration had occurred and that the frequency of the perceived peak was the same as $F^*$. If subjects preferred one-formant vowels for which $F^*$ was close to either $F_1$ or $F_2$ of the reference vowel, the experimenters concluded that integration had not occurred.

The general results concerning integration of formants which emerged from the Leningrad experiments are illustrated in Figure 6.6. As regards our first question, they provided evidence for a *critical distance* between formants of approximately 3 to 3.5 on the Bark scale. If two formant frequencies are

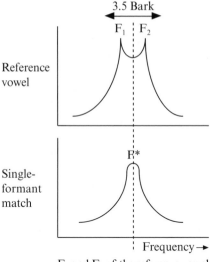

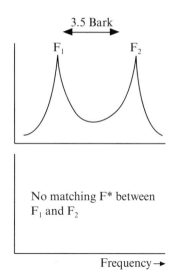

F$_1$ and F$_2$ of the reference vowel are less than 3.5 Bark apart. F* is between F$_1$ and F$_2$. In this example, F$_1$ and F$_2$ are equal in amplitude, and F* is halfway in between.

F$_1$ and F$_2$ of the reference vowel are more than 3.5 Bark apart. There is no matching F* between F$_1$ and F$_2$.

(a) *The spectral integration hypothesis.* If two formant peaks are separated by less than 3–3.5 Bark, they are integrated to give a single perceived peak.

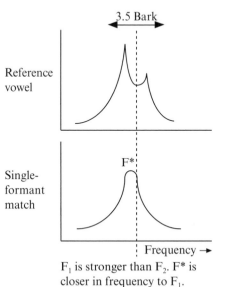

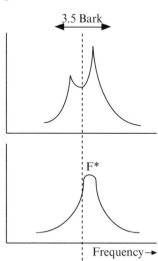

F$_1$ is stronger than F$_2$. F* is closer in frequency to F$_1$.

F$_2$ is stronger than F$_1$. F* is closer in frequency to F$_2$.

(b) *The centre of gravity effect.* When two formants are integrated, the frequency of the perceived peak will be closer to that of the stronger of the two.

FIGURE 6.6   The spectral integration hypothesis. (Note that the dashed line corresponds to a frequency half-way between F$_1$ and F$_2$.)

separated by less than 3–3.5 Bark, integration (fusion into a single peak) will occur. If they are separated by more than the critical distance, integration will not occur. This claim is known as the *spectral integration hypothesis*.

The results obtained by Chistovich and her colleagues also suggested an answer to our second question, concerning the frequency of the new combined peak. This was that the frequency of the new peak should depend on the relative amplitudes of the original peaks. If the two integrated formants were of equal amplitude, the perceived peak should be halfway in between. Otherwise, the perceived peak should be closer in frequency to the stronger of the two original peaks. This is known as the *centre of gravity* (*COG*) effect.

The spectral integration hypothesis has been of great interest to linguistic phoneticians. Firstly, it has interesting implications for vowel classification (Section 6.5). Secondly, this type of integration, if it does occur, is likely to be specific to speech and must take place *after* general processing in the auditory periphery, which applies to all types of sound (Sections 5.3, 5.4). Even if the proposed 3–3.5 Bark critical distance is rejected, it is still possible that some sort of special, speech-specific integration does occur. Thus, Rosner and Pickering (1994), who strongly reject Chistovich's hypothesis, argue in favour of another type of speech-specific integration. This serves to fuse together low-frequency harmonics into a single peak corresponding to $F_1$.

In any case, it is important to distinguish between the perceived formant frequencies and the 'real' formant frequencies. The terms *effective* and *nominal* are often used for this purpose. For example, *effective $F_1$* is the frequency of $F_1$ as perceived by the listener, whereas *nominal $F_1$* is the frequency of $F_1$ which could be measured from displays such as spectrograms, power spectra and LPC analysis.

### 6.4.1   *Integration of $F_2$ with other formants*

Let us now think about the possibilities for spectral integration. $F_2$ is the most important formant from this point of view. This is because the range of values taken by $F_2$ is so large – larger than that of any of the other formants. For example, in the set of Cardinal Vowels plotted in Figure 6.5, $F_2$ ranges from 700 Hz for [u] to 2300 Hz for [i]. $F_2$ thus serves as a sort of energy resource which can be used to provide an extra boost to either the low-frequency or the high-frequency part of the spectrum. If it is sufficiently low in frequency, it reinforces $F_1$; if it is sufficiently high in frequency, it reinforces $F_3$. In between these two possibilities is a middle ground, in which $F_2$, as it were, retains its identity as a separate peak.

The integration of $F_2$ with $F_3$ (and possibly also $F_4$) has been the subject of particular interest. The effective $F_2$ – which will be higher than the nominal ('real') $F_2$ in cases where it is integrated with $F_3$ – is often referred to as $F_2'$ (*$F_2$ prime*). Figure 6.7 shows a plot of $F_1$ vs. $F_2'$ for the set of Cardinal Vowels shown in Figure 6.5. The values of $F_2'$ were determined by means of a perceptual experiment which we shall not describe here (see Bladon 1983).

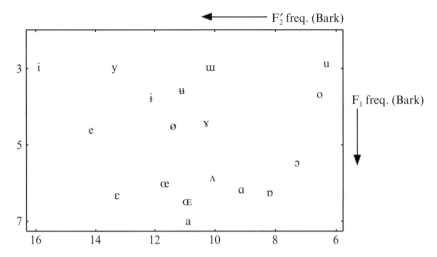

FIGURE 6.7 $F_1$–$F_2'$ plots for the set of Cardinal Vowels shown in Figure 6.5. As in Figure 6.5 (b), frequencies in Hz have been converted to Bark-scale values. Notice that substitution of $F_2'$ for $F_2$ changes the spacing between vowels in the horizontal dimension, particularly the front vowels.

The $F_2'$ values were determined experimentally. In the experiment, subjects were asked to match synthetic two-formant vowels with synthetic four-formant vowels. The $F_2$ value of the preferred two-formant vowel was taken to be $F_2'$ (Bladon 1983).

At the lower end of the spectrum, the possible integration of $F_1$ and $F_2$ has been the subject of fewer studies. However, the results of work by Beddor and Hawkins (1990), Assman (1991) and others suggest that the spectral integration hypothesis needs some modification when the formants concerned are in the lower part of the spectrum. As we have seen, it is in this part of the spectrum that individual harmonics are most clearly separated and where special mechanisms for identifying formant peaks might have to apply.

### 6.4.2 A role for $F_0$?

Although $F_0$ (the fundamental frequency) is not a formant, it is typically a prominent element in vowel spectra, and often constitutes a peak in its own right (as in the crude [ɑ]-like spectrum of Figure 3.1). Some researchers have suggested that this $F_0$ peak might interact with the $F_1$ peak in vowel perception. There are two hypotheses to be considered. Firstly, $F_0$ might be susceptible to integration with $F_1$ in accordance with the spectral integration hypothesis. Secondly, $F_0$, as well as $F_1$, might play a role in determining vowel height.

The idea that $F_0$ plays a role in the perception of vowel height is attractive because $F_0$ varies to some extent with vowel quality. This phenomenon is known as the *intrinsic pitch of vowels*. When high vowels are compared with low vowels pronounced in the same intonational (or tonal) context, the high vowels tend to have higher $F_0$. In other words, as we move down the vowel quadrilateral from high to low, $F_0$ and $F_1$ change in opposite directions – $F_0$ becomes lower while $F_1$ becomes higher. Accordingly, other things being equal, the difference between $F_0$ and $F_1$ will be smallest for high vowels and greatest for low vowels. Thus, $F_1$–$F_0$ might be a better measure of vowel height than $F_1$.

The matter is far from clear-cut and raises some rather complicated issues. $F_0$ goes up and down as required by the intonational (or tonal) pattern, so that phonologically high and low pitches can, in principle, be applied to any vowel. This means that the relationship between $F_0$ and $F_1$ can vary considerably, especially for speakers who employ a wide range of pitches ($F_0$ values). Another obvious problem is explaining the perception of whispered vowels, which are not voiced and which therefore have no $F_0$.

Unfortunately, experimental evidence relating to the interaction of $F_1$ and $F_0$ is correspondingly unclear. The hypothesis that listeners determine vowel height by comparing the frequencies of $F_0$ and $F_1$ was supported by some well-known experiments by Traunmüller (1981). For his study, the subjects were speakers of a variety of Austrian German, chosen for its five phonemically distinct vowel heights. For a contrasting result, we may cite the study of Hoemeke and Diehl (1994) with American English listeners. Although they found some evidence to support the hypothesis of $F_0$–$F_1$ integration, $F_1$ was more strongly correlated with perceived height than ($F_1$–$F_0$).

## 6.5  A system of binary features for vowels?

From the linguist's point of view, one interesting implication of the spectral integration hypothesis is that it provides for a classification of vowels in terms of binary categories or *features* (Section 1.4.2). Each of the possibilities for integration already mentioned ($F_1$ with $F_2$, $F_2$ with $F_3$, and also $F_1$ with $F_0$) divides vowels into two classes, depending on whether integration does or does not occur.

Such a classification has been carried out for American English vowels by Syrdal (1985) and Syrdal and Gopal (1986), using data from Peterson and Barney's (1952) study of American English vowels (from which the average formant values of Figure 6.2 were taken) together with a similar data base made available by the Speech Research Group of Texas Instruments (Dallas, Texas). They also took into account possibilities for integration of $F_4$ with $F_3$ and possibly also $F_2$. Their results are shown in the table below. In the right-hand column of the table, we have given the corresponding articulatory classification.

|                | Integration | Resolution |                                             |
| -------------- | ----------- | ---------- | ------------------------------------------- |
| $F_1–F_0$      | i u ɪ ʊ     | ɑ æ ʌ ɔ ɛ  | high vs. non-high ($/ɚ/$ is borderline)     |
| $F_2–F_1$      | ɑ ɔ         | others     | non-high and back vs. remainder             |
| $F_3–F_2$      | i ɪ ɛ æ ɚ   | ɑ ɔ ʊ u ʌ  | non-back vs. back                           |
| $F_4–F_3–F_2$  | i           | others     | high front vs. remainder                    |
| $F_4–F_3$      | others      | ɚ          | rhoticised vs. remainder (see Section 6.7.3) |

Although the spectral integration hypothesis primarily concerns vowel perception, it may also provide explanations for some historical shifts in vowel quality. The reasoning behind such proposals is rather complicated, and the reader is referred to the detailed discussion in Beddor (1991). An enthusiastic discussion of the implications of the spectral integration hypothesis for the structure of vowel systems may be found in Bladon (1986).

## 6.6   The traditional vowel quadrilateral revisited

The plot of Figure 6.7 was constructed with the aim of producing a visual analogue of an auditory two-dimensional vowel space. For some phoneticians, however, another criterion has had major importance. This is that vowel charts constructed from formant frequencies should, as far as possible, resemble the traditional quadrilateral used in impressionistic description. Since the use of $F_1–F_2$ plots for descriptive purposes is increasing, it is clearly desirable that they should correspond as closely as possible to the articulatory-based quadrilateral which they are coming to replace. At the same time, it must be remembered that the goal of reproducing a phonetician's impressionistic description of vowels is somewhat different from the goal of psychological reality. We cannot simply assume that the vowel quadrilateral which appears on the IPA chart corresponds to a universal perceptual vowel space.

In general, the correspondence between $F_1–F_2$ plots and the vowel quadrilateral is better in the height (vertical) dimension than in the backness (horizontal) dimension. As regards the backness dimension, an obvious shortcoming is that our $F_1–F_2$ plots are too symmetrical. In the traditional quadrilateral, the right-hand side, corresponding to the back of the vowel space, is vertical, while the left-hand side slopes downward to the right.

One solution to the problem is to plot the difference between the first and second formants ($F_2–F_1$) rather than simply $F_2$ on the horizontal axis. This system has been particularly advocated by Ladefoged (Ladefoged 1975; Ladefoged and Maddieson 1990), who also uses a pitch-based scale (the mel scale or the Bark scale, Section 5.4.1) for both axes. An example of this type of

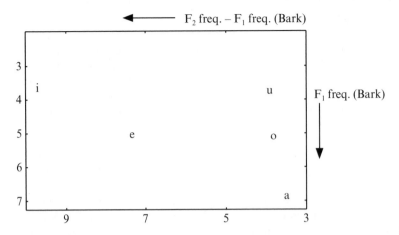

FIGURE 6.8    Average formant frequencies for the five distinctive vowels of KiMvita Swahili, pronounced by a male speaker from Mombasa (see Figure 6.1). Here, the difference between the frequencies of the first and second formants, rather than the second formant frequency, has been plotted on the horizontal axis.

chart, for the KiMvita vowels of Figure 6.1, is shown in Figure 6.8. Two steps are involved: (1) conversion of frequencies in Hz to the Bark scale and (2) calculation of $F_2$-$F_1$ from the Bark-scale values for each vowel.

In my view, the method of plotting ($F_2$-$F_1$) vs. $F_1$ is not very satisfactory because of its effect on the placing of central vowels. This is apparent in the plot of KiMvita vowels in Figure 6.8, which may be compared with Figure 6.1. The vowel /a/, which is, in traditional terms, low and central, appears to the right of the back vowels. For speakers whose back vowels are slightly centralised, with $F_2$ somewhat higher than expected, a low central /a/ will appear to be further back than vowels which are transcribed /ɔ/ or /u/; the effect can be more extreme for languages which have a back /ɑ/. In any case, as we have seen, the correspondence between $F_1$-$F_2$ plots and the vowel quadrilateral is straightforward only if front rounded and back unrounded vowels are left out of account.

A very different approach to the problem is proposed by Catford (1981), who suggests developing a new kind of $F_1$-$F_2$ plot which he calls *Cardinal Vowel Formant Charts*. This method involves devising a special frequency scale which ensures that the Cardinal Vowels are placed where they should be. It achieves the desired result but, in view of the complicated and somewhat *ad hoc* nature of the calculations, it is unlikely that it will come into general use.

## 6.7    Other dimensions of vowel classification

Height, backness and rounding were the three major articulatory dimensions used in the classification of vowels. If we think in purely acoustic terms, we have seen that the third dimension, that of rounding, does not appear to have a straightforward acoustic correlate. At present, it appears that rounded vowels are most easily distinguished from their unrounded counterparts by their distinctive formant frequencies rather than by other characteristics which might be defined independently of the formant frequencies.

Apart from rounding, there are other dimensions which may play a role in the classification of vowels. These are of two major types:

1  Lowering the soft palate. If the soft palate is lowered, allowing air to escape through the nasal cavity, a nasalised vowel will result.
2  Modification of the shape of the vocal tract tube away from its default shape. The traditional system of classifying vowels is based on the position of the highest point of the tongue hump. Implicit in this is an assumption that there is a usual or default overall shape for each possible tongue position. However, departures from this shape may occur. The pharynx may be expanded (by advancing the tongue root and/or lowering the larynx), to give *Advanced Tongue Root (ATR)* vowels. Conversely, the pharynx may be contracted (by retracting the tongue root and/or raising the larynx) to give *Retracted Tongue Root (RTR)* or *pharyngealised* vowels. A third possibility is that the vowel may be given an **R**-like quality (*rhoticity*), either by raising the tip of the tongue or by bunching up the body of the tongue and simultaneously constricting the pharynx.

As in the case of rounded vowels, we can ask two types of questions about these additional dimensions of vowel classification. On the one hand, we may ask what effect particular differences in articulation will have on a vowel's formant frequencies. On the other hand, we may look for differences which do not involve formant frequencies. Here, we shall concentrate on nasalised vowels and ATR vowels, and then give brief consideration to pharyngealisation and rhoticity.

### 6.7.1  Nasalised vowels

It has seemed obvious that nasal quality must involve some acoustic characteristic other than positioning of formant frequencies, if only because it is easily identified by people without phonetic training. At the same time, there is good reason to think that nasalisation cannot be totally independent of other aspects of vowel quality. Firstly, in languages which contrast nasalised and non-nasalised vowels, it is not uncommon for some oral vowels to lack nasalised counterparts, whereas no known language has more nasalised vowels than it has oral vowels. An extreme example is Standard French, which distinguishes at most four nasalised vowels (/ã/, /ɔ̃/, /ɛ̃/ and, for some speakers, also /œ̃/) beside its ten oral vowels (Figure 6.3a). This suggests that distinctions involving height, backness and/or rounding may be more difficult to perceive for nasalised vowels. Secondly, in some cases nasalised vowels have undergone historical shifts in quality. Typically, such shifts involve vowel height, with high vowels becoming lower and low vowels becoming higher (Beddor 1982). These tendencies cannot readily be explained in articulatory terms, since the position of the soft palate is, in principle, independent of the position and shaping of the tongue. It thus seems likely that nasalisation may affect the perception of vowel quality – in particular, vowel 'height' – and any account of the perception of nasalisation must provide some explanation for this.

We have seen (Section 4.6.1) that lowering the soft palate during the production of a vowel results in both new resonances (formants or poles) and new anti-resonances (antiformants or zeros) at certain frequencies, and that this affects the overall shape of the spectrum. The most prominent modifications are at low frequencies, in the region of $F_1$. For most vowels, the low-frequency peak associated with $F_1$ becomes broader and generally less well-defined.

This effect of nasalisation is illustrated in Figure 6.9, which shows a spectrogram of the Yorùbá minimal pair **ìrì** 'dew' and **ìrìn** (/ìrĩ/) 'walk' pronounced by a male speaker. In this language, intervocalic sonorant consonants, including the tapped /r/ ([ɾ]), are nasalised when they are followed by a nasalised vowel, and so the /r/ of the second word is also a nasalised sound. Below the spectrogram are narrow-band FFT spectra of the vowels in the second syllables. The oral vowel is on the left, while the nasalised vowel is on the right. In the oral vowel, the peak associated with $F_1$ is quite narrow and well-defined, while in the nasalised vowel, the slope down from the corresponding peak is more gradual, and there is an additional resonance ($F_N$) above $F_1$. This difference between the two vowels is also visible in the spectrogram. In the fully oral word on the left, the upper edge of the horizontal bar associated with $F_1$ is clearly defined. In the word on the right, the effects of nasalisation begin to appear towards the end of the first vowel, when an additional dark area appears above the $F_1$ bar. This continues throughout the /r/ and also the second vowel. Finally, we should note that there is a sharp dip in the spectrum of the nasalised vowel just above $F_N$, which is likely to reflect to the presence of the antiformant (zero).

The broadening and flattening of the low-frequency prominence associated with $F_1$ is an expected result of adding a paired resonance and anti-resonance (pole–zero pair) to the vocal tract filter function (Section 4.6.1). The effect may be simulated by simply adding energy to a synthetic vowel in the region of the first formant (Delattre 1954). There is some evidence that a broader and flatter $F_1$ prominence can be utilised by listeners as a cue for nasality (Hawkins and Stevens 1984). Alternatively, listeners might be sensitive to the presence of the extra peak associated with the nasal formant $F_N$ (Rosner and Pickering 1994). However, the possibility that listeners may utilise other cues, relating to higher-frequency parts of the spectrum, also needs to be investigated.

There has also been some interest in the implications of the spectral integration hypothesis for the perception of nasalised vowels. We cannot take up this matter here, and the reader is referred to articles by Beddor and her colleagues (Beddor 1982, 1991; Beddor *et al.* 1986; Beddor and Hawkins 1990).

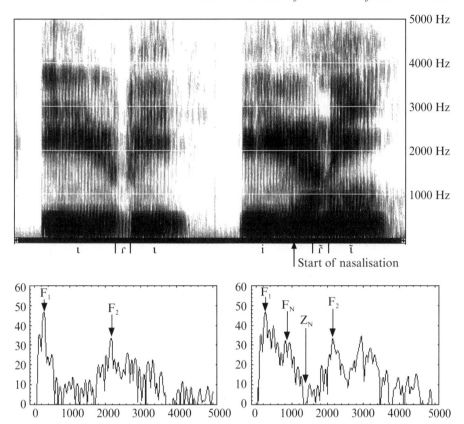

FIGURE 6.9    Broad band spectrograms of the Yorùbá words **ìrì** 'dew' and **ìrìn** (/ìrĩ̀/) 'walk' pronounced by a male speaker. Below each spectrogram is an FFT spectrum taken from the middle of the vowel of the second syllable. In the oral vowel (on the left), the narrow peak of the first formant dominates the lower part of the spectrum. In the nasalised vowel (on the right), an additional nasal formant $F_N$, appears to the right of $F_1$, making the downward overall slope of the spectrum more gradual. A sudden drop in amplitude, which would seem to reflect the presence of a nasal zero $Z_N$, is also visible. The effects of nasalisation, which begin before the end of the first vowel, can also be seen in the spectrogram.

### 6.7.2  Advanced Tongue Root (ATR) vowels

ATR vowels are characterised by a relatively large pharyngeal cavity. In general, expanding the pharyngeal cavity will cause lowering of $F_1$, and so we expect that [+ ATR] vowels will be located higher on a conventional $F_1$–$F_2$ plot than their non-ATR counterparts. This is indeed the case. Figure 6.10, taken from Ladefoged and Maddieson (1990, 1996), shows plots for the vowels of six 'ATR languages', five from West Africa (Nigeria and Ghana) and one from the Sudan (Dho Luo). The [+ ATR] vowels are picked out by the subscript diacritic ˌ. In accordance with Ladefoged's practice (Section 6.6), $(F_2$–$F_1)$ rather

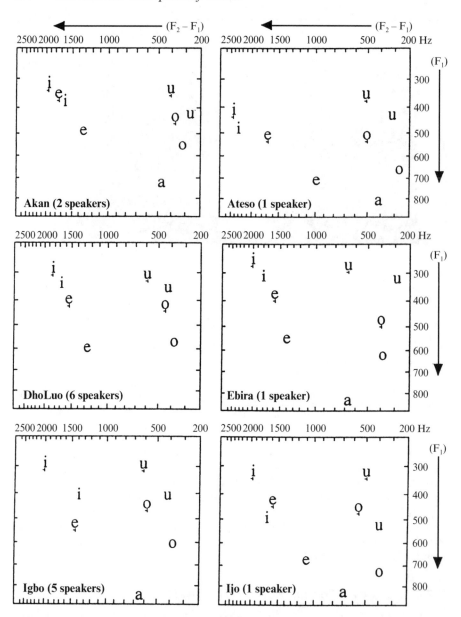

FIGURE 6.10  Average formant frequencies for the vowels of six African languages which distinguish [+ ATR] and [– ATR] vowels. These plots were constructed in the same way as the plot of Swahili vowels in Figure 6.8. The [+ ATR] vowels are picked out by the subscript diacritic ̧. From Ladefoged and Maddieson (1996).

than $F_2$ is plotted on the horizontal axis. Although the axes are labelled in Hz, they are scaled according to the Bark scale.

Without exception, each [+ ATR] vowel is higher (i.e. has lower $F_1$ frequency) than its [− ATR] counterpart on these plots. Another feature which requires mention is the somewhat centralised position of the [+ ATR] back rounded vowels, most frequently /u/ but also /o/. Ladefoged and Maddieson suggest that centralisation of these vowels relative to their [− ATR] counterparts might be diagnostic of ATR contrasts. This would contrast with the situation in languages such as English or German, which distinguish vowels which are conventionally transcribed with the symbols /u/ (as in **food**) and /ʊ/ (as in **good**). (The /u/–/ʊ/ contrast is often said to be similar to the [± ATR] /ʉ/–/u/ contrast.) It should be borne in mind, however, that any apparent centralisation of [+ ATR] /ʉ/ and /o̞/ will be exaggerated by the practice of plotting $(F_2-F_1)$ rather than $F_2$ on the horizontal axis. (If $F_1$ is lowered while $F_2$ remains stable, the distance between $F_1$ and $F_2$ will increase.) Also, it is possible that a vowel which is conventionally transcribed as /u/ may be equally centralised in a 'non-ATR' language. Southern British English (where the vowel /u/ found in words such as **food** is coming to be pronounced as a central vowel, especially among younger speakers) would be a case in point. Thus, it is doubtful that a central position of vowels transcribed as /u/ and/or /o/ relative to vowels transcribed as /ʊ/ and/or /ɔ/ can really be taken as diagnostic of a system with a [± ATR] contrast.

The question remains as to whether there is any feature intrinsic to the spectra of [+ ATR] vowels which serves to distinguish them from their [− ATR] counterparts. Such a feature may be related to perceived voice quality. A number of linguists who have worked on 'ATR languages' have reported that the two types of vowels typically exhibit distinctive voice qualities, the [+ ATR] type sounding more 'hollow' or 'breathy' than its [− ATR] counterpart.

The ATR contrast in Kwawu (an Akan language) has been studied from this point of view by Hess (1992), who reports that, at least for the speaker she studied, the most consistent difference between [+ ATR] and [− ATR] vowels lies in the bandwidth of the first formant, which is wider for the [− ATR] type. On the other hand, in a fuller study involving six speakers of another West African 'ATR language', Degema, Fulop (1996) found that the relative strength of $F_1$ and $F_2$ served, at least in most cases, to distinguish between the two types, with $F_1$ and $F_2$ being closer in amplitude in the [− ATR] vowels.

Both types of differences are illustrated in Figure 6.11, which shows two FFT spectra of the low-toned verbal prefix **bè** pronounced by a female speaker of another Akan language, Asante Twi. (This particle is pronounced with either a [+ ATR] vowel or a [− ATR] vowel, in agreement with the vowel of the root it is attached to.) In the [+ ATR] version, transcribed /e/, the $F_1$ peak is noticeably narrower than in the [− ATR] version, transcribed /ɛ/. At the same time, $F_1$ and $F_2$ are closer in amplitude in the [− ATR] version.

Hess' and Fulop's proposals need to be tested on more speakers of more languages before any firm conclusions can be reached. A final point is that the

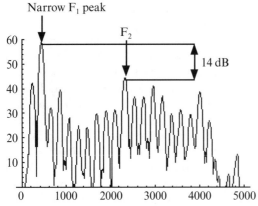

(a) /e/ in /òbètú/ 'He comes and digs it up.'

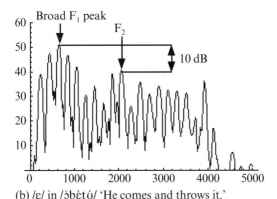

(b) /ɛ/ in /ɔ̀bɛ̀tʊ́/ 'He comes and throws it.'

FIGURE 6.11    FFT spectra of the vowels /e/ ([+ ATR]) and /ɛ/ ([– ATR]) pronounced by a female speaker of Asante Twi. The spectrum of /ɛ/ illustrates two reported characteristics of [– ATR] vowels: (1) a broader and less well-defined $F_1$ peak and (2) a smaller difference in amplitude between $F_1$ and $F_2$.

wider bandwidth of the first formant appears to function as a cue for nasalisation (Section 6.7.1). Since, at least in West Africa, many languages with ATR contrasts also make use of distinctive nasalisation, we must ask how the two dimensions interact. (In my experience, voice quality contrasts between [+ ATR] and [– ATR] vowels are considerably more difficult to hear when the vowels in question are nasalised.) This is a question for future research. A thorough investigation of the problem might shed more light on the nature of acoustic cues for nasality as well as on the natures of cues for the [± ATR] contrast.

### 6.7.3 Rhoticity and pharyngealisation

Rhoticised vowels are defined by their perceived **R**-like character. They are found in only a few languages, but, since one of those languages is American English, they have been the subject of a number of investigations.

American English has one phonemic rhoticised vowel, which is found in words such as **bird**, **fur** and **heard**, and is commonly symbolised /ɚ/. The most obvious acoustic characteristic of this vowel is its markedly low $F_3$, a feature which it shares with consonantal /r/ in both American and Southern British pronunciations (Section 7.8.4 and Figure 7.18). Presumably it is the low position of $F_3$ which gives this vowel its distinctive character. If the spectral integration hypothesis (Section 6.4) is correct, then /ɚ/ is highly unusual in showing a strong peak, resulting from integration of $F_2$ and $F_3$, in the middle of the range of possible $F_2$ values. In the classification scheme of Section 6.5, /ɚ/ stands out as unique because of the lack of integration of $F_4$ and $F_3$.

Interestingly, lowered $F_3$ has also been reported as characteristic of pharyngealised vowels (Catford 1983; Ladefoged and Maddieson 1996). The effects of pharyngealisation on the spectra of vowels, and the nature of similarities and differences between pharyngealisation and rhoticity are also interesting topics for future research.

## 6.8   Diphthongs

Diphthongs are vowels which change in quality. In impressionistic transcriptions, it is standard practice to represent diphthongs as a sequence of two vowels, one corresponding to the starting position and one to the ending position. For example, the diphthong of English **buy** is commonly transcribed /aɪ/. On spectrograms, we typically see a smooth and gradual transition from one quality to another. An example is the spectrogram of **buy** shown in Figure 6.12.

The extent to which languages vary in their realisation of the 'same' diphthongs remains a matter for further study. In the example of Figure 6.12, there are two identifiable steady states, corresponding to the /a/ and /ɪ/ portions of the diphthong and a relatively quick transition between them. It is also possible for diphthongs to occur in which the transition is relatively longer, taking up a greater portion of the whole. Correspondingly, the steady states are relatively shorter in such cases (Lindau *et al.* 1990). A historical overview of proposals for describing and classifying the diphthongs of American English, which could be extended to diphthongs in other languages, is provided by Gottfried *et al.* (1993).

## 6.9   Alternative approaches to vowel quality

From the beginning in this chapter, we have assumed that formant frequencies are the primary determinants of vowel quality. We have suggested that the three major articulatory dimensions of vowel classification (height, backness and rounding) might correspond to two dimensions of acoustic classification, namely effective $F_1$ and effective $F_2$. For the secondary articulatory dimensions (nasalisation, ATR, rhoticity, pharyngealisation), additional dimensions appear to be necessary. It is possible that these secondary characteristics are associated with other types of cues. For example, nasalisation might be associated with a

510 msec

a          Transition          ɪ

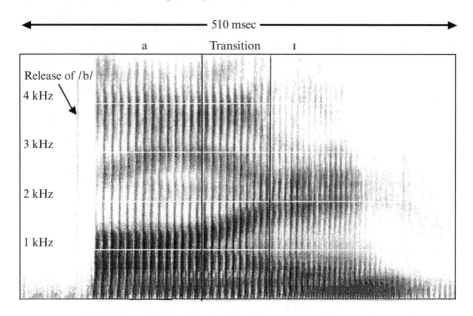

Release of /b/

4 kHz

3 kHz

2 kHz

1 kHz

FIGURE 6.12   Spectrogram of English **buy** (/baɪ/), pronounced by a male speaker. In this example, it is possible to pick out sections corresponding to the /a/ and /ɪ/ portions, and a transition which links the two. Some movement of the upper formants is visible following the release of /b/; this represents the transition from consonant to vowel (Section 7.2.1).

broadening and flattening of the spectral peak corresponding to $F_1$. Another possibility is that three spectral peaks need to be taken into account rather than two. For example, retroflex and pharyngealised vowels might be accounted for by a third acoustic dimension corresponding to effective $F_3$.

This is not the only possible approach to the study of vowel quality, and in this section we shall take note of a few alternatives. One possibility is that the overall spectral shape is of primary importance. This is adopted as a working hypothesis by Bladon and Lindblom (1981) in a well-known article which attempts to quantify perceptual distance between vowels by evaluating the degree of overlap of their auditory spectra. The idea that the overall shape of the spectrum as a whole is primary has also proved attractive to some phonologists. A good example of this is the discussion of phonological 'elements' in Harris (1994). Harris' theory postulates three primary elements I, A and U, all of which are defined in terms of spectral shape templates. This is dipping for I (prominence at both high and low frequencies), sloping downwards to the right for U (prominence at low frequencies) and peaking in the centre for A.

All of the approaches discussed so far are similar in that they focus on the static, steady-state part of the spoken vowel. Another, still more radically different possibility is to focus on the dynamic characteristics of vowels, in particular the formant trajectories in CVC syllables. Unfortunately, only a few perceptual studies have involved manipulating the time course of formant trajectories in synthesized words. A more common type of experiment involves the perception of 'silent centre' syllables, in which subjects are asked to identify syllables from which the central portions, containing the steady state of the vowel, have been removed. The fact that subjects do rather well in such tasks indicates that listeners can make use of dynamic as well as of static information about spectral structure – indeed, given that the spectrum of speech is constantly changing, it would be surprising if listeners did not make use of such information. Strange (1989a, 1989b) provides a good overview of studies based on this approach, which she terms *dynamic specification*.

## 6.10   The problem of normalisation

Nearly all of the vowel charts, and most of the examples, presented in this chapter have been based on male speakers. The problem of how to describe vowels becomes more difficult when women's and children's voices are taken into account. In general, women have higher formant frequencies than men and children have higher formant fequencies than women. This is because women and children have smaller vocal tracts. However, the magnitude of the difference also varies from vowel to vowel. For example, in a study based on data from American English and Swedish speakers, Fant (1973: 87) reports an average female $F_1$ / male $F_1$ ratio of 30% for American English /æ/ but a corresponding ratio of only 2% for American English /ɚ/. Such differences are due to the fact that the relative length of the pharyngeal cavity (considered as a portion of the whole) is smaller in women and children than in men (Fant 1973: Chapter 4).

The ability to abstract phonetic sameness from the diversity which exists across speakers is known as *normalisation*. The topic of normalisation is a complex one and may be approached in a variety of ways. A distinction is sometimes drawn between theories of *intrinsic* and *extrinsic* specification of vowel quality. Intrinsic specification means that all information necessary to identify a vowel is contained within the vowel itself. For example, Syrdal's (1985) and Syrdal and Gopal's (1986) studies of American English vowels (Section 6.5) had intrinsic specification as one of their main concerns. They argued that, when differences between pairs of formants ($F_1$ and $F_2$, $F_2$ and $F_3$, etc.) or between $F_1$ and $F_0$ were used to classify vowels, differences between talkers were greatly reduced. Accordingly, listeners might base their identification of particular vowels on distances between effective formant frequencies rather than on the effective frequencies themselves. Such a procedure, if it works, would eliminate the need for normalisation, since differences between talkers would be minimal.

By contrast, theories of extrinsic specification take it as given that the listener must adjust his or her vowel recognition procedures to the characteristics of the talker's voice. On this view, the boundaries of the talker's vowel space must be determined as needed from the immediately preceding context. For example, hearing someone say **hi** (/haɪ/) would give some clues as to what formant frequencies should be expected for low central-to-back and high front vowels. A good overview of intrinsic and extrinsic approaches to the normalisation problem may be found in Nearey (1989).

To conclude this section, we should note that normalisation is not a serious problem for some theories of speech perception. In the Direct Realist approach, which argues that the listener recovers the talker's articulatory gestures directly, there is no need to suppose that the listener must tune in to the talker's $F_1$–$F_2$ space. In the case of exemplar-based models, it is supposed that vowels (and speech sounds generally) will be recognised on the basis of their similarity to other vowels stored in the listener's memory. The exemplars stored in memory incorporate information about talker characteristics as well as about phonetic identity. The fact that a new vowel is similar to other vowels produced by the same speaker as well as to the 'same' vowel produced by different speakers, aids the listener in identification (Johnson 1997).

## 6.11   Predicting the structure of vowel systems

It is common practice among linguists to think of vowels not just as isolated segments but as members of a system of contrasts. For example, we might speak of 'the vowel system of Southern British English' or 'the vowel system of Parisian French'. Certain systems are extremely common and others rare or non-existent. For example, systems with five contrasting vowels of the type /i e a o u/ are found in many languages but no one has yet reported a language which has a five-vowel system consisting of /y ø ʌ ɤ ɯ/. It seems that languages show a striking preference for vowels around the periphery of the acoustic vowel quadrilateral, and it has long been supposed that this preference must reflect a tendency to maximise perceptual contrast. According to the *vowel dispersion hypothesis*, languages tend to disperse their vowels in the perceptual vowel space in such a way as to make them maximally contrastive; for example, the optimal three-vowel system would be /i a u/.

How can we test the hypothesis that vowel systems tend to be built around maximal perceptual contrast? One way is to develop a model to generate vowel systems based on maximum dispersion of vowels within a perceptual vowel space. For any given number of vowels, the model should predict what the most common vowel system(s) should be; for example, the optimal three-vowel system would be /i a u/. If the predictions are correct, we have evidence to support the hypothesis. There are three prerequisites to carrying out such an activity. Firstly, the space of possible vowels must be determined and each phonetic vowel quality must be defined. Secondly, it is necessary to be able to measure perceptual distance. Thirdly, enough data must be available about vowel systems from a wide variety of languages to enable tendencies to be picked out with confidence.

The most thorough investigations of this type have been carried out by Liljencrants and Lindblom (1972) and Lindblom (1986). In both cases, an articulatory model was used to generate the total space of possible vowel

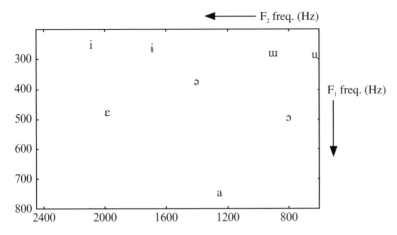

FIGURE 6.13 Optimal eight-vowel system, as predicted by Lindblom's *vowel dispersion model*. After Lindblom (1986).

articulations. The main difference between the earlier and later papers lies in the way in which perceptual distances were calculated. In the earlier paper, distances were based on differences between formant frequencies. In the later paper, a more sophisticated method was used, based on comparisons of entire spectra (see Section 6.8). A set of nineteen quasi-Cardinal Vowels, with formant frequencies appropriate for a male speaker, was taken as the starting point. Two types of transformed spectra were calculated, giving two separate but similar sets of results. 'Systems' of 3, 4, 5, 6, and so on, vowels were selected in such a way as to maximise the distance between all possible pairs in the system. Figure 6.13 shows the optimal eight-vowel system predicted by one of the two sets of calculations.

In its preference for peripheral vowels, the model agrees well with data from actual languages, but there are some discrepancies. The most serious of these is its preference for high 'interior' vowels, so that, for example, the seven-vowel system shows two vowels between [i] and [u] but no mid-central [ə]. (Contrast the not uncommon Amharic system of Figure 6.4.) The seven-vowel triangular system /i e ɛ a ɔ o u/ of languages such as Italian or Yorùbá is not predicted. Nor, as Disner (1984) points out in her discussion of vowel dispersion, do the calculations reflect a hierarchy observed in natural languages, whereby, of the three 'corner' vowels, /i/, /a/ and /u/, the last is most likely to be missing from a phonological inventory (/i/, /a/ > /u/). Still, despite such problems, Disner concludes that the agreement of phonological systems with the model is extremely good and 'a vowel dispersion theory correctly captures a principle governing the distribution of vowels in natural language' (Disner 1984: 154).

One unavoidable practical problem which arises in evaluating any predictions concerning vowel dispersion is the difficulty of relating the vowel qualities reported for actual languages to the qualities used for the purposes of the model. This issue is important because it is only possible to test a model by comparing its predicted systems with systems which are actually attested in languages. Two large-scale surveys of vowel systems, by Crothers (1978) and Maddieson (1984) (only the first of which was available to Lindblom), are now available, both based largely on published phonological descriptions. Such descriptions report vowel qualities in terms of phonetic symbols rather than formant frequencies or spectra, and there is often variation in the qualities associated with particular symbols. This is well-illustrated by the vowels commonly transcribed with the symbol **u**, which may have low $F_2$, close to $F_1$ (as in Thai) or higher $F_2$, more separated from $F_1$ (as in American – and also in Southern British – English or Amharic). Furthermore, as Maddieson (1997: 638) points out, the $F_1$–$F_2$ space may be smaller for languages with small numbers of distinctive vowels than for languages with large numbers of distinctive vowels. For example, the /u/ of a large vowel system may be higher and more back and have more extreme formant frequencies than the /u/ of a three-vowel system.

## 6.12  Summary

In acoustic studies of vowel quality, primary importance is attached to the frequencies of the vowel formants during the steady state of the vowel. This reflects not only the importance of formants in the source-filter theory of speech production, but also the probability that formants play a major role in vowel perception. A further reason for the emphasis on formants is the resemblance between acoustic vowel charts, based on plotting $F_1$ frequency vs. $F_2$ frequency, and the impressionistic vowel quadrilateral. This resemblance has made it possible to use $F_1$–$F_2$ plots for descriptive linguistic purposes. It has also raised questions about the relationship between the dimensions of impressionistic vowel description, measurable acoustic characteristics of vowels, and dimensions of vowel perception.

The impressionistic description of vowels is based on the three major dimensions of height, backness and rounding. On an $F_1$–$F_2$ plot, the placing of a vowel in the $F_1$ dimension appears to depend primarily on its height, whilst its placing in the $F_2$ dimension depends both on backness and rounding. As regards the other minor dimensions of vowel classification (nasalisation, ATR, pharyngealisation, rhoticity), these may have additional acoustic correlates which can be defined independently of a vowel's placing on an $F_1$–$F_2$ plot. For example, nasalised vowels appear to be characterised by a broad relatively flat low-frequency peak ($F_1$). More research is needed in this area. In the past, phoneticians engaged in descriptive linguistic work tended to concentrate exclusively on measuring formant frequencies. However, now that digital speech analysis has made other types of measurements (for example, formant bandwidths) easier, considerable progress can be expected in the near future.

As regards vowel perception, the idea that vowel formants might define a two-dimensional perceptual vowel space has proved to be an attractive one. In defining such a space, it is necessary to use the *effective* formant frequencies, perceived by the listener, rather than the *nominal* formant frequencies, which are what the techniques of speech analysis are designed to measure.

The hypothesized perceptual vowel space may also shed light on more purely linguistic problems. One idea which has been attractive is the vowel dispersion hypothesis, according to which languages tend to disperse their vowels in the perceptual vowel space in such a way as to make them maximally contrastive. We have also seen that the spectral integration hypothesis might provide a basis for a system of binary features for vowels. However, more work needs to be done with acoustic data recorded from actual languages (as opposed to models).

We have also seen that formant-based approaches to defining vowel quality are not entirely unproblematic. A major difficulty is explaining *normalisation*, that is, how listeners tune in to the vowel spaces of particular speakers. The role played by more dynamic aspects of vowels, in particular the transitions to and from flanking consonants, also needs to be clarified.

Another area of interest for linguists is the possibility of predicting the structure of vowel systems. It has long been observed that languages show a preference for vowels which are located around the periphery of the vowel quadrilateral. This has suggested the hypothesis that vowel systems must, as it were, be designed to maximise perceptual contrast. Various studies have attempted to determine the maximally dispersed vowel qualities for vowel systems of particular sizes (for example, the optimal seven-vowel system). In general, the results have been consistent with expectations, but some problems remain. These reflect both the theoretical difficulties inherent in calculating perceptual distance and the practical difficulties involved in relating theoretical systems obtained by calculation to descriptions of vowel systems which report vowel qualities in terms of impressionistic-phonetic symbols.

## 6.13  Further reading

Borden *et al.* (1994), Clark and Yallop (1990), Denes and Pinson (1993), Fry (1979), Johnson (1997), Kent and Read (1992), Lieberman and Blumstein (1988) and Pickett (1980) all provide introductions to vowel formants, vowel charts and vowel perception. Kent *et al.* (1996), devoted entirely to American English, is also to be recommended. Ladefoged and Maddieson's work (1990, 1996) is the most comprehensive from a cross-linguistic point of view and includes discussion of vowels from a wide spectrum of languages. Rosner and Pickering (1994) is a full-length and detailed work covering both production and perception, and includes a very full bibliography. Stevens (1998) includes an excellent account of production and perception, with a focus on acoustic aspects.

Measuring vowel formants can be more difficult than most elementary introductions suggest. Ladefoged (1967) and Ladefoged and Bladon (1982) are excellent discussions of the practical difficulties involved in measuring vowel formants. Ladefoged (1967) also includes an account of the history of vowel classification.

# Chapter 7

# The acoustic description of consonants

## 7.1 Introduction

From the point of view of acoustics and perception, consonants present more difficulties than vowels. It is no accident that the debate about the specialness of speech (Section 5.2.3) has centred around evidence concerning the perception of consonants. There are two main reasons for this.

Firstly, vowels contain more information about themselves within themselves. In Chapter 6, we saw that any vowel can be located in a two-dimensional vowel space on the basis of information derived from its formant pattern. The formant pattern is an inherent part of the vowel itself, and it exists all at once during the time when the vocal organs are in the target position for the vowel. By contrast, it is common for essential information about a consonant to appear in the acoustic signal before and/or after the vocal organs have assumed the target position for the consonant. For example, in the English words **spy**, **sty** and **sky**, the target positions for the stop consonants (/p/, /t/ and /k/) – in which there is a complete closure in the mouth and the vocal folds are not vibrating – will correspond only to silence in the acoustic signal. In order to distinguish between the three stop consonants (and the three words), it is necessary to attend to the transitions to the following vowel (/aɪ/). Because information relevant to individual consonants overlaps with preceding and following speech sounds, it is not possible to divide the acoustic signal up into neat segments, each complete in itself.

Secondly, the basic dimensions of the two-dimensional vowel chart are of the same type (they are based on frequency), and consequently are measured in the same units such as Hz or Bark. A two- or three-dimensional plot based on formant frequencies would be a straightforward and obvious visual display, even if it did not correspond so closely to the impressionistic vowel quadrilateral. By contrast, any acoustic classification of consonants must bring together a number of acoustic dimensions of different types, including not only frequency but also intensity and timing. Different acoustic dimensions are relevant in different cases. There is no simple and obvious way of converting acoustic measurements into general charts for consonants and there is no commonly accepted consonantal counterpart to the $F_1$–$F_2$ plot used for vowels.

Because of the great variety of consonants found in the world's languages and the great variety of acoustic dimensions which play a role in describing and classifying them, it is not possible to give a complete account of the acoustics of consonants in a short chapter. Since English is the best-studied language as regards the acoustics and perception of consonants, the discussion here will be largely (though not exclusively) concerned with English sounds. We shall also concentrate on single consonants between vowels.

## 7.2   General concepts

### 7.2.1   *Intervals and transitions*

The production of any consonant involves contact or at least close approxima-tion between two articulators at some 'place' between the larynx and the lips. This constriction is maintained for a certain length of time, and will have particular acoustic consequences. For example, Figure 7.1 shows the /ʃ/ of English **a shark**. The strong band of noisy energy, which fills the upper part of the spectrogram (above about 1500 Hz), represents the audible friction which is generated during the period of constriction. We shall refer to the time corres-ponding to the constriction as the *constriction interval*.

A consonantal constriction does not just happen; the articulators must move into their target position and then move away to the target position for the following sound. When a vowel precedes or follows, these movements will be reflected in movements of the vowel's formants from or to their steady-state values. These movements are known as the *formant transitions*. In the case of the vowel /ɑ/ of **shark** in Figure 7.1, the movements of $F_2$ and $F_3$ (the $F_2$

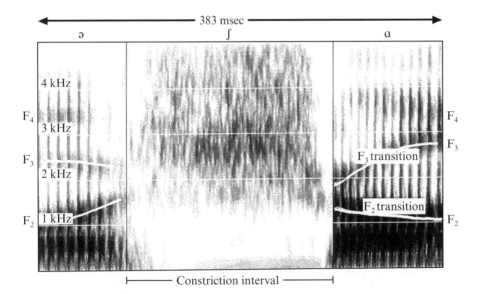

FIGURE 7.1   Spectrogram of English /ʃ/ in the sentence **We saw a shark**, pronounced by a male speaker.

*transition* and the $F_3$ *transition*) can be seen clearly at the onset of the vowel. Similar, though not identical, transitions, moving in the opposite direction, can be seen at the end of the preceding vowel /ə/. Of course, if there is no preceding or following vowel – for example if the consonant occurs after or before a pause – there will be no corresponding transitions.

Finally, we must consider the activity of the vocal folds and its acoustic consequences. If the consonant is voiceless the constriction interval will be accompanied by a voiceless interval, when the vocal folds are not vibrating and no low-frequency striations will be visible on the spectrogram (see Section 5.2.1). In our example /ʃ/, the constriction interval and the voiceless interval nearly coincide (though there is a slight gap between the end of the friction and the onset of voicing for the /ɑ/). In the case of aspirated consonants, the voiceless interval extends beyond the constriction interval, resulting in a long Voice Onset Time (Section 5.2.1).

### 7.2.2   Acoustic dimensions in the description and classification of consonants

We have already noted that, in contrast to vowels, the acoustic description of consonants depends not only on what happens during the constriction interval itself but also on what immediately precedes or follows. To begin, I shall list three general types of acoustic information which are relevant, both within and outside the constriction interval itself.

1   Presence or absence of aperiodic energy. For example, aperiodic energy – which may be continuous noise or transient (Section 2.3) – during the constriction interval distinguishes obstruent consonants (stops, fricatives and affricates) from voiced sonorants. Presence of continuous noise following the interval, overlapping with the formant transitions, is characteristic of aspirated (as opposed to unaspirated) consonants.[1]

2   Timing. For example, voiced obstruents tend to have shorter constriction intervals than voiceless obstruents. Outside the constriction interval, a contrast between quick and gradual formant transitions is important in distinguishing between semivowels on the one hand and voiced stops and nasals on the other (for example, [w] vs. [b] and [m]).

3   Spectral structure. For example, the nasal [n] and the lateral [l], which have some general characteristics in common, show differences in their spectra during the constriction interval. Outside the interval, for all consonants the starting points and trajectories of the formant transitions (both preceding and following) play a major role as cues for place of articulation.

All three of the main acoustic dimensions just mentioned (presence vs. absence of aperiodic energy, timing, spectral structure) are necessary to define the impressionistic-phonetic categories of place of articulation, manner of articulation and voicing in acoustic terms.

### 7.2.3  *Acoustic boundaries and consonants*

Another way of approaching the description of consonants, at least when they occur before vowels, is to compare the spectrum of the interval sound with the spectrum of the onset of the following vowel. For example, to compare /ʃ/ with /a/ in Figure 7.1, we should note that the lower edge of the band of noise in /ʃ/ (just below 2000 Hz) is at roughly the same height at the onset of $F_3$ for /a/. The darkest part of the band (just below 3000 Hz) is between $F_3$ and $F_4$.

The general hypothesis behind this approach is that the *acoustic boundary* between consonant and vowel is of particular importance for the listener. It is at acoustic boundaries that abrupt changes occur in the spectrum to which the auditory system may be particularly sensitive (Section 5.3.4). To quote Stevens (1985b: 253), 'Either the acoustic correlates of phonetic features consist of specification of how the spectrum is changing in this region, or the region provides a landmark that indicates where nearby spectral or temporal information is to be sampled.'

I shall now give an overview of the acoustic characteristics of various types of consonants, organised according to manner of articulation.

## 7.3  Stop consonants[2]

### 7.3.1  *General characteristics of stop consonants*

During the production of stop consonants, there is a complete closure somewhere in the vocal tract, cutting off the airstream from the lungs. The soft palate is raised, so that air cannot escape through the nasal cavity. If the vocal folds are not vibrating, no sound will be produced at all, resulting in a period of silence. On the other hand, during the closure period, air pressure is building up behind the closure. If a vowel immediately follows, release of the closure will be accompanied by a brief burst of noise, appropriately known as the *burst*. Stop consonants may also show release bursts when they occur before a pause or before another consonant, though this will vary depending on the language, the speaker and the speaking style.

The constriction interval for a stop consonant, accordingly, consists of silence or near-silence. It is often referred to as the *silent interval* or the *stop gap*. The interval ends with the release of pressure at the burst. This is generally easy to locate on a spectrogram, because it corresponds to a brief vertical spike, though it is weaker for labials than for other places of articulation. In contrast, the beginning of the interval is often difficult to locate precisely. This is not surprising when we remember that, unlike the burst, the blocking of the airstream is not a sudden event but occurs more gradually as the articulators come together. Also, although the articulators are together and the soft palate is raised, the seal may not be absolutely complete. Accordingly, some acoustic energy may be visible (as faint shading) during the interval itself. These general characteristics are apparent in the stop consonants illustrated in Figures 7.2–7.4.

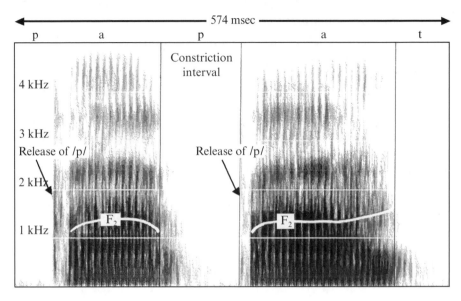

FIGURE 7.2    Spectrogram of the Javanese word **papat** 'four', pronounced by a male speaker from East Java.

### 7.3.2    *Voicing and aspiration*

Any account of voicing in stop consonants runs the risk of confusing the reader because the terms *voiced* and *voiceless* are used in two distinct ways. On the one hand, they may be used as phonetic terms to designate presence or absence of vocal fold vibration during the consonantal interval. On the other hand, they may be used to refer to opposed members of a phonological contrast which might or might not be pronounced as their labels suggest. For example, English /b d g/ are usually described as 'voiced stops' in opposition to 'voiceless' /p t k/ even though they may be produced without any vocal fold vibration during the closure. As in Section 5.2, I shall use *voiced* and *voiceless* as phonetic terms. When the terms are used in a more abstract, phonological way (as when referring to the contrast between English /p t k/ and /b d g/), I shall use [− voiced] and [+ voiced].

To illustrate voiceless unaspirated and fully voiced stops, I shall draw examples from languages other than English. Figure 7.2 shows a spectrogram of the Javanese word **papat** 'four', pronounced by a male speaker from East Java. The speaker paused both before and after the word, which was part of a counting sequence, and so there is no indication of where the constriction interval begins for the first /p/ or of when the constriction interval ends for the final /t/, which is unreleased. The bursts of the two /p/s, which are voiceless and unaspirated, are clearly visible, though the first is somewhat stronger than the second. The gap corresponding to the second /p/ is also clear, though it is somewhat difficult to say exactly where it begins. Similarly, it is difficult to pinpoint

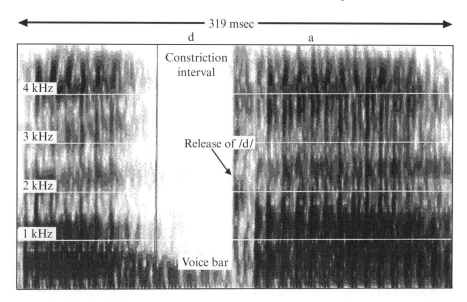

FIGURE 7.3    Spectrogram of Italian /d/ in the sentence **Dico d̲ata così**, pronounced by a male speaker from Sardinia.

the beginning of the constriction interval for the final /t/. In this particular instance, the end of the bars corresponding to the higher formants was taken to be the end of the vowel.

For fully voiced stop consonants, a low-frequency *voice bar* (Section 5.2.1) can be seen throughout the constriction interval. An example is shown in Figure 7.3, which shows the /d/ of Italian **data** 'date' extracted from the phrase **dico data** 'I say **data**', pronounced by a male speaker from Sardinia. The voice bar is darker at the beginning than at the end of the constriction interval. This reflects a general tendency for voicing to weaken and become more breathy in character over the course of the interval. Indeed, it is not uncommon for the voice bar to fade out altogether before the interval comes to an end. (The reasons for this will be discussed in Section 8.3.9.) Thus, even fully voiced stops may appear to be slightly aspirated. In my experience, such fading out is often less marked and is less commonly observed in absolute initial position. (In this regard, the /d/ of Figure 7.3 may be compared with the initial /d/ of Figure 5.2.) As already mentioned (Section 5.2.1), the English [+ voiced] stops /b/, /d/ and /g/ are frequently produced without voicing in absolute initial position.

It remains to give an example of an intervocalic voiceless aspirated stop. Figure 7.4 shows an example of English aspirated /k/ in **a car**. Here, the burst stands out as a dark spike at the beginning of the aspiration noise. In this case, the transitions can be seen as darker bands in the aspiration noise; by the time the striations appear, they have nearly reached their steady-state values. The spectrogram of English **tore** in Figure 5.1 provides an example of an aspirated stop in absolute initial position.

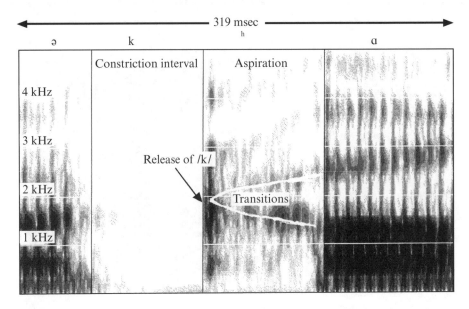

FIGURE 7.4   Spectrogram showing the English aspirated /k/ in the sentence
**We bought a car**.

To sum up, prototypical stop consonants are defined acoustically by a
constriction interval of silence which typically ends with the burst. The voiceless unaspirated and aspirated types differ in that, in the unaspirated case, the
voiceless interval comes to an end at about the same time as the constriction
interval, with the voicing for a following vowel beginning immediately after the
release. If there is aspiration, the voiceless interval extends beyond the constriction interval, overlapping with the formant transitions for the following vowel.
In the case of fully voiced stops, the constriction interval is not totally silent,
since the vocal folds continue to vibrate. Low-frequency striations, known as
the *voice bar*, will be visible.

### 7.3.3  Place of articulation

It should be clear that no information about place of articulation can be contained within the stop gap. Even if a voice bar is present, its acoustic character
will not differ from one place of articulation to another. The two most obvious
potential acoustic cues for place of articulation in stops are (1) the spectrum of
the burst and (2) the transitions to the following vowel. Perceptual experiments
have shown that both of these may indeed function as cues. However, both
have been problematic as regards lack of invariance (Section 5.2.2).

#### 7.3.3.1  Stop bursts

Typical examples of bursts for labial, alveolar and velar places of articulation
are illustrated in Figure 7.5. This shows spectrograms for the three English

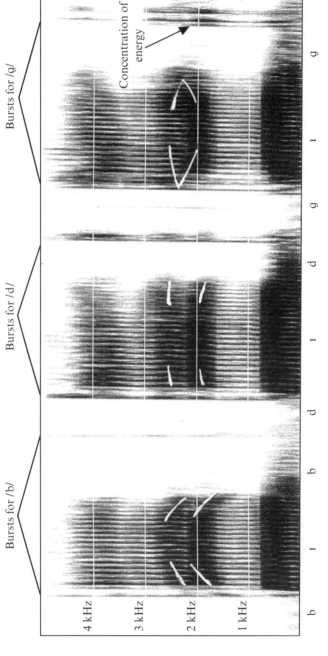

FIGURE 7.5    Spectrograms of the English words **bib**, **did** and **gig**, pronounced by a male speaker. The bursts for /b/ and /d/ are said to be 'diffuse', with energy spread out over a wide range of frequencies. By contrast, the bursts for /g/ are more 'compact', with energy concentrated in the middle of the frequency range. This is especially true for the /g/ in final position. The $F_2$ and $F_3$ transitions have been highlighted. Notice that both transitions are rising for /b/ but are more nearly level for /d/. The $F_2$ and $F_3$ transitions for /g/ converge, forming a wedge-like shape.

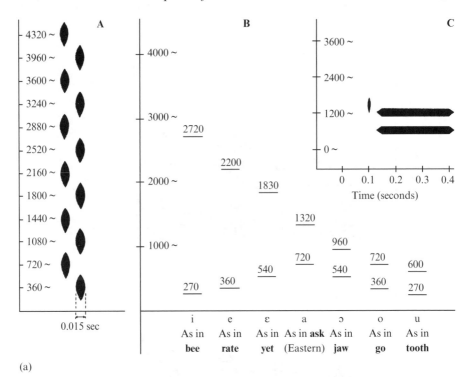

(a)

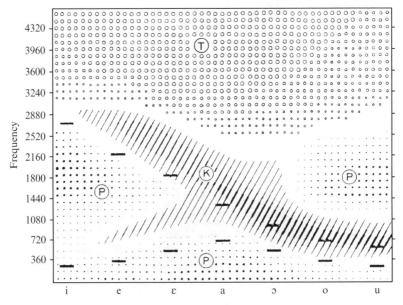

(b)

words **bib**, **did** and **gig**. The final consonant is released in all cases. Thus, there are two bursts for each consonant: one in word-initial position and one in final position before pause. There are several points to notice:

1 The bursts for /b/ are weaker than those for /d/ or /g/; the spike corresponding to the final /b/ is particularly faint.
2 The burst for final /b/ also shows somewhat more energy in the lower part of the frequency axis, and becomes particularly faint at the top of the display.
3 The bursts for /d/ have more energy at high frequencies than /b/ or /g/; both initially and finally, the spike is quite dark around 4000 Hz, and for the initial /d/ the darkness extends up to the top of the display (5000 Hz).
4 The bursts for /g/, especially pre-pausal /g/, show a concentration of energy in the middle of the frequency axis. For this reason, velars are sometimes characterised as *compact* (following Jakobson *et al.* 1952). By contrast, labials, dentals and alveolars are said to be *diffuse* because the energy in the burst is not so concentrated in a particular frequency region.
5 There is a difference between the initial /g/ and the pre-pausal /g/. For the initial /g/, the darkest area of the burst is around 2500 Hz, and there is also noticeable energy at higher frequencies. This makes the spectrum less compact since the energy spreads out, as it were, beyond the middle frequencies. For pre-pausal /g/, the darkest part of the burst is lower in frequency (around 2000 Hz) and there is little energy above 3000 Hz. In fact, the burst of the pre-pausal /g/ is more typical for the velar place of articulation. The character of the initial /g/, which has a more forward place of articulation, is due to the influence of the following front vowel.

Although the spectrum of a stop burst may be quite diffuse, it is possible to imitate stop bursts in synthetic speech using a narrower burst of noise. The earlist perceptual studies of stop bursts used this method. In a classic study carried out at Haskins Laboratories, Liberman *et al.* (1952) synthesised a series of CV syllables with simple noise bursts and two-formant vowels. The basic experimental design is illustrated in Figure 7.6 (a). There were twelve bursts, ranging in frequency from 360 Hz to 4320 Hz. Although the stylised spectrograms of the stimuli might appear quite crude in comparison with real spectrograms, listeners were able to hear the stimuli as the intended CV syllable and to

FIGURE 7.6 (*opposite*) Design (a) and results (b) of a classic experiment on the perception of place of articulation in stop consonants (Liberman *et al.* 1952). Twelve bursts, ranging in frequency from 360 Hz to 4320 Hz (A), were paired with two-formant versions of seven vowels (B), to give 84 CV syllables (as in C). Listeners were asked to identify the initial consonant of each syllable as /p/, /t/ or /k/.

The graph of (b) shows the dominant responses for each CV combination. Syllables with high-frequency bursts are uniformly identified as beginning with /t/. The lower part of the graph is, as it were, shared by /p/ and /k/. Notice that /k/ responses (slanted lines) dominate where the burst frequency is close to the $F_2$ of the following vowel.

classify the initial stop consonants as /p/, /t/ or /k/. The results are shown in Figure 7.6 (b). As might be expected, high-frequency bursts (above about 2800 Hz) were heard as /t/. However, the lower part of the diagram is, at it were, shared by /p/ and /k/. One general rule which emerges is that if the burst is near to the $F_2$ frequency of the vowel, listeners will tend to hear /k/. Nevertheless, the distribution of lower-frequency bursts between /p/ and /k/ is somewhat complicated. The results were regarded as encouraging because they showed that listeners could identify place of articulation on the basis of burst frequency alone. However, they were also seen as somewhat discouraging because the relationship between burst frequency and recognised phoneme was less straightforward than expected.

### 7.3.3.2  Formant transitions

Formant transitions provide the second obvious potential cue for place of articulation in stop consonants. It is easy to confirm that stop consonants can be identified from their transitions alone. If you extract and play the sequence of transition + vowel in a CV sequence beginning with a [+ voiced] stop (such as in the words **bay**, **day** or **gay**), you should have no difficulty in recognising the initial consonant, although the burst is missing. If the experiment is extended to words beginning with fricatives (such as **say**), you should find that, if you hear only the transitions and the vowel, the word in question sounds like it begins with a voiced stop as well. The transition + vowel part of **say** will sound like **day**.

Experiments with English native listeners have tended to concentrate on the [+ voiced] stops (/b/, /d/ and /g/) since aspiration typically overlaps with the transitions in voiceless /p/, /t/ and /k/ (Figure 7.4). Transitions are generally described with reference to CV sequences. For example, if we say that labials are associated with rising $F_2$ transitions, we mean that, in a syllable such as **bee** (/bi/), $F_2$ rises from consonant to vowel. It is understood that VC transitions (as in (**b)ib**) will be the mirror image of the corresponding CV transitions though the rate of formant movement may be different.

At least for places of articulation located in the mouth (as opposed to the pharynx), $F_1$ will rise in CV transitions. This is in line with theoretical considerations which suggest that during a stop closure in the oral cavity, $F_1$ should be 0. However, $F_2$ and $F_3$ may vary considerably with place of articulation. This is obvious in Figure 7.5. $F_2$ and $F_3$ rise steeply for the initial /b/ of **bib**, but rise only very slightly for the initial /d/ of did. For the initial /g/ of **gig**, $F_2$ is falling, but $F_3$ is rising, so that the two come together in a wedge-like shape. The situation begins to appear more complicated when other vowels are taken into account. This is evident if we compare Figure 7.5 with Figure 7.7, which shows bursts and formant transitions extracted from the beginnings of the words **barb**, **dart**, and **guard** (/bɑb/, /dɑt/, /gɑd/). This time, the $F_2$ transition for /b/ is more level (though the $F_3$ transition is still rising). For /d/, the $F_2$ transition falls steeply until it reaches the appropriate level for the steady state

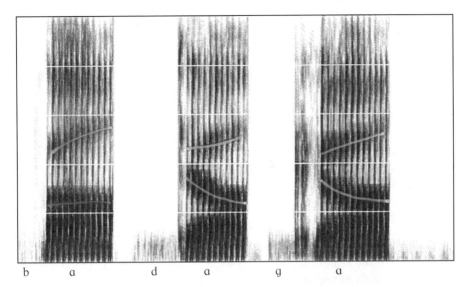

b    ɑ        d    ɑ        g    ɑ

FIGURE 7.7 Spectrogram showing bursts and formant transitions extracted from the English words **barb**, **dart** and **guard**, pronounced by a male speaker. As in Figure 7.5, the $F_2$ and $F_3$ transitions have been highlighted. Notice that, in contrast to the examples of Figure 7.5, the $F_2$ transition for /b/ is nearly level while the $F_2$ transition for /d/ is falling. The transitions for /g/ are similar to those of Figure 7.5 in that the $F_2$ and $F_3$ transitions converge, forming a wedge-like shape.

of the vowel /ɑ/. The $F_3$ transition is less clear, but it is more level. For /g/, the transitions resemble those of **gig** in Figure 7.5 in that $F_2$ and $F_3$ appear to start from the same point, the one falling and the other rising. However, the starting point is lower than for the transitions of **gig**. It is also useful to compare the /g/ of **guard** with the /k/ of **car** in Figure 7.4. In these two words, the burst and the transitions are very similar, though the transitions for the /k/ show up less well in the aspiration noise. The transitions for the /k/ of **car** appear slower, but this is because of the expanded time scale.

In general, for labial stops (/p/ and /b/), $F_2$ and $F_3$ transitions are level or rising. In the case of $F_2$, the rise is steepest when the following vowel is a front vowel with high $F_2$ (as in **bib**) and most nearly level when the following vowel is a back vowel with low $F_2$ (as in **barb**). For velar stops (/k/ and /g/), the $F_2$ transition commonly begins just above the vowel's second formant and falls; the $F_3$ transition begins at about the same point and rises, giving a distinct wedge-like shape as illustrated both in **gig** (Figure 7.5) and in **guard** (Figure 7.7). For alveolar stops (/t/ and /d/), the $F_2$ transition will generally be level or rising for front vowels (as in **did**, Figure 7.5) but falling for back vowels (as in **dart**, Figure 7.7). The $F_3$ transition will typically be level or falling. These general patterns were noted for spectrograms of natural speech by Potter *et al.* (1947). Early studies on the synthesis and perception of formant transitions focussed on the role of $F_2$.

The behaviour of $F_2$ transitions for /d/ is elucidated by the concept of *locus*. The locus is 'a place on the frequency scale at which a transition begins or to which it may be assumed to "point"' (Delattre *et al.* 1955: 769 n. 3). The qualification about 'pointing' is necessary because, in the case of stop consonants, the *very* beginnings of the transitions – corresponding to the beginning of the tongue's movement toward the position for the following vowel – are not visible on spectrograms.

The locus is essentially determined by the location of the closure (place of articulation). For example, in pronouncing the words **dart** and **did**, the tongue starts from roughly the same position but moves in different directions. Since the $F_2$ (and other) transitions reflect tongue and jaw movement, we might expect that they would start from the same position on the frequency axis but move in different directions. In the case of alveolar stops (/t/ and /d/), the $F_2$ locus is generally around 1800 Hz, at least for male speakers, and does not vary from vowel to vowel. Accordingly, if the vowel $F_2$ is above 1800 Hz (as in **did**), the transition will be rising, but if the vowel $F_2$ is below 1800 Hz (as in **dart** or **door**), the transition will be falling.

The concept of *locus* may also be applied to bilabials, which appear to have a locus in the region of 700–800 Hz. This fits in well with the observation that the $F_2$ transition rises steeply before front vowels but only a little or not at all before back vowels. The situation is less straightforward for the velars (/g/ and /k/). As we have just noted, the $F_2$ transitions for velars are generally falling (but not steeply falling), no matter what the identity of the following vowel. This reflects the tendency for the precise location of tongue contact for velars to vary according to the tongue position for the following sound.

In fact, the $F_2$ transitions for /g/ and /d/ may be quite similar before low vowels. This is certainly the case in our examples **dart** and **guard** (Figure 7.7), though the $F_3$ transitions are quite different. Accordingly, we might expect that the $F_3$ transition would play a crucial role in distinguishing between the two places of articulation. This was confirmed in another series of experiments reported in Harris *et al.* (1958).

Perhaps the best known of the perceptual experiments carried out at Haskins is one described by Liberman *et al.* (1957), which demonstrated that listeners could distinguish between /b/, /d/, and /g/ on the basis of the $F_2$ transition alone. It was also shown that, if the $F_2$ transition was varied while everything else was held constant, listeners would perceive the place of articulation contrast *categorically* (Section 5.2.3.1). This is probably the most frequently cited example of categorical perception.

### 7.3.3.3  Spectral templates as invariant cues

When individual cues to place of articulation such as simplified bursts or $F_2$ transitions are studied one at a time, the patterns which emerge are quite complicated. This is mainly because the same bit of acoustic information will be interpreted differently for different vowels. This acoustic variability in the face of evident articulatory sameness was a major inspiration for the development of the Motor Theory (Section 5.2.4.1). As an example, we may quote Liberman *et al.* (1967: 438), discussing the concept of *locus* for alveolars:

> Though the locus can be defined in acoustic terms – that is, as a particular frequency – the concept is more articulatory than acoustic . . . What is common to /d/ before all the vowels is that the articulatory tract is closed at very much the same point . . . it seems clear that though the locus is more nearly invariant with the phoneme than is the transition itself, the invariance is a derived one, related more to articulation than to sound.

Other researchers have been less pessimistic about the prospect of finding invariant cues for articulatory place, and have taken the view that such cues do indeed exist. However, it is necessary to approach the problem in a somewhat different way. Consider, for example, the velar stops (/k/ and /g/). It is usually easy to recognise these visually on a spectrogram. The $F_2$ and $F_3$ transitions typically start from about the same point and diverge, and this starting frequency is generally close to the burst frequency. Thus, the burst, the $F_2$ transition and the F3 transition all converge, as it were, into a small section of the frequency axis, resulting in the compact type of spectrum (Figures 7.5, 7.7). However, it is difficult to arrive at a notion of *compactness* if we study the effects of varying burst frequency, the $F_2$ transition and the $F_3$ transition one at a time and look for invariance in each one.

One way of giving formal explicitness to a notion such as *compact spectrum* is to develop a model shape, or template, with which actual spectra can be compared. This approach is particularly associated with the names of Kenneth Stevens and Sheila Blumstein. Their methodology has involved analysing LPC spectra (Section 4.5) with high-frequency pre-emphasis (Section 3.2.4), taken for a short (about 25 msec) time window beginning at the release burst. For English /b/, /d/ and /g/, the window generally includes the start of the formant transitions, whereas for /p/, /t/ and /k/, it does not.

Stevens and Blumstein's approach is illustrated in Figure 7.8. The spectra of alveolars should fit into a diffuse-rising template, while those of labials should fit into a diffuse-falling or diffuse-flat template. The spectra for velars should fit into a compact template. For the diffuse types (labial and alveolar), the templates are defined by a pair of dashed lines, which should, as it were, contain the outline of the spectrum. In the case of velars, a prominent mid-frequency peak must dominate the spectrum. It should be stressed here that the templates are intended to be valid across all vowel contexts. The approach is said to be based on *integration* of cues because information from the burst and information from the beginning of the transitions both contribute to the spectrum which is compared with the template.

The original templates of Stevens and Blumstein might be termed *static* in that only one template, unchanging over time, is said to be necessary to define each articulatory place. Other researchers have argued that templates should be defined in a more dynamic way. Thus, Kewley-Port (1983) argues that, if a

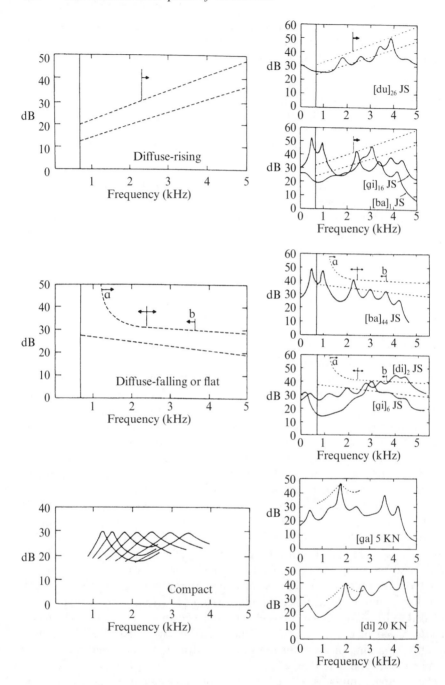

spectrum is to be classified as compact, it must not only have a mid-frequency peak at the moment of the burst, but also that the peak must extend over a time interval of about 20 msec. This would be true of both the /g/ of Figure 7.5 and the /g/ of Figure 7.7, where the central dark band of energy in the burst persists into the start of the $F_2$ and $F_3$ transitions.

Although spectral templates have seemed to work well for the three-way contrast between labials, alveolars and velars in English, there have been some problems in extending the approach to more complicated systems of contrasts. In a cross-linguistic study, Lahiri *et al.* (1984) found that the burst spectra of dentals could appear very similar to those of labials, and it did not seem possible to distinguish between them by means of spectral templates. Such results suggest that a more sophisticated notion of invariance is needed. Their proposal is that invariance is both *dynamic* and *relative*. *Dynamic* here refers to change through time. What matters is the way in which the spectrum changes across the acoustic boundary from the release burst to following vowel (as in the proposed definition of *compact* just mentioned). *Relative* refers to a comparison between the lower and upper parts of the spectrum. In the typical case, there is an increase in energy overall from burst to vowel onset. For dentals and alveolars, most of this increase involves the lower part of the spectrum whereas, for labials, the amount of change is more evenly split between the two. For example, in the spectrograms of **barb** and **dart** shown in Figure 7.7, the burst for /b/ is very weak, so that there is a large increase in intensity (darkness) at vowel onset for all frequencies. By contrast, the burst for /d/ shows a good deal of energy at high frequencies, so that there is little if any increase in intensity (darkness) at vowel onset in the upper part of the frequency range, though there is a noticeable increase in the lower part.

To sum up, the problem of identifying cues which may be utilised by listeners to identify the place of articulation for stop consonants is a difficult one. Three main cues have been extensively studied: the frequency of the burst, the $F_2$ transition and the $F_3$ transition. When these are investigated independently, the relationship between the acoustic signal and the corresponding speech sound (phoneme) appears to be highly variable. Alternative approaches have focussed

FIGURE 7.8    (*opposite*) Templates developed by Stevens and Blumstein to classify spectra as diffuse-rising (alveolars), diffuse-falling (labials) or compact (velars). The two panels to the right of each template show one spectrum which fits the template (above) and one spectrum which does not (below).

For the diffuse-rising template, an arrow pointing to the right from 2200 Hz (just above 2 kHz) indicates that, when comparing a spectrum with the template, a spectral peak above 2200 Hz must be made to coincide with the upper reference line. The remaining lower-frequency peaks must then fall between the reference lines. For the diffuse-falling template, there must be one peak between the reference lines in region (a) (1200–2400 Hz) and one peak in region (b) (2400–3600 Hz). For the compact template, a prominent mid-frequency peak must fit entirely within one of the contours of the template. From Stevens and Blumstein (1981).

on the overall spectrum in the neighbourhood of the burst and on changes across the acoustic boundary between a consonant and its adjacent vowel. These have been more successful in identifying characteristics which might serve as invariant cues.

A good overview of work on place of articulation up to the early 1980s is Syrdal (1983).

## 7.4  Fricatives

The rasping sound associated with fricative consonants is due to turbulent air flow, which occurs when the airstream emerges from the narrow constriction formed by the articulators. Accordingly, fricative consonants are defined acoustically by constriction intervals which are filled with noise rather than with silence. A good example is provided by the spectrogram of English /ʃ/ shown in Figure 7.1.

In the IPA chart, fricatives are classified using the two dimensions of place of articulation and voicing. It might be expected that each place should be associated with its own characteristic pattern of spectral peaks and valleys, rather as each vowel has its own characteristic formant pattern. The one exception is the glottal fricative [h]. This is because [h] does not involve any special positioning of the vocal organs above the larynx. The peaks and valleys in the spectrum of any particular [h] will generally match those of following or preceding vowels. In the case of intervocalic [h] between vowels which differ in quality, a gradual change in formant structure, linking the preceding and following vowels, is generally observed during the consonantal interval.

In addition to spectral shape, fricatives differ from one another in relative intensity and in the nature of their formant transitions. Relative intensity is particularly important for distinguishing between sibilant and non-sibilant fricatives; in English, for example, sibilant /s/ and /ʃ/ are clearly more intense than non-sibilant /f/ and /θ/. As regards formant transitions, these are similar in character to transitions for stop consonants, and reflect the movement of the tongue and jaw from the position for the fricative to the position for the following vowel.

We have seen that the waveforms of voiceless fricatives are aperiodic, without any repeating pattern (Section 2.3). Accordingly, FFT spectra (Section 3.4.2) and LPC spectra of fricatives are less stable than vowel spectra, and may vary considerably over even a small portion of the fricative. This is not to say that an overall pattern is lacking – for example, in the /ʃ/ of Figure 7.1, the overall visual impression is that the character of the spectrum remains more or less constant over the consonantal interval. In order to get the overall pattern to emerge, it is important to take as much of the consonantal interval into account as possible. This means that narrow band spectra are to be preferred to broad band spectra because they use a longer window (Section 3.4.2). A still better method is to average several spectra, taken over the course of the

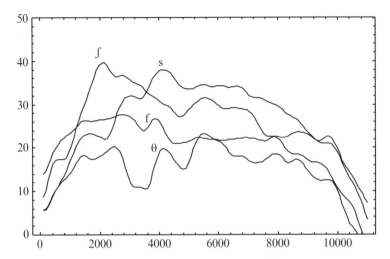

FIGURE 7.9   Averaged broad band spectra for the English voiceless fricatives /f/, /θ/, /s/ and /ʃ/, extracted from the words **fight, thigh, sigh** and **shy**, pronounced by a male speaker.

fricative, though not all speech analysis software provides for this possibility. Another point is that the spectra of fricatives – particularly [s] – may show prominent peaks above 5000 Hz. Accordingly, if fricatives are to be the object of study, it is important to use a higher sampling rate than 10,000 Hz (Section 3.4.1).

Figure 7.9 shows a comparison of averaged broad band spectra for the four non-glottal voiceless fricatives of English (/s/, /ʃ/, /f/, /θ/) produced by a single male speaker. In this case, the sampling rate was 22,000 Hz; frequencies up to 10,000 Hz are displayed. (The glottal fricative /h/ is excluded because it does not have its own characteristic spectrum.) Notice that (1) /s/ and /ʃ/ are more intense than /f/ and /θ/; (2) the main spectral peak for /s/ is higher in frequency than that for /ʃ/; and (3) /f/ and /θ/ are more diffuse in character, whilst /ʃ/ is more compact, with a prominent mid-frequency peak. Another difference which may be significant involves the slope of the overall spectrum; in this example, the curve for /ʃ/ rises steeply to its peak, while the curve for /s/ rises more gradually. A good discussion of the possible role of spectral slope in classifying sibilant fricatives may be found in Evers *et al.* (1998).

It should also be mentioned here that the spectra of English fricatives vary considerably from speaker to speaker, so that, while the observations just made are generally valid, it would be inappropriate to add more detail. At least for English, it has seemed appropriate to describe fricative spectra in terms of the general categories we might apply to the spectra of stop bursts (diffuse vs. compact, high-frequency prominent vs. low-frequency prominent) rather than in terms of specific formant frequencies, as would be the case for vowel spectra.

As regards perception, fricatives have been much less well-studied than stops. A classic study on English /s/, /ʃ/, /f/ and /θ/ was carried out by Harris (1958). She used naturally produced fricative + vowel syllables and also unnatural syllables, which she created by combining the fricative noise from one syllable with the transitions and vowel from another. The complete set of stimuli included all possible noise-transition combinations for five vowels. Her results suggested that there was a difference between sibilant and non-sibilant fricatives (/s/, /ʃ/ vs. /f/, /θ/). Sibilant fricatives could be identified correctly even when they were paired with the 'wrong' formant transitions. For the non-sibilants, however, the formant transitions played a more crucial role, so that, for example, when the noise interval for /f/ was combined with the transitions for /θ/, the listeners identified the fricative as /θ/ rather than as /f/. Further experiments have indicated that the sibilant–non-sibilant dichotomy may not be so clear-cut and that formant transitions do, in fact, play some role in the identification of sibilant fricatives. In languages with richer inventories of sibilants, formant transitions may be more important still. This result emerged from some perceptual experiments carried out by Bladon *et al.* (1987) involving speakers of Shona, a language with three distinctive sibilants (/s/, /ʃ/ and a labialised or labiodentalised /s$^w$/). Formant transitions were found to be an important cue to the distinction between /ʃ/ and /s$^w$/, for which the frequency of the main spectral peak is lower than for /s/.

Thus far, we have said nothing about voiced fricatives. As would be expected, these have a low-frequency voice bar across the bottom of the spectrogram. Above the voice bar, the overall pattern will be similar to that for the corresponding voiceless fricatives, but the intensity of the friction will be weaker. The duration of the friction will generally be shorter. A pattern of striations, corresponding to the individual vocal fold pulses, will be discernible, at least for low-pitched voices. An example is provided in Figure 7.10, which shows spectrograms for the English words **sip** and **zip**. In the case of weak non-sibilants (such as English /v/ or /ð/), it may be difficult to see anything corresponding to frication above the voice bar on a spectrogram.

It is also possible that changes in the spectrum across acoustic boundaries play a role in the perception of fricatives. This possibility is discussed both for the English /s/–/θ/ contrast and for the English /s/–/ʃ/ contrast by Stevens (1985b). He carried out some perceptual experiments that involved identification of synthetic fricative + vowel syllables (such as /sɑ/) by American English listeners. The results suggested that the frequency region around a vowel's $F_5$ may be crucial for distinguishing between /s/ and /θ/. If the friction noise for the fricative was stronger (that is, more intense) than the vowel in the $F_5$ region, listeners heard /s/. If the friction noise was weaker than the vowel in this region, listeners heard /θ/. Of course, we expect that the friction for /s/ will be more intense than that for /θ/ in any case. What is crucial here is that the fifth formant of the following vowel appeared to provide a standard of comparison against which the level of noise in the fricative could be assessed. As regards the /s/–/ʃ/ contrast, the crucial region of the spectrum was the area

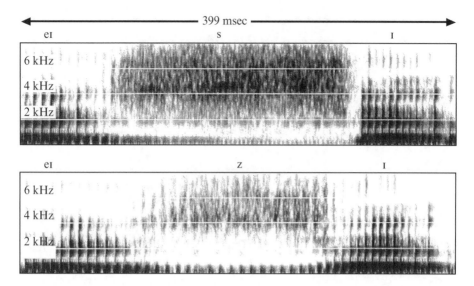

FIGURE 7.10 Contrasting spectrograms of English /s/ and /z/, extracted from the sentences **Did you say 'sip'?** and **Did you say 'zip'?** pronounced by a male speaker. Notice that the /z/ is shorter in duration, its friction is weaker, and a low-frequency voice bar is present.

around the vowel's $F_3$. A /s/ could be, as it were, turned into a /ʃ/ by adding a band of lower-frequency noise energy at the level of the vowel's $F_3$. For /ʃ/ identification, it was also crucial that the intensity of the noise should match or exceed that of the vowel $F_3$ peak.

## 7.5 Affricates

In purely phonetic terms, an affricate is a sequence of stop followed by fricative at the same place of articulation. As would be expected, the constriction interval for a voiceless affricate consists of two parts: silence followed by friction. The release burst of the stop provides a boundary between the two. This is illustrated in Figure 7.11, which contrasts the initial consonants of the English words **ship** and **chip**. Other things being equal, the duration of the stop portion of an affricate is less than that of the corresponding stop and the duration of the fricative portion is less than that of the corresponding fricative. In Figure 7.11, the total duration of the /t͡ʃ/ (236 msec) is only slightly longer than that of the /ʃ/ (212 msec).

I shall not give examples of voiced affricates, which are like combinations of voiced stops and voiced fricatives.

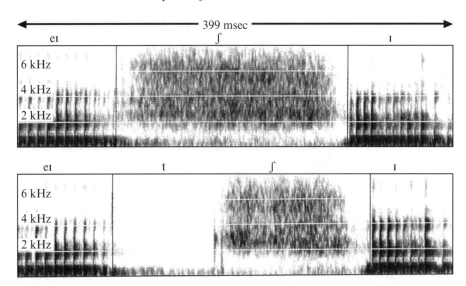

FIGURE 7.11    Contrasting spectrums of English /ʃ/ and /t͡ʃ/, extracted from the sentences **Did you say 'ship'?** and **Did you say 'chip'?** pronounced by a male speaker. The affricate includes a stop (/t/) portion and a fricative (/ʃ/) portion, but is only slightly longer than the fricative.

## 7.6    The fricative–affricate contrast

All obstruent consonants, voiced and voiceless, share the characteristic of noise during, or at the very end of, the constriction interval. In the case of stop consonants, this is entirely concentrated in the transient burst at the end. If we compare affricates with stops (in the same voicing category and at the same place of articulation), it appears that the noise portion is lengthened and the period of silence is shortened. Finally, in the case of fricatives, the noise portion fills the constriction interval and there is no period of silence.

A number of studies have been concerned with perception of the fricative–affricate distinction in English. Two minimal phonemic contrasts are involved (/ʃ/ vs. /t͡ʃ/ as in **share** vs. **chair**, and /ʒ/ vs. /d͡ʒ/ as in **leisure** vs. **ledger**). However, the second of these is rather limited since /ʒ/ never occurs word-initially or before a stressed vowel. Attention has thus been focussed on the /ʃ/–/t͡ʃ/ contrast. Also, the /ʃ/ vs. /t͡ʃ/ contrast seems more problematic because in absolute initial position the silent ([t]) part of /t͡ʃ/ will blend in to a preceding silence. By contrast, the [d] part of /d͡ʒ/ may stand out from a preceding silence because of its voice bar.

Not surprisingly, both the duration of the silent interval and the duration of the noise interval have been shown to function as cues in the affricate–fricative distinction. Lengthening the silent interval (when a vowel precedes) will elicit more affricate (/t͡ʃ/) responses from listeners whereas lengthening the noise interval will elicit more fricative (/ʃ/) responses; a good review of the evidence,

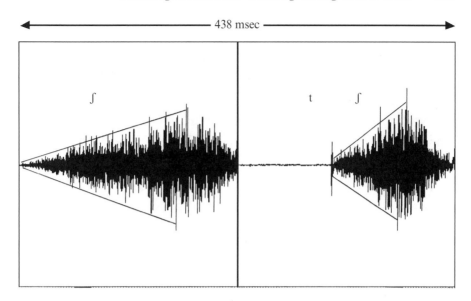

FIGURE 7.12   Comparison of waveforms for the initial consonants of English **share** (/ʃ/) and **chair** (/t͡ʃ/) pronounced in utterance-initial position by a male speaker. The *rise time* is the time from the onset of friction to its maximum amplitude. In this example, as is typically the case, the rise time is considerably shorter for /t͡ʃ/ than for /ʃ/.

including a discussion of the effect of speaking rate, may be found in Miller (1981). A third possible cue is the so-called *rise time*. This is defined as the time from the onset of the friction to its maximum amplitude. In fricative consonants, the amplitude of the friction typically builds up gradually, whereas in affricates the friction increases more rapidly from the beginning. This is illustrated in Figure 7.12, which presents a comparison of waveforms for the initial consonants of **share** and **chair**, pronounced in isolation by a male speaker. In some well-known experiments, Cutting and Rosner (1974) found evidence of categorical perception for the /ʃ/ vs. /t͡ʃ/ contrast based on listeners' categorisation of stimuli in a continuum with varying rise times. Moreover, similar results were obtained when listeners were asked to categorise stimuli in a rise time continuum based on string instruments as *bowed* (long rise time) or *plucked* (short rise time). They suggested that an ability to categorise sounds on the basis of rise time is a general property of the auditory system. More recently, this claim has come to be seen as controversial (Rosen and Howell 1987; Kluender and Walsh 1992).

## 7.7   Phonological contrasts involving voicing in obstruents

The phonological contrast between [+ voiced] and [− voiced] obstruents is one of the most discussed in the literature on acoustic phonetics. Although stops, fricatives and affricates are involved, the discussion has almost exclusively centred on stops. There are two main reasons for this. Firstly, the contrast in English is particularly complicated. As regards English stops, [– voiced] /p t k/ and [+ voiced] /b d g/ may vary considerably from one position in the word or phrase to another and, consequently, the acoustic cues to the distinction must also vary from one context to another. We have already seen (Section 5.2.3.2) that a number of cues have been identified and that they enter into trading relations with one another. More generally, five acoustic dimensions appear to be important in distinguishing between phonologically 'voiced' and 'voiceless' obstruents in English:

1  Vocal fold vibration (voicing):
   [+ voiced]: varies according to context from full voicing during closure to unvoiced
   [– voiced]: at most, partially voiced (and that only when the voicing is carried over from a preceding vowel)
2  Aspiration (stops only):
   [+ voiced]: if unvoiced, always unaspirated
   [– voiced]: varies according to context from unaspirated (short positive VOT) to aspirated (long positive VOT); onset of voicing is always later than for a [+ voiced] stop in the same context[3]
3  Duration of a preceding vowel and of the constriction interval itself:
   [+ voiced]: longer vowel, shorter constriction interval
   [– voiced]: shorter vowel, longer constriction interval
4  Intensity of burst (stops, if released) or friction noise (fricatives and affricates)
   [+ voiced]: less intense
   [– voiced]: more intense
5  $F_0$ and $F_1$ frequencies at the onset of immediately following vowels
   [+ voiced]: lower
   [– voiced]: higher

Secondly, it is not clear just how many types of [± voiced] contrast occur cross-linguistically. If we extend the discussion to other languages with two-way contrasts, then it appears that a good deal of variation is to be found, particularly with regard to dimensions (1) and (2). For example, in French, the [+ voiced] obstruents are fully voiced and the [– voiced] obstruents are unvoiced and (in the case of stops) unaspirated. As regards dimension (3), the general pattern is nearly universal, though the magnitude of the effect varies from language to language. It seems possible that still less cross-linguistic variation would be observed with regard to dimensions (4) and (5), though less data is available. Thus, there is evidence for both cross-linguistic diversity and cross-linguistic similarity. A good discussion of the issues involved may be found in Keating (1984a).

If we do recognise a cross-linguistic unity, then it must be admitted that the label [± voiced] is rather unfortunate, since it is precisely in the matter of presence or absence of vocal fold vibration that languages exhibit the most obvious variability. Possible alternatives might be *fortis/lenis* (as in Kohler 1979) or *high-pitched/low-pitched* (as in the proposed system of phonological elements illustrated in Figure 1.3). However, the terms *voiced* and *voiceless* are very well-established, and it is likely that phoneticians and phonologists will prefer to continue making a rather clumsy distinction between *phonetic voicing* and *phonological voicing* rather than adopt a new set of terms.

Questions of terminology aside, the most striking characteristic of the [± voiced] contrast is the consistency with which the five dimensions just listed pattern together across languages. For example, voicing during the closure interval goes with shorter duration (of the interval), weaker noise (of burst or of friction) and lower $F_0$. At least part of the explanation is to be found in the aerodynamics of voicing (Section 8.3.9.1). However, it also appears that the patterning serves to enhance the contrast between the two types, a matter which will be taken up in Section 7.9.

## 7.8   Sonorant consonants

In contrast to obstruents, sonorants are only rarely involved in phonemic voiced–voiceless contrasts, and so it is not surprising that acoustic and perceptual studies of sonorants have concentrated on voiced sonorants. Voiceless sonorants, like voiceless fricatives, are characterised acoustically by the presence of friction during the consonantal interval. In English, this chiefly affects the consonants /l/ and /r/, which are typically devoiced following voiceless stops and fricatives (as in **please** or **pray**).

### 7.8.1   Nasals

With regard to production, nasals share some characteristics with vowels on the one hand and with stop consonants on the other. As with vowels, their only source is air flow through the vibrating vocal folds. Thus, they have a recognisable pattern of formants, at frequencies which differ according to the place of articulation. The strongest formant in a nasal consonant is a low-frequency nasal formant (see also Section 6.7.1 and Figure 6.9). This is the resonance of the long double cavity formed by the pharynx and the nasal cavity. Above the strong low-frequency formant, the intensity of the formants is weak, reflecting the presence of zeros in the transfer (filter) function (Section 4.6.1) and also the absorption of acoustic energy by the slack walls of the nasal cavity. The sound which is emitted during a nasal consonant is, in essence, a hum. It is often referred to as the *nasal murmur*.

From an articulatory point of view, nasals are very similar to voiced stop consonants. The only difference is the lowered position of the soft palate. Accordingly, a nasal consonant will show stop-like formant transitions on either side of the constriction interval. The beginning of the constriction interval is typically marked by an abrupt reduction in amplitude and a sudden shift

◄─────────────────── 319 msec ───────────────────►

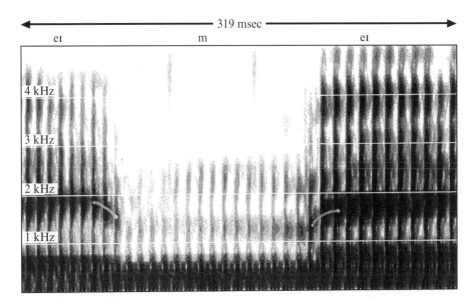

ei                    m                    ei

FIGURE 7.13    Spectrogram of English intervocalic /m/, extracted from the sentence **Did you say 'may'?** pronounced by a male speaker. The $F_2$ transitions have been highlighted. Notice the reduction in amplitude and the shift in the formant pattern which occur during the constriction interval.

in the formant pattern. At the end of the constriction interval, the shift back to a vowel-like spectrum is generally equally abrupt. All of these characteristics are evident in the spectrum of intervocalic English /m/ (in the phrase **say may**) shown in Figure 7.13.

As regards the perception of nasal consonants, a first and obvious hypothesis is that the murmur is a cue for manner of articulation whereas the transitions constitute the main cue for place of articulation. This hypothesis found some support in early experiments at Haskins, which showed that it was possible to synthesise recognisable nasal + vowel syllables (e.g. **ma** and **na**) by combining a standard nasal murmur with transitions appropriate to the corresponding voiced stops (**ba** and **da**). Other experiments used a splicing technique to mix and match murmurs and transitions, much as in Harris's experiments with fricatives described above (Malécot 1956; Recasens 1983). These indicated that, although the murmur did influence listeners' identifications to some extent, the transitions provided the dominant cue for articulatory place.

There is also reason to think, however, that the division of labour between murmur and transitions cannot be so neat as this. If the murmur is cut out of a nasal + vowel sequence, the result does not sound like a plain voiced stop. For example, if you record a word such as **mad** or **me**, cut out the nasal murmur, and play back the result, it will probably not sound like **bad** or **bee**; this is because a bit of nasalisation carries over into the vowel onset. More recently, Kurowski and Blumstein (1984) have argued that murmur and transitions (which, as just mentioned, include some nasalisation) are combined (*integrated*) rather than perceived separately in the perception of place of articulation.

### 7.8.2 Semivowels

The so-called semivowels or *glides* are the most vowel-like of all consonants. For example, the /j/ of English **yes** is very like a short version of the vowel [i], as in English **see**. Similarly, the /w/ of English **we** is very like a short version of the vowel [u]. It should be noted, however, that English /w/ is rather different from the English vowel which is commonly transcribed /u/. At least in current Southern British pronunciation, /u/ is a more central vowel with a relatively high $F_2$ in most contexts. More generally, both /w/ and /j/ may show a greater degree of constriction than their corresponding vowels. The relationship between semivowels and vowels in a number of languages is discussed by Maddieson and Emmorey (1985).

In phonological representations, it is generally considered that semivowel–vowel pairs such as /i/–/j/ have identical feature specifications but differ as regards their position in syllable structure (Section 1.4.2 and Figure 1.2). Vowels function as syllable nuclei whereas semivowels function as syllable onsets or syllable codas.

Spectrograms of semivowels may or may not show an identifiable consonantal interval. A more consistent defining characteristic is the slow transitions which link the semivowel with preceding and/or following vowels. This is very evident in the contrast between the English /m/ (of **say may**) shown in Figure 7.13 and the /w/ (of **say way**) shown in Figure 7.14. In this particular example, the /w/ does have a constriction interval which resembles that of a voiced stop (as in Figure 7.3). As regards the formant transitions, these appear to rise from a low-frequency starting point, as is typical of labial consonants. However, the transitions are rather slow and drawn out. In contrast, the transitions for the /m/ are very abrupt, making the change from consonant to vowel much quicker. A corresponding spectrogram of the semivowel /j/ (of **say yea**) is shown in Figure 7.15. It appears that the slow and gradual character of the transitions for semivowels can serve as a cue for listeners, distinguishing semivowels from voiced stops.

### 7.8.3 Lateral approximants (L-sounds)

In impressionistic-phonetic classification, lateral approximants are defined by the fact that the airstream is diverted from the centre of the vocal tract and is made to flow along one or both sides of the tongue. The approximation between the side(s) of the tongue and the roof of the mouth is not so close as to cause the turbulent air flow which is characteristic of fricatives. From the point of view of the source-filter theory, L-sounds are most similar to nasals, because

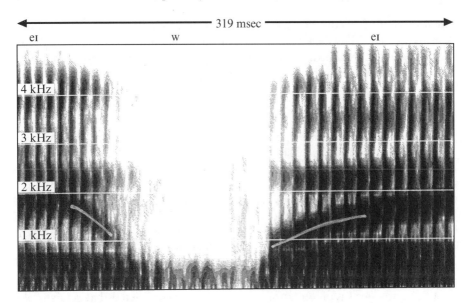

FIGURE 7.14   Spectrogram of English intervocalic /w/, extracted from the sentence **Did you say 'way'?** pronounced by a male speaker. The $F_2$ transitions have been highlighted. Notice the gradual character of the transitions as compared with the transitions for the /m/ of **may** in Figure 7.13.

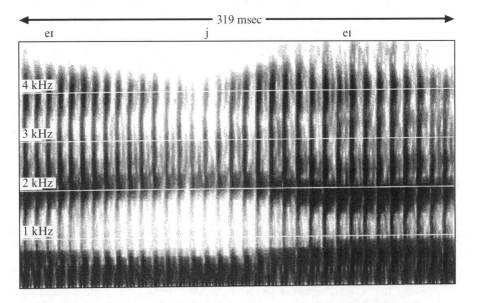

FIGURE 7.15   Spectrogram of English intervocalic /j/, extracted from the sentence **Did you say 'yea'?** pronounced by a male speaker. The /j/ shows an [i]-like formant structure, with high $F_2$ and gradual $F_2$ transitions. In this case, it is not possible to say exactly where the consonant begins and where it ends.

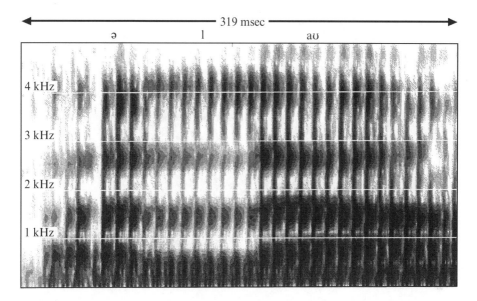

FIGURE 7.16   Spectrogram of English intervocalic *clear* /l/, extracted from the sentence **Did you say 'aloud'?** pronounced by a male speaker. As in the case of the /m/ of Figure 7.13, there is a reduction in amplitude and a shift in the formant pattern during the constriction interval.

the source is the same (air flow through the vibrating vocal folds) and the transfer (filter) function contains zeros. Since, for L-sounds, the soft palate is raised, there is no super-large cavity which will give rise to a strong low-frequency formant in the acoustic output. (This statement leaves the possibility of nasalised laterals out of account.)

Figure 7.16 shows a spectrogram of the intervocalic /l/ in English **aloud**. As with the /m/ of Figure 7.13, there is an abrupt reduction in amplitude and a shift in the formant pattern at the beginning of the constriction interval followed by an equally abrupt shift to a vowel-like pattern at the end of the constriction interval.

The formant patterns of the various allophones of a single /l/ phoneme may exhibit considerable variation. The English /l/ phoneme is well known for its *clear* and *dark* (velarised) allophones, at least in some dialects. The addition of velarisation gives the dark /l/ a more [u]-like character, and this is reflected in a lower $F_2$. However, English speakers may vary considerably with regard to degree of velarisation, and this is reflected in considerable variation in $F_2$ frequency. An extreme example of a dark /l/ is shown in Figure 7.17. It will be seen that, in this particular example, the transition from the vowel to the /l/ is more gradual and semivowel-like than that of the same speaker's clear /l/ shown in Figure 7.16.

Studies of the perception of laterals have focussed on the distinction between /l/ and /r/ rather than on, for example, the distinction between /l/ and

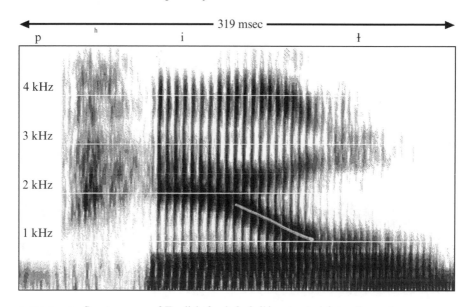

FIGURE 7.17    Spectrogram of English final *dark* /l/, extracted from the sentence **Did you say 'peal'?** pronounced by a male speaker. The $F_2$ transition (highlighted) is gradual, and may be compared with the transition following the semivowel /w/ (Figure 7.14).

/n/, though /l/ and /n/ appear more similar on spectrograms. This is probably because the distinction between /l/ and /r/ presents particular difficulties to some learners of English. The English /r/ sound is characterised by a markedly low $F_3$ (Section 7.8.4 and Figure 7.18), and it is not surprising that the frequency of $F_3$ should prove to be a very important cue for native English listeners (O'Connor *et al.* 1957; Miyawaki *et al.* 1975). In addition, as we have just noted, the transitions for /l/ in prevocalic position tend to be rapid and stop-like whereas the transitions for /r/ are more gradual and vowel-like. Accordingly, the tempo of the $F_1$ transition can also influence perception of the English /l/–/r/ contrast (Polka and Strange 1985).

### 7.8.4  Rhotics (R-sounds)

*Rhotic* is a general term for R-like sounds. That there should be a perceived unity to Rs is quite remarkable. Rs may be produced using a variety of articulations, and it is to be expected that the various types of R should exhibit a similarly broad variety of acoustic manifestations. Thus, in a detailed cross-linguistic study, Lindau (1985) concludes that there is no single acoustic property which *all* Rs have in common, though many are characterised by a low third formant.

The most common type of English /r/ is an approximant articulation and involves little tongue contact in most phonetic-phonological contexts. From an

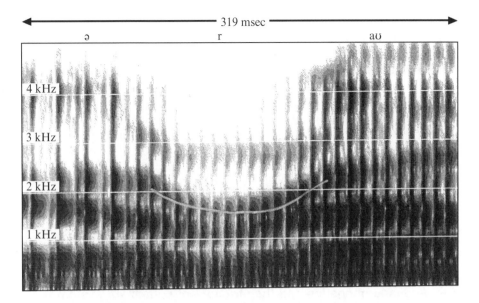

FIGURE 7.18 Spectrogram of English intervocalic /r/, extracted from the sentence **Did you say 'a_round'?** pronounced by a male speaker. Notice the dramatic lowering of $F_3$ (highlighted), which is very characteristic of this consonant. Here, $F_4$ shows considerable lowering as well.

acoustic point of view, it lacks the sudden weakening of the upper formants and shifts in the formant pattern which are so characteristic of the nasals and of (at least some types of) /l/. Its more gradual transitions make it more similar to the semivowels /w/ and /j/. The most salient characteristic of the English /r/, the one which distinguishes it from all other consonants in the language, is its unusually low $F_3$, a characteristic which it shares with the American English rhoticised vowels (Section 6.7.3). This is quite easy to pick out in spectrograms. An example is shown in Figure 7.18. An example of a very different kind of R-sound (a tap) can be seen in Figure 6.9 (Yorùbá **ìrìn**).

### 7.8.5 An overview of manner contrasts involving sonorants

We have seen that manner contrasts in obstruents (stops, fricatives and affricates) depend primarily on the distribution of aperiodic energy within the constriction interval. In stops, it is concentrated in the burst at the end, in affricates, it is more prominent continuous noise in the latter part of the interval, and in fricatives, it is long continuous noise which dominates the interval. In contrast, manner contrasts in sonorants (nasals, laterals, semivowels and rhotics) depend on timing and spectral structure.

At least in English (excluding varieties which use a tapped or trilled /r/ sound), the sonorant consonant which is most obviously distinct is /r/. As we have seen, it is distinguished from all the other sonorants by its low $F_3$. The

low $F_3$ occurs during the constriction interval; it also brings about characteristic transitions, as $F_3$ plunges to its unusually low value on either side of the
interval. In spectrographic terms, English /r/ is often very similar to /w/, with
which it shares gradual rather than abrupt formant transitions and a concentration of energy in the low-frequency part of the spectrum.

If we move on to consider the semivowels /w/ and /j/, we find that the
transitions appear to be of great importance. This is particularly true of /w/,
for which, as the example of Figure 7.14 illustrates, the constriction interval
can appear remarkably similar to the constriction interval of a voiced stop.

It remains to consider the nasals and the lateral approximant (/l/). The
constriction intervals of nasals and laterals (at least, clear /l/s in syllable-initial
position) can appear very similar on spectrograms. We have seen that both
typically show a sudden reduction in amplitude and shift in formant structure
in comparison with a preceding or following vowel. Nasals, however, are distinguished by the strong low-frequency formant which is absent from /l/.

## 7.9 Acoustic phonetics and the structure of consonant systems

Impressionistic-phonetic study teaches us that it is possible to produce a great
variety of consonants. However, some consonants appear much more frequently
in the consonantal inventories of languages than others. For example, most
languages contrast stops at labial, coronal and velar places of articulation
(e.g. /p/ vs. /t/ vs. /k/); most have a bilabial nasal (/m/) and an alveolar sibilant
fricative (/s/). The survey in Maddieson (1984), based on a data base of 317
languages, provides a good source of information about relative frequencies of
individual segment types and also about the structure of inventories as a whole.

Preferences for particular consonants might be compared to the preference
for /i/, /a/ and /u/ in vowel systems (Section 6.10). In the case of vowel systems,
it is clear that /i/, /a/ and /u/ are maximally spread out on a two-dimensional
vowel chart. It seems obvious that they should be maximally distinct from one
another. In the case of consonant systems, notions such as *maximally distinct*
or *more distinct* are much more difficult to formulate because the acoustic
dimensions involved in the description of consonants are so varied.

The most comprehensive account of why consonant systems should be struc-
tured as they are is provided by the theories of *auditory enhancement* developed
by Kenneth Stevens, together with his colleagues (Stevens *et al.* 1986; Stevens
and Keyser 1989) and by Randy Diehl together with his colleagues (Diehl and
Kluender 1989). The account which follows is based on Stevens and Keyser
(1989).

Stevens and Keyser's theory presupposes (1) a description of speech sounds
in terms of binary features (Section 1.4.2) and (2) the existence of invariant correlates for these features in the acoustic signal (Section 5.2.4.4). Both of these
propositions are somewhat controversial. However, if we accept them, we must
pose questions about preference somewhat differently. We should not ask, 'Why

do languages in general prefer particular consonants?' but rather, 'Why do languages in general prefer particular combinations of features?'

According to the theory of enhancement, the acoustic manifestations of some features are more perceptually salient than others. This leads to a distinction between more salient 'primary' features and less salient 'secondary' features. Languages will tend to make full use of the possibilities for contrast provided by the salient primary features. Especially in languages with small numbers of consonants, the secondary features will be used in such a way as to enhance the primary features.

For consonants, there are three primary features: continuant, sonorant and coronal.

The definition of *sonorant* is based on the low part of the spectrum, that is, the region of the first two harmonics (in the speaker's voiced sounds). This region is only the very bottom of a conventional spectrogram, but it is much more prominent in an auditory excitation pattern (Section 5.4.2). Consonant sounds which are [+ sonorant] show continuity with adjacent vowels at low frequencies. In contrast, sounds which are [− sonorant] show a reduction of amplitude at low frequencies. Nasals, laterals and semivowels are [+ sonorant]; stops, fricatives and affricates are [− sonorant]. In terms of impressionistic-phonetic classification, [− sonorant] is equivalent to *obstruent*.

The definition of *continuant* is based on the spectrum above the sonorant region, that is, above the first two harmonics. Sounds which are [− continuant] are characterised by an interval of weak amplitude relative to adjacent vowels. The boundaries of this interval are well defined, so that, if a vowel precedes, the decrease in amplitude is sudden. If a vowel follows, there is an abrupt increase in amplitude. As we have seen, the auditory system shows an enhanced response when stimulation follows silence in a particular frequency region (*adaptation*, Section 5.3.4), so [− continuant] sounds should have this property. By this definition, stops, nasals and laterals are [− continuant]; fricatives and semivowels are [+ continuant].

The definition of *coronal* is based on a comparison of higher and lower parts of the spectrum. Sounds which are [+ coronal] show greater spectrum amplitude at high frequencies than at low frequencies and/or an increase in amplitude at high frequencies relative to adjacent sounds. In articulatory terms, the high-frequency prominence can be related to the size of the cavity between the constriction and the lips (Section 4.6.2). If the cavity is sufficiently small, it will have a high resonant frequency, above that of an adjacent vowel's $F_3$. The more forward the constriction, the smaller the cavity. Accordingly, whether or not a sound will be classified as coronal by these criteria depends on its place of articulation. Dentals, alveolars and palatals are coronal while velars, and sounds articulated further back in the mouth, are not. Also, labials and labiodentals are not coronal (since the consonantal constriction is at the lips, there can be no cavity between the constriction and the lips).

The unaspirated [p]s of Figure 7.2 are [− sonorant] because they do not show continuity at low frequencies (amplitude decreases markedly during the stop gap). They are [– continuant] because there is a period of minimal amplitude (the stop gap) followed by an abrupt increase in amplitude (the burst and the onset of the following vowel). They are [– coronal] because of the diffuse-falling character of the burst and vowel onset (Section 7.3.3.3). In contrast, the [j] (y) of Figure 7.15 is [+ sonorant] because there is no reduction in amplitude at the very bottom of the spectrogram. It is [+ continuant] because the decrease and increase in amplitude at higher frequencies is gradual rather than abrupt. It is [+ coronal] because of its relatively prominent high frequencies.

As an example of a secondary feature, we shall consider the feature [± voiced]. Firstly, voicing (characterised by the feature [+ voiced]) is necessarily present in sounds which are [+ sonorant]. This is because sounds which are produced without vocal fold vibration lack the low-frequency energy which is the essential characteristic of [+ sonorant] sounds. On the other hand, voicing will weaken the [– sonorant] character of obstruent consonants. It should be easy to see why this is the case. Sounds which are [– sonorant] have reduced energy in the lowest regions of the spectrum. Accordingly, the strongest manifestation of [– sonorant] would be the absence of any low-frequency energy whatsoever, as is the case in voiceless stops, fricatives and affricates. If a voice bar is present, this will involve some low-frequency energy, which is more in tune with [+ sonorant] than [– sonorant]. Thus, the unaspirated [p] of Figure 7.2 and the aspirated [k$^h$] of Figure 7.4 are definitely [– sonorant] in character, whereas the [d] of Figure 7.3 is less clearly so. Such considerations suggest that, for example, [t] and [n] are more distinct from a perceptual point of view than are [d] and [n], which seems to make intuitive sense. More generally, we expect that voiceless obstruents should be more common in languages than voiced obstruents, because they will contrast more strongly with sonorant consonants. If a language has only a small number of obstruent consonants, these will tend to be voiceless.

Auditory enhancement may also be invoked to explain why certain phonetic characteristics tend to co-occur in the realisation of particular features. Not surprisingly, the [± voiced] contrast has received particular attention. Kingston and Diehl (1994, 1995) provide a more detailed discussion of auditory enhancement as it relates to the [± voiced] contrast in obstruents (Section 7.7). In their account, three general properties play a role in the [± voiced] contrast generally (across languages):

1   A *low-frequency property*, characterising [+ voiced] obstruents. Continuous voicing across the acoustic boundary between a consonant and the following vowel, lowered $F_0$, and lowered $F_1$ all contribute to this general effect, and, accordingly, are mutually enhancing. (This suggestion was first made by Stevens and Blumstein 1981.)
2   C/V duration ratio (smaller for [+ voiced], larger for [– voiced]). When voicing is present during a closure, listeners will perceive the closure as shorter and the preceding vowel as longer.

3   Aspiration, which may characterise [– voiced] segments. Although Kingston and Diehl do not discuss aspiration in detail, we might suppose that the presence of aspiration enhances [– voiced], since a delay in the onset of voicing (in a following vowel) is maximally different from continuous voicing across a consonant–vowel boundary.

From this brief description, it should be clear that the theory of enhancement makes predictions about the relative frequencies of classes of sounds, or of one sound relative to another. For example, it predicts that voiceless obstruents should be more frequent than voiced obstruents. However, in contrast to the vowel dispersion model, it does not make specific predictions about what consonants should make up an inventory of a particular size.

In any case, the predictions which emerge from such approaches to consonant systems can be compared with the data on phonological inventories published by Maddieson (1984). All of the languages in his data base contrast sonorant and obstruent consonants, and all have at least one stop consonant. All contrast continuant sounds (fricatives and/or semivowels) with non-continuants. All have at least one coronal consonant (dental or alveolar) and only one (Hawaiian) lacks a coronal stop. Voiceless obstruents (stops, fricatives and affricates) are considerably more common than their voiced counterparts.

## 7.10   Further reading

Most of the works mentioned in Section 6.12 are included here as well. Borden *et al.* (1994), Clark and Yallop (1990), Denes and Pinson (1993), Fry (1979), Johnson (1997), Kent and Read (1992), Kent, Dembowski and Lass (1996), Lieberman and Blumstein (1988) and Pickett (1980) all provide good introductions to the acoustics of consonants. Ladefoged and Maddieson (1996) is the most comprehensive from a cross-linguistic point of view and includes discussion of a wide variety of consonant types which could not be included here. Stevens (1998) includes an excellent account of production and perception, with a focus on acoustic aspects.

## Notes

1   This leaves out of account voiceless sonorants and sonorants produced with breathy voicing (see also Sections 2.3 and 8.3.6.4).
2   The term stop is used here as equivalent to IPA *plosive* (an oral stop produced with a pulmonic airstream mechanism). This usage has been common in writings on acoustic phonetics and speech perception.
3   This leaves out of account the fully voiced and flapped pronunciation of /t/ which is so characteristic of North American English (in words such as **writer** or **butter**) and the replacement of /t/ by glottal stop in similar contexts in a number of other dialects.

# Chapter 8

# Speech production

## 8.1 Introduction

Speech production is the process by which a linguistic representation in the brain of a speaker is translated into audible sound. This is accomplished by means of movement, including movement which is necessary to generate the airstream. The individual movements involved must be executed very quickly, and require precise coordination. We have already quoted Lenneberg's (1967) estimate that speaking may involve as many as 10–15 thousand neuromuscular events per minute (Section 1.3), and some researchers have estimated that there are over 70 different muscular 'degrees of freedom' (independently variable parameters) in the production of speech (Kent *et al.* 1996: 8). Accordingly, the major theoretical problem which arises in the study of speech production is understanding just how these very complex patterns of movement are organised and controlled.

From the perspective of theoretical linguistics, speech production is interesting from three distinct, though related, points of view.

1   A theory of phonological representation should, in principle, be able to account for all speech sounds of all human languages. Unfortunately, it is extremely difficult to determine just how many distinct sounds there are, and how many classificatory dimensions are necessary to describe them. This has traditionally been a concern of impressionistic phonetics and, as we have seen in Chapter 1, a framework for describing sounds existed before instrumental methods came to be widely used. Instrumental methods have served to extend this work, and provide clarification and documentation to supplement more traditional methods of articulatory classification. A good discussion of the issues involved may be found in Ladefoged (1997).

2   Within the phonologies of various languages, certain distinct sounds may pattern together. For example, a number of languages have vowel harmony systems in which vowels transcribed /i/, /e/, /o/ and /u/ pattern together as opposed to vowels transcribed /ɪ/, /ɛ/, /ɔ/ and /ʊ/. In such cases, the problem is to discover what common property defines the groupings. Most commonly, phoneticians have looked first to articulation (rather than acoustics) when trying to discover what such common properties might be. Instrumental techniques have been very important, particularly in cases

where the articulatory common ground is elusive. In the example just given, the articulatory property *Advanced Tongue Root* appears to unite the vowels in the first set (/i/, etc.). This was not proposed until the 1960s (Ladefoged 1964; Stewart 1967) and X-ray studies have played an important role in establishing its existence.

Both (1) and (2) are concerned with the general problem of linking phonemes or phonological features with phonetic segments. In both cases, the primary objective is to link abstract representations with articulatory descriptions directly, bypassing the problem of how the necessary movements are controlled. Research of this kind thus parallels research into speech perception in which acoustic cues are related directly to phonemes or features, bypassing questions of auditory processing (Section 5.2).

3   Phonological theories within the generative tradition assume a distinction between underlying and surface representations (Section 1.4.2). It is the surface representations which are assumed to be the input to speech production. Thus, a number of issues arise concerning just how surface representations are, as it were, translated into independent dimensions of articulatory movement. Most importantly, can we predict articulatory movements from surface representations? If not, how much additional information is necessary? Is such information part of an individual native speaker's knowledge of his or her language and, if so, how does this knowledge fit in with other aspects of linguistic knowledge? Such theoretical questions are inextricably linked with the more theoretical problem of how speech production is controlled.

Because the organs involved in speech production are so diverse, the specific questions involved in untangling the complications of how they work are also quite diverse. So are the instrumental techniques available for studying them. Some techniques are quite general in their application, others quite specific. Some require medical supervision, others do not. Some are uncomfortable or even dangerous for the subject whereas others are quite harmless. It should also be mentioned here that instrumental investigations of just about all aspects of speech production have been complemented by mathematical studies, based on models, and that these have played an important role in expanding our knowledge. In what follows, I shall give most attention to instrumental techniques which are widely available and do not require medical supervision. Excellent more detailed descriptions of most of the instrumental techniques are provided by Baken (1987), which assumes no background in electronics on the part of the reader.

Speech production is often divided into three major components – the airstream, the larynx and the vocal folds, and articulation proper – though in practice it is often difficult to separate them. I shall follow this basic scheme here.

## 8.2  The airstream

Speech is produced when movements of the articulators interact with the air-stream which human beings produce when they breathe out. As we have seen (Section 4.2), air flow is the source for all of the sounds of speech. The basic three types of sound waves (periodic, noisy and transient, Section 2.3) cor-respond to distinct types of flow. Accordingly, the study of the airstream in speech, known as *speech aerodynamics*, is essential to understanding how sound is generated in the vocal tract. A particular challenge for researchers has been understanding the nature of turbulent air flow, and how sound is generated in a turbulent airstream. This is crucial in the study of fricative consonants (Hixon 1966; Stevens 1971; Shadle 1990). Aerodynamics also plays an important role in the study of vocal fold vibration, as will be explained in Section 8.3.3.

An understanding of aerodynamics is also important if one is to evaluate the efficiency of an individual's voice or of a particular type of articulation. Since the air stored in the lungs is ultimately the 'power supply' for speech, it follows that speakers or articulations which get more sound for less expend-iture of breath are making more efficient use of their resources. Thus, breathy voice, in which air escapes through the vocal folds as they vibrate (Section 8.3.2), is less efficient than modal voice, where such leakage does not occur. It can also be argued that voiceless velar stops ([k]s) are more efficient than voiceless labial stops ([p]s). This is because it takes less air flowing up from the lungs to build up higher pressures in the smaller cavity behind the closure, which is relatively far back in the mouth (Section 8.2.1).

Much of the work done in speech aerodynamics is not very accessible to the general linguist, firstly because it is too heavily mathematical; secondly, since much of the modelling is done in terms of electric circuits, it presupposes some background in this area. At the same time, speech aerodynamics may be looked at in a more general way, with reference to a few basic principles which are not difficult to understand. For a general overview of aerodynamic aspects of speech, it is easiest to start from a simplified representation of the vocal tract, as shown in Figure 8.1. There are two major cavities: the oro-pharyngeal cavity (above the larynx) and the subglottal cavity (below the larynx), to which the nasal cavity may be added as a third. The subglottal cavity is by far the largest of these, and includes both the lungs and the trachea (windpipe). Although it is, in fact, quite complicated in structure, it is can be treated as a single cavity for the purposes of a general discussion. The oro-pharyngeal cavity comprises the mouth and the pharynx.

During speech, air flows from the lungs to the outside atmosphere, passing through the larynx and the oro-pharyngeal cavity as it does so. Along this path, the lungs are upstream, whereas the oro-pharyngeal cavity is downstream. The vocal folds, within the larynx, function as a valve, which may inhibit or cut off the flow of air between the two major cavities. There are two routes out of the oro-pharyngeal cavity, one via the lips and one via the nasal cavity. As regards the nasal cavity, it is the soft palate which functions as a valve and can

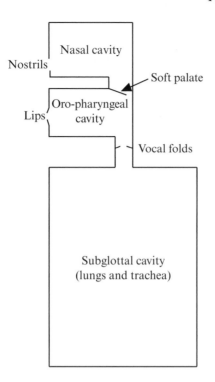

FIGURE 8.1 A simplified representation of the vocal tract, showing the three major cavities and the connections between them. Air flows from the lungs to the outside atmosphere, via the mouth and/or nose. Along this path, the lungs are 'upstream' while the oro-pharyngeal and nasal cavities are 'downstream'.

cut off the flow of air. The opening between the soft palate and the pharyngeal wall is often referred to as the *velopharyngeal port*. As regards the pathway via the lips, there is no single valve comparable to the soft palate, but the flow of air can be cut off or restricted at a number of locations and in a number of ways between the larynx and the lips. A constriction in the pharynx will also affect the possibilities for air flow through the nose.

### 8.2.1 Principles of air flow

The basic principles which account for air flow in the vocal tract are principles which govern the behaviour of liquids and gases generally. These spell out relationships between three types of quantities: pressure, flow rate and volume. Pressure is also affected by changes in temperature, but, since the temperature inside the body remains stable, it is not necessary to take this possibility into account. Pressure is usually represented by upper-case P, volume by upper-case V and flow rate by upper-case U. Subscripts are usually added to make these symbols more precise. Thus, $P_{sg}$ is often used for the subglottal pressure (in the cavities below the larynx), $P_o$ for the intraoral pressure (inside the oro-pharyngeal cavity), and $P_{atm}$ for the pressure of the outside atmosphere.

The following three principles are of primary importance:

1 For a fixed quantity of air (that is, a fixed number of air particles) enclosed in a container, pressure increases as volume decreases and vice versa. In other words, if the container becomes smaller, the pressure inside rises. If the container becomes bigger, the pressure inside falls. In fact, pressure and volume are inversely proportional, and their product ($P \times V$) remains constant (provided that the temperature also remains constant). This is known as *Boyle's Law*.

2 Air will always flow from a region of higher pressure to a region of lower pressure, taking whatever pathway is available. Flow will stop if and when the pressures in the two regions become equal.

3 When air flows through an orifice from a region of higher pressure to a region of lower pressure, the rate of flow will depend on both (a) the size of the pressure difference and (b) the size of the orifice. Other things being equal, the larger the pressure difference and/or the larger the orifice, the greater the rate of flow. (A tyre will deflate quickly if it is slashed but slowly if it has a small puncture.)

### 8.2.2  Respiratory function in speech

Principles (1) and (2) operate together in breathing in and breathing out. The lungs, which make up the greater part of the subglottal cavity, are often compared to a bellows. In the case of a bellows, the handles are pulled apart, causing the volume of the central air chamber to increase. Increasing volume brings about decreasing pressure (principle 1), and air rushes in until the inside of the cavity has a pressure equal to that of the air outside (principle 2). When the handles of the bellows are pushed together, the volume decreases and air flows out through the opening at the point, in the direction chosen by the user. The user can control the speed at which air flows in or out by moving the handles more quickly or more slowly.

Following up the analogy, air is made to flow into and out of the lungs by increasing and decreasing the volume of the chest cavity (*thorax*) which contains them. The lungs themselves contain no muscles, and it is movements of the walls of the chest cavity which make them expand and contract. As regards the chest cavity, it may be described as a beehive-shaped container, which has the rib cage as its sides. Its floor is a dome-shaped sheet of muscle, the diaphragm, which is also the roof of the abdominal cavity. The chest cavity can be expanded for inspiration (breathing in) by moving the rib cage upward and/or outward, by flattening the diaphragm, or both. All of these activities involve muscular effort, and all are opposed by restoring forces, which will tend to return the lungs to their original configuration.

The situation with regard to expiration (breathing out) is more complicated. Once the thorax has been expanded from its resting position, it can be returned to its resting position simply by 'letting go'. However, to let go is to relinquish all control, rather like putting the bellows down on their side, and letting gravity close them on its own. This is suitable for simple breathing in most situations, but it is not suitable for speech, which requires a controlled, steady airstream.

Research on breathing in speech has indicated, firstly, that expiration for speech is a highly controlled activity and, secondly, that the goal of this activity appears to be maintaining a stable baseline subglottal pressure ($P_{sg}$). The best-known and most influential work in this area was carried out in the 1950s by Peter Ladefoged, together with other colleagues (summarised in Ladefoged 1962, 1967). Their figure, reproduced here as Figure 8.2, appears in many textbooks on phonetics. It shows gradually and steadily decreasing lung volume and stable (though not absolutely constant) subglottal pressure. The figure also shows recordings of muscle activity. These indicate that the muscles of inspiration remain active during the first part of the expiration, thereby braking the contraction of the thorax. In the second part of the expiration, other muscles act to pull in on the walls of the thorax, ensuring that lung volume continues to decrease at the same rate. More recent work on respiration in speech has confirmed this basic result, despite some modification of views on the roles played by various muscles.

It also appears that the respiratory muscles do not simply work to ensure that lung volume decreases at a (nearly) constant rate but also speed up or slow down at various points in response to conditions downstream. Consider, for example, the effects of making a closure for a voiceless aspirated stop in the oral cavity. The soft palate is in a raised position (so that the velopharyngeal port is closed) and the glottis is open. When this happens, the outward flow of air from the vocal tract as a whole is cut off. If the respiratory muscles were to continue to contract the chest cavity at the same rate, $P_{sg}$ would continue to rise, possibly to a very high level. Accordingly, if a steady $P_{sg}$ is to be maintained, the respiratory muscles must slow down or even stop the movement of the walls of the chest cavity until the stop closure is released. Evidence from studies of chest wall movement in speech indicates that this is indeed what happens. In this way, $P_{sg}$ (and also $P_o$, the pressure in the oro-pharyngeal cavity) is prevented from rising above the baseline level.

The fact that subglottal pressure ($P_{sg}$) remains approximately constant has important implications for the interpretation of aerodynamic data. The easiest type of data to collect concerns flow rate at the lips and/or nostrils. In general, flow rate will alternately increase and decrease over the course of an utterance. From principle (3) above, we know that an increase in flow must reflect (a) an increase in the cross-sectional area of the passage through the supraglottal cavities and/or (b) an increase in $P_{sg}$ (more accurately, an increase in the *difference* between $P_{sg}$ and $P_{atm}$, the pressure of the outside atmosphere, which is assumed to remain constant). If we assume that the respiratory muscles are in control of $P_{sg}$ and are working to keep it at a constant level, then this effectively elminates the second possibility. Thus, a sudden increase in flow can

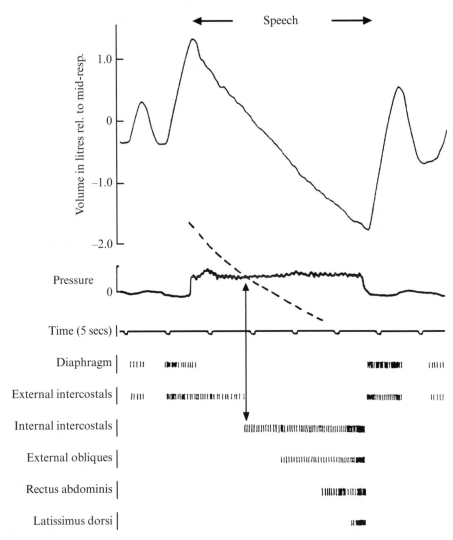

FIGURE 8.2 A record of respiratory activity during speech. The upper part of the figure shows a record of the changing volume of air in the lungs during respiration and speech (counting from 1 to 32 at a conversational loudness). Below this is a record of the subglottal pressure which, despite some variation, remains at roughly the same level over the course of the utterance. The dashed line, which is superimposed on the pressure record, shows the 'relaxation pressure' for the corresponding volume of air in the lungs; this is the pressure which would be observed if the lungs were allowed to return to their rest position in an uncontrolled way. It is equal to 0 when the amount of air in the lungs is the same as that at the end of a normal breath.

The bottom five lines of the diagram relate to muscular activity. In the first part of the expiration for speech, muscles which expand the thorax (the diaphragm and the external intercostals) remain active, slowing down the rate at which lung volume usually be assumed to reflect a widening of the air passage at the level of the larynx or above rather than a change in the activity of the respiratory muscles.

For the reasons just given, recordings of air flow are often used as a means of gaining information about the positions and movements of various articulators. They are particularly useful in investigations of nasality and the movement of the soft palate. If air is flowing out of the nostrils at all, the soft palate cannot be fully raised; otherwise the air could not have got into the nasal cavity in the first place. Although the relationship between the size of the opening and rate of flow is not entirely straightforward, the rate of nasal air flow can provide information about degree of nasalisation (good examples are Cohn 1990 and Huffman 1990). Less obviously, recordings of air flow can be useful in studying how movements of the vocal folds are coordinated with movements of the upper articulators (Section 8.2.3.2).

It remains to comment on two situations in which controlled increases or decreases in $P_{sg}$ occur. Firstly, it is well established that higher $P_{sg}$ is necessary for greater loudness. However, an increase in $P_{sg}$ can be accomplished either by making the thorax contract at a faster rate (controlled by the respiratory muscles) or by narrowing the opening between the vocal folds (controlled by the laryngeal muscles). It seems that either mechanism may be used. An interesting study in this regard is Gauffin and Sundberg (1989), whose results suggested that trained singers tended to control loudness, as it were, entirely from the lungs without changing the vocal fold configuration whereas subjects without vocal training tended to use a tighter vocal fold configuration when an increase in loudness was required.

Secondly, it is well established that, within an utterance, stressed syllables show raised $P_{sg}$ as compared with unstressed syllables. As in the case of overall loudness, an increase in $P_{sg}$ can be accomplished by respiratory activity, by laryngeal activity, or by some combination of the two, and it is possible that different speakers rely on different mechanisms. Another possibility is that the respiratory muscles are involved in cases of strong stress, whereas weaker stresses are regulated from the larynx (Ohala *et al.* 1979). A full overview of the issues involved and of published data which are relevant to the problem is provided by Dixit and Shipp (1985).

More controversial is the suggestion that talkers might regulate fundamental frequency ($F_0$) by increasing or decreasing $P_{sg}$ (Lieberman 1967). There is no doubt that, other things being equal, an increase in $P_{sg}$ results in an increase in $F_0$. However, it now seems that the laryngeal setting, rather than

FIGURE 8.2 (*cont'd*)
decreases. In the second part of the expiration, other muscles which serve to contract the thorax are activated. This ensures that lung volume continues to decrease at the same rate, maintaining a steady subglottal pressure. The change-over point corresponds to the point at which the subglottal pressure is equal to the relaxation pressure. More recent research has suggested an overlap in the activity of the two groups of muscles rather than a sudden change-over. From Ladefoged (1967).

$P_{sg}$, is likely to be of primary importance in this regard. There have also been suggestions that different types of respiratory activity might be associated with different syllable structures (Stetson 1951) or with aspirated and unaspirated consonants (Chomsky and Halle 1968), but these have not been borne out by experimental data.

### 8.2.3  *Measuring and quantifying pressure and flow*

#### 8.2.3.1  Pressure

Formal definitions of pressure refer to force per unit area. Accordingly, pressure may be measured in units such as dynes (force) per square centimetre or Pascals (= Newtons (force) per square metre). However, it is unusual to find such units in the literature dealing with pressures in speech. Phoneticians are normally not concerned with pressure in an absolute sense but with relative pressure. The term *relative* here has two senses. It can mean 'relative to other speech sounds', as in a comparison of intraoral pressures ($P_o$) for voiced and voiceless stops. It can also mean 'relative to the pressure of the outside atmosphere'. In the first case, arbitrary units of measurement may be used. In the second case, measurements are usually reported in *centimetres of water*, abbreviated *cm $H_2O$* or *cm Aq*. This scale of measurement is comparable to the scale of millimetres of mercury, used in reporting air pressures in weather forecasts. However, as just mentioned, such measurements report pressure relative to the pressure of the outside atmosphere, which is a convenient baseline for comparison.

A variety of specialised *pressure transducers*, which translate variations in pressure into variations in electrical voltage, are now available. The output of these devices is an electrical signal, the strength of which varies with pressure. The transducers can be connected to various recording devices in order to obtain a permanent record.

Whatever type of pressure transducer is used, the researcher must face the problem of how to connect the transducer to the cavity in which the pressure is to be measured. Measuring the pressure in the subglottal cavity involves particular difficulties which we shall not consider here (a good discussion is provided by Baken 1987). For measurements relating to the oro-pharyngeal cavity, connection is made by means of a narrow tube, a few millimetres in diameter. The end of the tube should be perpendicular to the direction of air flow and must be located behind the constrictions for all of the consonants which are included in the study. If measurements relate to labial and coronal consonants, the tube may be inserted through the mouth and curled round the back teeth. In such a case, the tube emerges from the corners of the lips but, because its diameter is small, it interferes only minimally with normal articulation. Another possibility is to introduce the tube into the pharynx via the nasal cavity. This will interfere less with articulation, but it may be unpleasant for the subject and also has the disadvantage of requiring a longer tube.

## 8.2.3.2 Flow

Measurement of flow, like measurement of pressure, involves translating (*transducing*) flow rate into an electrical signal. The process may be divided into two parts: firstly, collection of the air of which the flow is to be measured and, secondly, the transduction itself.

The most common means of collecting air for flow measurement is having the subject wear a mask, of the type usually used for anaesthesia. It is important that no air should be able to escape from around the sides of the mask, and use of a head harness is recommended to achieve a tight seal. For most research (as opposed to clinical) applications, it is desirable to separate oral and nasal flow. For this purpose, the basic mask may be partitioned into oral and nasal compartments. Additional care is necessary in order to ensure that no leakage occurs from one into the other. The second step in air flow measurement is the transduction of flow into an electrical signal. The most popular type of instrument for achieving this is the *pneumotachograph* (Greek *pneumo-* 'breath' + *tacho-* 'speed' + *graph* 'write').

For many applications, it is sufficient to observe where increases and decreases in rate of flow occur over the course of an utterance. If precise values are required, then it is necessary to calibrate the output of the transducer, and special equipment exists for doing this. Flow is measured as volume per unit time, usually millilitres per second (ml/sec) or litres per second (l/sec).

A modification of the pneumotachograph is the system developed by Rothenberg (Rothenberg 1973, 1977). This uses a special mask, which does not channel air through a single outlet, but is ventilated with fine wire mesh through a series of small holes around its circumference. The system will record even very small fluctuations of flow. Although developed with the application of inverse filtering in mind (Section 8.3.6.1), it is also used in more purely aerodynamic studies.

It remains to comment on the difference between filtered and unfiltered flow signals. The stream of air flowing out of the mouth (or nose) has small variations in flow rate superimposed on it. It is the small variations which will, as it were, be converted into small variations in air pressure and radiated as a sound wave (Section 4.2.4). The gross up and down movements of an air flow signal are often referred to as the *DC component* and the small variations which are superimposed are often referred to as the *AC component*. (DC and AC stand for *direct current* and *alternating current* respectively.) In aerodynamic studies, it is the gross up and down movements which are usually of interest. Accordingly, it is often convenient to filter out the small variations. This means filtering out the higher-frequency components. (Gross movements are slow; small superimposed variations are fast.) The result is a smoother curve, in which the overall pattern is easier to discern.

Figure 8.3 shows filtered and unfiltered oral air flow traces for the English sentence **We saw a shark**, pronounced by a male speaker. These were recorded simultaneously using a Rothenberg mask. The spectrogram is derived from

218    *Speech production*

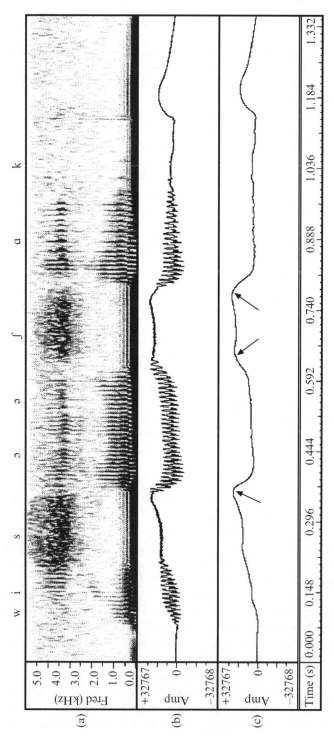

FIGURE 8.3   Unfiltered (b) and filtered (c) oral air flow traces for the English sentence **We saw a shark**, pronounced by a male speaker. These were recorded simultaneously using a Rothenberg mask. The spectrogram (a) is derived from the unfiltered signal. Notice that the unfiltered signal shows small variations in flow associated with the closing and opening of the vocal folds, while the filtered signal does not.

The arrows on the filtered trace (c) point to increases in flow at the beginning and ending of the fricative /s/, and at the end of the fricative /ʃ/. At these points, the glottis is being closed (or opened) while the constriction at the alveolar ridge is being released (or formed). For a brief interval of time, the vocal tract is relatively unconstricted, resulting in a brief increase in the flow rate.

the unfiltered signal, which looks like an ordinary pressure waveform super-imposed on an overall pattern of air flow. The portion relating to /ʃ/ may be compared with the spectrogram of Figure 7.1, which relates to an audio record-ing of the same utterance by the same speaker. In the filtered trace, the detail has been eliminated so that only the gross pattern is visible. This particular example is also interesting as an example of how an air flow recording can be used to obtain data on how movements of the oral articulators are coordinated with laryngeal activity.

The feature of interest in Figure 8.3 is the peaks in the flow trace which occur at the end of the /s/ and on either side of the /ʃ/, indicating a brief increase in flow rate. To understand why these should occur, it is necessary to think about the production of voiceless fricatives. At the level of the larynx, the glottis must be opened to allow a free passage of air. Further downstream, a fricative-like constriction must be formed in the oro-pharyngeal cavity. If the glottis is widened before the constriction is achieved or the constriction is released before the glottis returns to a closed position, then there will be a brief interval in which the passage through the oro-pharyngeal cavity is relatively unconstricted, resulting in an increase in flow. On the spectrogram of Fig-ure 7.1, this corresponds to the short gap which occurs at the end of the constriction interval before the onset of voicing for the /ɑ/.

The example of Figure 8.3 is also interesting because of what it reveals about the timing of vocal fold vibration. The oscillations which reflect the onset of voicing following /s/ begin just after the peak in the flow trace, when the glottis is still quite open. It can also be seen that the voicing for the vowel /ə/, which precedes the /ʃ/, continues until the flow trace reaches its peak.

## 8.3   The larynx and the vocal folds

Of all the organs involved in the production of speech, the vocal folds have the most diverse range of functions. For (voiced) vowels and sonorant consonants, modification of the airstream by means of vocal fold vibration is the only source of acoustic energy (Section 4.2.1). For these sounds, it is possible to vary the rate of vibration (fundamental frequency or $F_0$). This gives rise to perceived variation in pitch, which gives human language its melodic charac-ter. Perhaps less commonly, vowels and sonorant consonants may participate in contrasts based on phonation type, for example between breathy and non-breathy. For obstruent consonants, on the other hand, the vocal folds are responsible for distinctions between voiced, voiceless and aspirated varieties, and some less common types as well.

The vocal folds may serve as primary articulators in their own right, form-ing constrictions for [h] (and its voiced counterpart [ɦ]) and glottal stop ([ʔ]). Finally, the entire larynx may be moved up or down to compress or rarefy air which is trapped in the cavities above. These manœuvres are essential for the production of ejectives and implosives.

Experimental investigation of the larynx has revealed that laryngeal activity can be accounted for in terms of four basic gesture types (Sawashima and Hirose 1983; Hirose 1997). Two of these stand out as particularly important for speech, and might be termed primary: (1) opening-closing gestures, which regulate the degree of opening between the vocal folds and (2) stiffening-slackening gestures, which regulate the length, thickness and stiffness of the folds. Gestures of type (1) account for glottal stops and fricatives and also for phonation types. Gestures of type (2) account for $F_0$ variation. The two additional gesture types are: (3) raising-lowering gestures, which move the entire larynx up or down and (4) supplementary constricting gestures, which constrict the upper part of the larynx, above the vocal folds. These may also play a role in the glottal stop and, more generally, in sounds pronounced with glottal constriction.

Understanding just how the vocal folds work poses particularly difficult challenges. Firstly, the larynx and the vocal folds are not very accessible. Secondly, their structure is complicated. Thirdly, vocal fold vibration depends not only on the configuration of the folds themselves but also on aerodynamic factors. Fourthly, when the vocal folds vibrate, they move very quickly. Near the lower end of a low-pitched male voice, the folds might execute about 100 cycles of vibration per second (100 Hz), which is much too fast to be followed by eye. Fifthly, laryngeal activity must be coordinated with movements of the tongue and other structures above. The consequences of positioning the folds in any particular way will depend to some extent on events downstream in the vocal tract.

### 8.3.1   A simple description of the larynx

The larynx is a box of cartilage which continues the tube of the trachea and projects into the bottom part of the pharynx. The basic framework consists of four cartilages, the *cricoid*, the *thyroid* and the two *arytenoids*. Schematic drawings of these are shown in Figure 8.4. Notice in particular the *cricothyroid joint*, where the cricoid and the thyroid are hinged to each other. The two cartilages can rotate around this joint. If the front of the cricoid moves up, so that the gap between the two cartilages is narrowed, the top edge of the back must move downward and outward, taking the arytenoids with it. In this way, the distance from the arytenoids to the front of the thyroid will be increased. This manœuvre will have the effect of stretching the vocal folds, which run between the front of the thyroid and the arytenoids.

Figure 8.5 shows a schematic view of the vocal folds from above. As already mentioned, the folds run between the front of the thyroid cartilage at the front and the arytenoid cartilages at the rear. Each fold is attached to the *vocal process* of one of the arytenoids. The vocal processes project forward from the arytenoids. When they are brought together, they point towards the front of the thyroid cartilage. The extent to which the folds are together or apart at the rear depends on the positioning of the arytenoids in general and of the vocal

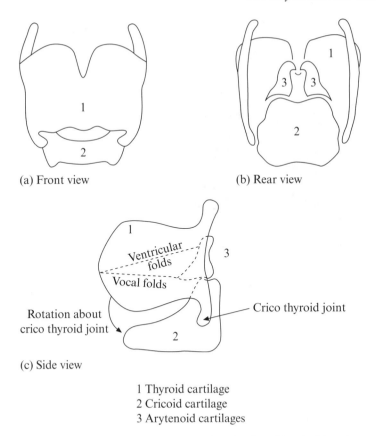

(a) Front view

(b) Rear view

(c) Side view

1 Thyroid cartilage
2 Cricoid cartilage
3 Arytenoid cartilages

FIGURE 8.4   Schematic diagrams showing the thyroid, cricoid and arytenoid cartilages as viewed from the front (a), read (b) and side (c). Adapted from Laver (1980).

The side view (c) shows the position of the vocal folds and the ventricular folds, which run from the thyroid cartilage at the front to the arytenoid cartilages at the rear. When the two cartilages are brought closer together at the front, the distance from the front of the thyroid to the arytenoids increases. As a result, the vocal folds are stretched.

processes in particular. By contrast, at the thyroid (front) end, the folds come together and cannot be moved apart.

We should also note that there is a second set of folds above the vocal folds (Figure 8.4). These are called the *ventricular folds* or *false vocal folds*. These also attach to the thyroid and the arytenoid cartilages, but they are somewhat further apart than the true vocal folds. In comparison with the true vocal folds, they contain much less muscle. The space between the true vocal folds and the ventricular folds is known as the *laryngeal ventricle* or the *ventricle of Morgagni*.

The true vocal folds are complex layered structures. The most detailed classification scheme is that of Hirano (Hirano 1977; Hirano 1981), who identifies five layers of soft tissue. However, these may be grouped into two, namely,

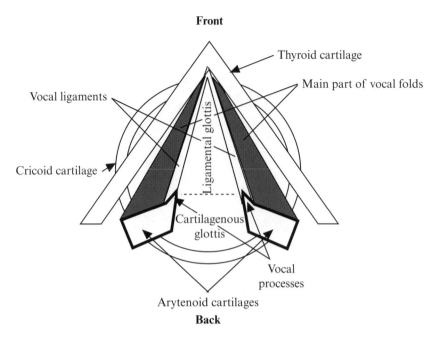

FIGURE 8.5    Schematic view of the vocal folds from above. The glottis is the space between the folds. It is bounded by the vocal ligaments (the inner edges of the vocal folds) at the front and by the arytenoid cartilages at the rear. Notice also the position of the vocal processes, which project forward from the arytenoids.

an outer *cover* and an inner *body*. The body and cover have very different mechanical properties. The cover, which contains no muscle, is relatively pliant and mobile whereas the body is relatively stiff and immobile.

In any case, the two vocal folds project inward from the sides. They may be pulled apart at the rear, allowing air to pass freely from the lungs to the pharynx. Or, they may be pulled together, protecting the entrance to the lungs. When vocal fold vibration (voicing) occurs, the folds move towards and away from each other. The frequency of vibration may be as low as 20 cycles per second (in low-pitched *creak*); at the other extreme, frequencies upwards of 1500 cycles per second are used in high soprano singing.

### 8.3.2   *Vocal fold vibration*

Figure 8.6 illustrates a cycle of vocal fold vibration seen in frontal cross-section and from above. Notice that: (1) The folds move vertically as well as horizontally. (2) There is a difference in timing between the upper and lower edges – in both closure (Frame 3) and opening (Frame 6), the lower edges of the folds are ahead of the upper. (3) The folds change in shape, owing to displacement of tissue. In Frames 5–8, when the folds are moving apart, the tissue which covers the inner margins is pushed upward and outward; in frames 1–4, the bump on

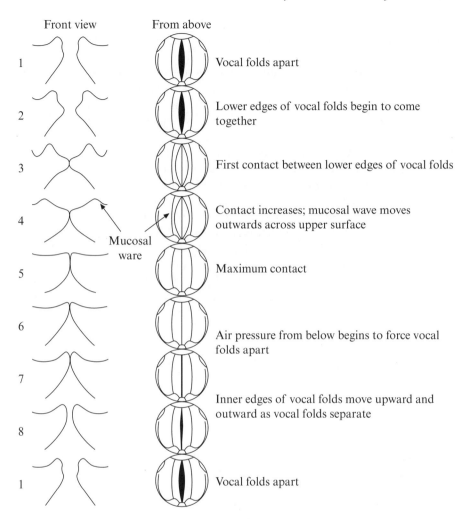

Front view     From above

1     Vocal folds apart

2     Lower edges of vocal folds begin to come together

3     First contact between lower edges of vocal folds

4     Contact increases; mucosal wave moves outwards across upper surface

Mucosal ware

5     Maximum contact

6     Air pressure from below begins to force vocal folds apart

7

8     Inner edges of vocal folds move upward and outward as vocal folds separate

1     Vocal folds apart

FIGURE 8.6   Schematic view of a single cycle of vocal fold vibration viewed in frontal cross-section (left) and from above (right). Adapted from Sundberg (1987).

the upper surface of the folds moves away from the midline. When the process is viewed from above, a wave (called the *mucosal wave* because the displacement involves the outer layer, or *mucosa*, of the folds) appears to travel across the surface of the folds, towards the sides of the tube.

This cycle of vibration is a prototypical example of *modal voice*. It is the sort of vibration which occurs when the speaker is in the low or middle part of his or her pitch range, with the folds relatively relaxed. It is also possible for vibration to occur under a variety of other conditions, resulting in different *phonation types*. For example, the folds may be brought more closely together than for modal voice. This typically results in a rather tense quality, which we

shall refer to here as *pressed voice*, though the term *creaky voice* is more frequently used. It is also possible for the folds to vibrate when they are somewhat
apart, so that complete closure does not occur and more air escapes during
each cycle of vibration. This results in *breathy voice*, as can often be heard in
intervocalic /h/ in English, for example in the word **behind**.

Discussions of phonation types are confusing for two reasons. Firstly,
different terms are used by different authors. We have already referred to the
use of the terms *pressed* and *creaky* to refer to a type of vocal fold vibration
in which the folds are held more tightly together than in modal voice;
*laryngealisation* and *glottalised phonation* have also been used for this phenomenon. In my view, *pressed* is a better designation since *creaky voice* and
*laryngealisation* may also imply the presence of irregularity like that found in
low-pitched *creak* (see below and Figure 8.9) while *pressed* suggests only a
greater degree of vocal fold adduction (cf. Gauffin and Sundberg 1989; Stevens
1988). It thus allows for a further distinction between presence or absence
of irregularity. Ladefoged has distinguished between more than one degree of
constriction. In Ladefoged (1971), three degrees are allowed for, but in later
publications this number is reduced to two (cf. Ladefoged 1973, 1993; Ladefoged
and Maddieson 1996). *Stiff voice* refers to the less constricted type (closer to
modal voice) while *creaky voice* and *laryngealisation* are alternative terms for
the more constricted type (closer to glottal stop).

For vibration with a greater degree of opening between the folds there is less
confusion. Ladefoged's classification has paralleled his classification of types
involving more constriction, with three degrees distinguished in Ladefoged
(1971) but only two degrees distinguished in later works. *Slack voice* is used for
the less open type (closer to modal voice) while *breathy voice* and *murmur* are
alternative terms for the type which shows a greater degree of opening. In this
way, phonation types may be placed on a continuum extending from fully closed
vocal folds (as in glottal stop) through modal voice to fully open vocal folds.

A second reason for confusion is that the number of dimensions used in
classifying phonation types may vary. In this book, all references to phonation
types are based on a one-dimensional classification of the type just described
(see also Section 4.3). This seems to work well for linguistic description; no
language has yet been reported which contrasts, for example, two types of
relatively pressed (creaky) phonation, produced by different mechanisms. A
one-dimensional classification is also presupposed by the system of laryngeal
features now commonly used by phonologists, which uses the features [spread
glottis] and [constricted glottis] (see Section 1.4.2 and Section 8.3.7). However,
much more research is needed on linguistic distinctions which involve phonation type, and it is possible that a one-dimensional classification will prove to
be inadequate.

More elaborate classifications allow for vibration in different parts of the
vocal folds, for different settings of the ventricular folds, and for production
of two or more phonation types simultaneously. The most elaborate system of
this type is Catford's classification (Catford 1964, 1977). Laver's classification

(Laver 1980, 1994) is also well-known among phoneticians. There is not space to discuss either of these here, though it is interesting to note that Laver's classification incorporates a continuum from *tense* (highly constricted) to *moderately breathy* which parallels Ladefoged's one-dimensional classification but which is said to be based on the overall tension of the laryngeal musculature rather than on phonation type proper (see Laver 1994: 418–420). Both Catford and Laver go beyond the needs of phonological description, and aim to provide a framework for describing types of voice production which might characterise individuals or social groups but which do not seem to be used contrastively in phonological systems.

At extremely low and extremely high pitches, modal vibration is no longer possible, and different mechanisms must be brought into play. These are known as *vocal registers*. A definitive description of register distinctions relevant to speech production has been given by Hollien (1974). (Finer distinctions between registers are often made in studies of singing.) For very low pitches, the rate of vibration is sufficiently slow for the individual taps of the vocal folds (when they snap shut) to be audible. There may be considerable irregularity in the duration of individual vibratory cycles (periods), giving the resulting sound a harsh, irregular character. This register is known as *creak*, *vocal fry* or *pulse*. In contrast, for extremely high pitches, *falsetto* or *loft* phonation would be used. Falsetto phonation is generally softer and breathier than modal phonation, and its pressure waveform more closely approximates a sine curve. A number of authors (for example, Laver 1994) treat *creak* and *falsetto* as phonation types rather than as registers.

### 8.3.3 Aerodynamics of vocal fold vibration

Aerodynamic factors play an important role in vocal fold vibration. When the folds are held loosely together, the airstream coming up from the lungs is obstructed, and air pressure builds up below them. When the pressure from below is sufficiently large, they yield to it and come apart (Figure 8.6, Frames 6–8). Once the folds have opened, however, other forces act to pull them together again. These are of two types: (1) elastic recoil force, which acts to restore the folds to their original position, and (2) the so-called *Bernoulli force* exerted by the airstream.

The Bernoulli force takes its name from the eighteenth-century Swiss mathematician Daniel Bernoulli, who developed a general theory of the motion of gases and liquids. When a flowing gas or liquid is made to travel faster, there is a drop in the pressure which it exerts perpendicular to the direction of flow. One case in which such an increase will occur is when the liquid or gas is made to flow through a narrow passage. The outward pressure on the sides of the passage drops, with the result that an inward force is exerted on the sides. A common situation in which the Bernoulli force is observed is when a wind blows down a corridor from which doors open off to the sides; the drop in pressure exerts an inward force, causing the doors to slam shut. In Figure 8.6, it is the Bernoulli force which causes the lower edges of the vocal folds to come together in Frame 3.

This account of vocal fold vibration, known as the *myoelastic-aerodynamic theory*, has been generally accepted since the 1950s, though subsequent research has led to a better understanding of both elastic and aerodynamic aspects. The important point is that voicing is the result of a complex interaction between the airstream and the vocal folds. The inward and outward movements of the folds are not controlled individually but depend on both aerodynamic factors and the laryngeal setting (controlled by the laryngeal muscles). In this regard, vocal fold vibration is like trilling the tongue tip, the uvula or the lips.

### 8.3.4   *Experimental investigation of the larynx*

Studies of the larynx may be divided into three main types. The first type is concerned with the overall laryngeal setting. Into this category come investigations of the length and thickness of the vocal folds, the width of the glottis and the activity of the laryngeal muscles. These generally require expensive equipment and the cooperation of skilled medical practitioners, and accordingly cannot be carried out on a large scale.

The second type involves more indirect methods of monitoring vocal fold vibration. Under this heading, we may include techniques for tracking the movements of the vocal folds and the patterns of air flow during vocal fold vibration. There has also been considerable interest in developing measures of phonation type which can be derived directly from acoustic waveforms and spectra. Techniques in this category are widely available and do not require medical supervision. The subject does not experience serious discomfort or danger. Accordingly, this kind of investigation is both much easier to carry out and much easier to find subjects for, and large-scale studies are possible.

The third type of study involves developing models of vocal fold activity. Models help to elucidate the relationships between aerodynamic conditions, the vocal fold setting, vocal fold movement and the output sound. Models of the vocal folds have been of greater interest to linguists than, for example, models of the tongue because they have played a role in developing a system of distinctive features (Section 1.4.2) to account for vocal fold activity.

### 8.3.5   *The laryngeal setting*

Three general types of techniques have been used in investigations of the laryngeal setting. These are direct observation, imaging and electromyography.

#### 8.3.5.1   Direct observation

Much of our understanding of the mechanics of vocal fold vibration has come from direct observation. *Direct observation* refers to situations where the investigator is able to look directly at the larynx. This involves using excised larynges – that is, larynges extracted from cadavers.

## 8.3.5.2 Imaging

*Imaging techniques* are techniques which register information about positions or movements of structures without actually contacting the structures (Stone 1997). Into this category come radiographic (X-ray) investigations and techniques based on viewing the larynx from above. We shall not discuss radiograhic techniques here, since X-ray investigations have been carried out only infrequently, at least in work of interest to linguistic phoneticians.

Viewing the larynx from above began in 1854 with the invention of the laryngeal mirror by the singing teacher Manuel Garcia. The idea is a simple one. A small circular mirror is inserted into the subject's mouth so that the mirror itself is at the back, over the pharynx. The larynx is directly below the mirror, and will be reflected in it, and (assuming sufficient illumination) the reflection can also be seen by the investigator looking into the mirror. The laryngeal mirror has now been superseded by modern *endoscopes* or *laryngoscopes*. These are like rigid telescopes, with an eyepiece for the investigator at the exterior end, which are inserted into the oral cavity. However, the basic idea – obtaining a view of the larynx from the top of the pharynx – is the same. The main shortcoming of the technique for the linguistic phonetician is that, because the mouth must be fully open and the tongue protruded, it is not possible to observe the larynx during the production of consonants or in running speech generally.

It is possible to view the larynx from above and leave the subject's mouth free if the larynx is viewed via the nasal cavity. This may be accomplished by means of a technique known as *fibre-optic laryngoscopy*, which makes use of the *flexible endoscope* or *fibrescope*. The fibrescope is a flexible tube which is inserted through the nasal cavity down into the pharynx. The tube contains two bundles of thin glass fibres, one to transmit light down to illuminate the folds and the other to transmit the image of the folds up to the eyepiece. The fibrescope has been much used in linguistic phonetic research, particularly to study laryngeal adjustments during consonant articulations. It has also proved useful as a means of obtaining information about the laryngeal setting above the level of the vocal folds, and also about the size of the pharyngeal opening and the position of the soft palate.

Whichever method is used to view the larynx, the image may be photographed, recorded on cine film, displayed on a video monitor or, as has recently become possible, digitised and displayed on a computer screen. Good discussions of methodology may be found in Baken (1987) and Hirose (1995), the second of which includes a description of a high-speed digital imaging system.

## 8.3.5.3   Electromyography

The third general method of investigating the laryngeal setting mentioned above involves recording the activity of the laryngeal muscles. This is accomplished via *electromyography* (*EMG*), which is a technique for detecting the electrical activity associated with muscle contraction.

It is well known that muscles initiate movement by contracting, bringing the structures to which they are attached closer together. It is also possible for contraction to occur without shortening (for example, if another, opposing, muscle contracts simultaneously). In the first case (contraction with shortening), the tension of the muscle remains the same, and the contraction is said to be *isotonic*. In the second case, although the length of the muscle remains unchanged, its tension increases. The contraction is said to be *isometric*.

Muscle contraction is always associated with electrical activity, and electrical activity occurs only if contraction is taking place. From this, it follows that if we can detect electrical activity in a particular muscle fibre, we know that it is contracting (though it is not possible to distinguish isometric from isotonic contraction). Electrical activity may be detected by means of electrodes, which must be in close proximity to the muscle fibres whose activity is to be recorded. Especially in the case of the laryngeal muscles, correct insertion of the electrodes requires a very high degree of experience and skill.

The laryngeal muscles, which we shall not discuss in detail here, control the setting of the vocal folds by positioning the various cartilages. The muscles are usually divided into two groups: the *intrinsic* muscles, which link the thyroid, cricoid and arytenoid cartilages to each other, and the *extrinsic* muscles, which attach to the thyroid cartilage and hyoid bone and link the entire laryngeal assembly to other structures above and below, including the *mandible* (jaw) and *sternum* (breastbone). The extrinsic muscles are sometimes referred to as the *strap muscles* (some authors restrict this term to the muscles which link the larynx and the hyoid with structures below). The intrinsic muscles are largely responsible for controlling the primary dimensions of stiffness and glottal width and also for constriction above the level of the vocal folds. The extrinsic muscles move the entire larynx up and down.

By far the greatest interest has attached to the intrinsic muscles, which, between them, are responsible for the two primary gesture types (opening-closing and stiffening-slackening). In discussions of stiffening and slackening of the vocal folds, referred to below, particular attention has focussed on the *cricothyroid* muscle and the *vocalis* muscle. When the cricothyroid muscle (CT) contracts and shortens, it brings about rotation about the cricothyroid joint (Figure 8.4). This has the effect of stretching the vocal folds, making them longer, thinner and stiffer. The vocalis muscle (VOC), which makes up the bulk of the inner body of the folds, is opposed to the cricothyroid. If it contracts and shortens, it brings the arytenoids closer to the front of the thyroid, thereby making the vocal folds shorter and thicker. Since the vocalis is internal to the folds, its contraction will typically affect the body (i.e. itself) and the

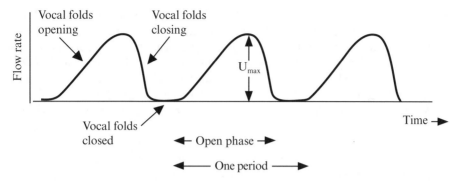

FIGURE 8.7    Schematic drawing of an idealised *flow glottogram*, obtained by inverse filtering. $U_{max}$ is the peak flow rate.

cover in different ways. (See Section 8.3.1.) In the case of an isotonic contraction (involving shortening but no change in tension), its own stiffness will remain unchanged but the cover will become thicker and slacker.

### 8.3.6    More indirect methods for monitoring vocal fold activity

Under this heading belong inverse filtering, electroglottography (EGG), photo-electric glottography (PGG) and acoustic measures of phonation types.

#### 8.3.6.1 Inverse filtering

The technique of inverse filtering is an application of the source-filter theory of speech production (Chapter 4). We have seen that the source waveform for voiced sounds is, in fact, a pattern of air flow through the glottis. By the time the airstream emerges from the lips, giving rise to a sound wave, the pattern has become more complicated due to effects of the vocal tract filter. The aim of inverse filtering is to start from the final output sound, or from a recording of air flow at the lips, and to undo the effects of the vocal tract filter, reversing the process diagrammed in Figure 4.3. The filter which reverses the effects of the vocal tract filter is called the *inverse filter*.

The output of the process is a waveform which estimates the rate of air flow through the glottis over time, rather like that shown in Figure 2.16. This is often referred to as the *flow glottogram*, abbreviated *FLOGG*. A schematic drawing of an idealised FLOGG for modal voice is shown in Figure 8.7. Each 'mountain' corresponds to a single opening and closing of the vocal folds. The left-hand side corresponds to vocal fold opening, when flow rate increases as glottal area increases. The right-hand side corresponds to vocal fold closing. Taken together, the opening and closing portions constitute the *open phase*, that is, the portion of the cycle when the glottis is open. The flat portion of the

FLOGG corresponds to that part of the vibratory cycle when the vocal folds are closed and no air can flow through the glottis. This is the *closed phase*.

Unfortunately, inverse filtering is more complicated than it sounds. In the example of Figure 4.3, we had the advantage of being able to choose the filter shape. In inverse filtering, the researcher has to deal with a real speech waveform 'warts and all', and does not know in advance what the filter is like. A good account of the difficulties involved may be found in Ní Chasaide and Gobl (1997).

Despite its attendant difficulties and limitations, inverse filtering has one major advantage which makes it the method of choice for many researchers. This is its close relationship to the source-filter theory. As we have just said, the FLOGG corresponds to the waveform of the glottal source. Accordingly, inverse filtering makes it possible to study the relationship between glottal activity and its acoustic consequences in a straightforward and mathematically rigorous way, which is not possible using other methods such as photoelectric glottography or electroglottography (Sections 8.3.6.2, 8.3.6.3).

### 8.3.6.2   Photoelectric glottography

*Photoelectric glottography* (*PGG*) is based on monitoring the amount of light which passes through the glottis. There must be a source of light below the glottis and a sensor above, or vice versa. During investigations of running speech, the component which lies above the glottis (whether light source or sensor) must be inserted via the nasal cavity, as with the flexible fibrescope. The component which lies below the glottis is able to sense or transmit light through the skin, and must be in contact with the skin at the appropriate place on the subject's neck. A good overview of the various techniques may be found in Gerratt *et al.* (1991).

If the glottis is fully closed, light will not pass through it. If, on the other hand, the glottis is fully open, a maximal amount of light will pass through. Intermediate degrees of opening should result in transmission of intermediate amounts of light. During normal vocal fold vibration, there will be one up-and-down movement of the PGG trace per cycle, reflecting opening (with increasing light) and closing (with decreasing light) movements of the vocal folds. PGG has been used in some important studies of vocal fold activity during obstruent consonants (a thorough overview is provided by Dixit 1989), but is now less popular than electroglottography.

### 8.3.6.3   Electroglottography (electrolaryngography)

The technique known as *electroglottography* (*EGG*) or alternatively as *electrolaryngography* or *laryngography* is used to monitor changing patterns of vocal fold contact during speech. It is becoming increasingly popular as a technique for investigating vocal fold activity. This is because it involves little or no discomfort and is not intimidating for the subject (or, in a clinical context, the patient). It is easy to use, and can be taken into the field.

In electroglottography, electrodes are placed on the neck, at either side of the subject's thyroid cartilage. A weak current is then passed between them. If the vocal folds are fully together (as in Frame 5 of Figure 8.6), the current can pass in a direct path across them. By contrast, if the folds are fully apart (as in Frames 1, 2, and 8 of Figure 8.6), the direct passage of the current will, as it were, be blocked by the intervening air. Between these two extremes, intermediate levels of current flow are possible.

If the vocal folds are vibrating, current flow will alternately increase and decrease as the extent of contact between the folds increases and decreases. To put the matter another way, resistance across the larynx alternately decreases and increases, and it is actually resistance which is measured by the apparatus. In any case, the output waveform shows a series of upward and downward movements, with each cycle corresponding to a cycle of vocal fold vibration. This waveform is often referred to as $L_x$ (for *larynx excitation*), following Fourcin (1974). It should also be mentioned that some systems display the waveform the other way round, with minimum contact (i.e. maximum resistance) at the top rather than at the bottom.

The question of overriding importance for EGG has been how to interpret the output waveform. Investigations of various types have confirmed that EGG provides a good indication of the amount of contact between the vocal folds. On the other hand, if the vocal folds are not in contact, EGG provides no information about the size of the glottal opening. Good overviews of the technique of EGG and the problems involved in interpreting EGG waveforms are provided by Baken (1992), Colton and Conture (1990) and Titze (1990).

It is possible to link various sections of the typical EGG cycle with various parts of the vocal fold cycle. A schematic illustration is given in Figure 8.8. The prototypical $L_x$ (EGG) cycle indicates increasing followed by decreasing contact area. The slope of the upward portion (corresponding to vocal fold closure) is rather steep. This may be followed by a sort of plateau (corresponding to a period of maximum contact). The slope of the downward portion (corresponding to vocal fold opening) is more gradual. Finally, a low plateau (trough) corresponds to the open part of the cycle, before the vocal folds snap shut.

Figure 8.9 shows examples of EGG ($L_x$) waveforms for prototypical (a) breathy and (c) pressed phonation. Both contrast with (b), which is closer to canonical modal voice. All three examples are sustained pronunciations of a low central vowel ([a]). Examples (a) and (b) were produced by a Korean female singer who specialises in the style known as *P'ansori*. In the lower part of her range, the qualities known as *T'ongsong* and *Agusong* are distinguished by phonation type. *T'ongsong* is very breathy, while *Agusong* is more modal. The waveform for the breathy type is shown in (a) and the waveform for the modal type is shown in (b). It will be seen that the breathy type (a) has small mountains separated by wide valleys, indicating a short closed phase and a

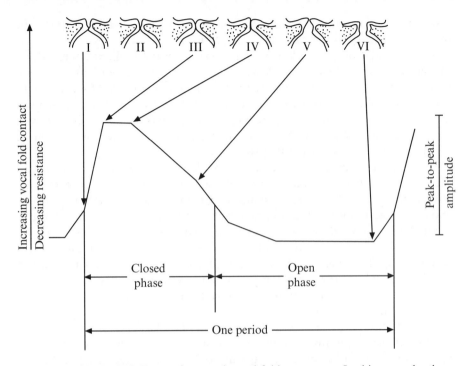

FIGURE 8.8    The $L_x$ (EGG) waveform and vocal fold movement. In this example, the beginning of the open phase is identified as the point at which the waveform descends to 30% of its peak-to-peak value. Adapted from Baken (1987).

long open phase. This is as expected, given the definition of breathy voice (Section 8.3.2), though it should also be noted that example (a) is a rather extreme case.

By contrast, example (c) illustrates a waveform for highly pressed (creaky) phonation. This was produced by an Egyptian professional reciter of the Qur'ān, who uses this type of phonation in the upper part of his range. The waveform shown in (d) is the exact opposite of that in (a), in that it shows broad plateaux separated by narrow valleys. This indicates a long closed phase and short open phase.

There is also a difference in the pressure waveforms for these vowels. In (a), there is one prominent peak at the beginning of each period, followed by rather small secondary peaks. In (b), the secondary peaks are more prominent, and in (c) they are more prominent still. These differences in the strength of the secondary peaks reflect the strength of the higher-frequency components in the spectrum, as will be seen in Section 8.3.6.4. We should also notice that there is a one-to-one correspondence between periods in the $L_x$ waveforms and periods in the audio waveforms. Each period of the audio waveform corresponds to a brief 'ripping' of the cavities above the larynx brought about by the snapping shut of the vocal folds (Section 3.3.2).

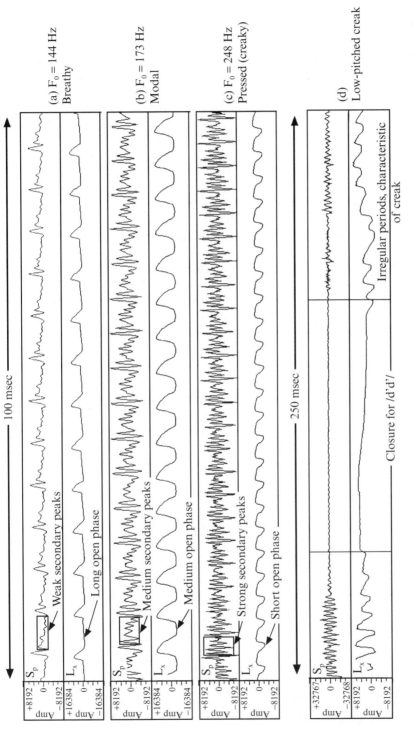

FIGURE 8.9   Example of $L_x$ (EGG) waveforms illustrating four phonation types. Examples (a), (b) and (c) are sustained productions of a low central vowel ([ɐ]). The breathy (a) and modal (b) examples were produced by a Korean female singer. The example of pressed (creaky) phonation was produced by a male professional reciter of the Qur'an from Egypt. Example (d) shows an intervocalic geminate glottalised /d'd'/ from the Gamo word /ʃod'd'e/ 'frog', pronounced by a male speaker from South West Ethiopia.

Figure 8.9 (d) shows a typical example of a fourth phonation type, low-pitched creak. The $L_x$ waveform relates to the pronunciation of glottalised geminate alveolar stop (/d'd'/) in Gamo, a language of South West Ethiopia. This consonant is pronounced with an accompanying glottal stop and is slightly implosive. At the beginning of the oral closure, there is a steep (though small) upward movement of the $L_x$ waveform to a peak. The corresponding valley does not appear until the end of the oral closure. Before the oral closure, the cycles become longer and increasingly asymmetrical whereas, on the right side of the closure, the waveform shows highly irregular alternation between longer and shorter cycles. It is the right-hand portion which is like prototypical creak.

Figure 8.9 (d) illustrates another feature of some EGG waveforms, that is, up and down movement of the trace as a whole. This would be described as the *DC component* of the waveform, whereas the smaller variations correspond to the *AC component* (Section 8.2.3.2). The interpretation of such gross movements is controversial, but it is possible that they may reflect vertical movements of the larynx. A more accurate means of determining larynx height is provided by the recently developed multichannel electroglottograph, which makes use of two pairs of electrodes (Rothenberg 1992).

Finally, it should be mentioned that both EGG and inverse filtering are very reliable methods for determining $F_0$. If we compare the $L_x$ waveforms of Figure 8.9 (a)–(c) with the examples of periodic waveforms in Figure 2.10, we can see that it would be much easier to determine precisely the duration of each individual period. Accordingly, no matter what method of $F_0$ extraction is used (Section 3.4.3), it will probably work better if applied to an EGG signal or to the output of an inverse filter than if applied to the speech signal itself. Introductions to EGG (electrolaryngography), which are usually aimed at clinical applications, typically concentrate on the use of EGG for $F_0$ extraction (Abberton and Fourcin 1984; Fourcin *et al.* 1995).

### 8.3.6.4    Acoustic measures of phonation types

In our account of the source-filter theory (Section 4.3), we said that breathier phonation is associated with a steeper slope of the source function, and, accordingly with weaker high-frequency harmonics. By contrast, more pressed (creaky) phonation is generally associated with a shallower slope of the source function and stronger high-frequency harmonics. These general characteristics remain evident in output spectra, in spite of the pattern of peaks and valleys superimposed by the vocal tract filter (Figure 4.6).

The extent to which the overall spectrum slopes downwards from low to high frequencies is known as the *spectral tilt*. Spectral tilt is a single dimension, and it marries well with a one-dimensional classification of phonation types from breathy (relatively open glottis) to creaky (relatively closed glottis) to glottal stop (fully closed glottis) (Ladefoged 1973; Ladefoged and Maddieson 1996). As we progress from breathy to pressed (creaky), we expect a change from relatively large (steep) spectral tilt to relatively small (shallow) spectral tilt.

Figure 8.10 shows narrow band spectra for the examples of Figure 8.9 (a)–(c). Notice that the high frequencies (above 3000 Hz) are relatively highest in amplitude for the example of very pressed (creaky) phonation (c) and lowest in amplitude for the example of breathy phonation (a). As already mentioned, the weakness or strength of the higher harmonics is evident in the relative prominence of secondary peaks in the acoustic waveforms of Figure 8.9 (a)–(c).

Such examples might suggest that measuring the relative prominence of the high-frequency end of the spectrum would be a good means of quantifying phonation type. In practice, however, it has proved difficult to come up with a generally accepted formula for doing this. A more popular approach has been to compare the prominence of individual harmonics at the lower end of the spectrum. One possible measure is the difference in amplitude between the second harmonic ($H_2$) and the first, or fundamental, harmonic ($H_1$ or $F_0$). In (a), $H_1$ dominates $H_2$, whereas in (b) the two are nearly equal and in (c) $H_2$ dominates $H_1$. Another possibility would be to compare the amplitude of the fundamental with the amplitude of the strongest harmonic in the first formant peak. Measures of this type must be used with caution because the amplitudes of individual harmonics will be influenced by the peaks and valleys of the vocal tract filter (Section 4.3). On the other hand, there is some evidence from perceptual experiments that vowels with a prominent fundamental ($H_1$) will sound more breathy (Bickley 1982). More research needs to be done in this area.

Two other types of measurements have been suggested as means of quantifying degrees of breathiness or creakiness. One noticeable characteristic of breathy voice is the presence of [h]-like friction which is, as it were, superimposed, on the basic sound quality. Accordingly, one way of quantifying breathiness would be to quantify the amount of friction present (Ladefoged *et al.* 1988). As regards creaky voice (at least low-pitched creaky voice), it may be characterised by considerable irregularity in the duration of individual periods. The example of Figure 8.9 (d), in which short periods alternate with long ones, is an extreme case. Variation of this type is known as *jitter*. Jitter also characterises some voice disorders, and there are standard methods for quantifying it (Baken 1987). Measurements relating to jitter in distinctively creaky vowels in Jalapa Mazatec (spoken in Mexico) are presented in Ladefoged *et al.* (1988).

### *8.3.7  Models of vocal fold vibration and features of the larynx*

Vocal fold vibration is particularly challenging because of the complicated interaction between aerodynamic factors and the properties of the folds themselves. It is only via models that a full understanding will be possible. In practice, individual approaches to modelling have focussed on either aerodynamic aspects or biomechanical aspects.

Probably the best-known and most influential model of vocal fold vibration is the *two mass model*, developed by Ishizaka and Matsudaira (1968). In this model, each vocal fold is represented by two masses and three springs, as in

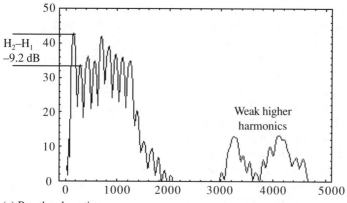

(a) Breathy phonation

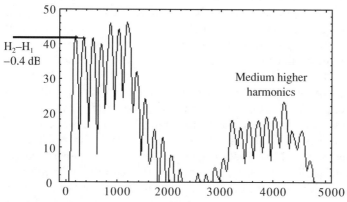

(b) Modal phonation

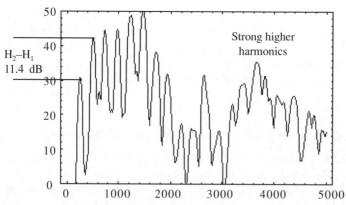

(c) Pressed phonation (creaky voice)

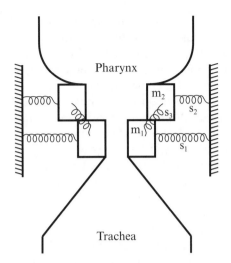

FIGURE 8.11    The *two mass model* of the vocal folds. In this model, each vocal fold is represented by two masses, $m_1$ and $m_2$, and three springs, $s_1$, $s_2$ and $s_3$. Two of the springs connect the masses to the pharyngeal walls, and the third spring connects them to each other. The masses move inwards and outwards, as do the vocal folds when they vibrate.

Figure 8.11. The masses move inwards and outwards, as do the vocal folds when they vibrate. The use of two masses rather than one (as in earlier models) makes it possible to represent the difference in motion between the upper and lower parts of the folds, illustrated in Figure 8.6. This difference between upper and lower parts is seen to play a crucial role in maintaining oscillation once it has started. More generally, the analysis of the aerodynamic contribution to vocal fold vibration is highly sophisticated. A good appreciation of how the model works may be gained by working through the step-by-step account in Broad (1979). The application of the model to breathy and pressed (creaky) types of phonation is discussed by Stevens (1988).

The two-mass model is familiar to linguists via the classic paper of Halle and Stevens (1971), though the revised version of Stevens (1977) is a better-considered presentation. Halle and Stevens present results of calculations

FIGURE 8.10    (*opposite*) Narrow band FFT spectra (effective bandwidth 40 Hz) for the low central vowels illustrated in Figure 8.9 (a)–(c). The amplitude of the high-frequency harmonics is lowest for breathy phonation (a) and highest for pressed phonation (c). The difference in amplitude between the first and second harmonics also changes with changing phonation type. In general, breathy phonation is associated with a strong first harmonic (fundamental) while in pressed (creaky) phonation the first harmonic is weak as compared with the second harmonic. In this case, the difference is exaggerated because the fundamental frequency of (c) is considerably higher than that of (a) and the second harmonic is closer to the first formant peak.

which determine whether or not vocal fold vibration will occur under conditions defined by three parameters: the pressure drop across the glottis ($\Delta P$), the average glottal width (w) and the stiffness of the spring $s_3$ which connect the two masses (k). The connecting springs are taken to correspond to the glottal walls (i.e. the inner edges of the vocal folds).

In order to derive their system of features, Halle and Stevens divided up both stiffness and glottal width parameters (k and w) into three levels, namely stiff-neutral-slack and spread-neutral-constricted. This gives nine possible combinations of stiffness and width levels (stiff, spread; stiff, neutral; stiff, constricted, etc.). These nine combinations can be identified with impressionistic-phonetic categories though the same cautions apply here as in the case of the vowel dispersion model (Section 6.10). Halle and Stevens express the nine categories in terms of four binary features ([± stiff vocal folds], [± slack vocal folds], [± spread glottis], [± constricted glottis]). The feature [+ spread glottis] is used to specify aspiration in the feature tree of Figure 1.3 (a).

More recently, attention has focussed on the mechanical properties of vocal fold tissue, as researchers have taken advantage of advances in the physics and mathematics of elasticity. This general approach to modelling is bearing fruit in a better understanding of how the laryngeal muscles regulate frequency and amplitude of vibration (Titze 1994). Another recent development has been the application of chaos theory to account for irregularities between cycles (Baken 1995).

Thus far, advances in vocal fold modelling have had no influence on phonological feature systems. This is probably because, unlike the two-mass model, more recent models have not lent themselves to reduction to a small number of simple dimensions. In the longer term, if vocal fold stiffness is to be a basic dimension in systems of phonological features, it will be necessary to take into account progress in our understanding of the nature of stiffness in vocal fold tissue.

### 8.3.8 Control of fundamental frequency

The frequency at which the vocal folds vibrate should depend primarily on their stiffness. We expect high $F_0$ from stiff, thin folds and low $F_0$ from slack, thick folds. The folds become both stiffer and thinner when they are stretched, and so increasing the amount of 'pull' on the folds should result in an increase in $F_0$. This expectation was confirmed by early studies based on X-ray imaging and the laryngeal mirror. These showed that, as fundamental frequency rose, the folds became both longer and thinner.

Elongation of the vocal folds is brought about by contraction of the cricothyroid (CT) muscle (Section 8.3.5.3). EMG studies have confirmed that, as expected, increases in $F_0$ are accompanied by increases in the level of CT activity. Unfortunately, the situation is more complicated because of the possibility of contracting the vocalis muscle, which forms the body of the folds. It is clear that the possibilities for interaction between the CT and the vocalis (VOC) are numerous and allow for fine control over the stiffness of both the body and the cover of the vocal folds. This, in turn, must account for the fine control which speakers (and singers) are able to exert over vocal pitch.

Two other factors also appear to play a role in determining the frequency of vibration. These are subglottal pressure and larynx height. Other things being equal, an increase in subglottal pressure will increase $F_0$. This relationship is quantified and discussed in some detail in Titze (1989, 1994). As regards larynx height, it has long been observed (and it is easy to verify oneself) that the larynx tends to be placed higher in the neck as $F_0$ increases. The nature of the relationship between larynx height and $F_0$ is still not well understood. One proposal is that, as the larynx is raised, more vertical pull is exerted on the membrane which lines the laryngeal airway and this increases the overall tension on the vocal folds (Stevens 1977; Ohala 1978; Hombert *et al.* 1979). It also seems likely that, as the larynx moves up and down, the relationship between the cricoid and thyroid cartilages will change, thereby changing the amount of pull on the vocal folds in the longitudinal (front–back) direction (Honda 1995).

### 8.3.9  *Control of voicing in obstruents*

The phonological contrast between [+ voiced] and [– voiced] obstruents has been a major preoccupation of linguistic phoneticians. Two related questions concerning these consonants have occupied researchers. The first question concerns how the contrast is implemented. The second question concerns the commonly observed differences in $F_0$ at the onset of vowels following the [– voiced] and [+ voiced] types. One possibility is that the differences in $F_0$ are simply automatic consequences of measures taken to inhibit or promote voicing and are not implemented independently. Another possibility is that the mechanisms which raise or lower $F_0$ are not necessary for implementing the [± voiced] contrast. On this view, differences in $F_0$ are, as it were, added on primarily for the purposes of *auditory enhancement* (Section 7.9).

#### 8.3.9.1  Problems of maintaining voicing: aerodynamic aspects

From an aerodynamic point of view, producing obstruent consonants, especially stops, with vocal fold vibration is somewhat problematic. During each cycle of vocal fold vibration, air pressure from below forces the vocal folds apart (Section 8.3.3). This can happen only if there is a sufficient pressure drop across the glottis (that is, if the pressure below the vocal folds, $P_{sg}$, is sufficiently greater than the pressure above, $P_o$). If there is a complete closure in the oro-pharyngeal cavity and the velopharyngeal port is closed, then any air particles which flow into the cavity will remain trapped there. This means that $P_o$ will rise. Since, as we have seen, $P_{sg}$ tends to remain approximately constant (Section 8.2.2), the difference between $P_{sg}$ and $P_o$ will lessen. In other words, the pressure drop across the glottis will decrease, and may become too small for voicing to continue. This is why voicing often becomes weaker or fades out altogether during stop consonants which are [+ voiced], particularly if they are phonologically long. An example is provided in Figure 8.12, which shows a spectrogram and $L_x$ waveform for the Arabic word /ʕaddad/ 'to count' pronounced by a male speaker of Egyptian Arabic.

In contrast, for vowels and sonorant consonants, air particles always have an escape route from the oral cavity (through the nasal cavity for nasals; around one or both sides of the tongue for laterals). Excessive air pressure does not build up in the oro-pharyngeal cavity. Accordingly, it should be possible to continue vocal fold vibration for as long as the speaker chooses to prolong the sound. Voicing that can be prolonged is sometimes referred to as *spontaneous voicing*, a term introduced by Chomsky and Halle (1968).

Modelling studies have been very important in determining just how long voicing can be maintained under various conditions. A much-cited study is that of Westbury (1983), who calculates that voicing can be maintained during a stop closure for about 60 msec if no active measures are taken by the speaker (Section 8.3.9.2).

### 8.3.9.2   Strategies for maintaining and inhibiting voicing

Since it is the building up of pressure in the oro-pharyngeal cavity which will tend to curtail voicing in [+ voiced] obstruents, any mechanisms which prevent pressure in the oral cavity from rising too rapidly will also tend to favour voicing. Three mechanisms which may serve this function are:

1   Lowering the larynx and/or advancing the tongue root, which will expand the pharynx (Section 8.2.1).
2   Incomplete closure of the velopharyngeal port. This will allow a bit of air to leak out, preventing the build-up of pressure. At the same time, the opening cannot be so great as for a proper nasal consonant.
3   Slackening the vocal folds, thereby reducing the size of the pressure drop needed to maintain vibration. This mechanism was suggested by Halle and Stevens (1971). The effect would be slower, breathier vocal fold vibration. However, the situation is complicated by the fact that the character of vocal fold vibration will change as the pressure drop across the glottis decreases, even without any active adjustment on the part of the speaker (Bickley and Stevens 1986).

All three of the mechanisms just mentioned are said to be *active* because they involve movements which are under the speaker's control. To these may be added the possibility of *passive expansion* of the oro-pharyngeal cavity. If the walls of the oro-pharyngeal cavity are slack and compliant, then an increase in the air pressure inside will exert a slight outward push, causing the cavity to expand and the pressure inside to lower. The extent to which this is possible depends on place of articulation. Passive expansion is greatest for bilabials, which have the largest oro-pharyngeal cavity and, accordingly, the

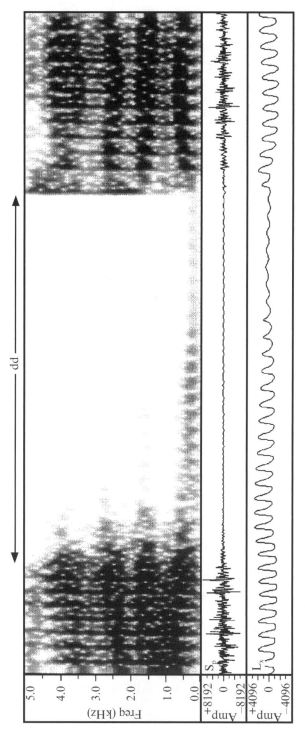

FIGURE 8.12 Spectrogram, audio waveform and $L_x$ waveform for geminate /dd/ in Arabic /ˤaddad/ 'to count', pronounced by a male speaker from Egypt. The voicing decreases in amplitude and becomes increasingly breathy during the closure interval.

largest surface area of compliant walls. It is smallest for velars, for the opposite reason.

By contrast, [− voiced] obstruents present the opposite kind of difficulty. If the vocal folds are vibrating, and there is no change in the laryngeal setting, they will continue to vibrate as long as aerodynamic conditions permit. It thus seems possible that, in producing [− voiced] obstruents, speakers take active steps to turn off voicing. There are two main possibilities: (1) opening the glottis, thereby allowing more air to flow into the oral cavity so that $P_0$ rises more quickly and (2) stiffening the vocal folds, thereby increasing the size of the pressure drop needed to maintain vibration. To these may be added the possibility of stiffening the walls of the oro-pharyngeal cavity in order to prevent passive expansion.

From this brief summary, it should be clear that a wide variety of experimental techniques have been involved in investigating the possibilities. Whether or not the velopharyngeal port is open during [+ voiced] stops can be determined by recording air flow through the nose (as in Nihalani 1975) or by means of a fibrescope (Section 8.3.5.2) inserted into the nasal cavity. Spectrograms may also provide evidence for incomplete velopharyngeal closure if left-to-right bars resembling nasal formants are present. An example is shown in Figure 8.13, which shows a spectrogram and $L_x$ waveform for a geminate /dd/, in the word **keddi'** 'coward', in Madurese (spoken in Madura and East Java, Indonesia); notice that, in this case, the voicing does not come to an end in the middle of the consonant (though it does decrease in amplitude) and that the 'formants' of the consonant continue throughout its duration.

Evidence for active expansion of the oro-pharyngeal cavity during [+ voiced] stops has come from radiographic studies (Perkell 1969; Kent and Moll 1969; Westbury 1983) as well as from more specialised investigations of larynx height (Riordan 1980). There has been particular interest in the position of the larynx. This is because a lower larynx position is commonly associated with lower $F_0$ (Section 8.3.8). Accordingly, it is possible that lower $F_0$ at vowel onset following a [+ voiced] stop is an automatic consequence of the lower larynx position, adopted as a voicing-maintaining strategy, though this remains controversial (Hombert *et al.* 1979; Kingston and Diehl 1994).

As regards [− voiced] obstruents, evidence that the vocal folds may open during the closure interval has come from fibre-optic studies. An example is shown in Figure 8.14, which is taken from a study of Hindi stop consonants by Kagaya and Hirose (1975). The graph shows changing glottal width over time for the three consonants /p/ (plain voiceless), /pʰ/ (voiceless aspirated) and /bʱ/ (voiced with a breathy-voiced release). (The Hindi system also includes plain voiced stops, but these have the glottis closed for voicing throughout.) The three graphs are aligned with respect to the release of the bilabial closure. Notice that in the case of /p/ the vocal folds open but are closed again by the time of the release. By contrast, the curve for /bʱ/ is similar in duration and in degree of opening but the timing is very different; in /bʱ/ the opening begins only at the release. Experiments such as these have also shown that voiceless

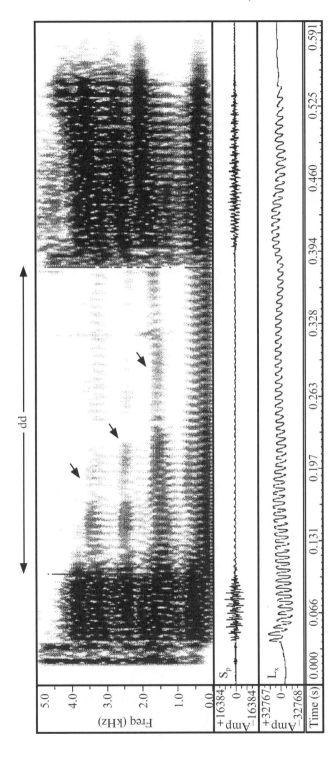

FIGURE 8.13   Spectrogram, audio waveform and $L_x$ waveform for geminate /dd/ in Madurese **keddi'** 'coward', pronounced by a male speaker. In this case, voicing continues throughout the closure interval, which has a duration of 279 msec. The bars running from left to right across the consonantal interval of the spectrogram (picked out by arrows) may be identified as nasal formants and would seem to reflect some velopharyngeal opening.

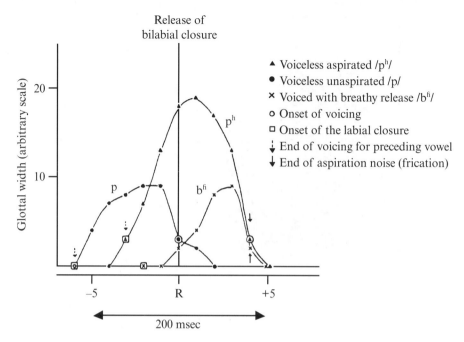

FIGURE 8.14   A record of changing glottal width during the production of Hindi bilabial stop consonants. The three consonants in question are /p/ (plain voiceless), /pʰ/ (voiceless aspirated) and /bʱ/ (voiced with a breathy-voiced release). The numbers along the horizontal axis are frame numbers on the cine film. The frames for each consonant have been numbered so that the frame corresponding to the release of the articulatory closure is frame 0. The interval between frames is 20 msec.

Notice that in the case of /p/, the vocal folds open but have closed again by the time of the release. The curve for /bʱ/ is similar as regards duration and in degree of opening, but the timing is very different: the opening begins only at the release. As regards /pʰ/, the glottal opening is much wider at its maximum point. The timing is such that the point of maximum opening coincides, or nearly coincides, with the release. This is typically the case for voiceless aspirated stops. Adapted from Kagaya and Hirose (1975).

aspirated stops are associated with an open glottis; the curve for /pʰ/ is taller than the other two and the timing is such that the point of maximum opening nearly coincides with the release.

Perhaps the most controversial aspect of the [± voiced] contrast has been the suggestion that the vocal folds might be stiffened actively as a means of inhibiting voicing during [− voiced] obstruents. In such a case we should expect involvement of the cricothyroid (CT) muscle, which, as we have seen, is the stiffener *par excellence* and is also primarily responsible for raising $F_0$. Cricothyroid activity can be studied only by means of electromyography, and the results of the relevant studies have not been entirely consistent. A good overview of studies in this area is provided by Löfqvist *et al.* (1989).

## 8.4  Articulation

The study of articulation includes the positions and movements of the speech organs above the larynx. As the terms *positions* and *movements* imply, there are both static and dynamic aspects to be taken into account.

The positions of interest are the target positions which are the basis of impressionistic-phonetic classification (Section 1.2). For example, the target position for the English vowel /i/ requires that the front of the tongue should be making a constriction of appropriate closeness along the hard palate and that the lips should be at least moderately spread. However, target positions do not just happen; the vocal organs must be moved to them from what precedes and moved away from them to what follows. For example, in a word such as English **seem** (/sim/), the talker must move his or her vocal organs from the /s/ position to the /i/ position and from the /i/ position to the /m/ position. This involves coordinating the tongue, the lips and the soft palate (and also the vocal folds and the respiratory muscles). Another approach to describing the activity would be to regard the movements as primary and the supposed target positions as consequences of the way in which the movements are coordinated.

The study of articulation is, in many ways, more straightforward than the study of laryngeal activity. This is because the organs involved are bigger, the movements are slower, and the aerodynamic aspects are less complex. Following Stone (1996, 1997) it is useful to make a major division between *imaging techniques*, *point-tracking techniques*, *palatography* and *electromyography* (in Stone's articles, the last two are grouped together as techniques for 'measurement of complex behaviors'). To these may be added modelling and the statistical technique of factor analysis. Electromyography was described briefly above (Section 8.3.5.3), and, accordingly, we shall concentrate on the others.

### *8.4.1  Imaging techniques*

As already mentioned (Section 8.3.5.2), imaging techniques are techniques which register information about positions or movements of structures without actually contacting the structures. Another general characteristic of imaging techniques is that they do not commit the researcher to a particular type of measurement. For example, we might take a film of the lips viewed from the front with a view to measuring the distance between the upper and lower lips at the midpoint. However, after the film had been taken, we could decide to measure the width of the mouth opening from corner to corner as well. By contrast, if we use a point tracking technique (Section 8.4.2) to record the movement of a single point on the lower lip, there is no possibility of deciding to look at something else after the recording has been made. In practice, this type of flexibility can be a mixed blessing, since it may be difficult to decide what to measure; it is possible to end up with so much data that no clear-cut, general result emerges from it.

Historically, the most important imaging technique used in the study of articulation has been radiography, and we shall focus our attention upon it here. Other techniques which have played a more limited role are photography (for recording labial activity), ultrasound and, more recently, magnetic resonance imaging (MRI).

X-rays are, in essence, similar to light rays, and, like light rays, can be used to expose photographic film. However, they can 'see through' some materials which would be impenetrable to light. The extent to which X-rays are able to pass through any given material will depend on that material's density, so that, for example, the cheeks and other soft tissues will be transparent whereas the teeth and bones will not.

X-ray equipment is both expensive and potentially dangerous, and can only be used under specialist medical supervision. It is also well known that over-exposure to radiation can have adverse effects on health and should be avoided. For these reasons X-ray imaging is now available for phonetic research only in highly exceptional circumstances. However, such severe restrictions on the use of X-rays are relatively recent. Much published (and unpublished) material, gathered in earlier, less scrupulous times, is still available to – and still used by – phoneticians. For example, in an important paper on the articulatory and acoustic characteristics of palatal and velar consonants, Keating and Lahiri (1993) base their articulatory analysis primarily on published x-ray profiles.

It is necessary to distinguish between radiography proper and the more indirect method of *fluorography*. In radiography, the X-rays themselves expose the photographic film directly after passing through the subject's body. In fluorography, on the other hand, the image is produced by arranging for the X-rays to strike a fluoroscopic screen rather than photographic film. In this way, the image produced by the x-radiation is, as it were, translated into a fluorescent image. This image is rather weak, but an *image intensifier* may be used to enhance its quality. This intensified image may be observed in real time by the experimenter, and may be recorded on cine film or videotape for future playback. One of the main advantages of fluorography is that it requires lower doses of radiation. A more detailed account of the various radiographic techniques may be found in Ball (1984).

Once radiographic images have been collected – either as stills or as frames of a cinefilm – it is usual to project them and trace the outlines of the structures onto tracing paper. It is the resulting line drawings which are usually published. If the purpose of the investigation is purely qualitative description, the report on the research will simply describe what is observed. If, on the other hand, measurements are to be taken, they will usually be taken from the tracings.

### 8.4.2  Point-tracking techniques

In contrast to imaging techniques, point-tracking techniques are very focussed. Particular points on the surface of one or more articulators are chosen for tracking at the start of the investigation. The motion of these points, in one, two or, in some cases, three dimensions, is then recorded, and is taken to be representative of the motion of the articulators as a whole so that, for example, the motion of a point at the centre of the lower lip would be taken as representative of the motion of the lower lip. The output is not a picture, but a trajectory.

Over the past 15–20 years, instruments for tracking motion during speech have become more sophisticated and more widely available. On the one hand, this reflects an increased interest in dynamic aspects of speech production. On the other hand, the availability of the equipment has served to stimulate interest in dynamic aspects of speech production. The types of point-tracking systems most commonly used in linguistic-phonetic studies are listed below.

1   *Optical systems.* In optical systems, small light-emitting diodes (LEDs) are attached to the chosen point or points on the subject's face. Special sensors, themselves fixed in position, are used to track the positions of the LEDs, which emit infra-red signals. However, such systems cannot be used to track points inside the vocal tract, since, if the LEDs were placed inside the mouth, the reception of their signals by the sensors would be blocked.

2   *Electromagnetic systems.* Electromagnetic systems track motion by determining the distance between generator coils, which produce alternating magnetic fields, and sensor coils. The magnetic fields serve to induce a voltage in the sensor coils, which varies inversely with the distance from the sensor to the receiver. If a single sensor coil is made to respond to two or more generators, operating at different frequencies, the sensor can be located in space relative to two or more reference points and its position can be determined precisely. It is also possible to use several sensors at the same time, and thus monitor the motion of several points simultaneously.

   Electromagnetic systems have an important advantage over optical systems in that the sensors can be used inside the mouth. They can thus, in principle, be used to record the motion of points on the tongue, velum, or pharynx wall, provided that the subject is able to tolerate the coils in those places.

3   *X-ray microbeam.* As its name implies, the X-ray microbeam system uses a very thin (0.44 mm) X-ray beam. The beam tracks the motion of small metal pellets, which are attached at the points of interest, and which may be located inside the subject's mouth. For example, a series of pellets might be fixed to the midline of the tongue. The location of each pellet, specified by x and y (horizontal and vertical) coordinates, is recorded (sampled) in turn by a computer, with up to 1000 pellet positions recorded per second. In this way, it is possible to obtain a very accurate record of the movements of the pellets and accordingly of the movements of the points at which they are attached. The X-ray dosage required is very small, so a considerable amount of data can be gathered from a single subject without risking overexposure to radiation.

   The X-ray microbeam system would probably be the instrument of choice for tracking articulator movement were it not for the fact that it is extremely

expensive to build and to maintain. At present, such a system exists only at
the University of Wisconsin, and users must travel there to avail themselves
of it.

More detailed accounts of various systems are provided by Stone (1996, 1997)
and Baken (1987).

### 8.4.3  Palatography

*Palatography* is a group of techniques used to record contact between the
tongue and the roof of the mouth. In the context of experimental phonetics,
palatography has a relatively long history, going back to the 1870s, and it has
remained popular among phoneticians.

A major distinction may be drawn between *direct* and *indirect* palatography.
In direct palatography, a marking substance is sprayed or painted onto the
roof of the mouth; a mixture of powdered charcoal and powdered chocolate
has been frequently used for this purpose. The speaker pronounces the sound
of interest – for example, an alveolar [t] – in an appropriate context. The
substance on the roof of the mouth will be wiped off in places where there is
contact between the tongue and the roof of the mouth (in this particular example, along the alveolar ridge) but will be left undisturbed where no contact
has occurred. The subject must then keep his mouth open while a record is
made of the *wipe off*; this is usually done by taking a photograph. Since the
marking substance will adhere to the tongue, a *linguogram*, recording which
parts of the tongue were involved in the articulation, may also be made. In an
alternative version of the technique, the marking substance is painted onto the
tongue and is transferred to the upper surface of the mouth. This method is
preferred by Ladefoged (1997a), who recommends a mixture of olive oil and
powdered charcoal as the marking substance. Provided that a suitable marking
substance and suitable photographic equipment are to hand, palatograms can
be made in the field with a minimum of preparation.

The methodology of indirect palatography is essentially the same as that of
direct palatography, but the subject wears a custom-made artificial palate,
which can be removed immediately after the articulation has been completed,
leaving the mouth free. The indirect method has several disadvantages. Firstly,
the presence of the artificial palate may interfere with natural articulation.
Secondly, since the artificial palate does not cover the teeth and usually only
extends as far back as the soft palate, the range of articulations which can be
examined is smaller. Thirdly, the technique requires that a palate be made for
each subject. This last disadvantage effectively rules out its use in the field.

Both direct and indirect techniques share the disadvantages that articulations can only be recorded one at a time and that it is not possible to study the
timing of the contact pattern. The number of contexts which may be observed
is also very limited, since care must be taken to avoid words containing two
articulations which use the same part of the palate. For example, English

words such as **sat** or **stop** would be unsuitable for a palatographic study of either /s/ or /t/ because /s/ and /t/ are both alveolar articulations and it would be unclear whether any wipe-off in the alveolar region was due to one, the other, or both. These limitations are overcome by *electropalatography* (*EPG*). EPG is now widely available and is becoming increasingly popular as a technique for investigating the positions and movements of the tongue.

Electropalatography is a type of indirect palatography in that the subject wears an artificial palate. In this case, however, a number of electrodes are embedded in the palate. These serve as sensors for tongue contact. The system is controlled by a computer, which samples and records the pattern of tongue contact 100 or more times per second. The patterns can then be printed out and/or subjected to various kinds of quantitative analysis. A further advantage is that EPG is easy to use in combination with other methods of investigation such as air flow recording (pneumotachography, Section 8.2.3.2), or electroglottography (Section 8.3.6.3).

Although EPG provides direct information about the palate, most investigators have been keen to interpret that information in relation to the tongue. Two assumptions are involved. Firstly, it is assumed that each part of the tongue will contact that part of the palate which lies immediately above it. (This does not apply for retroflex consonants, which are produced by curling the tongue back.) Secondly, it is assumed that the greater the contact area, the higher the tongue position; this makes sense, since if the tongue is not contacting the palate in a particular region it must be relatively lower than in a situation where contact is observed.

As an example, we may consider an EPG printout for English /t͡ʃ/, in the phrase **the chap**, recorded by a male speaker, shown in Figure 8.15. The first contact is at the very front of the palate, in frame 452. This is assumed to involve the tip or the front of the blade. Between frame 452 and frame 459, contact in the front-to-middle part of the palate increases, suggesting raising of the front part of the tongue body. At the same time, the contact in the first row decreases after frame 455, from which we can infer that the tongue tip is being lowered. Overall, we can say that the tongue configuration becomes more convex (with higher body and lower tip) over the course of the articulation. Notice that it is the tongue body contact, in the middle and back parts of the palate, which is the last to be released. In frame 462, we see evidence of a narrow central channel, as would be expected for a grooved fricative articulation.

### 8.4.4  *Identifying articulatory dimensions: the case of vowels*

As already mentioned (Section 8.1), one of the main problems in the study of articulation is determining how many independent articulatory dimensions are necessary to account for the speech sounds which occur in the languages of the world. A good example is the case of vowel sounds, which have been particularly problematic from this point of view. A classic discussion of vowel features is Lindau (1978).

First contact between tongue
and alveolar ridge for [t]
↓

| 448 | 449 | 450 | 451 | 452 | 453 | 454 | 455 | Front of palate |
|---|---|---|---|---|---|---|---|---|
| ...... | ...... | ...... | ...... | 000.0. | 000.0. | 000000 | 000000 | |
| ........ | ........ | ........ | ......0. | 00..0000 | 00000000 | 00000000 | 00000000 | |
| ........ | ........ | ........ | ........ | ......0 | 0......0 | 0.....00 | 00...000 | |
| ........ | ........ | ........ | ........ | ........ | ......0 | 0......0 | 0......0 | |
| ........ | ........ | ........ | ........ | ........ | ........ | 0......0 | 0......0 | |
| ........ | ........ | ........ | ........ | ........ | .......0 | .......0 | 0......0 | |
| ........ | ........ | ........ | ........ | ........ | .......0 | .......0 | 0......0 | Back of palate |
| ........ | ........ | ........ | ........ | ........ | .......0 | .......0 | .......0 | |

Narrow channel for [ʃ]
↓

| 456 | 457 | 458 | 459 | 460 | 461 | 462 | 463 |
|---|---|---|---|---|---|---|---|
| 00000. | 000.0. | 000... | 00.... | ...... | ...|.. | ...... | ...... |
| 00000000 | 00000000 | 00000000 | 00000000 | 00000000 | 000..000 | 000..000 | 00....00 |
| 000..000 | 000..000 | 000.0000 | 000.0000 | 000..000 | 000..000 | 000..000 | 000...00 |
| 0......0 | 00.....0 | 00.....00 | 000...00 | 000...00 | 000...00 | 000...00 | 000...00 |
| 0......0 | 0......0 | 00.....0 | 00.....0 | 00....00 | 00....00 | 00....00 | 00....00 |
| 0......0 | 0......0 | 0......0 | 0......0 | 0......0 | 00.....0 | 00.....0 | 00.....0 |
| 0......0 | 0......0 | 0......0 | 0......0 | 0......0 | 0......0 | 0......0 | 0......0 |
| .......0 | 0......0 | 0......0 | 0......0 | 0......0 | 0......0 | 0......0 | 0......0 |

| 464 | 465 | 466 | 467 | 468 | 469 | 470 | 471 |
|---|---|---|---|---|---|---|---|
| ...... | ...... | ...... | ...... | ...... | ...... | ...... | ...... |
| 0......0 | 0....... | ........ | ........ | ........ | ........ | ........ | ........ |
| 00...00 | 00.....0 | 0....... | 0....... | ........ | ........ | ........ | ........ |
| 00.....0 | 00.....0 | 00.....0 | 0......0 | 0....... | 0....... | ........ | ........ |
| 00.....0 | 00.....0 | 00.....0 | 0......0 | 0......0 | 0....... | 0....... | ........ |
| 00.....0 | 0......0 | 0......0 | 0......0 | 0......0 | 0......0 | 0......0 | ........ |
| 0......0 | 0......0 | 0......0 | 0......0 | 0......0 | 0......0 | 0......0 | .......0 |
| 0......0 | 0......0 | 0......0 | 0......0 | 0......0 | 0......0 | .......0 | .......0 |

FIGURE 8.15    EPG printout for English /t͡ʃ/ in the phrase **the chap**, recorded by a male speaker. The printout shows a series of *frames*, representing a sequence of tongue contact patterns. The interval between frames is 100 msec.

Each dot or zero corresponds to a single electrode on the artificial palate; the zeros are used to represent electrodes for which tongue contact is registered. It should also be noted that the electrodes at the front of the palate (in the first four rows) are closer together than the electrodes at the back of the palate. The fourth row (counting from the top) corresponds (roughly) to the back of the alveolar ridge.

Few topics have occasioned so much discussion and dispute among phoneticians as the description of vowels. The impressionistic vowel quadrilateral has the height and backness of the highest point of the tongue hump as its basic dimensions. This system of vowel classification dates back to the nineteenth century, prior to the discovery of X-rays. Once radiographic imaging became available, it was possible to test claims about the height and backness of the highest point of the tongue hump in an objective way. Unfortunately, the X-ray evidence brought to light several potential problems with, and objections to, the classification scheme.

Probably the most-discussed problem is the existence of mismatches between vowel height (as implied by the symbol used in an impressionistic transcription) and the relative height of the highest point of the tongue hump (as determined from an X-ray tracing). For example, the tongue hump might be higher for a 'low' vowel, transcribed /ɑ/ or /a/, than for a 'mid' vowel, transcribed /o/ or /ɔ/ (Wood 1975). Whether or not such examples of height inversion are very numerous or very serious has been a matter of controversy (Lindau 1978; Catford 1981). Nor is it clear that they reveal weaknesses in the basic classification scheme itself (as opposed to weaknesses in the way it is implemented).

At the same time, we cannot simply assume that the vowel quadrilateral represents the best way of describing vowel articulation within the context of speech production as a whole. Here I shall mention three alternative approaches. The first is to start from simple models of the vocal tract (Sections 4.4.1, 4.4.3). This naturally leads to the suggestion that constriction location and constriction degree should be central to the articulatory description of vowels. This proposal was made by Wood (1979) on the basis of both X-ray and EMG data. In his framework, the vocal tract tube is divided into four zones: the hard palate, the soft palate, the upper pharynx and the lower pharynx. Each of these is associated with a particular type of muscle activity. For example, in the case of the palatal vowels ([i], [e], [ɛ]), muscles at the base of the tongue, known as the *genioglossi*, push the tongue upward and forward. In Wood's view, constriction location and constriction degree should also form the basis for the phonological specification of vowels. His ideas have proved attractive to some phonologists.

The second alternative approach is to generate vocal tract shapes from a small number of basic parameters or basic shapes. X-ray profiles are essential to this enterprise, since they generally provide the output shapes which the model must generate. A well-known example is the model proposed by Lindblom and Sundberg (1971). They were able to generate two-dimensional tongue profiles for the distinctive vowels of Swedish by combining four basic shapes. These corresponded to the vowels [a], [i], [u] and a neutral position. Lindblom and Sundberg's approach is similar in spirit to theories of phonological distinctive features which describe vowels as combinations of a small number of *particles* or *elements* (e.g. Schane 1984).

The third approach is similar but works the opposite way round, starting from the output tongue shapes and arriving at the basic shapes by means of statistical techniques. This has been particularly developed by Ladefoged and his colleagues at UCLA. The most thorough study of this type is Jackson (1988), which also contains a good summary of models of vowel articulation. Thus far, this type of approach appears to have had little impact on theories of phonological features.

As regards classificatory dimensions which might form the basis for systems of features, still another possibility is to regard acoustic dimensions as basic (Chapter 6). This does not eliminate the need for an economical description of vowel articulation, since the talker must, in this case, be able to convert his or her acoustic-based representations into articulations.

## 8.5   Wider issues: relating phonological representations to speech production

As we have seen (Section 5.2.3), one of the main controversies in the study of speech perception is whether or not 'speech is special' – that is, does the processing of an incoming speech signal involve a different mode of perception from the processing of other types of sounds? A comparable question might be asked with regard to speech production – that is, are mechanisms unique to speech involved in the planning and execution of spoken utterances? Perhaps surprisingly, the question is not often posed, at least in these terms. It has seemed more useful to ask other, yet closely related, questions. To what extent is the planning of articulatory movement part of a talker's linguistic knowledge? Is it linked to the generation of surface forms in the phonological component of the native speaker's internal grammar? Or is it a separate process which takes place only after the phonological component has done its work?

A concrete example of data which might have some bearing on this general problem is shown in Figure 8.16. This is concerned with the phenomenon of assimilation in English. It is well known that word-final alveolar consonants may assimilate in place of articulation to the initial consonants of following words, particularly in rapid or casual styles; for example **bad boy** may be pronounced as **ba[b] boy** or **ten girls** as **te[ŋ] girls**. In a more phonological treatment, it would be said that the features relating to place of articulation spread from one consonant to the other, as in Figure 1.4.

The examples of Figure 8.16, taken from Nolan (1992), are printouts from an electropalatographic study. Examples (a), (b) and (c), relate to pronunciations of the phrase **boat covered** (where the final /t/ of **boat** could undergo assimilation to the following /k/), whereas example (d) illustrates a pronunciation of **oak cupboard** (where the first word has underlying final /k/) for comparison. In (a), described by Nolan as *full alveolar*, the tongue contact pattern provides clear evidence of an alveolar /t/ closure. In (b), described as *residual alveolar*, there is some evidence of contact between the tongue tip and the alveolar ridge, but no full closure occurs. In (c), described as *zero alveolar*, the EPG printout provides no evidence for alveolar contact at all; indeed, (c) and (d) are remarkably similar. As Nolan points out, it is still possible that some slight movement of the tongue towards the alveolar ridge has taken place without resulting in increased tongue contact.

The significance of the data of Figure 8.16 is in their demonstration that assimilation may be *gradient* – that is, it is possible that a final /t/ is not fully

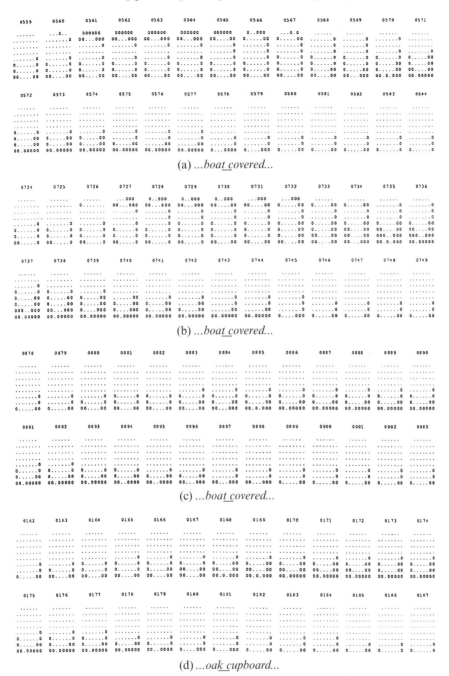

(a) ...*boat covered*...

(b) ...*boat covered*...

(c) ...*boat covered*...

(d) ...*oak cupboard*...

FIGURE 8.16    EPG printouts for various pronunciations of /t/ + /k/ sequences across word boundaries (a)–(c) and for a /k/ + /k/ sequence (d) for comparison. From Nolan (1992).

articulated but also that it is not fully replaced by something else. Of course, it would be incorrect to imply that phoneticians were unaware of such possibilities before such instrumental investigations of articulation and spectrographic analysis became possible (cf. Laver 1970). However, instrumental articulatory data has revealed more cases of gradience than might otherwise have been detected, and has challenged researchers to account for them in a precise and principled way.

In at least some cases, gradience is an obvious consequence of the dynamic character of speech. For example, in the English word **team** (/tim/), the first consonant should be pronounced with the soft palate in the raised position whereas the final nasal consonant should be pronounced with the soft palate in a low position. It is clear that the soft palate must be lowered during the /i/ portion of the word if it is to be fully low for the /m/. Thus, not only will the vowel be partially nasalised but the degree of nasality will increase over the course of its duration. This example would be described as *coarticulation*, because characteristics of the /m/ (a lowered soft palate) overlap with the preceding vowel.

It is often convenient to present information about overlapping articulations, whether obtained from an instrumental record or from introspection, in a *parametric phonetic representation*. A parametric phonetic representation is a multi-tiered graph in which the movements of various articulators (for example, up and down movements of the tongue tip and the soft palate) are plotted one above the other and the temporal coordination between them can be examined. The plot of Figure 8.17 (b) below, showing movements of various articulators, is a sort of parametric representation.

In its dynamic and gradient character, actual articulation contrasts markedly with the surface phonological representations. Surface phonological representations are assumed to be *categorical*. For example, in the examples involving English final /t/ of Figure 8.16, the final consonant would have to be specified either as alveolar or as something else; it could not be partially alveolar. Furthermore, surface phonological representations are conceived of as sequences of discrete specifications (Section 1.4.2).

The problems posed by the disparity between gradient and dynamic speech and the categorical and discrete character of surface phonological representations are complex and have been the subject of much discussion. For many researchers, it has been convenient to think in terms of going from a phonological feature tree (as in Figure 1.3 (a) or (b)) to a parametric phonetic representation. A good introduction to various viewpoints is a special number of *Journal of Phonetics* (volume 18, no. 3) dedicated to the question of 'phonetic representation'.

One possible position is that taken by Chomsky and Halle (1968) in their influential *Sound Pattern of English*. In their proposals, each distinctive feature of phonological representation was intended to correspond to an 'independently controllable aspect of the speech event' (p. 298). The first stage in going from an underlying representation to a phonetic representation involves deriving fully specified matrices of features, in which each feature has the value '+' or '−' for each segment. Next, the '+' and '−' values are converted, by phonological rules, to gradient values which are the basis for instructions to articulators. Chomsky and Halle's approach is distinctive on two grounds. Firstly, it assumes a particularly close link between features and the control of speech production (each feature corresponds to a single articulatory dimension); evidence concerning the number of independently controllable aspects of speech would, accordingly, have to be taken into account when determining the total number of features. Secondly, it assumes that the discrete character of phonological representation projects, as it were, down into the phonetics of production. A sequence of gradient feature values comes first; the details of timing and movement are added only at the final stage.

A position opposite to that of Chomsky and Halle would involve, as it were, projecting the dynamic character of speech up into the level of underlying representation. This is the essence of the theory of *Articulatory Phonology*, which is most closely associated with the names of Catherine Browman and Louis Goldstein (cf. Browman and Goldstein 1986). In their view, the basic units of phonological representation are not discrete features or elements but dynamic gestures. In this way, the production of any particular utterance can be described as a one-stage process rather than as a two-stage process requiring a translation from abstract, timeless phonological units to physically real events within the vocal tract. A special number of the periodical *Phonetica* (volume 49, no. 3–4) is devoted to papers on Articulatory Phonology by proponents and sceptics and this provides a good introduction to the details of Browman and Goldstein's proposals.

Articulatory Phonology is closely linked to the *Task Dynamics* model, which provides the framework for defining gestures and relating them to the movement of specific articulators. Task Dynamics is a general model of the control of skilled movement which was originally developed to account for non-speech tasks such as reaching. The essence of the model is its concern with overall regularity rather than with the details of specific patterns of muscle activity. For example, raising the tongue tip to form a constriction with the alveolar ridge is an example of a gesture. The general trajectory of the tongue tip is quite similar no matter where it starts from, but the details of which muscles are involved and to what degree may differ considerably from one instance to another.

The gestures involved in any particular word or utterance, together with their relative timings, are specified in a *gestural score*. An example, taken from Browman and Goldstein (1989), is shown in Figure 8.17. This shows a gestural score for the word **palm**, transcribed [pʰɑm]. Each level of the score corresponds to a single *tract variable*. On each level, boxes are used to mark out the time intervals when particular gestures are active. The height of each box reflects the degree of aperture. In the lower part (b), the movements of the tract variables

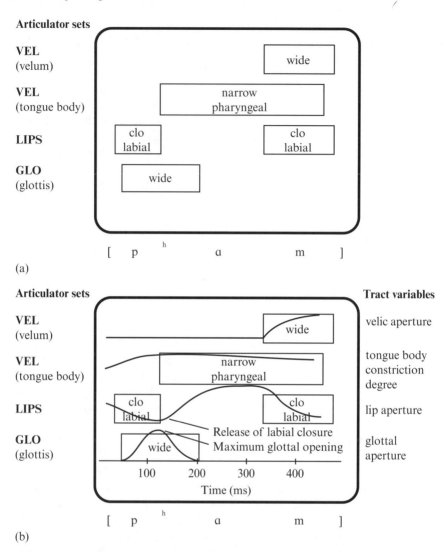

FIGURE 8.17  *Gestural score* for the English word **palm**, adapted from Browman and Goldstein (1989: 212). The diagram in (a) is the score itself, which specifies in an abstract way how the various gestures involved in an utterance are coordinated. On the vertical axis, the tiers represent the sets of articulators involved, while the horizontal axis represents time. The boxes correspond to the individual gestures, and the extent of each box in the horizontal dimension corresponds to the interval of time during which the particular gesture is active. Gestures involving the velum or the glottis are specified in terms of their constriction degree only. For example, a wide opening of the velum (achieved by lowering the soft palate) is specified at the end of the score, where the nasal [m] occurs. Gestures involving articulators in the mouth are specified in terms of both their location and their degree. For example, the two closures of the lips (for [p] and [m]) must be specified both as labial (location) and as complete closure (degree).

are also computed and are superimposed on the boxes. Thus, the gestural score provides a basis for computing the trajectories of the individual articulators. Although no example is provided here, it should be clear that data on the movements of individual articulators, such as can be provided by point-tracking systems, have been crucial to developing and testing this theory.

A further look at Figure 8.17 makes it clear how coarticulation is dealt with in the Articulatory Phonology framework. In the gestural score, the lowering of the soft palate starts before the labial closing gesture for /m/, and so must overlap with the pharyngeal narrowing associated with /a/. The resulting nasality is not treated as an inherent feature of /m/ which spreads to /a/. Rather, the overall pattern results from the relative timing of the various gestures. This approach also provides a good framework for accounting for various kinds of assimilations, a matter which cannot be gone into here.

A third possibility as regards the question of relating phonological representations to speech production is to assume that a native speaker's internal grammar contains a separate 'phonetic component' which serves to translate surface phonological representations into parametric phonetic representations. This approach has been pursued by Patricia Keating in a number of papers (Keating 1985, 1988, 1990a, 1990b). In her view, the surface phonological representations (termed *categorical phonetic* in Keating 1990a) provide a sequence of targets, which are then connected up by processes of interpolation. It should be noted, however, that targets may be rather loosely specified, allowing for a certain amount of variation.

The conversion from categorical phonetic feature tree to an articulatory target may vary from language to language. For example, English vowels would not have a target of 'fully raised soft palate'. Instead, the target would be a range of possible positions of the soft palate, allowing a relatively low (but still not fully open) position in cases where a vowel is between two nasal consonants, as in the word **man**. The range of possibilities – termed a *window* in Keating (1990b) – might be different in a language which had a phonemic contrast between nasalised and non-nasalised vowels. Other aspects of the conversion are language-specific – or even speaker-specific – as well. For example, in some languages categorical phonetic specifications [+ voiced] and [– voiced] would affect the duration of the preceding vowel (see Section 7.7), whereas in others they would not.

FIGURE 8.17   *(cont'd)*

From the specifications for each gesture, it is possible to calculate the corresponding trajectory for the relevant vocal tract variable using a task-dynamic model. For example, the tract variable corresponding to the labial closure gesture would be the vertical distance between the upper and lower lips (lip aperture). In (b), estimated trajectories have been drawn in, and a time scale has been added. Thus, (b) represents a possible realisation of the abstract score presented in (a). Notice that the peak of the glottal opening gesture nearly coincides with the release of the labial closure for the aspirated [pʰ], as in the experimental data of Figure 8.14.

One implication of Keating's approach, which allows a single feature to correspond to more than one articulatory parameter and vice versa, is that the nature of articulatory parameters and their control need not impose any constraints on phonological representations. For example, either the feature tree of Figure 1.3 (a) or the tree of Figure 1.3 (b) could, in principle, be translated into a parametric phonetic representation. The question of whether there is a one-to-one relationship between features and major articulators or whether the features are more abstract simply does not arise. At the same time, it seems clear that more abstraction in the surface phonological (categorical phonetic) representation must entail more complex procedures in the phonetic component which performs the conversion. The implications of this still need to be explored.

In this section, we have been able to give only a brief view of some of the issues involved in relating surface phonological representations to the complications of speech production. It should be clear, however, that the debate is a lively one, and will continue to be so for some time to come.

## 8.6   Further reading

Borden *et al.* (1994) and Lieberman and Blumstein (1988) are good starting points for further reading about speech production. For more advanced reading, the collections of articles by Lass (1996) and Hardcastle and Laver (1997) provide comprehensive coverage and are good sources of bibliography. Lass's collection includes articles on models of speech production by Kent, Adams and Turner, on the larynx by Orlikoff and Kahane, on breathing by Warren, and on instrumentation by Stone. Hardcastle and Laver's volume has particularly good articles on articulatory processes, coarticulation and theories and models of speech production by Perkell, Farnetani and Löfqvist respectively. The articles on aerodynamics by Shadle, on the voice source by Ní Chasaide and Gobl, and on instrumentation by Stone (similar to her contribution to Lass's volume) are also to be recommended.

Outside of these volumes, Hawkins (1992) provides an excellent readable introduction to the task dynamics model. Byrd (1994) is a good introduction to the practicalities of interpreting electropalatographic data. Ohala (1983) considers the influence of vocal tract constraints on sound patterns. Hardcastle and Marchal (1990) also contains a number of good papers on speech production, of which we shall mention particularly Ohala's excellent account of respiratory function and Lindblom's thought-provoking discussion of speech production. Schneiderman (1984) is a well-illustrated introduction to the anatomy and physiology of speech production.

As regards the larynx, Sundberg (1987) is a very good, readable and non-technical introduction, which will be of particular interest to readers with an interest in singing. Hayward (1992), which is generally available, provides an introduction to the larynx and phonation types on video.

For technical aspects, Baken (1987) provides excellent overall coverage of techniques which are currently relevant to clinical work. Code and Ball (1984) contains a number of useful articles, of which we shall mention particularly Abberton and Fourcin on electrolaryngography, Anthony and Hewlett on aerometry and Ball on radiographic techniques.

**Appendix**

# An overview of impressionistic-phonetic classification

One of the main assumptions of impressionistic-phonetic classification is that every segment can be specified uniquely with reference to a target. Impressionistic-phonetic classification is thus based on specifying target positions of the speech organs. With the exception of the lateral sounds, these positions are (at least roughly) symmetrical around the midline of the body. They are commonly represented in two dimensions on a mid-sagittal section of the head and neck. A somewhat schematic mid-sagittal section of the entire vocal tract is shown in Figure A.1.

A first observation is that the vocal tract is made up of four major cavities: (1) the lungs and trachea, below the larynx; (2) the pharynx, immediately above the larynx; (3) the nasal cavity; and (4) the oral (mouth) cavity.

## A.1 Preliminaries: air flow in the vocal tract

Although the most obvious activity involved in speech production involves movement in the mouth, the process of speaking actually begins in the lungs. In normal circumstances we speak while breathing out, although it is possible to speak while breathing in. In any case, speech cannot take place without an airstream.

The lungs provide a reservoir of air. The rate at which that air is allowed to flow out to the outside atmosphere is controlled by muscles located in the chest cavity. Whether or not speech sounds are produced, and what kind of sounds are produced, depends on what happens to the air during its passage to the outside atmosphere.

As Figure A.1 illustrates, all air leaving (or entering) the lungs must travel via the *trachea*, a tube made up of rings of cartilage which is also appropriately called the *windpipe*. It must then pass through the larynx, a box of cartilages which is both the end of the trachea and the beginning of the pharyngeal cavity. The most important component of the larynx is the vocal folds. These are a pair of flange-like structures of soft tissue, which project inward from the sides of the larynx and run horizontally from back to front across the top of the trachea. They are fixed in position at the front, but may be moved apart or together at the back. They may also be stretched and lengthened or compressed and shortened. The space between the folds is known as the *glottis*. If the folds are held tightly together (a position known as a *glottal stop*), no air

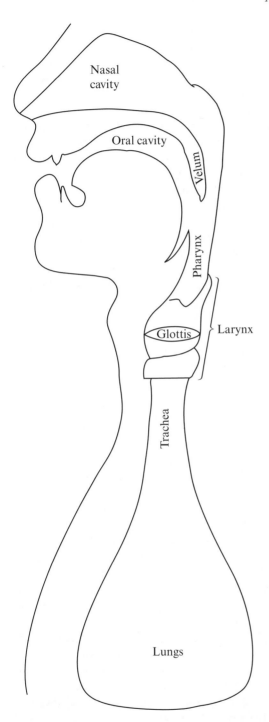

FIGURE A.1 A schematic mid-sagittal section of the vocal tract.

can pass through the larynx in either direction. Conversely, the folds must be held apart if air is to flow freely from the lungs into the oral cavity.

Between the open and closed positions of the glottis, there is an important intermediate possibility. The folds may be held loosely together so that they are set into vibration by the airstream from the lungs. Vibration of the vocal folds involves their moving apart and together so that the air passes through in a series of small puffs rather than as a continuous stream. Vocal fold vibration is a very efficient means of producing sound and consequently plays an important role in speech production. In phonetic terminology, vocal fold vibration is called *phonation* or *voice*, and a major distinction is made between *voiced* sounds, which are produced with vocal fold vibration, and *voiceless* sounds, which are produced without it. Voicing gives language its musical character and is essential for the art of singing. The rate at which the vocal folds vibrate determines the pitch of the sound, faster vibrations being associated with higher pitch and slower vibrations with lower pitch. In addition, the overall character of the voicing, known as the *phonation type*, can be varied. If the vocal folds do not come together completely when they vibrate, more air is able to pass through the glottis, resulting in *breathy voice*. Conversely, the vocal folds may be held together rather tightly (but not so tightly as to make vibration impossible), resulting in *creaky voice* or *pressed phonation*.

Once the airstream has got past the larynx, it has two possible exit routes – via the mouth and via the nose. From the point of view of phoneticians, the mouth is the main route. There is only one route into the nose, via the back of the mouth. The entrance to the nasal cavity may be closed off by raising the soft palate or *velum*, which, as Figure A.1 illustrates, is part of the roof of the mouth, at the very back end of the oral cavity and the top of the pharynx. The adjective *velic* is used to refer to the passage between the soft palate and the back wall of the pharynx; thus, *velic closure* refers to the closure formed by raising the soft palate. Although the soft palate may, in principle, assume any position from fully raised to fully lowered, phonetic classification distinguishes only two possibilities: up and down. If the soft palate is up and the nasal cavity is shut off, the speech sound in question is said to be *oral*. If the soft palate is down, the sound will be either *nasal* or *nasalised* (see below).

The lungs can hold a large quantity of air, and are able to maintain a steady, controlled airstream which will support several seconds of speech. All speech sounds produced with lung air are called *pulmonic* (from Latin *pulmo*, 'lung'), though this is usually left unspecified as it is by far the most common situation. For quick and unsustained movement of small quantities of air, there are alternative possibilities. For example, if the lips are smacked to produce a kissing sound, a small amount of air is sucked into the mouth. It is this sudden movement of air which is responsible for the sound; the lungs are not involved at all. Such alternative airstreams are called *non-pulmonic*. They are not suitable for sustained speech or even for single vowel sounds, but they can be used to produce some types of consonant sounds.

We now move on to consider the possibilities for modulating the airstream by means of movement of structures in the mouth and pharynx. This is known as *articulation*. Articulation determines how the airstream will be modified once it has passed through the larynx and thus it determines each sound's specific character. It is generally assumed that sounds can be divided into two general types, vowels and consonants. These are described using different sets of dimensions.

## A.2    Consonants

When pronouncing a consonant sound, it is usually possible to feel, and sometimes also to see, that two (or, in some cases, more) parts of the mouth are touching or in any case are very close to one another. These are the *articulators* for the consonant. The target position which they assume is called the *articulation*. For example, for the /p/ of English **pan** the articulators are the two lips and they come together to form an articulation involving complete closure. No air can escape through the mouth until the lips are opened again, in other words until the closure is released. The vocal folds are not vibrating.

These observations give us the basis for a three-dimensional classification of **p**. The first dimension is voicing, which distinguishes between voiced sounds (produced with vocal fold vibration) and voiceless sounds (produced without vocal fold vibration). English /p/ is voiceless because the vocal folds are not vibrating. The second dimension is *place of articulation*, i.e. where in the mouth and by means of which articulators is it produced. In this case, the articulators are the two lips and the articulation is said to be *bilabial*. The third dimension is *manner of articulation*, i.e. what kind of constriction is involved. In this case, the lips form a complete closure, blocking the airstream's escape through the mouth, and the manner is said to be a *stop* or, more specifically, a *plosive* (see below). The three dimensions may be put together to give a three-term label for the sound, in this case *voiceless bilabial stop* or *voiceless bilabial plosive*.

This three-dimensional voice-place-manner classification provides the framework of the IPA Consonant Chart (Figure A.2). The columns correspond to place, and the rows correspond to manner. Voiceless sounds are on the left of their boxes, while voiced sounds are on the right. Thus the box containing **p** is at the intersection of the bilabial column and the plosive row. Within the box, the symbol **p** is to the left of symbol **b**, which represents its voiced counterpart.

### A.2.1    Sonorants and obstruents

One obvious feature of the chart is that some boxes have two symbols and others contain only one. If there is only one symbol, the sound is voiced, and the symbol stands at the right of its box. This reflects tendencies observed across languages. Some types of sounds typically come in voiced–voiceless pairs in languages, while others do not. The first type are known as *obstruents* while the second type are known as *sonorants*. For example, in the bilabial plosive box, English contrasts voiceless /p/ and voiced /b/ (**pan** vs. **ban**) but in the bilabial nasal box, English has voiced /m/ only. Although it is perfectly

## THE INTERNATIONAL PHONETIC ALPHABET (revised to 1993, corrected 1996)

CONSONANTS (PULMONIC)

|  | Bilabial | Labiodental | Dental | Alveolar | Postalveolar | Retroflex | Palatal | Velar | Uvular | Pharyngeal | Glottal |
|---|---|---|---|---|---|---|---|---|---|---|---|
| Plosive | p b |  |  | t d |  | ʈ ɖ | c ɟ | k ɡ | q ɢ |  | ʔ |
| Nasal | m | ɱ |  | n |  | ɳ | ɲ | ŋ | N |  |  |
| Trill | ʙ |  |  | r |  |  |  |  | R |  |  |
| Tap or Flap |  |  |  | ɾ |  | ɽ |  |  |  |  |  |
| Fricative | ɸ β | f v | θ ð | s z | ʃ ʒ | ʂ ʐ | ç ʝ | x ɣ | χ ʁ | ħ ʕ | h ɦ |
| Lateral fricative |  |  |  | ɬ ɮ |  |  |  |  |  |  |  |
| Approximant |  | ʋ |  | ɹ |  | ɻ | j | ɰ |  |  |  |
| Lateral approximant |  |  |  | l |  | ɭ | ʎ | L |  |  |  |

Where symbols appear in pairs, the one to the right represents a voiced consonant. Shaded areas denote articulations judged impossible.

CONSONANTS (NON-PULMONIC)

| Clicks | Voiced implosives | Ejectives |
|---|---|---|
| ʘ Bilabial | ɓ Bilabial | ' Examples: |
| ǀ Dental | ɗ Dental/alveolar | p' Bilabial |
| ǃ (Post)alveolar | ʄ Palatal | t' Dental/alveolar |
| ǂ Palatoalveolar | ɠ Velar | k' Velar |
| ǁ Alveolar lateral | ʛ Uvular | s' Alveolar fricative |

OTHER SYMBOLS

ʍ Voiceless labial-velar fricative

w Voiced labial-velar approximant

ɥ Voiced labial-palatal approximant

ʜ Voiceless epiglottal fricative

ʢ Voiced epiglottal fricative

ʡ Epiglottal plosive

ɕ ʑ Alveolo-palatal fricatives

ɺ Alveolar lateral flap

ɧ Simultaneous ʃ and X

Affricates and double articulations can be represented by two symbols joined by a tie bar if necessary.

k͡p t͡s

DIACRITICS    Diacritics may be placed above a symbol with a descender, e.g. ŋ̊

| | | | | | | |
|---|---|---|---|---|---|---|
| ̥ Voiceless | n̥ d̥ | ̤ Breathy voiced | b̤ a̤ | ̪ Dental | t̪ d̪ |
| ̬ Voiced | s̬ t̬ | ̰ Creaky voiced | b̰ a̰ | ̺ Apical | t̺ d̺ |
| ʰ Aspirated | tʰ dʰ | ̼ Linguolabial | t̼ d̼ | ̻ Laminal | t̻ d̻ |
| ̹ More rounded | ɔ̹ | ʷ Labialized | tʷ dʷ | ̃ Nasalized | ẽ |
| ̜ Less rounded | ɔ̜ | ʲ Palatalized | tʲ dʲ | ⁿ Nasal release | dⁿ |
| ̟ Advanced | u̟ | ˠ Velarized | tˠ dˠ | ˡ Lateral release | dˡ |
| ̠ Retracted | i̠ | ˤ Pharyngealized | tˤ dˤ | ̚ No audible release | d̚ |
| ̈ Centralized | ë | ̴ Velarized or pharyngealized | ɫ | | |
| ̽ Mid-centralized | e̽ | ̝ Raised | e̝ (ɹ̝ = voiced alveolar fricative) | | |
| ̩ Syllabic | n̩ | ̞ Lowered | e̞ (β̞ = voiced bilabial approximant) | | |
| ̯ Non-syllabic | e̯ | ̘ Advanced Tongue Root | e̘ | | |
| ˞ Rhoticity | ɚ a˞ | ̙ Retracted Tongue Root | e̙ | | |

VOWELS

Where symbols appear in pairs, the one to the right represents a rounded vowel.

SUPRASEGMENTALS

ˈ Primary stress

ˌ Secondary stress

ˌfoʊnəˈtɪʃən

ː Long    eː

ˑ Half-long    eˑ

̆ Extra-short    ĕ

| Minor (foot) group

‖ Major (intonation) group

. Syllable break    ɹi.ækt

‿ Linking (absence of a break)

TONES AND WORD ACCENTS

| LEVEL | | CONTOUR | |
|---|---|---|---|
| e̋ or ˥ | Extra high | ě or ˩˥ | Rising |
| é ˦ | High | ê ˥˩ | Falling |
| ē ˧ | Mid | e᷄ ˧˥ | High rising |
| è ˨ | Low | e᷅ ˩˧ | Low rising |
| ȅ ˩ | Extra low | e᷈ ˧˩˧ | Rising-falling |
| ↓ Downstep | | ↗ Global rise | |
| ↑ Upstep | | ↘ Global fall | |

FIGURE A.2    The International Phonetic Alphabet. From the *Handbook of the International Phonetic Association* (1999).

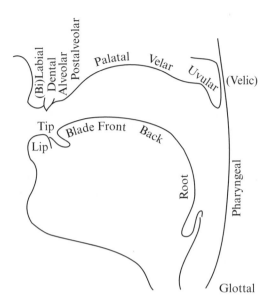

FIGURE A.3    Mid-sagittal section of the supralaryngeal vocal tract showing active articulators and places of articulation. From Nolan (1995).

possible to pronounce a voiceless [m] (by closing the lips and blowing out through the nose) and such sounds do occur in some languages, voiced [m] is very much the norm. When it is necessary to write a voiceless [m], a modification (*diacritic*) is added to the **m** symbol, in this case a subscript circle (m̥).

### A.2.2    The place dimension

The dimension with the greatest number of categories is *place of articulation*. 'Place' is usually said to refer to location (as above), but it also, at least implicitly, refers to the articulators involved in making the constriction. For such purposes, general designations such as 'the tongue' or 'the roof of the mouth' are inadequate, and so it is necessary to use a more detailed terminology to refer to parts of the tongue and parts of the roof of the mouth. Most of the terms used are illustrated in the mid-sagittal section of the head and neck shown in Figure A.3. It will be seen that all but two of the column labels on the IPA chart are represented, the exceptions being *labiodental* and *retroflex*.

In discussing the place dimension, it is useful to make a distinction between *active* and *passive* articulators. The active articulator moves while the passive articulator remains fixed in position. The tongue and the lower lip (supported by the lower jaw) are mobile and can function as active articulators. By contrast, the roof of the mouth and the back wall of the pharynx are immobile and can only play a passive role in articulation. (For these purposes, it is convenient to ignore vertical movement of the soft palate, contraction of the pharyngeal passage and protrusion of the upper lip which plays a role in lip rounding.) The difference between active and passive articulators is reflected in Figure A.3. It will be seen that the passive locations have been labelled with adjectives, while the mobile active articulators have been labelled with nouns.

There is not space to go through all of the place categories one by one, but I shall distinguish two general types:

1    The active articulator moves towards that part of the roof of the mouth or the pharyngeal wall which is opposite to it. This is by far the most common situation, and might be considered to be the default. In such cases, the place of articulation is designated using the appropriate adjective from Figure A.3 (in the case of *bilabial*, the prefix *bi-* species that the two lips are involved). For example, if the tip or blade of the tongue moves up to make contact with the alveolar ridge (just behind the teeth), the articulation is said to be *alveolar*. If the front of the tongue moves up to make contact with the hard palate, the articulation is said to be *palatal*. If the root of the tongue is pulled back towards the back wall of the pharynx, the articulation is *pharyngeal*. For the lower lip, the only possibility is to move up, making contact with the upper lip.

2    The active articulator moves to a point of contact which is outside of its default territory. There are two main examples. The first is the case of *retroflex* sounds, which are formed by bringing the tip (or even the underside) of the tongue back to make contact with the back of the alveolar ridge or the hard palate (the term refers to the tongue's curled back, concave posture). Retroflex consonants are particularly associated with languages of the Indian subcontinent.

The second example is the case of *labiodental* articulations, in which the lower lip moves up and back to make contact with the upper teeth. English /f/ and /v/ are both examples of labiodental sounds.

It remains to mention the terms *apical*, *laminal* and *coronal*. The first two refer to the tip (*apex*) and blade (*lamina*) of the tongue respectively, and are usually used to make the place label more specific – for example, an apical alveolar plosive (stop) would be a plosive made by raising the tip of the tongue to the alveolar ridge. The term *coronal* is often used as a general place term on its own, and refers to any articulation for which the active articulator is the tip or blade of the tongue. The category of coronals includes dental, alveolar, postalveolar and retroflex places.

### A.2.3  The manner dimension

The IPA Consonant Chart has eight rows, corresponding to eight manners of articulation. Although manner is usually treated as a single dimension, it involves a complex intersection of potentially distinct dimensions, as listed below.

1 Degree of stricture in the oral or pharyngeal cavity. There are three distinct degrees of stricture: (a) complete closure, which completely blocks air flow; (b) very narrow stricture, which results in turbulent air flow, which in turn produces sound with a rasping quality known as *audible friction*; (c) more open stricture which does not bring about turbulent air flow, but is still close enough for the introspecting speaker to feel that there is a constriction in the vocal tract. Category (a) includes plosives and nasals, category (b) includes fricatives and lateral fricatives, and category (c) includes approximants and lateral approximants.

2 Nasality. The opening vs. closure of the velic passage distinguishes the *nasal* manner from the *plosive* manner within category (a). In the case of plosives, both nasal and oral passages are blocked, and this results in a build-up of pressure inside the oral cavity when air flows into the pharynx and mouth from the lungs. A small explosion, or *burst*, occurs when the closure is released. Since, in the case of nasals, the nasal passage is open, the build-up of pressure does not occur, and there is no burst. In English, /p/ and /b/ are bilabial plosives, while /m/ is a bilabial nasal.

The term *stop* is also frequently used to refer to plosive sounds. Strictly speaking, *stop* is a more general category, and includes various non-pulmonic sounds as well as plosives.

3 Central vs. lateral passage of air. This binary dimension subdivides the fricative and approximant categories. The distinguishing characteristic of lateral (L-) sounds is that the airstream is diverted from the midline of the vocal tract. Instead, it flows along one or both sides of the tongue. In *lateral fricatives*, as in fricatives generally, the passage is sufficiently narrow to cause audible friction; in *lateral approximants*, it is not. Non-lateral fricatives and approximants have the more usual central passage of air. English /s/ is a fricative, while English /j/ (orthographic **y**) is an approximant. English /l/ is a lateral approximant. Lateral fricatives do not occur in English; for English speakers (at least in the British Isles), the most familiar example of a lateral fricative is the sound which is written **ll** in Welsh ([ɬ]), as in the place name **Llangollan**.

The other manner categories, *trills* and *taps/flaps*, stand outside the categories identified above. Trills are produced when one articulator is made to vibrate against another by the airstream. The possibilities are effectively limited to the lips, the tip of the tongue and the uvula; of these, the tongue-tip trill is most common cross-linguistically. Taps and flaps are defined by their short duration; one articulator (usually the tongue tip) simply taps against another rather than forming a sustained closure. From a strictly logical point of view, taps and flaps ought to be described as very short plosives, but they are most typically perceived as a kind of R-sound (*rhotic*). This is reflected in the use of symbols based on the letter R to represent them.

For many phoneticians and linguists, the terms *tap* and *flap* are synonymous. When the two are distinguished, *flap* is used to single out cases in which the tongue tip strikes the roof of the mouth in passing, usually as part of a back-to-front movement (Ladefoged and Maddieson 1996: 231). This gives flaps an affinity with retroflex stops.

Both tapped and trilled R-sounds are commonly associated with Scottish English. However, the best-known example of a tap in English is the American English pronunciation of orthographic **t(t)** and **d(d)** following a stressed vowel, as in **writer**, **rider**, **latter**, **ladder**.

### A.2.4  Simultaneous and sequential articulations

Some sounds do not have a single place of articulation, but are produced with two simultaneous articulations. A good example is [w], which is not found in the main body of the chart. The body of the tongue must be brought towards the soft palate – as for a very 'lazy' [k] – and at the same time the lips must be rounded. Thus, [w] involves two simultaneous approximants, one labial and one velar. Accordingly, it is called a *labial-velar approximant*. In cases where the IPA provides no special symbol (as it does for [w]), double articulations are represented by writing two symbols tied together by a ligature. For example, doubly articulated voiceless labial-velar stops, which are found in a number of West African languages, are represented as [k͡p].

Sometimes, a sequence of two consonant sounds appears to function as a single sound in the system of a particular language. There are two types of cases:

1   *Affricates.* These involve sequences of stop + fricative at the same place of articulation. A good example is the English sound represented by the letters **ch** which occurs in words such as **church**. This is a *post-alveolar affricate*. Affricates are represented by compound symbols joined by a tie bar – in this case as [t͡ʃ].
2   *Prenasalised stops.* These involve sequences of nasal + stop at the same place of articulation. For example, in Swahili, the sequence [mb] functions as a single sound, as in **mbuzi** 'goat'. Prenasalised stops are also represented by compound symbols joined by a tie bar – in this case as [m͡b].

Both affricates and prenasalised stops are sequences of *homorganic* sounds, that is, of sounds having the same place of articulation. However, not all homorganic sequences function as single sounds. For example, the [mb] of English **number** and the [ts] of English **cats** are not usually considered to be single sounds. The criteria which are used to decide whether a homorganic sequence functions as a single sound cannot be discussed here.

### A.2.5  Non-pulmonic consonants

We have already said that some consonant sounds are produced without using the airstream from the lungs and that, for this reason, they are said to be *non-pulmonic*. There are three types, known as *ejectives*, *implosives* and *clicks*.

In earlier versions of the IPA chart, ejectives and implosives were given their own rows at the bottom of the main consonant chart, but the current version lists them in a separate table, together with the clicks. All three types of sounds are somewhat 'exotic' from an English point of view, but all function as normal speech sounds in at least some other languages. Ejectives and implosives are widely attested in regions as diverse as the Caucasus and the Americas, while clicks are almost entirely confined to southern Africa.

Ejectives and implosives are similar to more common pulmonic consonants but differ in that the airstream is produced by moving the larynx up or down rather than by lung action. This technique for producing an airstream is referred to as the *glottalic air stream mechanism*.

Ejective stops differ from plosives in the way in which air pressure is built up in the mouth. We have seen that, in plosive consonants, this is caused by air flowing out from the lungs. In ejectives, the vocal folds close tightly, forming a glottal stop, and the entire larynx is raised. This makes the oro-pharyngeal cavity smaller and, consequently, causes the pressure inside to rise. Before the larynx descends again, the closure in the mouth is released. It is possible to generate very high pressures inside the mouth cavity in this way, and the explosion may sound quite strong. (One way of demonstrating this is to breathe out all the air in the lungs and try to make a strong **k**-sound.) The same mechanism can be used to produce fricatives and affricates.

Implosives are produced in the opposite way, by moving the larynx down rather than up. This has the effect of lowering the air pressure inside the mouth so that, when the stop closure in the mouth is released, air is sucked into the mouth.

Because a glottal stop is essential for the production of ejectives, it is not possible for the vocal folds to vibrate simultaneously. For this reason, all ejectives are voiceless. However, the requirements for producing implosives are less strict, and both voiced and voiceless varieties have been reported. Prototypical, 'textbook' implosives are produced with voicing. Particularly good examples are to be found in the Sindhi language (spoken in Pakistan).

Ejectives and implosives may be thought of as strongly emphasised variants of more common speech sounds, but clicks are *sui generis*. Examples of clicks are the sound made by sliding the blade of the tongue backwards along the upper teeth (as in pronouncing the interjection which is sometimes written **tut-tut**) and the sound used to encourage horses, which involves sliding one side of the tongue inward along the edge of the upper surface of the mouth.

The technique for producing clicks is known as the *velaric air stream mechanism*. The tongue is used to seal off a small pocket of air just below the roof of the mouth and is then lowered to create a suction. The production of a click requires a [k]-like (velar) closure, which serves to seal off this small pocket of air at the back end. This back closure remains in place while the more obvious movements involved in lowering the tongue are performed, and is only released afterwards. It is these more obvious movements which determine the click's place of articulation. For example, because the **tut-tut** click involves sliding the blade of the tongue back along the upper teeth, it is said to have a dental place of articulation.

### A.2.6   Refinements

The main IPA chart provides symbols for general categories to which more detail may be added. For example, in an impressionistic transcription, we would wish to note that English /p/ is aspirated in certain circumstances. The presence of aspiration may be expressed by adding a superscript **h** to the appropriate symbol, for example, [pʰ]. English /l/, when it occurs word-finally or before another consonant (i.e. in a syllable rhyme) has a 'dark' quality which results from raising the back of the tongue towards the soft palate. Raising the back of the tongue in this way is like superimposing an approximant articulation on a more neutral [l] sound and is known as *velarisation*. It can be represented by adding a superscript ɣ (the symbol for a voiced velar fricative), for example [lˠ], or by drawing a tilda through the main symbol, for example [ɫ]. Such modifications to the basic symbols are known as *diacritics*. An extensive list of diacritics, which cannot be discussed in detail here, is given at the bottom of the chart.

### A.2.7   Impossible and unattested sound types

It remains to comment on another very obvious feature of the chart. Some of the boxes contain no symbols and some of these empty boxes are shaded. The shaded boxes correspond to place-manner combinations which are thought to be impossible. For example, it is not possible to make a glottal nasal, because a nasal, by definition, requires that air should pass out through the nose while a glottal stop cuts off the airstream at the larynx, making it impossible for air to pass out through the nose. The unshaded empty boxes correspond to place-manner combinations which are not judged to be impossible but which have not been observed as sounds in language. For example, although it may be possible to trill the lower lip against the upper teeth, a *labiodental trill* has yet to turn up in a language.

We shall now move on to consider the classification of vowels.

### A.3   Vowels

We have already said that vowels are classified using dimensions different from those used to classify consonants. This is because of the difficulties involved in identifying a vowel's *place of articulation*. For example, in the English word **sad**, it is easy to feel that the [s] and the [d] involve contact between the tongue and the alveolar ridge, but the vowel in between is not so readily placeable.

For consonants, the tongue, as it were, puts into port somewhere on the coastline of the mouth space, defined by the roof of the mouth and the back wall of the pharynx, while for vowels it ventures out into the open sea. The phonetician aims to construct a two-dimensional map of possible tongue locations, using a system which has been compared to geographical mapping using lines of latitude and longitude. Of course, since the tongue is a large structure which takes up a good deal of space inside the mouth, it does not really make sense to speak of a precise location of the tongue in the mouth. Rather, one must determine the location of a reference point on the surface of the tongue. This reference point is conventionally taken to be the highest point of the tongue.

### A.3.1  Dimensions of vowel classification

The mapping of tongue positions depends on the idea of a *vowel space*, which is a two-dimensional area on a mid-sagittal section of the mouth. The vowel space includes all possible positions assumed by the highest point of the tongue in forming vowel sounds. It is commonly represented as a quadrilateral, as can be seen in Figure A.2. The vertical dimension of the quadrilateral is *height* and the horizontal dimension is *backness*. The height dimension ranges from *close* at the top to *open* at the bottom or, in a popular alternative terminology, from *high* to *low*. The horizontal dimension ranges from *front* at the left to *back* at the right. It will also be noticed that the quadrilateral is wider at the top than at the bottom, and that the left-hand side is longer than the right-hand side.

The four corners of the quadrilateral are defined by four extreme vowel articulations, [i], [u], [ɑ] and [a]. The first three of these are defined by an approximation of the appropriate part of the tongue to the hard palate ([i]), the soft palate ([u]) and the lower pharynx ([ɑ]); the approximation must be close, but not so close as to result in audible friction. In the case of [u], the lips are also rounded. The fourth vowel, [a], is not so easily specified, but involves a maximally low and front position of the tongue hump.

Since these four articulations represent the extreme possibilities, it follows that all other articulations (as represented by the highest point of the tongue) must be located somewhere in between. To aid in the placement of tongue positions, the quadrilateral is divided by grid lines. These provide for two intermediate levels along the height dimension and one intermediate level along the backness dimension. Some phoneticians would take the view that the basis for the division is auditory, while others would maintain that it is articulatory. The intermediate heights are *close-mid* (or upper-mid) and *open-mid* (or lower-mid), and the intermediate level between front and back is *central*. Symbols are provided for vowel qualities which correspond to intersections of the grid lines. A few commonly used symbols which correspond to qualities between the lines are also included. For example, the symbol *schwa* (ə) which is, in practice, the most frequently used symbol for vowels with mid-central qualities, is placed in the very centre of the chart. It is unfortunate that the chart provides no symbol for a low central vowel, since such vowels are found in a wide variety of languages. In practice, the symbol **a** is often used to represent vowels of this type.

Thus far, we have said nothing about the position of the lips. The basic IPA classification allows for two possibilities: *rounded* and *unrounded*. Rounding functions as a third dimension, which is independent of height and backness. In other words, all possible tongue positions may be pronounced with either rounded or unrounded lips. This dimension is represented in the same way that the voicing dimension is represented for consonants. With a few exceptions involving commonly used symbols, vowel symbols are provided in pairs. The left member represents an unrounded vowel, while the right member represents a rounded vowel. For example, the symbol [y] represents a vowel with the tongue position of [i] pronounced with rounded lips (as in French **tu** 'you').

The IPA vowel symbols may be understood in either a *broad* or a *narrow* way. For example, the symbol ɑ may be used to refer to an ɑ-region of the chart (which would border on an **a**-region and an ʌ-region). It may also be used in a more specific way, to refer to the one unique point at the corner of the chart, which is maximally open and maximally back. On the first interpretation, [ɑ] is quite a suitable transcription for the vowel of English **palm**. On the second interpretation, it would be necessary to add one or more diacritic marks to indicate that the vowel is somewhat more forward than the reference vowel (for example, [ɑ̟]). If the vowel symbols are understood in the second, more specific, way, they provide a set of cardinal reference points to which other vowels can be compared.

The idea of using specific vowel qualities as reference points is particularly associated with the great twentieth-century British phonetician Daniel Jones, who was also responsible for designing the vowel quadrilateral. Jones designated eight vowels around the periphery of the chart ([i], [e], [ɛ], [a], [ɑ], [ɔ], [o], [u]) as *Primary Cardinal* vowels, and the ten remaining peripheral vowels ([y], [ø], [œ], [ɶ], [ɒ], [ʌ], [ɤ], [ɯ], [ɨ], [ʉ]) as *Secondary Cardinal* vowels. These vowels were defined in universal phonetic terms rather than with reference to the vowels of any specific language, and Jones's own pronunciation (taught directly to his students, and later recorded on a grammophone record) has continued to provide a definitive point of reference.

### A.3.2  Refinements

Unmodified IPA symbols represent oral vowels (produced with the soft palate in the raised position). Vowels may also be produced with a lowered soft palate, in other words, *nasalised*. A tilde placed over a vowel symbol marks nasalisation; for example, [ẽ] represents a nasalised [e].

Implicit in the IPA system is the idea that, for each position of the highest point of the tongue, there is a unique normal or default overall tongue shape. There are three possible departures from this shape: (1) *Advanced Tongue Root* (*ATR*), in which the root of the tongue is more forward; (2) *Retracted Tongue Root* (*RTR*), in which the root of the tongue is further back; and (3) *rhoticity*, or R-colouring (like that evident in the American English vowel of **bird**) which may be achieved by curling up the tip of the tongue (retroflexion) and/or by additional constriction in the lower pharynx.

Of these, ATR has been of particular interest because it provides the basis for systems of vowel harmony. In vowel harmony systems, vowels within a word or some part of a word must agree with regard to some given classificatory dimension. For example, in Turkish, vowels in suffixes must agree in frontness or backness with the final vowel of the root word they are attached to. The suffix meaning 'to' thus has both a front form /e/ and a back form /a/ as in **deniz-e** 'to the sea' and **yol-a** 'to the road'.

In a typical ATR harmony system, vowels are divided into two sets, which are usually represented as (1) /i/, /e/, /o/, /u/ and (2) /ɪ/, /ɛ/, /ɔ/, /ʊ/ (these symbols do not have their IPA values). Low [a]-like vowels are typically neutral as regards the distinction. Within a word, all of the vowels must be taken from either one set or the other. For example, in Asante Twi (spoken in Ghana) the verbal prefix which marks agreement with a 3rd person singular subject has the form /o/ or /ɔ/, depending on whether the root it attaches to contains a vowel from set 1 or set 2. Thus, /òtú/ 'he digs up' contrasts with /ɔ̀tʊ́/ 'he throws'. There is now a specific diacritic for ATR vowels, a subscript ˌ.

### A.3.3  Diphthongs

Many languages have *diphthongs*, or vowels which change from one quality to another over the course of their duration. In IPA notation, a diphthong is represented as a sequence of two vowels, the first representing the starting point and the second representing the ending point. For example, the vowel of English **boy** is a diphthong which starts from an [ɔ]-like position and ends somewhere in the neighbourhood of [ɪ].

This concludes our review of the IPA framework for classifying segments. We shall conclude our review of IPA classification with a brief look at the so-called *suprasegmentals*.

## A.4  Suprasegmentals (prosodic features)

*Suprasegmentals* and *prosodic features* are general terms used to refer to patterned variation in pitch, force (*stress*) and duration – in other words, to the properties which spoken language shares with music. Pitch variation gives spoken language its melody, while stress provides a sense of beat. Contrasts between long and short duration (quantity) may also contribute to the perceived rhythmic character of a language. It is not surprising, therefore, that suprasegmentals have been considered as different in kind from the segmental properties which serve to define vowel and consonant articulations.

Of the three suprasegmentals, stress has proved to be both the most straightforward to analyse impressionistically and the most difficult to define in purely phonetic terms. Stress picks out certain syllables as more prominent than others. Phoneticians have differed as to how many levels of stress they allow for. The IPA chart of Figure A.2 provides a three-level system: primary stress, secondary stress and unstressed (unmarked). Despite general agreement as to the rhythmic and hierarchical nature of stress, its phonetic nature has remained elusive. Other things being equal, stressed syllables may have longer duration, higher pitch, greater acoustic intensity and more carefully articulated vowel and consonant sounds than unstressed syllables. However, none of these properties will consistently and unambiguously distinguish stressed from unstressed syllables.

By contrast, both pitch and duration are extremely simple to define in physical terms; duration needs no special definition, while the auditory sensation of pitch can be correlated with the fundamental frequency of the voice in a straightforward way. However, pitch and duration function in numerous and interrelated ways within linguistic systems, making it difficult to formulate a universally valid framework for recording them in a systematic way in transcription. Apart from their possible contributions to stress, we may distinguish three general types of functions:

1   As contributors to contrasts which primarily involve segmental properties. For example, in English, vowels are higher in pitch (at least at the beginning) following voiceless consonants than following voiced consonants (compare **peat** and **beat**). Vowels are longer before voiced consonants than before voiceless consonants (compare **bead** and **beat**).

2   As contrasting properties in their own right, serving to distinguish between individual segments or syllables. In many languages (so-called *tone languages*), each morpheme has its own characteristic pitch, and changing the pitch can result in a change in meaning; for example, in Thai, the syllable /maa/ may mean 'dog', 'come' or 'horse', depending on whether it is pronounced with rising, mid level, or high level pitch. Similarly, many languages contrast long and short vowels and/or consonants.

3   As properties which vary over, and help to delimit, whole phrases. As regards pitch, this function is known as *intonation*. English has a particularly complex system of intonation tunes. For example, a simple sentence such as **John smokes** can be uttered with a large number of melodies depending on whether the emphasis is on John or the smoking, and also on the attitude of the speaker. Characteristic patterns of speeding up and slowing down (resulting in shorter and longer durations of individual segments) also play a role in linguistic phrasing.

Not all of these functions are equally well catered for by the IPA, which is oriented toward the recording of segmental rather than phrasal variation in pitch and duration. This orientation reflects the lack (as yet) of a generally agreed universal system of categories for classifying intonational and temporal aspects of phrasing. As can be seen from the bottom right of the chart, there is an elaborate system of accents and 'tone letters' for recording the pitch of individual sounds. There is also provision for four degrees of duration: extrashort, short (unmarked), half-long and long.

## A.5 Using the IPA

The IPA is intended to be a flexible system of notation, which can be used for a wide variety of purposes. By making full use of the available diacritics, it is possible to represent a good deal of detail about pronunciation in an unbiased way (so far as that is humanly possible). This is usually done as a first step in analysing the phonological system of a language, particularly if the language has not been described before.

A more common use of the IPA has been to provide symbols for phonemic (systematic) representation, allowing the user to define conventions which will apply in the interpretation of various symbols and to take account of variation between individuals or between dialects. This kind of usage is found in the 'Illustrations of the IPA', which are published regularly in the *Journal of the International Phonetic Association*. For example, in the Illustration of Hebrew (Laufer 1990), the 'conventions' note that while the R-sound, represented as /r/, is usually an alveolar trill ([r]) in the Oriental dialect, it is usually a uvular approximant ([ʁ]) in the Non-Oriental dialect. The same symbol, /r/, is used in the example texts for both dialects.

The fact that individual symbols can be re-defined in this way sometimes gives the impression that some practitioners of IPA transcription are not really committed to IPA usage. However, flexibility has been the Alphabet's strength. It has allowed the Association to be a 'broad church' as regards what we might call the 'philosophy of transcription'. It has also made the IPA very useful for practical applications, such as representing pronunciation in dictionaries or language teaching, where typographical simplicity may be a factor in choosing a system of notation.

## A.6 Further reading

General references on impressionistic-phonetic classification are given in Section 1.7 of Chapter 1. The most authoritative introduction to the IPA symbols and their use is the *IPA Handbook* (International Phonetic Association 1999). Nolan (1995), which is published as Volume 25 of the *Journal of the International Phonetic Association*, is a preliminary version. The reader may also be interested in the more personal views of the nature of phonetic transcription published by Abercrombie (1985) and Ladefoged (1990).

# Bibliography

Abberton, E. and A. Fourcin (1984). Electrolaryngography. In Code and Ball (1984), 62–78.

Abberton, E., D. Howard and A. Fourcin (1989). Laryngographic assessment of normal voice: a tutorial. *Clinical linguistics and phonetics* 3, 281–296.

Abercrombie, D. (1954). The recording of dialect material. *Orbis* 3, 231–235.

Abercrombie, D. (1957). Direct palatography. *Zeitschrift für Phonetik* 10, 21–25.

Abercrombie, D. (1967). *Elements of General Phonetics.* Edinburgh: Edinburgh University Press.

Abercrombie, D. (1985). Daniel Jones's teaching. In Fromkin (1985), 15–24.

Abercrombie, D., D. B. Fry, P. A. D. MacCarthy, N. C. Scott and J. M. Trim, eds. (1964). *In Honour of Daniel Jones.* London: Longman.

Abramson, A. (1962). *The Vowels and Tones of Standard Thai: Acoustical Measurements and Experiments.* Bloomington: Indiana University Research Center in Anthropology, Folklore, and Linguistics, Publication 20.

Abramson, A. S. and L. Lisker (1970). Discriminability along the voicing continuum: cross-language tests. In Hála *et al.* (1970), 569–573.

Abramson, A. S. and L. Lisker (1973). Voice-timing perception in Spanish word-initial stops. *Journal of Phonetics* 1, 1–8.

Abry, C., L.-J. Boë and J.-L. Schwartz (1989). Plateaus, catastrophes, and the structuring of vowel systems. *Journal of Phonetics* 17, 47–54.

Allen, W. S. (1953). *Phonetics in Ancient India.* London: Oxford University Press.

Anthony, J. and N. Hewlett (1984). Aerometry. In Code and Ball (1984), 79–106.

Archangeli, D. and D. Pulleyblank (1994). *Grounded Phonology.* Cambridge, MA: MIT Press.

Ashby, P. (1995). *Speech Sounds.* London: Routledge.

Asher, R. E. and E. J. A. Henderson, eds. (1981). *Towards a History of Phonetics.* Edinburgh: Edinburgh University Press.

Assmann, P. F. (1991). The perception of back vowels: centre of gravity hypothesis. *Quarterly Journal of Experimental Psychology* 43A, 423–448.

Baken, R. J. (1987). *Clinical Measurement of Speech and Voice.* London: Taylor and Francis Ltd.

Baken, R. J. (1992). Electroglottography. *Journal of Voice* 6, 98–110.

Baken, R. J. (1995). Between organization and chaos: a different view of the voice. In Bell-Berti and Raphael (1995), 233–245.

Ball, M. (1984). X-ray techniques. In Code and Ball (1984), 107–128.

Beckman, M. E. and J. Pierrehumbert (1999). Interpreting 'phonetic interpretation' over the lexicon. To appear in *Papers in Laboratory Phonology VI.*

Beddor, P. S. (1982). *Phonological and Phonetic Effects of Nasalization on Vowel Height.* Ph.D. Dissertation, University of Minnesota.

276

Beddor, P. S. (1991). Predicting the structure of phonological systems. *Phonetica* 48, 83–107.

Beddor, P. S. and S. Hawkins (1990). The influence of spectral prominence on perceived vowel quality. *Journal of the Acoustical Society of America* 87, 2684–2704.

Beddor, P. S., R. A. Krakow and L. M. Goldstein (1986). Perceptual constraints and phonological change: a study of nasal vowel height. *Phonology Yearbook* 3, 197–217.

Bell-Berti, F. and L. J. Raphael, eds. (1995). *Producing Speech: Contemporary Issues. For Katherine Safford Harris.* New York: American Institute of Physics.

Bickley, C. (1982). Acoustic analysis and perception of breathy vowels. *Working Papers, MIT Speech Communication Group* 1, 71–81.

Bickley, C. A. and K. N. Stevens (1986). Effects of a vocal-tract constriction on the glottal source: experimental and modelling studies. *Journal of Phonetics* 14, 373–382.

Bladon, A. (1983). Two-formant models of vowel perception: shortcomings and enhancements. *Speech Communication* 2, 305–313.

Bladon, A. (1986). Phonetics for hearers. In McGregor (1986), 1–24.

Bladon, A., C. Clark and K. Mickey (1987). Production and perception of fricatives: Shona data. *Journal of the International Phonetic Association* 17, 39–65.

Bladon, R. A. W. and G. Fant (1978). A two-formant model and the cardinal vowels. *Royal Institute of Technology, Speech Transmission Laboratory, Stockholm, Quarterly Progress and Status Report* 1, 1–8.

Bladon, R. A. W. and B. Lindblom (1981). Modelling the judgment of vowel quality differences. *Journal of the Acoustical Society of America* 69, 1414–1422.

Bless, D. M. and J. H. Abbs, eds. (1983). *Vocal Fold Physiology: Contemporary Research and Clinical Issues.* San Diego: College-Hill Press.

Borden, G. J., K. S. Harris and L. J. Raphael (1994). *Speech Science Primer* (3rd edn). Baltimore: Williams and Wilkins.

Broad, D. J. (1979). The new theories of vocal fold vibration. In Lass (1979), 203–256.

Browman, C. P. and L. Goldstein (1986). Towards an articulatory phonology. *Phonology Yearbook* 3, 219–252.

Browman, C. P. and L. Goldstein (1989). Articulatory gestures as phonological units. *Phonology* 6, 201–251.

Byrd, D. (1994). Palatogram reading as a phonetic skill: a short tutorial. *Journal of the International Phonetic Association* 24, 21–34.

Catford, J. C. (1964). Phonation types: the classification of some laryngeal components of speech production. In Abercrombie *et al.* (1964), 26–37.

Catford, J. C. (1977). *Fundamental Problems in Phonetics.* Edinburgh: Edinburgh University Press.

Catford, J. C. (1981). Observations on the recent history of vowel classification. In Asher and Henderson (1981), 19–32.

Catford, J. C. (1983). Pharyngeal and laryngeal sounds in Caucasian languages. In Bless and Abbs (1983), 344–350.

Catford, J. C. (1988) *A Practical Introduction to Phonetics.* Oxford: Clarendon Press.

Chistovich, L. A. (1985). Central auditory processing of peripheral vowel spectra. *Journal of the Acoustical Society of America* 77, 789–805.

Chomsky, N. and M. Halle (1968). *The Sound Pattern of English.* New York, Evanston and London: Harper & Row.

Clark, J. and C. Yallop (1995). *An Introduction to Phonetics and Phonology* (2nd edn). Cambridge, MA, and Oxford: Blackwell.

Code, C. and M. Ball, eds. (1984). *Experimental Clinical Phonetics*. London and Canberra: Croom Helm.

Cohn, A. C. (1990). *Phonetic and Phonological Rules of Nasalization. UCLA Working Papers in Phonetics* 76.

Coleman, J. (1998). Cognitive reality and the phonological lexicon: a review. *Journal of Neurolinguistics* 11, 295–320.

Colton, R. H. and E. G. Conture (1990). Problems and pitfalls of electroglottography. *Journal of Voice* 4, 10–24.

Connell, B. and A. Arvaniti (1995). *Phonology and Phonetic Evidence. Papers in Laboratory Phonology IV*. Cambridge: Cambridge University Press.

Cooper, F. S., P. C. Delattre, A. M. Liberman, J. M. Borst and L. J. Gerstman (1952). Some experiments on the perception of synthetic speech sounds. *Journal of the Acoustical Society of America* 24, 597–606.

Crothers, J. (1978). Typology and universals of vowel systems. In Greenberg, Ferguson and Moravcsik (1978), 93–152.

Cutting, J. E. and B. S. Rosner (1974). Categories and boundaries in speech and music. *Perception and Psychophysics* 16, 564–570.

Davenport, M. and S. J. Hannahs (1998). *Introducing Phonetics and Phonology*. London: Arnold.

David, E. E. Jr. and P. B. Denes, eds. (1972). *Human Communication: A Unified View*. New York: McGraw-Hill.

Delattre, P. (1954). Les attributs de la nasalité vocalique et consonantique. *Studia Linguistica* 8, 103–109.

Delattre, P. (1981). *Studies in Comparative Phonetics. English, German, Spanish and French. Edited and Introduced by Bertil Malmberg*. Heidelberg: Julius Gross Verlag.

Delattre, P., A. M. Liberman, F. S. Cooper and L. J. Gerstman (1952). An experimental study of the acoustic determinants of vowel color: observations on one- and two-formant vowels synthesized from spectrographic patterns. *Word* 8, 195–210.

Delattre, P. C., A. M. Liberman, and F. S. Cooper (1955). Acoustic loci and transitional cues for consonants. *Journal of the Acoustical Society of America* 27, 769–773.

Delgutte, B. (1997). Auditory neural processing of speech. In Hardcastle and Laver (1997), 507–538.

Delgutte, B. and N. Y. S. Kiang (1984a). Speech coding in the auditory nerve: I. Vowel-like sounds. *Journal of the Acoustical Society of America* 75, 866–878.

Delgutte, B. and N. Y. S. Kiang (1984b). Speech coding in the auditory nerve: III. Voiceless fricative consonants. *Journal of the Acoustical Society of America* 75, 887–896.

Denes, P. B. and E. N. Pinson (1993). *The Speech Chain: The Physics and Biology of Spoken Language* (2nd edn). New York: W. H. Freeman and Company.

Diehl, R. and K. Kluender (1989). On the objects of speech perception. *Ecological Psychology* 1, 123–144.

Disner, S. F. (1984). Insights on vowel spacing. In Maddieson (1984), 123–155.

Dixit, R. P. (1989). Glottal gestures in Hindi plosives. *Journal of Phonetics* 17, 213–237.

Dixit, R. P. and P. F. MacNeilage (1980). Cricothyroid activity and control of voicing in Hindi stops and affricates. *Phonetica* 37, 397–406.

Dixit, R. P. and T. Shipp (1985). Study of subglottal air pressure during Hindi stop consonants. *Phonetica* 42, 53–77.

Docherty, G. J. and D. R. Ladd, eds. (1992). *Papers in Laboratory Phonology II. Gesture, Segment, Prosody*. Cambridge: Cambridge University Press.

Ehret, G. (1992). Preadaptations in the auditory system of mammals for phonetic recognition. In Schouten (1992), 99–112.

Eimas, P. and J. Miller, eds. (1981). *Perspectives on the Study of Speech*. Hillsdale, NJ: Lawrence Erlbaum.

Evers, V., H. Reetz and A. Lahiri (1998). Crosslinguistic acoustic categorization of sibilants independent of phonological status. *Journal of Phonetics* 26, 345–370.

Ewan, W. G. and R. Krones (1974). Measuring larynx movement using the thyroumbrometer. *Journal of Phonetics* 2, 327–335.

Fant, G. (1956). On the predictability of formant levels and spectrum envelopes from formant frequencies. In Halle *et al.* (1956), 109–119.

Fant, G. (1960). *Acoustic Theory of Speech Production*. The Hague: Mouton.

Fant, G. (1973). *Speech Sounds and Features*. Cambridge, MA, and London: MIT Press.

Fant, G. (1985). The vocal tract in your pocket calculator. In Fromkin (1985), 55–77.

Farnetani, E. (1997). Coarticulation and connected speech processes. In Hardcastle and Laver (1997), 371–404.

Fischer-Jørgensen, E. J., J. Rischel and N. Thorsen, eds. (1979). *Proceedings of the Ninth International Congress of Phonetic Sciences, Volume I*. Copenhagen: University of Copenhagen Institute of Phonetics.

Fodor, J. A. (1983). *The Modularity of Mind*. Cambridge, MA: MIT Press.

Fourcin, A. J. (1974). Laryngographic examination of vocal fold vibration. In Wyke (1974), 315–333.

Fourcin, A. J., E. Abberton, D. Miller and D. Howells (1995). Laryngograph: speech pattern element tools for therapy, training, and assessment. *European Journal of Disorders of Communication* 30, 101–115.

Fowler, C. A. and L. D. Rosenbaum (1990). Duplex perception: a comparison of monosyllables and slamming doors. *Journal of Experimental Psychology: Human Perception and Performance* 16, 742–754.

Fowler, C. A. and L. D. Rosenbaum (1991). The perception of phonetic gestures. In Mattingly and Studdert-Kennedy (1991), 33–67.

Fromkin, V. A., ed. (1978). *Tone. A Linguistic Survey*. New York: Academic Press.

Fromkin, V. A., ed. (1985). *Phonetic Linguistics: Essays in Honour of Peter Ladefoged*. Orlando, FL: Academic Press.

Fry, D. B. (1979). *The Physics of Speech*. Cambridge: Cambridge University Press.

Fujimura, O., ed. (1988). *Vocal Physiology: Voice Production, Mechanisms and Functions*. New York: Raven Press.

Fulop, S. A. (1996). An acoustic study of the tongue root contrast in Degema vowels. *UCLA Working Papers in Phonetics* 93, 13–46.

Gauffin, J. and J. Sundberg (1989). Spectral correlates of glottal voice source waveform characteristics. *Journal of Speech and Hearing Research* 32, 556–565.

Gernsbacher, M. A., ed. (1994). *Handbook of Psycholinguistics*. San Diego: Academic Press.

Gerratt, B. R., D. G. Hanson, G. S. Berke and K. Precoda (1991). Photoglottography: a clinical synopsis. *Journal of Voice* 5, 98–105.

Goldinger, S. D. (1997). Words and voices: perception and production in an episodic lexicon. In Johnson and Mullennix (1997), 33–66.

Goldinger, S. G., D. B. Pisoni and P. A. Luce (1996). Speech perception and spoken word recognition: research and theory. In Lass (1996), 277–327.

Goldsmith, J. (1994). *The Handbook of Phonological Theory*. Cambridge, MA, and Oxford: Blackwell.

Gottfried, M., J. D. Miller and D. J. Meyer (1993). Three approaches to the classification of American English diphthongs. *Journal of Phonetics* 21, 205–229.

Greenberg, J. H., C. A. Ferguson and E. A. Moravcsik, eds. (1978). *Universals of Human Language 2: Phonology*. Stanford: Stanford University Press.

Greenberg, S. (1996). Auditory processing of speech. In Lass (1996), 362–407.

Gussenhoven, C. and H. Jacobs (1998). *Understanding Phonology*. London: Arnold.

Hála, B., M. Romportl and P. Janota (1970). *Proceedings of the Sixth International Congress of Phonetic Sciences, September 1967*. Prague: Academia.

Halle, M. (1985). Speculations about the representation of words in memory. In Fromkin (1985), 101–114.

Halle, M., H. Lunt and H. MacLean, eds. (1956). *For Roman Jakobson*. The Hague: Mouton.

Halle, M. and K. Stevens (1971). A note on laryngeal features. *Quarterly Progress Report MIT Research Laboratory of Electronics* 101, 198–213.

Handel, S. (1989). *Listening*. Cambridge, MA: MIT Press.

Hardcastle, W., W. Jones, C. Knight, A. Trudgeon and G. Calder (1989). New developments in electropalatography: a state-of-the-art report. *Clinical Linguistics and Phonetics* 3, 1–38.

Hardcastle, W. J. and J. Laver, eds. (1997). *The Handbook of Phonetic Sciences*. Cambridge, MA, and Oxford: Blackwell.

Hardcastle, W. J. and A. Marchal, eds. (1990). *Speech Production and Speech Modelling*. Dordrecht: Kluwer Academic Publishers.

Harris, J. (1994). *English Sound Structure*. Oxford and Cambridge, MA: Blackwell.

Harris, K. S. (1958). Cues for the discrimination of American English fricatives in spoken syllables. *Language and Speech* 1, 1–7.

Harris, K. S., H. S. Hoffman, A. M. Liberman, P. C. Delattre and F. S. Cooper (1958). Effect of third-formant transitions on the perception of the voiced stop consonants. *Journal of the Acoustical Society of America* 30, 122–126.

Hawkins, S. (1992). An introduction to task dynamics. In Docherty and Ladd (1992), 9–25.

Hawkins, S. and K. N. Stevens (1985). Acoustic and perceptual correlates of the non-nasal–nasal distinction for vowels. *Journal of the Acoustical Society of America* 77, 1560–1575.

Hayward, K. (1992). *Phonation Types Seen by Fibreoptic Laryngoscopy: Hausa, Korean, and Gujarati*. Video, SOAS, University of London.

Hess, S. (1992). Assimilatory effects in a vowel harmony system: an acoustic analysis of advanced tongue root in Akan. *Journal of Phonetics* 20, 475–492.

Hirano, M. (1977). Structure and vibratory behavior of the vocal folds. In Sawashima and Cooper (1977), 13–27.

Hirano, M. (1981). *Clinical Examination of Voice*. Wien and New York: Springer-Verlag.

Hirose, H. (1995). Imaging of the larynx – past and present. In Bell-Berti and Raphael (1995), 247–257.

Hirose, H. (1997). Investigating the physiology of laryngeal structures. In Hardcastle and Laver (1997), 116–136.

Hirose, H., C. Y. Lee and T. Ushijima (1974). Laryngeal control in Korean stop production. *Journal of Phonetics* 2, 161–180.

Hixon, T. (1966). Turbulent noise sources for speech. *Folia Phoniatrica* 18, 168–182.

Hoemeke, K. A. and R. L. Diehl (1994). Perception of vowel height: the role of $F_1$–$F_0$ distance. *Journal of the Acoustical Society of America* 96, 661–674.

Hollien, H. (1974). On vocal registers. *Journal of Phonetics* 2, 125–143.

Hombert, J.-M., J. J. Ohala and W. G. Ewan (1979). Phonetic explanations for the development of tones. *Language* 55, 37–58.

Honda, K. (1995). Laryngeal and extra-laryngeal mechanisms of $F_0$ control. In Bell-Berti and Raphael (1995), 215–232.

Hong, K., S. Niimi and H. Hirose (1991). Laryngeal adjustments for Korean stops, affricates, and fricatives – an electromyographic study. *Annual Bulletin, Research Institute of Logopedics and Phoniatrics* 25, 17–31.

Huffman, M. K. (1990). *Implementation of Nasal: Timing and Articulatory Landmarks. UCLA Working Papers in Phonetics* 75.

International Phonetic Association (1999). *Handbook of the International Phonetic Association. A Guide to the Use of the International Phonetic Alphabet.* Cambridge: Cambridge University Press.

Ishizaka, K. and M. Matsudaira (1968). What makes the vocal cords vibrate? In Kohasi (1968), B9–B12.

Jackson, M. T. T. (1988). *Phonetic Theory and Cross-Linguistic Variation in Vowel Articulation. UCLA Working Papers in Phonetics* 71.

Jacoby, L. L. and L. R. Brooks (1984). Nonanalytic cognition: memory, perception and concept learning. *The Psychology of Learning and Motivation* 18, 1–47.

Jakobson, R., C. G. M. Fant and M. Halle (1952). *Preliminaries to Speech Analysis.* Acoustics Laboratory, Massachusetts Institute of Technology.

Javkin, H. R. (1996). Speech analysis and synthesis. In Lass (1996), 245–273.

Johnson, K. (1997). *Acoustic and Auditory Phonetics.* Cambridge, MA, and Oxford: Blackwell.

Johnson, K. (1997). Speech perception without speaker normalization: an exemplar model. In Johnson and Mullennix (1997), 145–165.

Johnson, K. and J. W. Mullennix, eds. (1997). *Talker Variability in Speech Processing.* San Diego: Academic Press.

Kagaya, R. and H. Hirose (1975). Fiberoptic, electromyographic, and acoustic analyses of Hindi stop consonants. *Annual Bulletin, Research Institute of Logopedics and Phoniatrics* 9, 27–46.

Katamba, F. (1989). *An Introduction to Phonology.* London and New York: Longman.

Keating, P. A. (1984a). Phonetic and phonological representation of stop consonant voicing. *Language* 60, 286–319.

Keating, P. A. (1984b). Physiological effects on stop consonant voicing. *UCLA Working Papers in Phonetics* 59, 29–34.

Keating, P. A. (1985). Universal phonetics and the organization of grammars. In Fromkin (1985), 115–132.

Keating, P. A. (1988). The phonology–phonetics interface. In Newmeyer (1988), 281–302.

Keating, P. A. (1990a). Phonetic representations in a generative grammar. *Journal of Phonetics* 18, 321–334.

Keating, P. A. (1990b). The window model of coarticulation: articulatory evidence. In Kingston and Beckman (1990), 451–470.

Keating, P. A., ed. (1994). *Phonological Structure and Phonetic Form. Papers in Laboratory Phonology III.* Cambridge: Cambridge University Press.

Keating, P. and A. Lahiri (1993). Fronted velars, palatalized velars, and palatals. *Phonetica* 50, 73–101.

Kelly, J. and J. Local (1989). *Doing Phonology.* Manchester and New York: Manchester University Press.

Kenstowicz, M. (1994). *Phonology in Generative Grammar*. Cambridge, MA, and Oxford: Blackwell.

Kent, R. D., S. G. Adams and G. S. Turner (1996). Models of speech production. In Lass (1996), 3–45.

Kent, R. D., J. Dembowski and N. J. Lass (1996). The acoustic characteristics of American English. In Lass (1996), 185–225.

Kent, R. D. and K. L. Moll (1969). Vocal-tract characteristics of the stop cognates. *Journal of the Acoustical Society of America* 46, 1549–1555.

Kent, R. D. and C. Read (1992). *The Acoustic Analysis of Speech*. San Diego: Whurr Publishers.

Kewley-Port, D. (1982). Measurement of formant transitions in naturally produced stop consonant–vowel syllables. *Journal of the Acoustical Society of America* 72, 379–389.

Kewley-Port, D. (1983). Time-varying features as corelates of place of articulation in stop consonants. *Journal of the Acoustical Society of America* 73, 322–335.

Kingston, J. and M. E. Beckman (1990). *Papers in Laboratory Phonology I. Between the Grammar and Physics of Speech*. Cambridge: Cambridge University Press.

Kingston, J. and R. L. Diehl (1994). Phonetic knowledge. *Language* 70, 419–454.

Kingston, J. and R. L. Diehl (1995). Intermediate properties in the perception of distinctive feature values. In Connell and Arvaniti (1995), 7–27.

Kiritani, S., H. Hirose and H. Fujisaki, eds. (1997). *Speech Production and Language. In Honor of Osamu Fujimura*. Berlin and New York: Mouton de Gruyter.

Klatt, D. H. (1989). Review of selected models of speech perception. In Marslen-Wilson (1989), 169–226.

Kluender, K. R. (1994). Speech perception as a tractable problem in cognitive science. In Gernsbacher (1994), 173–217.

Kluender, K. R. and M. A. Walsh (1992). Amplitude rise time and the perception of the voiceless affricate/fricative distinction. *Perception and Psychophysics* 51, 328–333.

Kohasi, Y., ed. (1968). *Proceedings of the Sixth International Congress on Acoustics, Vol. 2*. New York: American Elsevier.

Kohler, K. J. (1984). Phonetic explanation in phonology: the feature fortis/lenis. *Phonetica* 41, 150–174.

Kuhl, P. K. (1981). Discrimination of speech by nonhuman animals: basic auditory sensitivities conducive to the perception of speech-sound categories. *Journal of the Acoustical Society of America* 70, 340–349.

Kuhl, P. K. and J. D. Miller (1978). Speech perception by the chinchilla: identification functions for synthetic VOT stimuli. *Journal of the Acoustical Society of America* 63, 905–917.

Kurowski, K. and S. E. Blumstein (1984). Perceptual integration of the murmur and formant transitions for place of articulation in nasal consonants. *Journal of the Acoustical Society of America* 76, 383–390.

Ladd, D. R. (1996). *Intonational Phonology*. Cambridge: Cambridge University Press.

Ladefoged, P. (1962). Sub-glottal activity during speech. In Sovijärvi and Aalto (1962), 73–91.

Ladefoged, P. (1964). *A Phonetic Study of West African Languages*. Cambridge: Cambridge University Press.

Ladefoged, P. (1967). *Three Areas of Experimental Phonetics*. London: Oxford University Press.

Ladefoged, P. (1971). *Preliminaries to Linguistic Phonetics*. Chicago and London: University of Chicago Press.

Ladefoged, P. (1973). The features of the larynx. *Journal of Phonetics* 1, 73–83.

Ladefoged, P. (1975). *A Course in Phonetics* (1st edn). New York: Harcourt Brace Jovanovich.

Ladefoged, P. (1983). The linguistic use of different phonation types. In Bless and Abbs (1983), 351–360.

Ladefoged, P. (1990). Some reflections on the IPA. *Journal of Phonetics* 18, 335–346.

Ladefoged, P. (1993). *A Course in Phonetics* (3rd edn). Fort Worth: Harcourt Brace College Publishers.

Ladefoged, P. (1996). *Elements of Acoustic Phonetics* (2nd edn). Chicago and London: University of Chicago Press.

Ladefoged, P. (1997a). Instrumental techniques for linguistic phonetic fieldwork. In Hardcastle and Laver (1997), 137–166.

Ladefoged, P. (1997b). Linguistic phonetic descriptions. In Hardcastle and Laver (1997), 589–618.

Ladefoged, P., J. F. K. Anthony and C. Riley (1971). Direct measurement of the vocal tract. *UCLA Working Papers in Phonetics* 19, 4–13.

Ladefoged, P. and A. Bladon (1982). Attempts by human speakers to reproduce Fant's nomograms. *Speech Communication* 1, 185–198.

Ladefoged, P. and I. Maddieson (1990). Vowels of the world's languages. *Journal of Phonetics* 18, 93–122.

Ladefoged, P. and I. Maddieson (1996). *The Sounds of the World's Languages*. Cambridge, MA, and Oxford: Blackwell.

Ladefoged, P., I. Maddieson and M. Jackson (1988). Investigating phonation types in different languages. In Fujimura (1988), 297–318.

Lahiri, A., L. Gewirth and S. E. Blumstein (1984). A reconsideration of acoustic invariance for place of articulation in diffuse stop consonants: evidence from a cross-language study. *Journal of the Acoustical Society of America* 76, 391–404.

Lass, N. J., ed. (1979). *Speech and Language. Advances in Basic Research and Practice* 2. New York: Academic Press.

Lass, N. J., ed. (1983). *Speech and Language. Advances in Basic Research and Practice* 9. New York: Academic Press.

Lass, N. J., ed. (1996). *Principles of Experimental Phonetics*. St Louis: Mosby-Year Book.

Laufer, A. (1990). Hebrew. *Journal of the International Phonetic Association* 20, 40–43.

Laver, J. (1970). The production of speech. In Lyons (1970), 53–75.

Laver, J. (1980). *The Phonetic Description of Voice Quality*. Cambridge: Cambridge University Press.

Laver, J. (1994). *Principles of Phonetics*. Cambridge: Cambridge University Press.

Lehiste, L., ed. (1967). *Readings in Acoustic Phonetics*. Cambridge, MA, and London: MIT Press.

Lenneberg, E. H. (1967). *Biological Foundations of Language*. New York: John Wiley & Sons, Inc.

Liberman, A. M. (1996). *Speech: A Special Code*. Cambridge, MA, and London: MIT Press.

Liberman, A. M., F. S. Cooper, D. P. Shankweiler and M. Studdert-Kennedy (1967). Perception of the speech code. *Psychological Review* 74, 431–461.

Liberman, A. M., P. Delattre and F. S. Cooper (1952). The role of selected stimulus variables in the perception of unvoiced stop consonants. *American Journal of Psychology* 65, 497–516.

Liberman, A. M., K. S. Harris, H. S. Hoffman and B. C. Griffity (1957). The discrimination of speech sounds within and across phoneme boundaries. *Journal of Experimental Psychology* 54, 358–368.

Liberman, A. M. and I. G. Mattingly (1985). The motor theory of speech perception revised. *Cognition* 21, 1–36.

Lieberman, P. (1967). *Intonation, Perception, and Language (Research Monograph No. 38)*. Cambridge, MA: MIT Press.

Lieberman, P. and S. Blumstein (1988). *Speech Physiology, Speech Perception and Acoustic Phonetics*. Cambridge: Cambridge University Press.

Liljencrants, J. and B. Lindblom (1972). Numerical simulation of vowel quality systems: the role of perceptual contrast. *Language* 48, 839–862.

Lindau, M. (1978). Vowel features. *Language* 54, 541–564.

Lindau, M. (1985). The story of /r/. In Fromkin (1985), 157–168.

Lindau, M., K. Norlin and J.-O. Svantesson (1990). Some cross-linguistic differences in diphthongs. *Journal of the International Phonetic Association* 20, 10–14.

Lindblom, B. (1986). Phonetic universals in vowel systems. In Ohala and Jaeger (1986), 13–44.

Lindblom, B. (1990). Explaining phonetic variation: a sketch of the H&H theory. In Hardcastle and Marchal (1990), 403–439.

Lindblom, B. E. F. and J. Sundberg (1971). Acoustical consequences of lip, tongue, jaw, and larynx movement. *Journal of the Acoustical Society of America* 50, 1166–1179.

Lisker, L. (1986). 'Voicing' in English: a catalogue of acoustic features signaling /b/ versus /p/ in trochees. *Language and Speech* 29, 3–11.

Lisker, L. and A. S. Abramson (1964). A cross-language study of voicing in initial stops: acoustical measurements. *Word* 20, 384–422.

Lisker, L. and A. S. Abramson (1967). Some effects of context on Voice Onset Time in English stops. *Language and Speech* 10, 1–28.

Lisker, L. and A. S. Abramson (1970). The voicing dimension: some experiments in comparative phonetics. In Hála *et al.* (1970), 563–567.

Löfqvist, A. (1997). Theories and models of speech production. In Hardcastle and Laver (1997), 405–426.

Löfqvist, A., T. Baer, N. S. McGarr and R. S. Story (1989). The cricothyroid muscle in voicing control. *Journal of the Acoustical Society of America* 85, 1314–1321.

Lyons, J., ed. (1970). *New Horizons in Linguistics*. Harmondsworth: Penguin Books.

MacDonald, J. and H. McGurk (1978). Visual influences on speech perception processes. *Perception and Psychophysics* 24, 253–257.

MacNeilage, P., ed. (1983). *The Production of Speech*. New York: Springer-Verlag.

Maddieson, I. (1984). *Patterns of Sounds*. Cambridge: Cambridge University Press.

Maddieson, I. (1997). Phonetic universals. In Hardcastle and Laver (1997), 619–639.

Maddieson, I. and K. Emmorey (1985). Relationship between semivowels and vowels: cross-linguistic investigations of acoustic differences and coarticulation. *Phonetica* 42, 163–174.

Malécot, A. C. (1956). Acoustic cues for nasal consonants. An experimental study involving a tape-splicing technique. *Language* 32, 274–284.

Marslen-Wilson, W., ed. (1989). *Lexical Representation and Process*. Cambridge, MA: MIT Press.

Massaro, D. W. (1987). *Speech Perception by Ear and Eye: A Paradigm for Psychological Inquiry*. Hillsdale, NJ: Lawrence Erlbaum.

Massaro, D. W. (1994). Psychological aspects of speech perception. Implications for research and theory. In Gernsbacher (1994), 219–263.

Massaro, D. W., M. M. Cohen, A. Gesi, R. Heredia and M. Tsuzaki (1993). Bimodal speech perception: an examination across languages. *Journal of Phonetics* 21, 445–478.

Mattingly, I. G. and M. Studdert-Kennedy, eds. (1991). *Modularity and the Motor Theory of Speech Perception.* Hillsdale, NJ: Lawrence Erlbaum.

McGregor, G., ed. (1986). *Language for Hearers.* Oxford: Pergamon Press.

McGurk, H. and J. MacDonald (1976). Hearing lips and seeing voices. *Nature* 264, 746–748.

Miller, J. (1981). Effects of speaking rate on segmental distinctions. In Eimas and Miller (1981), 39–74.

Miyawaki, K., W. Strange, R. Verbrugge, A. M. Liberman, J. J. Jenkins and O. Fujimura (1975). An effect of linguistic experience: the discrimination of [r] and [l] by native speakers of Japanese and English. *Perception and Psychophysics* 18, 331–340.

Moore, B. C. J. (1989). *An Introduction to the Psychology of Hearing* (3rd edn). London: Academic Press.

Moore, B. C. J. (1997). Aspects of auditory processing related to speech perception. In Hardcastle and Laver (1997), 539–565.

Moore, B. C. J. and B. R. Glasberg (1983). Suggested formulae for calculating auditory-filter bandwidths and excitation patterns. *Journal of the Acoustical Society of America* 74, 750–753.

Myers, T., J. Laver and J. Anderson, eds. (1981). *The Cognitive Representation of Speech.* Amsterdam: North-Holland Publishing Company.

Nearey, T. M. (1989). Static, dynamic, and relational properties in vowel perception. *Journal of the Acoustical Society of America* 85, 2088–2113.

Nearey, T. M. (1995). A double-weak view of trading relations: comments on Kingston and Diehl. In Connell and Arvaniti (1995), 28–40.

Newmeyer, F. J., ed. (1988). *Linguistics: The Cambridge Survey. Volume I. Linguistic Theory: Foundations.* Cambridge: Cambridge University Press.

Ní Chasaide, A. and C. Gobl (1993). Contextual variation of the vowel voice source as a function of adjacent consonants. *Language and Speech* 36, 303–320.

Ní Chasaide, A. and C. Gobl (1997). Voice Source Variation. In Hardcastle and Laver (1997), 427–461.

Nihalani, P. (1975). Velopharyngeal opening in the formation of voiced stops in Sindhi. *Phonetica* 32, 89–102.

Nolan, F. (1992). The descriptive role of segments: evidence from assimilation. In Docherty and Ladd (1992), 261–280.

Nolan, F. (1995). *Preview of the IPA Handbook. Journal of the International Phonetic Association* 25.

O'Connor, J. D. (1973). *Phonetics.* Harmondsworth: Penguin.

O'Connor, J. D., L. J. Gerstman, A. M. Liberman, P. C. Delattre and F. S. Cooper (1957). Acoustic cues for the perception of initial /w, j, r, l/ in English. *Word* 13, 25–43.

O'Grady, W., M. Dobrolovsky and F. Katamba, eds. (1997). *Contemporary Linguistics: An Introduction* (3rd edn). London: Longman.

Ohala, J. J. (1978). The production of tone. In Fromkin (1978), 5–39.

Ohala, J. J. (1983). The origin of sound patterns in vocal tract constraints. In MacNeilage (1983), 189–216.

Ohala, J. J. (1990). Respiratory activity in speech. In Hardcastle and Marchal (1990), 23–53.

Ohala, J. J. (1997). The relation between phonetics and phonology. In Hardcastle and Laver (1997), 674–694.

Ohala, J. J. and J. J. Jaeger, eds. (1986). *Experimental Phonology*. Orlando, FL: Academic Press.

Ohala, J. J., C. J. Riordan and H. Kawasaki (1979). Investigation of pulmonic activity in speech. In Fischer-Jørgensen *et al.* (1979), 205.

Orlikoff, R. F. and J. C. Kahane (1996). Structure and function of the larynx. In Lass (1996), 112–181.

Patterson, R. D., J. Holdsworth and M. Allerhand (1992). Auditory models as preprocessors for speech recognition. In Schouten (1992), 67–83.

Perkell, J. S. (1969). *Physiology of Speech Production: Results and Implications of a Quantitative Cienradiographic Study*. Cambridge, MA: MIT Press.

Perkell, J. S. (1997). Articulatory processes. In Hardcastle and Laver (1997), 333–370.

Perkell, J. S. and D. H. Klatt, eds. (1986). *Invariance and Variability in Speech Processes*. Hillsdale, NJ: Lawrence Erlbaum.

Peterson, G. E. and H. L. Barney (1952). Control methods used in a study of the vowels. *Journal of the Acoustical Society of America* 24, 175–184.

Pickett, J. M. (1980). *The Sounds of Speech Communication*. Baltimore: University Park Press.

Pinker, S. (1994). *The Language Instinct*. London: Penguin Books.

Polka, L. and W. Strange (1985). Perceptual equivalence of acoustic cues that differentiate /r/ and /l/. *Journal of the Acoustical Society of America* 78, 1187–1197.

Potter, R. K., G. A. Kopp and H. C. Green (1947). *Visible Speech*. New York: D. Van Nostrand.

Recasens, D. (1983). Place cues for nasal consonants with special reference to Catalan. *Journal of the Acoustical Society of America* 73, 1346–1353.

Remez, R. E. (1994). A guide to research on the perception of speech. In Gernsbacher (1994), 145–172.

Riordan, C. J. (1980). Larynx height during English stop consonants. *Journal of Phonetics* 8, 353–360.

Roach, P. (1991). *English Phonetics and Phonology: A Practical Course* (2nd edn). Cambridge: Cambridge University Press.

Robins, R. H. (1989). *General Linguistics: An Introductory Survey* (4th edn). London: Longman.

Roca, I. (1994). *Generative Phonology*. London and New York: Routledge.

Roca, I. and W. Johnson (1999). *A Course in Phonology*. Oxford: Blackwell.

Rosen, S. and P. Howell (1987). Is there a natural sensitivity at 20ms in relative tone-onset-time continua? A reanalysis of Hirsch's (1959) data. In Schouten (1987), 199–209.

Rosen, S. and P. Howell (1991). *Signals and Systems for Speech and Hearing*. London: Academic Press.

Rosner, B. and J. Pickering (1994). *Vowel Perception and Production*. Oxford: Oxford University Press.

Rothenberg, M. (1968). *The Breath-Stream Dynamics of Simple-Released-Plosive Production*. Basel and New York: S. Karger.

Rothenberg, M. (1973). A new inverse-filtering technique for deriving the glottal airflow waveform during voicing. *Journal of the Acoustical Society of America* 53, 1632–1645.

Rothenberg, M. (1977). Measurement of airflow in speech. *Journal of Speech and Hearing Research* 20, 155–176.

Rothenberg, M. (1992). A multichannel electroglottograph. *Journal of Voice* 6, 36–43.

Russell, G. O. (1970/1928). *The Vowel: Its Physiological Mechanism as Shown by X Ray.* College Park, MD: McGrath.

Sawashima, M. (1977). Fiberoptic observation of the larynx and other speech organs. In Sawashima and Cooer (1977), 31–46.

Sawashima, M. and F. S. Cooper, eds. (1977). *Dynamic Aspects of Speech Production.* Tokyo: University of Tokyo Press.

Sawashima, M. and H. Hirose (1983). Laryngeal gestures in speech production. In MacNeilage (1983), 11–38.

Sawusch, J. R. (1996). Instrumentation and methodology for the study of speech perception. In Lass (1996), 525–550.

Schane, S. (1984). The fundamentals of particle phonology. *Phonology Yearbook* 1, 129–155.

Schneiderman, C. R. (1984). *Basic Anatomy and Physiology in Speech and Hearing.* San Diego: College-Hill Press.

Schouten, M. E. H., ed. (1987). *The Psychophysics of Speech Perception.* Dordrecht: Martinus Nijhoff.

Schouten, M. E. H., ed. (1992). *The Auditory Processing of Speech. From Sounds to Words.* Berlin and New York: Mouton de Gruyter.

Sekiyama, K. and Y. Tohkura (1993). Inter-language differences in the influence of visual cues in speech perception. *Journal of Phonetics* 21, 427–444.

Shadle, C. H. (1990). Articulatory–acoustic relations in fricative consonants. In Hardcastle and Marchal (1990), 187–209.

Shadle, C. H. (1997). The aerodynamics of speech. In Hardcastle and Laver (1997), 33–64.

Silverman, D. (1997). Laryngeal complexity in Otomanguean vowels. *Phonology* 14, 235–261.

Sinex, D. G., L. P. McDonald and J. B. Mott (1991). Neural correlates of nonmonotonic temporal acuity for voice onset time. *Journal of the Acoustical Society of America* 90, 2441–2449.

Sovijärvi, A. and P. Aalto, eds. (1962). *Proceedings of the Fourth International Congress of Phonetic Sciences.* The Hague: Mouton & Co.

Spencer, A. (1996). *Phonology. Theory and Description.* Cambridge, MA, and Oxford: Blackwell.

Stetson, R. H. (1951). *Motor Phonetics: A Study of Speech Movements in Action* (2nd edn). Amsterdam: North Holland Publishing Co.

Stevens, K. N. (1971). Airflow and turbulence noise for fricative and stop consonants: static considerations. *Journal of the Acoustical Society of America* 50, 1180–1192.

Stevens, K. N. (1972). The quantal nature of speech: evidence from articulatory–acoustic data. In David and Denes (1972), 51–66.

Stevens, K. N. (1977). Physics of laryngeal behavior and larynx modes. *Phonetica* 34, 264–279.

Stevens, K. N. (1981). Constraints imposed by the auditory system on the properties used to classify speech sounds: data from phonology, acoustics and psychoacoustics. In Myers, Laver and Anderson (1981), 61–74.

Stevens, K. N. (1983). Design features of speech sound systems. In MacNeilage (1983), 247–261.

Stevens, K. N. (1985a). Spectral prominences and phonetic distinctions in language. *Speech Communication* 4, 137–144.

Stevens, K. N. (1985b). Evidence for the role of acoustic boundaries in the perception of speech sounds. In Fromkin (1985), 243–255.

Stevens, K. N. (1988). Modes of vocal fold vibration based on a two-section model. In Fujimura (1988), 357–371.

Stevens, K. N. (1989). On the quantal nature of speech. *Journal of Phonetics* 17, 3–45.

Stevens, K. N. (1997). Articulatory-acoustic-auditory relationships. In Hardcastle and Laver (1997), 462–506.

Stevens, K. N. (1998). *Acoustic Phonetics.* Cambridge, MA and London: MIT Press.

Stevens, K. N. and S. E. Blumstein (1981). The search for invariant acoustic correlates of phonetic features. In Eimas and Miller (1981), 1–38.

Stevens, K. N. and A. S. House (1955). Development of a quantitative description of vowel articulation. *Journal of the Acoustical Society of America* 27, 484–493.

Stevens, K. N., S. Kawasaki, and C. G. M. Fant (1953). An electrical analogue of the vocal tract. *Journal of the Acoustical Society of America* 25, 734–742.

Stevens, K. N. and S. J. Keyser (1989). Primary features and their enhancement in consonants. *Language* 65, 81–106.

Stevens, K. N., S. J. Keyser and H. Kawasaki (1986). Towards a phonetic and phonological theory of redundant features. In Perkell and Klatt (1986), 426–449.

Stevens, S. S. and J. Volkman (1940). The relation of pitch to frequency: a revised scale. *The American Journal of Psychology* 53, 329–353.

Stewart, J. M. (1967). Tongue root position in Akan vowel harmony. *Phonetica* 16, 185–204.

Stone, M. (1996). Instrumentation for the study of speech physiology. In Lass (1996), 495–524.

Stone, M. (1997). Laboratory techniques for investigating speech articulation. In Hardcastle and Laver (1997), 9–32.

Strange, W. (1989a). Dynamic specification of coarticulated vowels spoken in sentence context. *Journal of the Acoustical Society of America* 85, 2135–2153.

Strange, W. (1989b). Evolving theories of vowel perception. *Journal of the Acoustical Society of America* 85, 2081–2087.

Summerfield, Q. and M. Haggard (1977). On the dissociation of spectral and temporal cues to the voicing distinction in initial stop consonants. *Journal of the Acoustical Society of America* 62, 436–448.

Sundberg, J. (1987). *The Science of the Singing Voice.* DeKalb, IL: Northern Illinois University Press.

Syrdal, A. K. (1983). Perception of consonant place of articulation. In Lass (1983), 313–349.

Syrdal, A. K. (1985). Aspects of a model of the auditory representation of American English vowels. *Speech Communication* 4, 121–135.

Syrdal, A. K. and H. S. Gopal (1986). A perceptual model of vowel recognition based on the auditory representation of American English vowels. *Journal of the Acoustical Society of America* 79, 1086–1100.

Titze, I. R. (1989). On the relation between subglottal pressure and fundamental frequency in phonation. *Journal of the Acoustical Society of America* 85, 901–906.

Titze, I. R. (1990). Interpretation of the electroglottographic signal. *Journal of Voice* 4, 1–9.

Titze, I. R. (1994). *Principles of Voice Production.* Englewood Cliffs, NJ: Prentice Hall.

Titze, I. R., E. S. Luschei and M. Hirano (1989). Role of the thyroarytenoid muscle in regulation of fundamental frequency. *Journal of Voice* 3, 213–224.

Traunmüller, H. (1981). Perceptual dimension of openness in vowels. *Journal of the Acoustical Society of America* 69, 1465–1475.

Traunmüller, H. (1990). Analytical expressions for the tonotopic sensory scale. *Journal of the Acoustical Society of America* 88, 97–100.

Wakita, H. J. (1996). Instrumentation for the study of speech acoustics. In Lass (1996), 469–494.

Warren, D. W. (1996). Regulation of speech aerodynamics. In Lass (1996), 46–92.

Westbury, J. R. (1983). Enlargement of the supraglottal cavity and its relation to stop consonant voicing. *Journal of the Acoustical Society of America* 73, 1321–1336.

Whalen, D. H. and A. M. Liberman (1987). Speech perception takes precedence over nonspeech perception. *Science* 237, 169–171.

Wood, S. (1975). The weakness of the tongue-arching model of vowel articulation. *Phonetics Laboratory, Department of Linguistics, Lund University Working Papers* 11, 55–107.

Wood, S. (1979). A radiographic analysis of constriction location for vowels. *Journal of Phonetics* 7, 25–43. Reprinted in Wood (1982).

Wood, S. (1982). X-Ray and Model Studies of Vowel Articulation. *Phonetics Laboratory, Department of Linguistics, Lund University Working Papers* 23.

Wyke, B., ed. (1974). *Ventilatory and Phonatory Control Systems*. New York: Oxford University Press.

Zwicker, E. and E. Terhardt (1980). Analytical expressions for the critical-band rate and critical bandwidth as a function of frequency. *Journal of the Acoustical Society of America* 68, 1523–1525.

# Index